Library of
Davidson College

Winthrop Sociology Series
Scott G. McNall, *editor*

The Capitalist State
and the Politics
of Class

The Capitalist State and the Politics of Class

Albert Szymanski
University of Oregon

Winthrop Publishers, Inc.
Cambridge, Massachusetts

Library of Congress Cataloging in Publication Data

Szymanski, Albert
    The capitalist state and the politics of class.

    Includes bibliographical references and index.
    1.   Political sociology.   I.   Title.
JA76.S95   301.5'92   77-11604
ISBN 0-87626-105-5

Cover design by Karyl Klopp.

©*1978 by Winthrop Publishers, Inc.*
  17 Dunster Street, Cambridge, Massachusetts 02138

All rights reserved. No part of this book may be reproduced in any form or by any means without permission in writing from the publisher. Printed in the United States of America.

10 9 8 7 6 5 4 3 2

*To the NLFSV
and to Juan Linz.*

*Without them
this book would not
have been.*

Contents

Preface / xi

1 Introduction / 1

The Contending Perspectives within Political Sociology / 1
The Fundamentals of the Marxist Perspective / 20
Summary / 32

2 The Politics of the United States Capitalist Class / 33

The Wealth of the Capitalist Class / 33
The Capitalist Class as a Social Class / 38
The Political Conservatism of the Capitalist Class / 40
Political Differences within the Capitalist Class by Type of Industry / 40
A Look at the Politics of Some Specific Industries / 45
New Money Versus Old Money / 48
Protestants, Catholics, and Jews / 49
Liberals Versus Conservatives / 50
Summary and Conclusion / 53

3 Political Differences within the Working Class / 55

Income Level and Politics / 55
Skill Level and Politics / 58
The Effect of Unemployment / 60
Intraclass Communication / 62
Mobility / 66
The Effect of Trade Unions / 70
The Politics of White-Collar Workers / 73
The Politics of Rural Wage Laborers / 76
Summary / 78

4 The Politics of the Petty Bourgeoisie / 81

The Politics of Small Business / 83
The Politics of Professionals / 86
The Politics of College Students / 89
The Politics of Independent Farmers / 92
Summary / 96

5 The Politics of Sex, Race, and Age / 99

The Politics of Sex / 99
The Politics of Minorities / 108
The Politics of Age / 115
Summary / 118

6 Elections and Political Parties / 121

The Role of Elections / 121
The Effect of Electoral Systems / 125
The Role of Political Parties / 128
Variations in Party Structure / 129
Communist Party Organization / 132
Summary / 135

7 The Origins of the Capitalist State / 137

The Development of the Capitalist State / 143
The Historical Development of Parliamentary Forms / 147
The Development of the Capitalist State in the United States / 151
Summary / 161

8 The Functions of the Capitalist State / 163

Part One: Implementing and Tempering the Capitalist-Class Will, Funding the State, Preserving Law and Order, and Maintaining Legitimacy

The State Bureaucracy and the Financing of the Capitalist State / 164
The Formation and Tempering of the Capitalist-Class Will / 171
The Preservation of the Legitimacy of the System / 176

The Protection of Private Property and the Maintenance of Order / 179
Summary / 182

9 The Functions of the Capitalist State / 183

Part Two: The Facilitation of Capital Accumulation

The Provision and Regulation of the Labor Force / 183
The Facilitation of Commerce / 188
Ensuring Sufficient Buying Power in the Economy / 189
Countercyclical Policies / 201
Direct and Indirect Subsidization of Private Corporations / 202
State-Sanctioned Self-Regulation of the Corporations / 204
Advancing the Overseas Interests of the Corporations / 206
Summary / 212

10 The Mechanisms of Direct Domination of the State by Capital / 215

The Selection of Top Governmental Personnel / 216
Lobbying / 225
The Process of Forming Public Policy / 228
Summary / 234

11 The Mechanisms of Indirect Domination of the State by Capital / 237

Ideological Hegemony as a Mechanism of Control / 238
The Logic of Capitalist Relations as a Mechanism of Control / 262
Military Intervention as a Mechanism of Control / 264
Political and Social Disruption as a Mechanism of Control / 266
Structural Determination of State Policies / 267
The Role of Direct and Indirect Mechanisms of Domination of the State / 272

12 Fascism / 275

Fascist Movements / 276
Fascist Regimes / 278
The Nazis / 281
Fascistic Movements in the United States / 286
Summary / 290

13 Revolution and Socialist Movements in the Capitalist State / 293

The Conditions for Revolution / 295
Future Revolutionary Possibilities in the United States / 309
Summary and Conclusion / 316

Index / 319

Preface

This book is about the primary questions of our time. Questions of the state's role in society, of which groups have the greatest influence in determining state policies, of the causes and power of social movements, of the determinants of political behavior, are absolutely basic to understanding the world around us. All conscious human beings have ideas on these topics. The newspapers, television, and the schools from the primary through the graduate level are permeated with strongly held positions on the questions this book considers.

I need not convince the reader of the importance of this book's subject matter. What may be controversial, however, is not the questions I pose, but the analysis I make. My purpose is to synthesize the best in the academic tradition of political sociology — and there is much empirical work of great value in this tradition — within the theoretical framework of Marxism to understand better the nature of power and political movements. I have tried as best as I can to shed light on political processes that are too often mystified and obscured by those who exercise political power and benefit from that power. If I have failed, I hope this reflects on my own inadequacies as a scholar and not on the validity of the project.

Political sociology is implicitly premised on the assumption that the disciplinary boundaries — especially those between political science and sociology, but also between these fields and history and economics — are invalid and serve only to prevent the comprehensive understanding necessary to explain adequately the state and political movements and processes. To think that the role and functioning of the state can be understood without reference to history and economic processes is nonsense. The differentiation of the various "social sciences" within the nineteenth-century European university structure was caused by social forces having to do with both the nature of European universities and the demands on social science for mystification. It has nothing to do with any actual and semiautonomous sets of phenomena in the world corresponding to such things as a "polity" or "economy." Thus, the approach that must be adopted by any serious social analysis must be *uni*disciplinary. A unidisciplinary approach is used in this book. A problem is posed and the answer is looked for wherever the problem directs, irrespective of the nature of the academic degrees (or lack thereof) of those who produced the sources on which I rely.

Another major obstacle to the scientific study of the state and politics is the artificial distinction between theory and empirical research. The need for the unity of the two should be obvious. Nevertheless, since the 1930s empiricist or positivist *and* theoretical camps have grown up within each of the so-called social sciences. The empiricists emphasize hard data, rigorous methods, computer techniques, and mathematical models, but for the most part apply these high-power techniques to only the most theoretically trivial concerns. The theorists emphasize reading Parsons, Hegel, Habermas, Althusser, or whomever, look down on empirical confirmation or data, and thus doom themselves to obscurantism and irrelevance even if they have fun debating the theoretically important questions. Any actual contribution to political sociology must operate within the absolute unity of theory and research. All theory must be made concrete enough to have empirical implications that can be confirmed or disconfirmed, and the facts observed must be made to address the basic theoretical issues in the field. This approach has been the model for this book.

It might be objected by some that a "bias" permeates this book — that I unfairly have imposed Marxist interpretations. Those who might raise such an objection probably would contend that a "value-free" perspective is proper and is the standard they themselves approach in their own work. But a "value-free" approach to political sociology is a logical impossibility, a contradiction in terms. The study of the state and politics is the study of the most controversial area of contemporary human life. Every political ideology, whether of the right, left, or center; whether pluralist, parliamentary democratic, aristocratic, the Divine Right of Kings, Socialist, anarchist, Communist, or whatever, makes definite and usually well-defined claims about the role of the state, political movements, the role of the masses in decision making, and so on. Because the subject matter of political ideologies to which every conscious human being subscribes is virtually identical to the subject matter of political sociology, it logically and necessarily follows that the theories developed and held to by political sociologists — whether on the basis of their interests and preconceptions *or* on the basis of purely objective and abstract scientific research — must necessarily either coincide or conflict with (or perhaps partially conflict and partially coincide with) *all* of the various contending political ideologies. Whether a truly objective study of the state determines that the state is the instrument of a small group of economically privileged people or is in fact a democratic instrument of the whole people, this finding will necessarily and equally conflict with or support the various contending political ideologies about the nature of the state. The *only* difference is which political ideologies (radical, liberal, or reactionary) an objective analysis supports. Characterizations of a work as "biased" as opposed to "value-free" often then reduce to nothing other than the statement that "the findings of your work conflict with my political ideology."

This is not to say that sloppy scholarship is not often a factor in works by both mainstream political sociologists and academic Marxists. Such is most definitely the case, and probably occurs today with equal frequency in both camps. The work of political sociologists must be subject to the most rigorous empirical examination to determine its validity. This must be true of the work of Marxists as well as of the work of pluralists and functionalists. The scientific validity of the claims of this book can only be substantiated by such a rigorous examination. In the real world of political conflict and struggle, however, realists understand that theoretical positions are not held to, and do not triumph, because of their intellectual power as much as because of the power of their adherents.

I would like to thank those who generated my interest in political sociology: Ralph England, George Wittenburg and my other teachers at the University of Rhode Island, and my professors at Columbia University, especially Terry Hopkins, Immanuel Wallerstein, Thomas O'Dea, and, above all, Juan Linz. Although we have a few theoretical differences, I owe more to Juan Linz than to any other teacher I have ever had. He not only excited my interest in the field, taught me the methods of doing political sociology, opened up a vast literature to me and was the source of innumerable ideas, but he served as the model of scholarship and seriousness which the subject deserves. My debt to him is immense.

I thank my parents, Al and Verna. From the latter I learned my respect for books, from the former, my attitude to work. For both I am eternally grateful. Without what they taught me, to say nothing of their emotional and financial support through my college years, this work would not have been possible.

I wish to thank the readers of this manuscript, especially Peter Dreier and, above all, Scott McNall, for the many helpful suggestions that have made this a much stronger manuscript than it otherwise would have been. I would like to thank the members of the various political organizations and collectives in which I have worked during the time the ideas in this book germinated for the stimulation and discussion that is manifested in this book: the University of Rhode Island Students for Democratic Action, the Columbia Committee to End the War in Vietnam, the Columbia Students for a Democratic Society (SDS), the Graduate Sociology Student Union at Columbia, the Columbia and Oregon chapters of the New University Conference, the Anna Louise Strong Collective and the *Insurgent Sociologist*. Others who have had a personal impact (through both stimulation and support) in helping me develop the ideas in this book include Judy Cashin, Carol Cofone, Andy Colonna, Michael Doyle, Gerry Duguay, John Evansohn, the Feminist Theory Collective, Paul Fitzgerald, Richard French, Harry Humphries, Sue Jacobs, Steve Johnson, Bert Knorr, Jerry Lembcke, Martha Older, Lonnie Raithel, Mark Rudd, Joe Schoenfeld, David Wellman, Erik Wright, and the students in my political sociology, issues and movements, and social stratification courses at the University of Oregon since 1970.

I wish to thank those whose help has made this book possible: Doris

Boylan, who typed and retyped the manuscript as well as so much of my other work, for whose care I am most thankful; the secretaries of the University of Oregon Sociology department, who have given me support in so many ways; the University of Oregon research librarians at the social science and government documents desks, whose assistance in locating information has been invaluable; Paul O'Connell, Alison Mills, and others at Winthrop Publishers, for all they have done and, finally, all those who produced the paper, set the type, and transported and sold the copies, who of necessity must remain nameless, but without whom my name would not be on the manuscript.

Important influences on me have included the editors of the journal *Monthly Review* and especially Paul Sweezy, who played such an important role in providing analysis and a source of Marxist literature to those of us graduate students who became radicalized in the 1960s. The absence of the *Monthly Review* during these years might have been fatal to the intellectual development of a generation of radical scholars. Other important intellectual influences on me as well as many others during the 1960s include *Studies on the Left, The National Guardian,* and the writings and example of C. Wright Mills.

There are two important intellectual currents of the 1970s that have been important in shaping my thinking on the state and to which I am especially indebted: (1) the tradition of power structure research, especially as tirelessly pursued by the North American Congress on Latin America and G. William Domhoff (whose books, particularly *Who Rules America?*, have had a major impact on this work); and (2) the ideas of the Kapitalistate Collective, which has popularized and synthesized many of the ideas of continental theorists of the state in North America. While recently the latter school of thought has been challenging the former, and must be thanked for clarifying certain key questions, it has probably made too many claims about the worthlessness of power structure research. This book attempts to provide a balance and synthesis between the contributions of these apparently antagonistic trends.

Intellectual work is a collective project. Intellectuals in capitalist society enjoy the illusion of their own importance and genius. In fact, the ideas we express are those of classes, institutions, and traditions. Any originality in our ideas must be attributed to the fact that we are living in a time of conflict and crisis which is calling forth the development of existing theoretical systems and in some cases (although not as often as we imagine) the creation of new understandings. No century has witnessed greater change than ours. In the short span of sixty years over one third of the world has opted out of the capitalist world system and adopted socialism, and the former colonies of the Third World have gained at least formal independence from Europe. The masses of working people are in motion everywhere to achieve control of their lives. If the world survives another sixty years it is probable that most of it will be socialist. If there is a nuclear war, a distinct possibility, it is almost certain that the survivors will organize themselves according to socialist principles — witness the great expansion of socialism after the first and second world wars. This is the milieu within which we work in the 1970s. It is in support of, and in response to, the various classes and interests involved in these struggles on one side or the other that all political sociologists write. This work is in this regard no different from the works of others.

Given this reality, it would be a lie to think that my intellectual debt is mainly to my teachers and those with whom I have come into personal contact. My real debt is to the traditions (and to the class forces and interests they represent) that come together in this work. First of all I am obviously greatly indebted to the American tradition of political sociology, developed more than anywhere else at Columbia University in the post-World War II period, of which Seymour Martin Lipset is both the leading force and the most articulate spokesperson. Although we have never had a discussion, the impact of Lipset and the "Columbia tradition" on this work is pervasive. In my opinion, Lipset's writings have made a greater contribution than those of any other non-Marxist academic sociologist in the United States today.

While American sociology largely degenerated in the 1950s into rationalizing ideology, refined intelligence-gathering techniques for the powers that be, and methodological trivia, Lipset and his tradition (despite a flirtation with Parsonianism) continued to relate concrete theory to theoretically important data, refusing to mystify their methods or obscure their theory, to both address and offer answers to many of the key theoretical and practical problems of our times. I am perpetually grateful for having stumbled into this tradition in my pursuit of C. Wright Mills.

The Lipset tradition was considerably affected by the events of the 1950s; if it had not been, it would not have survived. In the 1940s Lipset was a Marxist; by the 1960s he was a leading liberal establishment sociologist whose work offered considerable ideological legitimation to the status quo. But it is to the Marxist tradition in which Lipset became a sociologist that he owes the categories, problems, ideas and original impetus for his political sociology. And it is, of course, to that tradition and to the social forces of which it is the intellectual manifestation that I too owe the most.

While I was becoming a political sociologist the foremost political struggle in the world, and the struggle which had the greatest impact on my political and intellectual development as well as on that of a whole generation, was the struggle of the people of Vietnam against the imperial aggression of the government of the United States of America and the corporate ruling class which was behind it. As an activist throughout the 1960s and early 1970s in the movement to get the United States out of Vietnam, my political development, specifically my transformation from being a liberal supporter of "peace" and "civil rights" in the early 1960s to becoming a Marxist by the end of the decade, must be attributed more than anything else to these involvements.

Through involvement in the antiwar movement and increasing identification with the struggles of the Vietnamese and other Third World peoples, I came to understand the analytical power of Marxist theory and the wisdom of its tradition. Marxism grew up and became an intellectual force in the latter part of the nineteenth century as a manifestation of the rapidly growing working-class movements of Europe. In the first half of the twentieth century it provided the intellectual guidance to the Russian, Chinese, and other revolutions and spread throughout the world to become the world's leading intellectual perspective. Everywhere where more than a handful of intellectuals subscribes to its basic ideas, it is working people who are primarily its adherents. This appears to be the case because Marxism seems to account best for their situation and offer the best hope for change. Thus, in the final analysis I am indebted to the working people of the world, whose struggles are in a very real sense the ultimate source of my ideas, my perspective, the problems this book addresses, and the energy for doing the book at all. Whether this book will prove to have been worth doing will depend on whether it can make any contribution to repaying its most important debt.

The Capitalist State and the Politics of Class

1

Introduction

Political sociology primarily considers three questions: (1) What is the source of political ideas and political behavior? (2) Who or what controls the state and state policies? and (3) What role does the state play in society? The answers to these questions vary among the contending theoretical approaches within the field. This book argues that: (1) the experiences of people as structured by their economic position in society ultimately determine their politics; (2) the class which owns and controls the corporate economy dominates the state in the United States and other advanced capitalist countries; and (3) the state plays a central and growing role in stabilizing society (largely through securing the loyalty of the masses), in facilitating the profit-making process, and in increasing economic productivity and growth of the corporate interests.

This book attempts to synthesize much of the research done in the last generation within academic political sociology from a Marxist theoretical perspective. It tries to reconceptualize the diverse theoretical and empirical studies and systematically lay out a new orientation to the field.

This chapter first summarizes the leading contending perspectives within political sociology as well as the major objections raised to each approach. Then it summarizes the basics of the Marxist orientation, which is the framework of the remaining chapters. Finally, it illustrates the basic relation between politics and class.

The Contending Perspectives within Political Sociology

Pluralism

The dominant tendency within political sociology over the last generation has been pluralism (also variously described as the theory of balance or equilibrium theory).[1] Pluralists define society as an aggregate of dissimilar and to a large extent equally influential special interest groups and associations with highly diverse and often conflicting interests. Corporations, business associations, professional associations, labor unions, religious groups, hobby clubs, PTAs, youth associations, women's groups, sporting clubs — thousands of different groups and interests — make up society.

Each of these diverse groups attempts to influence governmental policy (which pluralists define as the product of the conflicting pressures of all these groups, no one of which is dominant). The balance between the various conflicting claims on the state is represented by state policy. The various interest groups negotiate and bargain with one another to reach a mutually agreeable outcome for each contested issue. The "equilibrium" or "balance" found in the political process thus tends to maximize the interests and concerns of all participants.

Each group trades off positions on issues of lesser importance to achieve victories on issues of greatest concern. Outcomes of these issues are not only a result of compromise, but also a product of shifts in temporary alliances among groups. Different coalitions emerge on different issues; therefore no stable block of groups can consistently dominate the political process. State policy thus is not predominantly a result of business, labor, religious, or any other given interest or pressure; rather, it is a compromise among *all* such interests and pressures.

The father of American pluralism, Arthur Bentley, expressed the essence of the pluralist idea rather eloquently in his classic book, *The Process of Government*:

> *Pressure, as we shall use it, is always a group phenomenon. It indicates the push and resistance between groups. The balance of the group pressures is the existing state of society. Pressure is broad enough to include all forms of the group influence upon group, from battle and riot to abstract reasoning and sensitive morality. It takes up into itself "moral energy" and the finest discriminations of conscience as easily as bloodthirsty lust of power. It allows for humanitarian movements as easily as for political corruption. Groups exert their pressure, whether they find expression through representative opinion groups or whether they are silent, not indeed with the same technique, not with the same palpable results, but in just as real a way....*[2]

[1] Some of the more influential works in the pluralist tradition include David Truman, *The Governmental Process* (New York: Alfred Knopf, 1951); Alexis de Tocqueville, *Democracy in America* (New York: Alfred Knopf, 1945); Robert Dahl, *Who Governs?* (New Haven: Yale University Press, 1961); Nelson Polsby, *Community Power and Political Theory* (New Haven: Yale University Press, 1963); Arnold Rose, *The Power Structure* (New York: Oxford University Press, 1967); David Easton, *The Political System* (New York: Alfred Knopf, 1971); and V. O. Key, *Parties, Politics and Pressure Groups* (New York: Crowell, 1954).

[2] Arthur Bentley, *The Process of Government* (Cambridge, Mass.: The Belknap Press of Harvard University, 1908, 1967), pp. 258–259.

> *In governments like that of the United States we see these manifold interests gaining representation through many thousands of officials in varying degrees of success, beating some officials down now into delegate activity, intrusting representative activity (in the narrow sense) to other officials at times in high degree, subsiding now and again over great areas while "special interests" make special use of officials, rising in other spots to dominate, using one agency of the government against another, now with stealth, now with open force, and in general moving along the route of time with that organized turmoil which is life where the adjustments are much disturbed. . . .[3]*
>
> *One might work out a picture of the adjustments, "normal" for the given society, not in terms of a providence that filled every mouth, nor of a morality projected to ideality from any given point of view, but in terms of the adjustment of actual strengths in the given society, in terms of such a process that every interest forcing itself beyond the point of endurableness to the remainder of the interests would be checked before its excess had provoked violent reaction.[4]*

Pluralists thus consider social groups to be the units that comprise the political process, which distinguishes them from classical democratic theorists, who believed state policy was determined by the rationally arrived-at *individual* vote. Policy outcomes for the pluralists are a result of group processes. Social groups are essentially autonomous and democratic agents, each reflecting its special social situation. Their structure, interests, goals, and commitments are considered inherent to their existence, rather than examined as products of more basic social factors.

Social groups have a considerable degree of overlapping membership. This is a major force holding the political process together, since it provides people with a means of feeling that they are in touch with the whole process, thereby mitigating and moderating the intensity of conflicts between each social group. Some business leaders belong to one church, others to another; likewise with labor leaders. Businesses as a group therefore cannot form a firm alliance with one church; nevertheless, business and labor leaders have a strong common bond in belonging to the same churches.

The complex web of "cross-pressures" operating in society guarantees that no systematic conflict develops that endangers the stability of the political system itself. It ensures that virtually all contestants for governmental policy are somewhat ambivalent about victory, consider other groups' viewpoints, and do not want to totally destroy their opposition. And together with the general internalization of democratic values and norms, it tends to institutionalize respect for "the rules of the game."

Another central pluralist idea is the notion of "veto groups" or mutual

[3] Ibid., p. 453.
[4] Ibid., p. 458.

restraint. While no one block of groups such as business or labor is considered to be powerful enough to get its way, generally such groups are considered typically to possess enough power to prevent other groups from consistently getting their way. That is, groups can more easily prevent events from happening that are against their perceived interest than they can get events to happen that favor their interests. This is a further force causing all participants in the political process to make mutually advantageous compromises that do the minimum of harm to all contending groups.

Pluralism, although it stresses the group rather than the individual, argues that the state in capitalist society is authentically democratic since (1) its policies are a result of interaction among society's constituent groups, to which almost all people belong; (2) the groups are internally democratic, or at least as "voluntary associations" they accurately reflect the interests and concerns of their members; and (3) the balance among these forces, reflected in state policy, is an essentially fair and true equilibrium among all the various interest groups, with no great and consistent bias in any direction.

The group operates on the political process both through the act of voting and during the day-to-day process of forming, administering, and adjudicating state policies. The individual, who is not in most cases realistically able to gather all the information necessary to make a truly rational and informed decision in voting, tends to go along with the opinion of those he respects — the leaders of the voluntary associations — his union, business associates, church, etc. Of course, lobbyists for the various interest groups work at state and federal legislatures, fund candidates in campaigns, channel self-serving studies to political leaders and the media, organize letter-writing campaigns, hold demonstrations, threaten and organize strikes and boycotts, etc. — all of which are calculated to influence, and in the aggregate determine, the governmental process.

Critiques of pluralism

There are two primary criticisms of pluralism.[5] The pluralist assumption that society is composed of a wide diversity of equally powerful groups reflecting the interests of most people can be challenged on many grounds. There is considerable evidence to show that (1) only about half the people in the population belong to as many as one voluntary association; (2) most of the voluntary associations people are connected with are at best only peripherally interested in politics — that is, most memberships are in fraternal and social clubs, church-connected groups,

---

[5] Some of the better criticisms of the pluralist perspective include: G. William Domhoff, *The Higher Circles* (New York: Vintage Books, 1970), especially chapter 9; C. Wright Mills, *The Power Elite* (New York: Oxford University Press, 1957), chapter 11; Peter Bachrach, *The Theory of Democratic Elitism* (Boston: Little, Brown, 1967); Richard Hamilton, *Class and Politics in the United States* (New York: John Wiley & Sons, 1972), chapter 2; Henry Kariel, *The Decline of American Pluralism* (Stanford, Calif.: Stanford University Press, 1961); and Grant McConnell, *Private Power and American Democracy* (New York: Alfred Knopf, 1966).

athletic associations, youth service groups, cultural or hobby clubs, and so on; (3) the voluntary associations to which most people belong make their decisions without consulting most of their membership, and often such decisions are made against their interests — for example, most union members in the United States rarely attend union meetings or otherwise participate in their union's activities except through paying dues; and (4) voluntary associations are asymmetrical in the amount of power they wield per member — for example, the AFL-CIO, with over 15 million members, does not have as much clout as the Council on Foreign Relations (the leading business group dealing with foreign affairs), which has only about 1300 members, because of the tremendous economic power and the political connections of the latter group. Business people and corporations are far more organized, politically conscious, politically active, and able to influence politics through money, connections, and prestige than are union members. The critics of pluralism argue that there is such an asymmetrical distribution of power among participants in the struggle among interest groups that in the end state policies reflect interests of the various corporations and business associations almost exclusively. While a pluralism of sorts may exist, it is primarily a pluralism among only the very powerful business-related groups in society, which equally share in the struggle over state policy.

A second major criticism of pluralism is directed against its conception of the functioning or output of the state. The equilibrium (or balance) theory of the pluralists assumes that the output of the state is an automatic and accurate resultant of the relative strength of the various interest groups. Pluralism suggests that virtually any state policy is a possibility, since the determination of state "output" is a matter of the "input" of the various groups attempting to influence it. In fact, there are only a limited number of effective policies that the state can follow in any area without causing general social or economic disruption of the society. Given the basic operating principles of capitalism or class society, only certain policies designed to reduce inflation, decrease unemployment, or increase production will actually work. Although various interest groups may want other policies, these policies might not be feasible.

Those who run and advise the state (leading state officials and the more farsighted, class-conscious, and influential business people and experts), perhaps through a process of trial and error, perhaps through observing what has happened in other societies, or perhaps through an analysis of what is likely to happen in their society, are able to mediate the process of decision making and policy implementation to modify what would be the unimpeded result of the equilibrium of forces. If this does not happen an ineffective policy will be tried, will fail, and a new solution adopted — probably after a number of interests come to see that their initial proposals were inadequate.

By whichever mechanism, state policy is more a result of the basic political and economic conditions than of conscious decision making. This can be seen in the general continuity of state policies whether Democrats, Republicans, liberals, conservatives, or even social democrats are in office, and regardless of the influence of any particular groups in an administration. The period since 1960 has seen liberals following conservative economic and military policies (for example, Johnson), and conservatives following liberal economic and military policies (for example, Nixon). During the 1964 election campaign, Johnson promised to keep the United States out of a major war and won, whereas during the 1972 campaign McGovern promised to withdraw from Vietnam and lost. Yet immediately after their respective elections, Johnson and Nixon proceeded to implement exactly the opposite policies from those with which they had won their elections.

The imperatives of the system thus seem to be more important than the balance of interests within the political process as the actual determinants of state policies. History has also seen fascist and "Socialist" governments (for example, in the 1920s Mussolini in Italy and MacDonald in England) following identical liberal economic policies as the only possible solution within the basic parameters of the capitalist system.

Parsonian functionalism

Functionalism, whose most influential figure has been Talcott Parsons, represents a second major perspective within political sociology.[6] Parsonian functionalism can be characterized by two basic premises: (1) that the state, like all social institutions, is essentially functional for the society as a whole — that is, that the "output" of the state generally benefits the other basic institutional orders of society, such as the economy, the family, religion, etc. — and advances both the general social interest and that of the individuals within it (thus political analysts must look at the role of the state and the people's relationship to political processes in these terms); (2) that in the last analysis, the values, norms, and attitudes held by people are the most important determinant of both individual behavior and the logic of social institutions.

Parsons's own work on the state and political processes focuses on the functions of political power, leadership, the concentration of power, and the state. Parsons's definition of power emphasizes that (1) it is the ability to get things done, and (2) it is directed to performing collective goals, thereby encompassing both of the basic characteristics of Parsonianism — the positive functioning of all institutions, and idealism (that is, the reduction of explanations to conscious goals or collective commitments).

---

[6] For statements of Parsons's position see his *The Social System* (New York: The Free Press of Glencoe, 1964); *The System of Modern Societies* (Englewood Cliffs, N.J.: Prentice-Hall, 1971); "The Distribution of Power in American Society," in *Structure and Process in Modern Societies* (New York: The Free Press, 1960) (this is Parson's review of C. W. Mills, *The Power Elite*); "On the Concept of Political Power," *Proceedings of the American Philosophical Society*, 107, no. 3 (June 1963); and *Politics and Social Structure* (New York: The Free Press, 1969). Other influential functionalist statements include: Kingsley Davis, *Human Society* (New York: Macmillan, 1949); and Kingsley Davis and Wilbert Moore, "Some Principles of Stratification," *American Sociological Review* 10, no. 2 (April 1945); and Robin Williams, *American Society* (New York: Alfred Knopf, 1970).

Parsons sees power not as a finite thing which can only be divided or won (what he calls the "zero sum conception of power"), but primarily as a thing which can and has to be generated, thus varying according to the ability to mobilize groups and actors to follow a given course. He compares political power to money, arguing that both are "generalized mediums" largely dependent on people's "faith" that in a pinch they will be backed up (in the case of paper money by gold, and in the case of political power by force). In both cases the greater people's faith in the certainty of what would happen in a pinch, the greater the ratio of paper to gold or political power to force that can exist stably. But when people's confidence declines, the lower that ratio becomes. Elections are "deposits of power" by which the people, by expressing their confidence in a government, increase its power or capacity to mobilize them. Thus the source of power is also the degree to which the people consider the government to be legitimate.

Parsons's definition of the state parallels his definition of power. Parsons defines the state as the social institution which specializes in the society's "collective goal attainment" — that is, in achieving the goals of the people in society. He also considers the state to be what he calls an "institutionalized power system," by which he means "a relational system within which certain categories of commitments and obligations are treated as binding." Again we see that these definitions consist of the two basic Parsonian postulates: the state is defined as being concerned with achieving *society's* ends (as opposed to those of any component group or class within society), and those ends are defined in terms of ideas (collective commitments, obligations, and conscious goals).

Parsons goes further to argue that considerable social, economic, and political inequality is a functional necessity of "complex, industrial society" for realizing the collective goals. Social inequality is a mechanism by which society ensures that the most important positions are conscientiously filled by the most qualified people. High income, power, and prestige are in part the reward for undergoing arduous training and the burdens of performing important functions, and are a guarantee that the best, most qualified people will find their way into the most important jobs in society and perform their jobs well once they are in these positions. The larger the scale of society and the more specialized industrial societies become, the greater is the need for a specialized and powerful leadership group. Even "democracies," he argues, need a functional equivalent to aristocracy to provide centralized, and hence effective, leadership. Effective leadership in pursuit of social goals and collective commitments is a product of effective organization, which in turn requires the firm and stable institutionalization of authority and power. It is "out of the question," he argues, "that power should be diffused equally among an indefinite number of very small units."

In all salient respects, the modern economy has moved very far from the Jeffersonian ideal. The pace-setting units have become both large and specialized. Their development has been part of a general process of structural differentiation in the society which has led to greater specialization in many fields. An essential aspect of the process of development of the economy as a system in both *these senses is greater specialization on at least three levels: first, the specialization of organizations in the functions of economic production as distinguished from other functions; second, the specialization of functions within the economy; and third, the specialization of the roles of classes of individuals within the organization.*

Leadership is an essential function in all social systems which, with their increase of scale and their functional differentiation, tend to become more specialized. I think we can, within considerable limits, regard the emergence of the large firm with operations on a nation-wide basis as a "normal" outcome of the process of growth and differentiation of the economy. Similarly, the rise to prominence within the firm of specialized executive functions is also a normal outcome of a process of growth in size and in structural differentiation....[7]

Power is a generalized facility or resource in the society. It has to be divided or allocated, but it also has to be produced and it has collective as well as distributive functions. It has the capacity to mobilize the resources of the society for the attainment of goals for which a general "public" commitment has been made, or may be made. It is mobilization, above all, of the action of persons and groups, which is binding *on them by virtue of their position in the society.*[8]

In his critique of C. Wright Mills's *The Power Elite* he argues that there is in fact a concentration of power in a relatively few hands in the United States — he thus basically agrees with Mills's description. However, he argues that such concentration is both inevitable *and* desirable. The great concentration of power in the United States is, he maintains, a product of the "dynamic of a mature industrial society" as well as a just and expected response to the changed international position of the United States, especially to the "danger of world Communism." Of course, he adds, a well-defined elite group has developed in the business world, for how else could the giant corporations and financial institutions be guided in performing their social functions of producing and distributing wealth? It is not true, Parsons argues, that this great and growing concentration of power is a bad thing. The only way the state, the military, and the economy can efficiently perform their functions is through such a concentration of power; in fact, it has been this functional need that has resulted in the concentration of power.

Parsons's essential agreement with Mills's thesis of the concentration of political power is, however, compatible with his view that the state in capitalist society nevertheless is democratic, both in the sense of furthering the goals held by the masses — respecting their commitments, norms, and values — and in being a

[7] Parsons, *Structure and Process*, pp. 207–208.
[8] Ibid., p. 221.

product of an electoral process which invests state officials with the power to act in the interests of the people. Since one of the basic postulates of the Parsonian system is that basic values determine social phenomena, Parsons does not question where the goals and commitments of the masses expressed in elections come from, what effect elections actually have in determining state policies, or what happens when elections fail to verify the goals and commitments of powerful interests in society. The idealism and functionalism of Parsons's system thus fit together quite nicely.

Critiques of Parsonian functionalism

There are at least four criticisms of Parsonian functionalism.[9] Its insistence that the existing state and government in a society is necessarily operating in the interest of the society as a whole, and that power is a resource to be used in collective betterment, is open to challenge. While it is true that states and ruling groups often do serve the general social interest given the historically and structurally possible options, it is by no means true that this is always or necessarily the case. Whether a given state, government, or ruling class is or is not serving the general social interest must be examined. Such a concrete study of the social contribution of the capitalist class would — at least in the eyes of Marxist critics of Parsonian functionalism — find that upper-class control of the state in the eighteenth and nineteenth centuries may well have served the general social welfare in rapidly advancing the development of the forces of production, spreading much of the benefit of increasing wealth to all classes of the population, and establishing basic democratic rights such as the abolition of slavery and serfdom, the freedom of religion, speech, and association. However, the rule of this class now acts as an obstacle to further historical progress. Racism, war, exploitation, environmental destruction, production for its own sake, or lack of control over our lives can be attributed to capitalist rule in an era when these things are no longer a necessary consequence of the level of technological development.

A second criticism of Parsonian functionalism is directed against its failure to understand the class basis of the state and the role of class struggle in the determination of state policy. Parsonianism offers a rather technocratic view of the state as merely a group of disinterested experts and officials pursuing the general social interest. In fact one could argue that even when the state is serving the general social interest, it is being directed by a social class acting in its own interest. Further, Parsonian functionalism, by assuming all groups in society have a common interest, fails to understand the continual and ongoing conflict among the various classes and segments of classes within society. It does not see class struggle as having an effect on state policies, but rather views things in a

---

[9] Some of the works critical of Parsonian functionalism include: C. Wright Mills, *The Sociological Imagination* (New York: Oxford University Press, 1959), chapter 2; Albert Szymanski, "The Value of Sociology: An Answer to Lidz," *Sociological Inquiry* 40, no. 1 (Winter 1970): 21–25; and Albert Szymanski, "Dialectical Functionalism: A Further Answer to Lidz," *Sociological Inquiry* 42, no. 2 (Spring 1972): 145–153.

technocratic way. Functionalism thus can be seen as the opposite of pluralism, which by neglecting the requisites of effective state policies, considers only the impact of interest groups on the state. In fact, one could argue that both the (historically specific) necessary functions of the state and the struggle of classes and segments of classes play roles in the determination of state policy.

A third criticism of Parsonian functionalism as well as of all the varieties of the "political culture" and "political behavior" schools is directed against the idealism of these perspectives. Defining political phenomena as ultimately a result of the values, perceptions, or norms held by individuals, rather than as a result of the requirements or logic of social structures (material conditions), this perspective has difficulty accounting for historical change — especially the rise and development of new social movements and revolutionary regimes. If ideas are the basic determining element, and each generation socializes the next into its values, attitudes, and perspectives, we would expect no basic changes except in the degree to which the goals inherent in the various value systems transmitted from generation to generation are realized, or the consistency among values and goals is increased, or those values that promote economic development and hence superior military force (which then results in the conquest and suppression of other cultures) are enhanced. Thus, Parsonian attempts to interpret history — especially the history of Socialism, fascism, and other mass movements — in these terms is inadequate. Changes which run against the normal development of value systems appear to indicate that they have to be accounted for by the existence of processes occurring within the social structure of the society, and that values, perceptions, and norms ultimately arise from the social structure.

This brings us to the fourth criticism of Parsonian functionalism — the narrow and one-sided positive nature of its functionalism. Parsons views everything in society as working for the benefit and advancement of everything else. All social forces that operate with, rather than against, one another to the mutual benefit of all contribute to the general equilibrium. Again, such a positive conception of systematic functionalism has difficulty accounting for change, except in the direction of still greater harmony and effectiveness. Some critics also argue that the Parsonian conception of functionalism distorts the operation of social institutions and creates a mystique concerning the actual sources of systematic social change. Although social institutions generally are structured to operate in the interests of the existing system of social relationships, at the same time they accomplish their positive functions they nevertheless generate negative consequences that tend to undermine the system — precisely because they are functioning correctly. (Marxists call these processes contradictions.) These necessary negative consequences or contradictions within a system are the impetuses for change within the system and for the eventual qualitative transformation which a system undergoes. For example, one can argue that a gigantic military budget is functionally necessary to advance U.S. corporate interests around the world and to ensure that the United States remains the number one economic power in the world. But the cost of this gigantic expenditure is the slowing down of the rate of increase in productivity and economic growth in the United States (by directing most research and development to nonproductive military uses), thereby undermining the economic basis of being number one.¹⁰ The notions of contradiction and qualitative change are alien to the Parsonian system.

The elite theory

A third major contending school within political sociology consists of the closely related theories of "elitism" and "mass society." These are to be found in both aristocratic varieties (for example, the work of Pareto, Michels, Mosca, and Baltzell) and radical varieties (for example, the work of C. Wright Mills).¹¹

The aristocratic school of elite theory maintains that all (at least all large) societies have "elites" which rule the vast majority. The state, according to this position, cannot be anything other than the organ of a minority that will necessarily rule in its own interests. The majority is considered to be permanently incapable of government because of its lack of interest or inherent incapacity to govern itself. Leaders are considered to be indispensable. Without them society could not be organized, and effective cooperation would be impossible. Economic, military, social, or any other activity must be led by small numbers of individuals with the will, ability, and interest in putting things together and inspiring the masses. This is the only way things can ever get done.

> *Among the constant facts and tendencies that are to be found in all political organisms, one is so obvious that it is apparent to the most casual eye. In all societies — from societies that are very meagerly developed and have barely attained the dawnings of civilization, down to the most advanced and powerful societies — two classes of people appear — a class that rules and a class that is ruled. The first class, always less numerous, performs all political functions, monopolizes power, and enjoys the advantages that power brings, whereas the second, the more numerous class, is directed and controlled by the first in a manner that is now more or less legal, now more or less arbitrary and violent, and supplies the first, in appearance at least, with material means of subsistence and with the instrumentalities that are essential to the vitality of the political organism.¹²*

---

¹⁰ For the development of this argument, see the last part of chapter 13. Also see Albert Szymanski, "Military Spending and Economic Stagnation," *American Journal of Sociology* 79, no. 1 (July 1973): 1—14.

¹¹ The essential works in the conservative elitist tradition include Vilfredo Pareto, *The Mind and Society* (New York: Dover Publications, 1935, 1963); Gaetavo Mosca, *The Ruling Class* (New York: McGraw-Hill, 1939); Roberto Michels, *Political Parties* (New York: Collier, 1915, 1962); E. Digby Baltzell, *The Protestant Establishment* (New York: Random House, 1964); and E. Digby Baltzell, *Philadelphia Gentlemen* (New York: The Free Press, 1958). The radical variety of elitist theory is best represented by Mills, *The Power Elite*. The work of G. William Domhoff is also considered by some to be within the tradition of radical elitist theory. See, for example, G. William Domhoff, *Who Rules America?* (Englewood Cliffs, N.J.: Prentice-Hall, 1967) and *The Higher Circles*.

¹² Mosca, *The Ruling Class*, p. 50.

Elite theory generally assumes that individuals have an inborn drive for power. That power is sought after and jealously guarded once obtained. When leaders from the masses attain positions of power, they tend to become willing to do anything to avoid returning to the humble conditions of the masses. Even leaders with the most sincere and firm equalitarian and reformist commitments necessarily become transformed into jealous guardians of their own privilege once they obtain power.

The elite of leaders, moreover, has the means to maintain its position. These leaders occupy the command posts of the major institutions of society and can manipulate the resources they have at their disposal to secure their position. They control the press, mass media, education, the state, and religion. They can mobilize the popular religions and patriotic and racist sentiments to manipulate the helpless masses in virtually any manner they choose. Elites become adept at using demagogic appeals to the masses to keep themselves in power. Different elites tend to justify their power and privilege by different ideologies subscribed to by the masses — some rely primarily on religion (for example, the Divine Right of Kings), some on patriotism, some on fear of communism, others on the personal quasi-mystical qualities of their leaders, still others on the myth of the ballot box. The choice of "political formula" rests more on which particular appeal the masses will buy.

Governing elites also vary by the relative degree of physical force, chicanery, and moral or ideological appeal they use to control the masses. Some types of elites use considerably more manipulation, and some considerably more violence than others. But in all cases, and at all times, the elite always dominates the masses. Even when a revolutionary overthrow of a given elite occurs, it is led by another elite that soon transforms itself into just as powerful and privileged a group as its predecessors. The masses are constitutionally incapable of governing themselves.

The radical version of elite theory is closely identified with C. Wright Mills. Mills also sees society as divided between the politically dominant elite and the passive masses who are manipulated by the elite. The power of the members of the elite comes from their structural position at the "command posts" of the society. Their power has grown greater in recent years because society has become more centralized and the social institutions have grown larger and more powerful. Because of common interests, common background, and common contemporary patterns of association, the elite makes decisions (only in part through actually getting together and working out agreements) which generally benefit its own interests at the expense of the masses.

Mills, like the aristocratic elite theorists, sees the masses as manipulated, but he does not claim that this is because they are constitutionally incapable of governing themselves. Instead he attributes their passivity to the atomization of nonelite individuals and the pervasive manipulative influence of the mass media. Although his book is permeated with hostility toward the elites, and although he does not argue that elitism is a necessary aspect of society (as do the conservative elitists), neither does he argue that a society without elites is possible, or that the masses can actually govern themselves. His argument then does not differ much from that of Pareto, Mosca, Michels et al., except in its tone.

The theory of mass society

Closely related to elite theory is the theory of mass society.[13] In the work of Mills, Kornhauser, and Nisbet (although not in the work of Mosca, Pareto, and Michels) they are unified as part of one argument. Contrary to what pluralists believe, mass society theorists view society as an amorphous set of atomized individuals or small individual families facing the consolidated power of elites (of the state or big corporations) without the benefit of strong associations to guide and protect them. Because of the absence of a strong network of "intermediate" associations that mediate between the individual and the elite, a healthy political process is impossible. In the eyes of the radicals, this situation means that the masses are helpless before the power of the media and the state, and thus become passive pawns before the juggernaut of the ruling elites that are able to manipulate them at will. In the eyes of the conservatives, this means that the masses engage in "irrational mass behavior" (that is, making socialist revolutions, rioting for food or national self-determination) unconstrained by traditional influences like the church, which traditionally secured law and order by tying the individual into stable social relationships.

The elitist theory of democracy

A variant of elitism is what has been called "the elitist theory of democracy." Conservative theorists sympathetic to the idea that governing elites are both inevitable and desirable have developed a sophisticated defense of the parliamentary form of state. Joseph Schumpeter and Seymour Martin Lipset are perhaps the best known proponents of this position.[14] Schumpeter argues that the classical theory of democracy is absurd. The classical theory made three assumptions — each, he maintains, is invalid: (1) individuals in society have a definite political will; (2) individuals have the ability to observe and interpret the facts; and (3) individuals will make a rational choice, on the basis of their will and knowledge,

---

[13] The classical works in the theory of mass society include: Jose Ortega y Gasset, *The Revolt of the Masses* (New York: W. W. Norton, 1960); Emile Lederer, *The State of the Masses* (New York: W. W. Norton, 1940); Sergei Chakotkin, *The Rape of the Masses* (New York: Alliance Press, 1940); Robert Nisbet, *The Quest for Community* (New York: Oxford University Press, 1953); William Kornhauser, *The Politics of Mass Society* (Glencoe, Ill.: Free Press, 1959); Hannah Arendt, *The Origins of Totalitarianism* (New York: Harcourt, Brace, 1966); and Herbert Marcuse, *One Dimensional Man* (Boston: Beacon Press, 1964). For one of the better critiques of this position see Hamilton, *Class and Politics*, chapter 2.

[14] See Joseph Schumpeter, *Capitalism, Socialism and Democracy* (New York: Harper Brothers, 1950), part IV; and Seymour Martin Lipset, *Political Man* (Garden City, N.Y.: Doubleday, 1960), chapter 2.

of representatives who will implement their will. Schumpeter argues that most people (1) do not have a clear conception of what they want from the state; (2) are incapable of objectively assessing and interpreting facts; and (3) are irrational in their reasoning processes, thus making them constitutionally unable to intelligently choose representatives who carry out their wills.

Rather than drawing the same conclusion as do Pareto, Michels, and Mosca (that the democratic process is a deception and a sham), Schumpeter takes the tack of redefining democracy to fit in with the "reality" of constitutionally incompetent masses. He defines democracy as "the institutional arrangement for arriving at political decisions in which individuals acquire the power to decide by means of a competitive struggle for power." The meaning of democracy is thus changed from a government of the people in which the people authentically decide the policies of their state, to the existence of competition among elites to control the state. However, Schumpeter's argument essentially amounts to an indirect statement of the aristocratic elitist position.

Following Schumpeter, Seymour Martin Lipset, the most influential figure in contemporary political sociology, offered his own definition of democracy in response to the obvious fact that the masses were not governing themselves. Lipset defines a democracy as a political system, which supplies regular constitutional opportunities for changing the governing officials, and a social mechanism, which permits the largest possible part of the population to influence major decisions among contenders for political office. The only significant difference between Lipset's and Schumpeter's definitions is the phrase in Lipset's definition "which permits the largest possible part of the population to influence major decisions." While making the definition more palatable to his American audience, the substance of his redefinition of democracy is the same as Schumpeter's. No criteria are given of "influence" other than the vote of the people itself, an idea which is already included in Schumpeter's definition. The question left begging by both definitions is how the vote is determined and what actual role voting plays in determining the decisions made by the state. Their "up-to-date" definitions seem to reduce to descriptions of competition among elites within parliamentary forms for the power and privileges of governing society, utilizing the democratic ideology to mobilize support. The classical substantive criteria of whether a society is democratic — the correspondence between the interests of the people as determined through autonomous, careful, and rational study and analysis on the part of the masses, and the policies of the state — have been lost, but the idea that advanced capitalist societies are "democratic" (now merely a word which evokes good feelings) is maintained.

Critiques of elite theory

Probably the most serious objection raised to elite theory is to its contention that elites normally *control* the masses and the functioning of society.[15] Elites decide

---

[15] For critiques of elite theory see Herbert Aptheker, *The World of C. Wright Mills* (New York: Marzani and Munsell, 1960); G. William Domhoff and Hoyt Ballard, *C. Wright*

how things will be, the argument goes, and their will is usually implemented. Critics of the elite theory maintain that by arguing that the masses are totally controlled and manipulated by elites, the power of the dominant group(s) in society is greatly exaggerated. In reality, people continually resist domination, sometimes quite successfully — either on a specific issue when they force the dominant group to retreat, or occasionally altogether in a social revolution. Elite theory (and its companion, mass society theory) makes it difficult to understand how such resistance and ongoing struggle over policies is possible. It thus makes change, especially change involving the masses of people, difficult to understand. Contrary to what elitist theory implies, politics is a matter of struggle. No one group, however well positioned, can be totally in control. The masses of people are not as passive or manipulatable as the theory of mass society presumes.

Elite theory argues that the urge to dominate or the drive for power on the part of elites is the motivating force underlying the inevitable development of controlling elites. Both assumptions are debatable on empirical grounds. It is open to question whether a general urge to dominate or will to power can be demonstrated empirically. Also, it is problematic whether all societies are equally dominated by small elites that act in their own interest against the masses of people. While all societies and groups may have leaders, these leaders in fact could be motivated by a wide variety of concerns that vary considerably by society, time, class, function of the group, and personality of the leaders — an abstract urge to power does not seem to be a universal motivation. Similarly, societies and groups vary considerably in the degree to which the masses actively and authentically participate in the determination of policies and in the degree to which state policies serve the people's interest. The critics maintain that there is no more an inherent tendency for elites to appropriate the power of the people than there is an inherent tendency in the opposite direction. Rather than an "iron law" applying to all societies at all times, the relative distribution of power and privilege is a product of historically specific forms of social organization.

Two specific theoretical notions

The three general perspectives that have been outlined here (pluralism, Parsonian functionalism, and elite theory) — as the three leading theoretical approaches within contemporary American political sociology — are manifested in a wide range of theoretical formulations. In addition to these broad perspectives there are, of course, more limited theoretical notions that exert considerable influ-

---

Mills and the Power Elite (Boston: Beacon Press, 1968); Nicos Poulantzas, *Political Power and Social Classes* (London: New Left Books and Sheed and Ward, 1973); Sabine Sarbei-Biermann et al., "Class Domination and the Political System: A Critical Interpretation of Recent Contributions by Claus Offe," *Working Papers on the Kapitalistate*, no. 2 (1973); John Mollenkopf, "Theories of the State and Power Structure Research," *The Insurgent Sociologist* 5, no. 3 (Spring 1975); Claus Offe, "The Abolition of Market Control and the Problem of Legitimacy," *Working Papers on the Kapitalistate*, no. 1 and no. 2 (1973).

ence within more delimited areas. Two of these — the Marxian revisionist view of the working class, and the idea of group pressures — are discussed in the sections that follow.

The Marxian Revisionist View of the Working Class Since the 1930s, Marxian ideas have had a considerable influence within political sociology — for example, the idea of the centrality of class position in determining political attitudes and behavior; the idea that politics is largely a reflection of class struggle; the idea that business has a disproportionate impact on determining state policy; and the concern with the effect of state policy on social classes. The Marxian revisionists integrate these notions into a generally pluralist framework.[16] The working class is *not* considered to be the agent of historical progress, but rather just one among many social classes, all with legitimate interests and contributions to make. In fact, in this tradition there is a tendency to view the middle class as the major defender of democratic institutions, civility, moderation, rationality, and all that is good and desirable in politics.

Lipset's classic statement, *Political Man* (1959), is undoubtedly the most influential work within political sociology. It, more than any other book, summarizes the case for the Marxian revisionist position. Three chapters (chapters 6, 7, 8) summarize the principles of the revisionist version of the group voting perspective and the effect of social position — especially occupational or class position — on the determination of political attitudes. For the most part Lipset's argument differs little from an orthodox Marxist analysis of voting. The major exception most Marxists would take to Lipset's class analysis concerns his drawing of class lines. In his work, as well as in that of most others in Lipset's tradition, the working class is defined as those in *manual* occupations, while the middle class is defined as those in nonmanual occupations.

Marxists define class not by the nature of the work done, but rather by the relationship to the means of production. Thus Marxists consider lower level white-collar workers in offices and salesrooms as well as most service workers (excluding the police) to be part of the working class or proletariat. Only those who either own the means of production or exercise functional ownership through actual control over the labor power of others and/or themselves are considered to be middle class or petty bourgeois. While most Marxists consider the industrial working class (Lipset's manual occupations) to be potentially the most leftist and politically the most important sector of the working class, the two groups are not coterminous. When the class lines are drawn according to this conceptualization rather than according to the revisionist approach, approximately 75 percent of the people in

---

[16] Classic statements of revisionist Marxism include: Eduard Berstein, *Evolutionary Socialism* (New York: Schocken, 1909, 1970); and Lipset, *Political Man*. Also see Thomas Marshall, *Class, Citizenship and Social Development* (Garden City, N.Y.: Doubleday, 1964); Kurt Mayer, *Class and Society* (Garden City, N.Y.: Doubleday, 1955); Robert Alford, *Party and Society* (Chicago: Rand McNally, 1963); and Daniel Bell, *The End of Ideology* (Glencoe, Ill.: Free Press, 1960).

advanced industrial society (compared with the approximately 35 percent proposed by the Marxian revisionists) are part of the "working class." This could make a significant difference in one's interpretation of the dynamic and future of class struggle.

A second related idea proposed in chapters 6 to 8 of Lipset's book (as well as in the introductory and concluding chapters) is the "embourgeoisment" of the working class.[17] Lipset argues that one of the principal determinants of workers' politics is their level of skill, while the primary determinant of the degree of democracy of a society is its wealth. According to the embourgeoisment argument, the working class is being integrated into society as the differences in income, type of labor, life-style, and attitudes between the working class and the middle class evaporate. As society becomes wealthier it can afford to bring most of the working class in, leaving only a relatively small number of marginal low-paid workers and farmers (among whom minority groups such as blacks and Latins are concentrated) out of the mainstream of middle-class life in America. Although Lipset does not fully develop the embourgeoisment thesis in *Political Man*, others who have picked up where he left off have attempted to demonstrate that the gap between working-class and middle-class life-styles and political attitudes is shrinking as the working class adopts those of the middle class. (Several British studies empirically test this thesis.[18]) They argue that the process of embourgeoisment undermines the basis for the continuation of class struggle politics in the advanced capitalist countries.

Even if Marxists were to concur with the notion that there is a convergence in life-styles and politics between the working class and the middle class, they would argue that this reflects, not an adoption of middle-class values by the working class, but rather the evolution of a new working-class life-style and politics (different from that of the early twentieth century) shared by industrial, white-collar, and service workers — a new homogeneous life-style and political culture common to all sectors of the working class. This new working-class culture is made possible now, for the first time, by the increasing similarity of the relation to the means of production and conditions of labor of all sectors of the working

---

[17] For one of the most influential statements of the "embourgeoisment" thesis, see Kurt Mayer, *Class and Society* (New York: Random House, 1955) and his "Recent Changes in the Class Structure of the United States," *Transactions of the Third World Congress of Sociology* vol. 3, 1956, pp. 66–80. For refutations of this thesis see S. M. Miller and Frank Riessman, "Are Workers Middle Class?," *Dissent* 8 (Autumn 1961): 507–516; S. M. Miller and Frank Riessman, "The Working Class Subculture: A New View," *Social Problems* 9 (Summer 1961): 86–97; Richard Hamilton, "The Income Difference Between Skilled and White Collar Workers," *British Journal of Sociology* 14 (December 1963): 363–373; John Goldthorpe et al., *The Affluent Worker: Political Attitudes and Behavior* (Cambridge, England: Cambridge University Press, 1967–1968); and John Goldthorpe et al., "The Affluent Worker and the Thesis of Embourgeoisment," *Sociology* 1, no. 1 (January 1967). See chapter 3 for a detailed treatment of the factors that influence working-class politics.

[18] See sources listed in f.n. 17.

class. This argument establishes the groundwork for a *sharpening* of class struggle politics because of the polarization implicit in the undermining of differences *within* the working class.

Chapters 4, 5, and 12 of *Political Man* complete the argument against the classic Marxist insistence that the working class is the historical agent of reason and human progress, while the middle class is the agent of reaction and irrationality. Lipset argues that the working class tends to be "authoritarian" — intolerant of civil liberties and prone to dictatorial, irrational, intemperate, and uncivil behavior. The middle class, Lipset maintains, is the main defender of moderation, civility, and respect for political differences and, further, represents the voice of reason and progress. While chapter 4 marshalls empirical evidence to show that working-class people are incapable of guiding society, chapter 5 is dedicated to refuting the theory, very popular in the 1930s and 1940s, that fascism is primarily a middle-class phenomenon — which is a natural corollary of the position that this class is the agent of civility and democracy.

By advancing a study of an "exceptional case" of a truly democratic union, chapter 12 adds to the argument that the working class and its organizations are incapable of providing guidance to all classes in the establishment of a genuine democratic society. According to Lipset, his study proves the rule that working-class unions and parties must of necessity be bureaucratic and dictatorial. Accepting the argument of the elite theorist Roberto Michels, Lipset implicitly poses the rhetorical question — If the working class is unable to make its own organizations democratic, how could it ever play the role of a "vanguard" or guiding force in bringing democracy to the whole of society? Lipset thus lays the groundwork for the current leading position within political sociology on this issue: The middle class is the agent of reform and democracy not only in the advanced capitalist countries, but also in the countries of Asia, Africa, and Latin America, whereas the working class is incapable of guiding even itself, let alone all society.

The Idea of Group Pressures Another specific theory commonly accepted by both the radical (most prominently represented by Richard Hamilton and Maurice Zeitlin) and the more conservative theorists (such as Lipset, Berelson, Campbell, Lazarsfeld et al.) is the idea of group pressures. This theory stresses the importance of the role social groups play in determining one's political attitudes and behavior.[19] Many pluralists use the group-voting concept as a sub-

[19] Classic statements of the group-influence thesis and empirical works based on this idea include: Bernard Bereleson et al., *Voting* (Chicago: University of Chicago Press, 1954); Angus Campbell et al., *The Voter Decides* (Evanston, Ill.: Row Peterson, 1954); Lipset, *Political Man*; Elihu Katz and Paul Lazarsfeld, *Personal Influence* (Glencoe, Ill.: Free Press, 1955); Richard Hamilton, *Affluence and the French Worker* (Princeton, N.J.: Princeton University Press, 1967); Hamilton, *Class and Politics*; Paul Lazarsfeld et al., *The People's Choice* (New York: Columbia University Press, 1960); and Maurice Zeitlin, *Revolutionary Politics and the Cuban Working Class* (Princeton, N.J.: Princeton University Press, 1967).

stitute for the ideal of formal voluntary associations as the primary constituent element in the equilibrium of social forces. Some radicals use the idea as a substitute for the concept that organized class-conscious organizations and the fully developed class consciousness they stimulate are the primary factors behind the political struggles of the oppressed classes. The pluralists have to face a very serious problem when it is pointed out that most people are not active in voluntary associations, that most voluntary associations are not particularly concerned with politics, that most members of voluntary associations play a most marginal role in the process of decision making within them, and that there is a wide disparity in the political clout of voluntary associations.

Marxists — at least in the United States — also have a serious analytical problem. They do not believe that the working class and other oppressed groups are completely manipulated by the ruling class, for to do so would reduce their theory to elitism. Yet they cannot argue that the class consciousness and militancy of the oppressed in the United States are sufficiently developed for a social revolution to occur. This is inconsistent with the available evidence and could cause those who base their political practices on such an analysis to formulate faulty political strategies. In both theoretical schema, the idea of the centrality of group processes represents a sharp contrast to the notion (of mass society theory) that individuals are atomized, and hence subject to total manipulation, *and* to the idea that political behavior is a rational individual reaction to factors which affect individual people.

The central idea of the group pressures theory is that people are firmly rooted in a network of small, mostly informal groups that insulates the individual from direct influence from the elite groups in society. A person's position within social groups, perhaps the most important of which are those which grow up around the person's job, imposes upon him/her attitudes, values, and perceived interests that may or may not realistically reflect the person's interests. The structure of social relationships within which the person is implanted determines how the person perceives economic, social, and political forces, and how the person responds to such forces. The groups of which the person is a part consist of the typical patterns of social relationships and communications of people similarly positioned in society. The pressures these similarly positioned people put on each other produces and reinforces a common consciousness and common forms of behavior. Social group pressure is thus the primary and immediate determinant of political attitudes and behavior. Since similar situations produce similar social relationships and communications, one can expect that the political behavior and attitudes of a social group represent rational responses to each member's personal situation — even though the derivation of their politics did not have a classically rational basis.

The Marxist and Marxian variants of the group pressures school argue that the most salient social groups grow up around the job. Work is the very center of the person's life, and thus the social processes in which one is involved at work play the most important role in structuring one's life experiences and perceptions. The group pressures theory thus explains how one's relationship to the means of production operates to produce political consciousness, and how, in the absence of a class-conscious Marxist party, the working class can nevertheless "spontaneously" have class consciousness.

The pluralist proponents of the group pressures thesis reject the idea that one's "occupational role" determines the relative salience of group pressures which in turn determine the individual's politics. They emphasize instead the multiplicity of different social groups and the overlapping group memberships of individuals. They see most individuals as belonging to different social groups, which pressure the individual to adopt *different* perceptions, values, attitudes, and behavior. They see people who are subject to the least cross-pressures as the firmest in their political commitments and the most politically active. People subjected to the greatest cross-pressures, however, are the most ambiguous and least active. The stability of "democratic systems" and political flexibility is viewed as dependent on the prevalence of the latter type of people.

The Fundamentals of the Marxist Perspective

The perspective used in this book incorporates many of the insights contained in the competing perspectives just reviewed. It agrees with the pluralists that politics is a matter of struggle among contending interests (although heavily biased in favor of the capitalist class). It agrees with the elite theorists that a rather small, powerful group dominates (but does not control) society. It agrees with the functionalists that the leading group within the state must either service the general social interest or have its rule become unstable (and eventually be overthrown). And it agrees with the Marxian revisionists and the theorists of group pressure that the group involvements of people as structured by their economic roles largely determine political attitudes and behavior. However, this book argues that although these other perspectives — perspectives which as of 1977 enjoyed more currency within the field of political sociology than Marxism — have achieved partial understandings of political processes, they each fail to give us a complete and scientific understanding. This book maintains that Marxism is the theoretical system best able to incorporate the various strong points of the contending theories, avoid their weaknesses, and successfully interpret the empirical studies undertaken by political sociologists over the last generation.

According to Marxist theory, the state plays a central role in society.[20] A

---

[20] The classic Marxist works on state include: Karl Marx, *The Eighteenth Brumaire of Louis Napoleon*, in *Selected Works in One Volume* (New York: International Publishers, 1968); Friedrich Engels, *The Origin of the Family, Private Property and the State* (New York: International Publishers, 1972); Friedrich Engels, *Anti-Duhring*, (Moscow: Foreign Languages Publishing House, 1962); and V. I. Lenin, *The State and Revolution*, in *Selected Works in Three Volumes*, vol. II (Moscow: Foreign Languages Publishing House, 1960).

Marxist political sociology must thus give careful and detailed consideration to the nature of the state. We begin by defining exactly what we mean by the term *state*. The state is a social institution consisting of a group of *full-time* decision-making and administrative officials and specialists in the use of physical violence. This group successfully exerts hegemonic military force within its territorial area, and is consequently the arbitrator of conflicts, the securer of social order, and the guarantor of existing social relationships.[21] The exercise of superior military force in a territory is the essence of the state.

In the words of Lenin, "The state is the product and the manifestation of the irreconcilability of class antagonism. The state arises when, where, and to the extent that class antagonisms objectively cannot be reconciled."[22] The state is an instrument by which the exploitation of the economically subordinate class is secured by the economically dominant class that controls the state (what is called "the ruling class"). In the language of the *Communist Manifesto*, "Political power, properly so classed, is merely the organized power of one class for oppressing another."[23] In Lenin's words, "The state . . . is a class concept. The state is an organ or instrument of violence exercised by one class against another."[24] The social relationships and the social order that the state guarantees are thus the social relationships of inequality and the order of property and exploitation. The historically specific manifestation of the state is always a product of the means and mode of production prevailing in society. Thus in capitalist society we speak of *the capitalist state*.

To understand fully these statements it is necessary to understand exactly how Marxists use the terms *class* and *capitalist*. A class consists of all those individuals who share a similar relationship to property or the means of production. Thus in a slave society, such as the pre-Civil War South in the United States, the two major classes were the slaves and the slave owners. In feudal Europe the two major classes were the serfs and the feudal landlords. And in capitalist society the two major classes are the capitalist class and the working class (or proletariat). Each basic type of class society tends to have a dominant class that owns the primary means of production (for example, the slaves, the land, the machines), and a subject class that directly produces most of the goods and services.

Every society also has secondary classes, such as small independent landowners, self-employed artisans and merchants, and the permanently unemployed. In capitalist society the most important of these secondary classes is called the *petty bourgeoisie* — those people who *own* or *control* their own means of production (as do the capitalists) *and* who work them themselves (as do proletarians). Those who legally do *not* have ownership rights in the means of production, but

---

[21] For an excellent analytical discussion of the nature of the state, see Engels, *Origins of the Family, Private Property, and the State*, chapter 9.
[22] Lenin, *The State and Revolution*, p. 306.
[23] Marx and Engels, *The Communist Manifesto*, in *Selected Works*, p. 54.
[24] Lenin, *Can the Bolsheviks Retain State Power?* in *Selected Works*, vol. II, p. 447.

who have control over the labor power of others and relative control over their own work process, are members of the petty bourgeoisie — for example, most business executives and higher level professionals.

Capitalist society is that type of society in which most of the producer class does not own the means of production, is itself neither the property of another class (as are slaves) nor tied to the land (as are serfs), and consequently is able to, and must (to feed itself) sell its labor power to those who own the means of production but who do not themselves set these means of production in motion.

Even those states which are set up by conquest, revolution, or coup d'état and whose leadership consists of military people, popular rebel leaders, religious figures, or fascist parties normally settle into the normal pattern. A new ruling class (whether established by military force, insurrection, political abilities or manipulation of religious ideology) typically transforms itself into the new owners of the means of production (for example, the Germanic invaders of the Roman empire who became the new feudal lords, or the barbarian conquerors of India and China who became despots in their own right). The effect of the mode by which a new regime was established soon becomes socially irrelevant, as it comes to be manifested only in ceremonial forms.[25]

The general rule that all states are the instruments of the economically dominant class is only clearly operative when there *is* one dominant economic class. In times of economic contention between two powerful classes, each with considerable economic assets, the state bureaucracy is able to establish a degree of independence from *both* contending forces (since they largely cancel each other out). The state bureaucracy then can come to have an independent life of its own. However, such situations are temporary. They occur in periods of transition from one form of social organization to another. According to Engels:

> *... periods occur in which the warring classes balance each other so nearly that the state power, as ostensible mediator, acquires, for the moment, a certain degree of independence of both. Such was the absolute monarchy of the seventeenth and eighteenth centuries, which held the balance between the nobility and the class of burghers; such was the Bonapartism of the First, and still more of the Second French Empire, which played off the proletariat against the bourgeoisie and the bourgeoisie against the proletariat. The latest performance of this kind, in which ruler and ruled appear equally*

---

[25] Engels provides a masterful defense of this position in his *Anti-Duhring*. In maintaining that the mode of production is the primary organizing element in class society, Marx argued: "This much, however, is clear, that the middle ages could not live on Catholicism, nor the Ancient World on politics. On the contrary, it is the mode in which they gained a livelihood that explains why here politics, and there Catholicism, played the chief part. For the rest, it requires but a slight acquaintance with the history of the Roman republic, for example, to be aware that its secret history is the history of its landed property. On the other hand, Don Quixote long ago paid the penalty for wrongly imagining that knightly errantry was compatible with all economic forms of society." Karl Marx, *Capital*, vol. I (Moscow: Foreign Languages Publishing House, n.d.), p. 82.

ridiculous, is the new German Empire of the Bismarck nation: here capitalists and workers are balanced against each other and equally cheated for the benefit of the impoverished Prussian cabbage junkers.[26]

Karl Marx also devoted a lengthy study, *The Eighteenth Brumaire,* to an analysis of one such regime, that of the second Napoleon in France.[27]

A state does not rely exclusively on the use of physical force to maintain its hegemony. Physical force, in fact, is normally used against most members of a class society only as a last resort. States normally guarantee obedience to their rule through religion, nationalism, personal loyalties, voter apathy, and feelings that the state is operating in the interest of the society as a whole. The state propagates the idea that its domination is legitimate — that it is right that people follow its dictates because to do so is to follow God's will or the will of the people, or because it has expert knowledge, and so on. The state creates a cult around itself through its control over education, military training, and public ceremonies. This cult of the state is furthered by the social institutions run by the economically dominant class that dominates the state.[28]

Unlike the elite theorists, Marxists do not maintain that the capitalist class fully controls the other classes in society, nor do they maintain that it can have the state do anything it wants. Rather, the capitalist class is considered to be politically dominant or hegemonic. It normally either gets its way or is able to so deflect and integrate the pressures coming from other classes as to turn them to its own uses. But it does not control all aspects of society. It is merely the typical dominant force in the class struggle, and the force that is dominant within the state.

There are two fundamentally different ways by which the interests and will of the capitalist class are realized against the state. First, through *direct* means or "input" channels, and second, through the *indirect* means of *structuring* the environment in which the state must operate. In most cases both forces are operating at once to guarantee doubly that the state does the bidding of the capitalist class.

One of the direct mechanisms by which the state in capitalist society is directly dominated by the capitalist class is through the actual selection of the incumbents for top governmental office. Leading officials tend to be either leading members of the capitalist class (such as Franklin Roosevelt, John Kennedy, or Nelson Rockefeller); famous celebrities who have been carefully picked and closely advised by members of the upper class, who finance and manage their campaigns and surround them with advisers (for example, Dwight Eisenhower, Ronald Reagan, or John Glenn); or small-time politicians who have worked their way up the ladder by years of service to big business interests, who reward and promote them by funding campaigns and opening doors for them (for example,

---

[26] Engels, *The Origin of the Family*, pp. 320, 321.
[27] Marx, *The Eighteenth Brumaire*, in Marx and Engels, *Selected Works*.
[28] See Lawrence Krader, *The Formation of the State* (Englewood Cliffs, N.J.: Prentice-Hall, 1968).

Richard Nixon, Lyndon Johnson, and Gerald Ford). What applies to the presidents generally also applies to their cabinet officials, and to the upper level managers of the leading governmental agencies.

A second direct mechanism of achieving dominance is through the process of lobbying. Business interests employ thousands of people who have considerable resources at their disposal to influence members of Congress and members of the regulatory and administrative agencies. A third mechanism is the process of forming public policy. Exclusive capitalist-class organizations, such as the Council on Foreign Relations (CFR), actually formulate public policies. These are then transmitted to the appropriate state agencies for implementation, either through the placement of members of these exclusive groups in top government office (for example, Henry Kissinger, a member of the CFR) or through the influence that the prestige of these organizations' reports, studies, conferences, seminars, and advice has on government officials.

The capitalist nature of the state is also guaranteed by another set of processes. Even if the capitalist class exercised no direct control over the state by any of the three mechanisms described earlier, the state would behave in the same way (at least in "normal" conditions). Although if this were the case the state might be more willing to experiment with different policies before settling on those most advantageous to the largest segments of the business community if not the capitalist class as a whole. The state must operate within an ideological, economic, military, and political environment structured by capitalist relations of production. If state officials are to succeed in their careers, if the agencies they command are to operate smoothly, if the state is to prevent social crisis and promote prosperity, and if it is to be successful militarily, then there are certain imperatives that it *must* follow. This is true as long as it stays within the parameters established by the nature of the capitalist system. And it cannot step outside of those parameters to other fundamentally different modes of production without the massive energy of a social revolution behind it sufficient to mobilize the people for a total reorganization of society (and the state).

There are four mechanisms of indirect control over the state:

1. Capitalist values permeate the society and are propagated through the schools, military, media, and churches. Officials typically accept capitalist ideology as their own and authentically act as if capitalist rationality were the only rationality. Attempts by state officials to enact measures that would violate capitalist ideology would generate considerable opposition, even from the oppressed, as long as they accept capitalist ideas.

2. If the state attempts to follow policies that business doesn't like, businesses can move to other countries *or* they may curtail production, lay off workers, or follow other restrictive policies, thereby promoting an economic crisis for which the state would be blamed. Businesses can refuse to invest unless the state follows probusiness policies. Banks have the special advantage of refusing to make loans to the state unless the state follows policies directed by them. Such

actions by business might not be malicious, but might be merely economically rational and dictated by the necessity of maximizing profits.

3. States that attempt anticapitalist policies are subjected to the threat of military intervention, either by foreign states that want to prevent the abolition of capitalism, or by their own military, which may well be closely tied to the capitalist class.

4. Officials who follow anticapitalist policies may be cut off from campaign financing, slandered in the capitalist-class-controlled media, and forced to face well-financed and promoted opponents in their campaigns for reelection as well as being confronted with embarrassing demonstrations, disruptions, and possible social and political crises.

The mere *threat* of the use of these last three mechanisms by the capitalist class is normally sufficient to keep the state on its course even when the state officials themselves have no personal commitment to capitalism.

The state in capitalist society is a capitalist state by virtue of its domination by the capitalist class *and* in that it functions most immediately in the interests of capital. The capitalist state has five basic functions for capitalism: (1) the state operates to preserve the existing class relations in society through guaranteeing private property and law and order; (2) the state makes continual capital accumulation and profitability possible through regulating the labor force, ensuring sufficient buying power in the economy, regulating the economy, and otherwise helping business; (3) the state secures the legitimacy of capitalist society through its control over the schools, its management of the cult of patriotism, and the ideological function of voting to persuade people that the state is being run by and for them, when the reality is quite different; (4) the state operates to "aggregate" the diverse interests and wills of the different segments of the capitalist class — that is, form the capitalist class will — so that the state can implement unified compromise policies tempered by the demands of other classes (this is part of the function of the Congress and the various regulatory and administrative agencies); (5) the state raises the money to fund the bureaucracy and otherwise acts to maintain the apparatus required to perform the first four functions.

Marxism takes a *materialist* position on the formation of political attitudes and the motives for political behavior. It rejects the idealist position, current in many sectors of the social sciences, that values, political socialization, and norms are the ultimate explanations of social phenomena. Marxists look beyond the values and attitudes that motivate people to *why* people believe what they do, and beyond the conscious reasons given for political action to the structural conditions that determine and direct it. Since most people's lives are both centered and anchored in their jobs (or in their relation to the means of production) this factor plays the most important role in structuring our experiences and interests, as well as our formal and informal social groups. Most of our waking hours are spent working, preparing to go to work, or recovering from work. Most of our friends and acquaintances come from our work or from other activities we engage in because of our work. Where we live, our hobbies, even our religion are largely determined by the types of job we and our immediate family have.

People in similar class situations are very likely to develop a common culture that includes similar political attitudes and behavior — that is, to become a *social class*. A social class is typically composed of a set of freely intermarrying families, whose head or heads share the same relation to the means of production, and who share the distinctive traditions common to their social position. A social class is composed of many more people than its core members, who usually are directly relating to the means of production in similar ways. It also includes those who are temporarily unemployed, those who used to have the typical relation to the means of production, but because of disability, retirement, or training programs are not currently employed, and the mates and dependent children of those who are directly relating to the means of production in the class-typical way.

Similarly class-positioned people are further inclined to become *class conscious* — that is, to develop an accurate understanding of their place in society, their collective interest, and their relationship to other classes, and to act as a class to advance their collective interest against other classes.

There are four social classes in the United States: (1) the capitalist class, which owns and controls the major means of production; (2) the petty bourgeoisie (professionals, small-business people, and independent farmers and artisans); (3) the working class of industrial, rural, and white-collar workers, who must sell their labor to live and who do not have authority over other people on the job; and (4) the lumpen proletariat, or people who do not regularly work for a living, but rather live through welfare, crime, or hustling.

Social class is the primary determinant of political attitudes and behavior. Class factors operate to produce consciousness — both directly, through the experience and reasoning of the individual, and indirectly, by the mechanisms outlined in the discussion of the group pressures thesis that produce shared political attitudes and behavior. A "political culture" is produced in the different classes and among the various subgroups within each class (also defined by the special relationship to the means of production of the various segments of a class) that is rooted ultimately in the experiences and interests inherent in their social position.

The objective conditions of life tend to make members of the wealthy capitalist class the most conservative (that is, supportive of the status quo) class in society, and the working class the most leftist or progressive (that is, supportive of change in the direction of greater equality). The petty bourgeoisie, whose conditions of life are intermediate between these two classes, consequently have politics that typically are also intermediate. Because it lacks a structural relation to the means of production, the lumpen proletariat tends not to have stable or consistent politics.

These structurally determined political differences are the basis of the political struggle among the classes. The various types of capitalists tend to have somewhat different interests and experiences, as do the various types of workers and the petty bourgeoisie. These differences also produce political conflict and struggle. The political differences within the various classes — because they generally are not as serious as the differences among classes, and because a common class culture ties the divergent interests within a class together — do not normally lead to as much struggle as intraclass differences.

Struggles within society over state policies are thus understood by Marxists to be rooted in differences in material conditions of life. The analysis of the social basis of politics in chapters 2, 3, 4, and 5 reflects this understanding. Political outcomes are the result of the relative size, social location, consciousness, degree of organization, and strategies followed by classes and segments of classes in their ongoing struggles. No one class or segment of a class is ever able totally to control all aspects of society. State policy is always influenced to some extent by the various classes, even while it is normally under the domination of the class that owns and controls the means of production, and even when other classes have no formal representation in the organs of government. The ruling class must take into account both the demands and likely responses of other classes when it makes state policy. If it does not it may suffer very serious consequences, including social revolution.

The content and outcome of class struggle, however, is not a matter of the strength of will or the abstract consciousness of the various classes. The factors that determine the outcome of political struggle among classes and segments of classes are in turn determined by the logic of the prevailing mode of production and its stage of development. The size of a class, its interests, the size of the relative component parts of a class, the factors that produce its common consciousness, the political skills available to a class, the degree of its organization, the strategies that make sense to these organizations, and the probability of success, are products of basic social forces. Similar outcomes of the political class struggle tend to occur in separate societies at similar stages of development (for example, the situations of the rich capitalist countries or the poor countries of the Third World, or the trend toward dictatorship in the 1930s and toward Communist-led revolution in the Third World in the 1970s). This shows that the results of class struggle are not unique products of the special conditions of each society, but rather are structured by factors inherent in the capitalist mode of production and its historical development.

Marxism accepts the functionalist argument that as long as the special interest of the dominant economic class coincides with the interests of other classes, there is no objective basis for sharp class struggle or for a revolutionary overthrow of its rule. As long as capitalist class dominance of the state resulted in freeing serfs and slaves, wiping out extreme poverty, advancing literacy, undermining mysticism, defending the rights of speech, assembly, press, and religion, full employment and a rising standard of living, and conquering disease and nature, all classes of the population benefited and there was no cause for revolutionary opposition.

But every mode of production has its "contradictions." When these contradictions become manifest in wars between countries, depressions, environmental destruction, racism, stagnation in living standards, high crime rates, rising mental illness, general unhappiness, and rampant competitive individualism, the net effect of capitalist rule on other classes becomes negative.

Marxists believe these contradictions are caused by the need of capitalist enterprises to maximize their profits. Thus, far from being examples of "deviance," malfunction, or accidents, these contradictions are an organic and necessary part of the capitalist system that cannot be eliminated without removing their cause — the capitalist mode of production itself.

Capitalism, because of conflicting demands on it, is unable to solve these problems successfully and thus has to be transcended as a social system to meet the needs of other classes and society in general. Marxists say that at such a point, the capitalist class is no longer "progressive," but now acts as a fetter on historical development. They also argue that another class, the working class, will step forward to provide leadership to society in solving its increasingly serious problems, allowing historical advance to continue. It is only in periods of general social crisis induced by the capitalist class's inability to solve the contradictions of its system that a thorough overturn of class relations is possible.

Class and political attitudes

The basic idea underlying each chapter of this book is the notion that classes and struggles among classes are the essence of political sociology. It is therefore necessary to establish the basis for this claim from the beginning.

The most fundamental (but not always the most immediate) determinant of political attitudes is *social class*, which, in turn, is rooted in its members' relation to the means of production.[29] Thus, more than anything else, politics reflects a conflict among classes and segments of classes. People (at least in the United States) often identify themselves more in terms of factors such as their religion, nationality, region, sex, and marital state, than as members of a class. But these factors in good part ultimately reduce to underlying class factors.[30] As a general rule the lower a social class is in the class structure of a country, the more leftist (that is, in favor of more equality and less privilege) will be its politics. This phenomenon can be illustrated with data from a number of countries (see table 1−1).

Wherever there are large Communist, Socialist, or Labor parties, the lower classes in general and the manual working class in particular give them disproportionate support, while the more privileged classes disproportionately support the more conservative parties.[31] This is illustrated in table 1−1, where electoral

---

[29] Several good general discussions of the social effect of class, especially of the effect on working-class life, are: Arthur Shostak, *Blue-Collar Life* (New York: Random House, 1969); and Seymour Martin Lipset and Reinhard Bendix, ed., *Class, Status and Power*, 1st ed. (Glencoe, Ill.: Free Press, 1953).

[30] This is developed further in chapters 2 to 5.

[31] Throughout this book I use the terms *revolutionary, leftist, liberal, conservative,* and *reactionary* to describe different types of politics. By revolutionary I mean advocacy of a fundamental and discontinuous change in political and economic institutions that takes

Table 1–1 Support of Communist, Socialist and Labor Parties by Class[a]

	W. Germany[1] 1967 (S)[b]	France[2] 1956 (C)[b]	Italy[3] 1958 (C+LS)[b]	Belgium[4] 1968 (C+S)[b]	Norway[5] 1965 (C,LS+L)[b]	Sweden[6] 1968 (S+CJ)[b]	Finland[7] 1966 (C+S)[b]	Britain[8] 1968 (L)[b]	Canada[9] 1965 (L)[b]	Ireland[10] 1969 (L)[b]	Japan[11] 1960 (S)[b]
Large Businessmen, Executives	—	—	—	—	—	—	—	(9%)	—	—	—
Professionals	(5%)	1%	1%	12%	(3%)	{14%	{15%	18	{21%	{10%	20
Small Businessmen	14	6	6	17	24	31	38	23	13	15	44
Office and Sales Workers	34	21	31	27	42	44	{38	37	47	27	43
Urban Manual Workers	49	49	62	47	55	77	80	52	—	—	18
Farmers	(4)	11	10	5	76	6	17	—	5	4	—
Farm Workers	(21)	29	77	—	57	57	70	—	—	—	—

Sources: 1. Richard Rose, ed., *Electoral Behavior: A Comparative Handbook* (New York: The Free Press, 1974), p. 147. Data in parentheses are from Seymour Martin Lipset and Stein Rokkan, ed., *Party Systems and Voter Alignments: Cross-National Perspectives* (New York: The Free Press, 1967), p. 287. (These data are for 1953.)
2. Lipset and Rokkan, *Party Systems*, p. 157.
3. Lipset and Rokkan, *Party Systems*, p. 158.
4. Rose, *Electoral Behavior*, p. 83.
5. Rose, *Electoral Behavior*, p. 334. Datum in parentheses is from Allan Barton study of the 1949 election. Cited in Juan Linz and Seymour Martin Lipset, "The Social Bases of Diversity in Western Democracy" (Stanford: Center for Advanced Study in the Behavioral Sciences, 1956, mimeographed), chapter 8, p. 4.
6. Rose, *Electoral Behavior*, p. 401.
7. Rose, *Electoral Behavior*, p. 294.
8. Rose, *Electoral Behavior*, p. 502. Datum in parentheses is from John Bonham, *The Middle Class Vote* (London: Faber and Faber, 1954), p. 129. This datum is for 1951.
9. Rose, *Electoral Behavior*, p. 584.
10. Rose, *Electoral Behavior*, p. 631.
11. Lipset and Rokkan, *Party Systems*, p. 448.

[a] The definition of the various classes varies from study to study. In some countries the data are for men only, in some other countries housewives are considered to be part of their husbands' class. Thus the figures for the different countries are not exactly comparable. The support for one or another party fluctuates from one election to another giving these figures more a general than a precise character. In those countries where the Communist Party and left wing Socialists are strong, respondents sympathetic to these parties often lie to interviewers about their political support of such groups thus producing an artificially low support percentage for them. Because of all these problems the data reported above should be interpreted to have only very general usefulness in indicating the ranking of various classes in their support of the left parties within each country.

[b] (S) indicates the figures are for the main socialist or social democratic party in the country.
   (C) indicates the figures are for the Communist Party.
   (L) indicates that the figures are for the Labor Party.
   (LS) indicates that the figures are for the left Socialist Party.

data from West Germany, France, Italy, Belgium, Norway, Sweden, Finland, Britain, Canada, Ireland, and Japan are reported. Similar results have been found for the Netherlands and Australia.[32] Indeed, almost all countries from which data are available reflect the same phenomena.[33]

The United States is the only advanced capitalist country of any size anywhere in the world with a parliamentary system that does not have a massive Communist, Socialist, or Labor party.[34] But even in the United States the lower classes, especially the working class, are more leftist than the more privileged classes. In the United States the near-universal tendency of the working class to be the most leftist (that is, the most equalitarian) is manifested in its disproportionate support for the Democratic party (of the two major parties the one with the equalitarian *popular image*) and for liberal economic and social policies. In 1968, 43 percent of American manual workers voted for Humphrey, the liberal Democratic candidate, as compared with 36 percent of professionals, 37 percent of business people, and 38 percent of clerical and sales workers.[35] In the 1964 elections, only 20 percent of nonsouthern, white, married, manual workers supported Goldwater in contrast to 51 percent of the upper middle class (professionals, higher salaried employees, and business people).[36] In 1968, 70 percent of manual workers outside of the South identified themselves as Democrats, in contrast to 25 percent of independent professionals, 51 percent of managers and officials, 43 percent of salaried professionals, 57 percent of independent business people, and 67 percent of clerical and sales people.[37]

The relative leftism of American workers is also revealed in their attitudes about social questions. In 1968 a nationwide sample survey inquired into the attitudes of people toward federally guaranteed jobs and a decent standard of living, and toward federal guarantees of low-cost medical care. Forty-five percent of

---

power away from one class or group of classes and gives it to another class or classes. Leftism refers to support of equalitarian measures that reduce the differences in power, wealth, and privilege among classes and strata (the term *progressive* can be used synonomously). Liberal means advocacy of relatively minor and slow changes in the direction of equalitarianism (while radical refers to advocacy of more basic and rapid change). Conservative refers to support of the status quo. Reactionary means advocacy of a real or imagined *status quo ante*, belief in restoring the old order, or reversing the recent course of political and economic events (fascism is one variety of reaction).

[32] Data for the Netherlands can be found in Richard Rose, ed., *Electoral Behavior: A Comparative Handbook* (New York: The Free Press, 1974), p. 244. Data for Australia can be found in Robert Alford, *Party and Society* (Chicago: Rand McNally, 1963), p. 102.

[33] See Lipset, *Political Man*, part II.

[34] For a discussion of the exceptional situation of the United States, see the last part of chapter 13.

[35] Rose, *Electoral Behavior*, p. 702.

[36] Richard Hamilton, *Restraining Myths: Critical Studies of U.S. Social Structure and Politics* (New York: John Wiley and Sons, 1975), p. 159.

[37] Hamilton, *Restraining Myths*, p. 47.

manual workers favored a federal governmental job and living-standard guarantee in contrast to 26 percent of independent business people, 43 percent of independent professionals, 22 percent of managers and officials, 37 percent of salaried professionals, and 39 percent of clerical and sales people. Seventy-three percent of manual workers favored federal support of medical care, compared with 58 percent of independent business people, 60 percent of independent professionals, 66 percent of managers and officials, 52 percent of salaried professionals, and 58 percent of clerical and sales people.[38]

The greater leftism of the manual working class and other less privileged groups reflects their material interest in social equality. The Communist, Socialist, and Labor parties (and even to a degree, the Democratic party in the United States — "the party of the working man") support, and are identified in the popular mind with, measures designed to improve the living standards and working conditions of the poor and working classes, diminish the degree of inequality in society, and defend the rights of the less privileged. Therefore, these parties get most of their support from those who would gain from governments led by them. It should come as no surprise that those who stand to benefit from equalitarian policies support them. What would seem more difficult to explain is why some members of the lower classes do *not* support equalitarian measures that would benefit them.

The correlation between class and political attitudes is far from perfect, however, since class factors do not operate in an unmediated way on politics. The most serious obstruction to the operation of class factors is the influence of the most powerful groups in society on the rest of the social classes. Through control of the media, education, religious institutions, the structure of jobs, and military indoctrination, the upper class intervenes in the process of the creation of political attitudes to block the operation of class factors.[39] The less privileged classes are thus subject to considerable conflicting pressure coming from their shared economic experiences and interests on one side, and their cultural experiences and subjection to authoritarian relationships on the other. Which set of factors predominates at any given time for a class or section of a class is a function of specific historical factors examined later. Consequently, fundamental political disagreement among the lower classes, even in periods of massive upheaval from below, is considerable. The upper class of a society, on the other hand, is subjected to the least cross-pressures, since its immediate economic experiences and social milieu are reinforced by the media and education to which it is exposed, as well as by its positions of command in the structure of authority. Consequently, its politics are usually the most consistent of any class.[40]

---

[38] Ibid., p. 55.

[39] See chapters 3 and 11 for a full discussion of the effect on the working class of ideological hegemony by the capitalist class.

[40] The conservative upper-class parties benefit from the fact that people tend to see themselves in the most favorable light. If people have any attribute which they believe is that of an upper-class or upper-middle-class person, they have a tendency to think of them-

Summary

This chapter has outlined the major contending perspectives and theoretical notions within contemporary political sociology. It has also outlined an alternative perspective — that of Marxism — which is the perspective presented by this book. Pluralism (the idea that politics is the result of compromise among a wide variety of equal groups), Parsonian functionalism (the idea that political institutions necessarily serve society as a whole, and that political values and norms play a leading role in political behavior), and elite theory (the idea that all societies are necessarily ruled by a very small number of individuals who act in their own interest) have each been discussed. The strengths and weaknesses of each have been presented. Two more delimited notions — the revisionist Marxian idea of the backwardness of the working class, and the widespread and influential notion of group pressures — were also outlined because of their considerable influence in contemporary political sociology. A Marxist approach to political sociology was outlined which synthesized the strengths of the pluralist, functionalist, and elitist approaches with the basic ideas of the Marxist tradition. The three essential ideas in this latter tradition (which form the core of this book) are (1) the idea that the state is dominated, and basic state policies structured by the capitalist class; (2) the idea that state policies normally facilitate and advance the interests of the capitalist class, although there are contradictions between what the state is required to do and various capitalist-class interests; and (3) the idea of the class basis of politics. Empirical support was brought to bear on this latter point. It was argued that class is the most fundamental determinant of political behavior and attitudes. Data from voting studies were used to show the virtually universal positive association between leftism and the manual working class.

The last two sections of this introductory chapter have attempted to summarize the general argument of the book. The remainder of the chapters will develop this argument, using considerable empirical evidence — evidence collected by all schools of political sociology — to support this position.

---

selves as upper class or upper middle class regardless of the lower-class nature of the rest of their characters and life-styles. The tendency to see oneself in the most favorable light thus operates to generate support for the conservative parties, which are popularly identified with the most prestigious upper classes. Many people thus tend to switch their political allegiance once they get a promotion, come to own a little property, inherit a little stock, or otherwise come to feel that they are developing a stake (even when they remain in the manual working class). See Lipset, *Political Man*, chapter 7; and Juan Linz and Seymour Martin Lipset, "The Social Bases of Diversity in Western Democracies," Center for Advanced Study in the Behavioral Sciences, Stanford, Calif., 1956, mimeographed, chapter 5.

The Politics of the United States Capitalist Class

The capitalist class is that class of people which owns and controls the major factories, mines, farms, transportation and communications enterprises, merchandizing companies, and financial institutions in the United States. The size of the capitalist class in the United States can be estimated to be at most 0.5 percent of the population, and at minimum those people who, by being listed in the *Social Registers* of the various U.S. cities, have become socially acceptable as members of the social upper class. Approximately 110,000 individuals (or 0.05 percent) are listed in the *Social Register*.[1] The broader estimate includes many relatively wealthy people who are not exceptionally privileged, economically powerful, or socially integrated into the American upper class. The narrower definition excludes some economically powerful and privileged individuals who, because they are self-made people, highly-paid employees of the corporations, have the wrong religion or nationality, or for some other reason are not generally socially acceptable among the rich.

The Wealth of the Capitalist Class

Capitalist-class wealth comes from employment of the labor power of those who do not own the means of production. In 1975 only about 8 percent of the economically active people in the United States worked for themselves. Most of the rest worked, not for enterprises owned by middle-class small-business people

---

[1] For descriptions of the upper class, see Domhoff, *Who Rules America?*, chapter 1, and *The Higher Circles*, chapter 1.

and farmers, but for the big capitalist-class controlled corporations that dominate the American economy or the state. Ownership and control of most of the productive economy of the United States gives the capitalist class immense wealth and privilege. It also serves as the economic basis for the development of a distinctive social class which has its own exclusive social institutions and traditions.

Capitalists, naturally, only hire labor power when it is profitable for them to do so. The working class produces almost all of the wealth in the economy, but receives as wages only a portion of what it produces. The difference between wealth produced and wages (called *surplus value*) goes to the capitalists as the return on their investment in the labor power of the worker. The worker has to agree to be paid less than what he or she produces — the alternative in capitalist society means no work and extreme poverty. The surplus value acquired from the working class becomes the private property of the capitalist class, which thus grows ever richer. It uses this surplus value (that is, its profits) to hire more workers, who then produce still more surplus value for the capitalists, who as a result become still richer. The logic of this process results in the capitalist class accumulating increasing wealth.[2]

The richest 1 percent of all adults in the United States holds about 25 percent of all the privately held wealth, and the richest 0.5 percent about 20 percent of total wealth. This latter figure suggests an extreme concentration of wealth. The trends over the years indicate that the very richest's share of the national wealth declined in the period from the end of World War I to the end of World War II, rose through the 1950s, and was essentially constant through the 1960s (see table 2—1).

In 1971 the wealthiest 1 percent of people owned 51.1 percent of the value of all corporate stock, compared with 51.7 percent in 1958 and 61.5 percent in 1922.[3] This overwhelming concentration of ownership in the corporations is the basis of both the wealth and power of this class.

The wealthiest families in the capitalist class own billions of dollars worth of assets and, because of their superior economic positions, control many times more in other people's wealth. In the mid 1960s the DuPont family was the wealthiest family in America, with an estimated family fortune of $7.629 billion dollars. The next wealthiest families were the Mellons at $4.768 billion, and the Rockefellers at $4.742 billion (see table 2—2). Also among the wealthiest billionaire families were the Fords and Pews. Because of its concentration in key banks and corporations, the economic power of such family fortunes allows the billionaires to control smaller fortunes that have total values greatly exceeding the wealth of any one billionaire family. The Rockefellers' wealth enables them to control assets of over fifteen times their personal wealth, thus making their for-

---

[2] See Marx, *Wage Labor and Capital* in *Selected Works*.

[3] See Robert J. Lampman, *The Share of Top Wealth-Holders in National Wealth* (Princeton, N.J.: Princeton University Press, 1962), p. 209; and Marshall Blum et al., "Stockownership in the U.S.: Characteristics and Trends," *Survey of Current Business*, November 1974, p. 27.

Table 2–1 The Share of Personal Wealth (Equity) Held by the Top Wealth-Holders, Selected Years

Year	Top 1 Percent of Adults	Top 0.5 Percent of All Persons
1922	31.6	29.8
1929	36.3	32.4
1933	28.3	25.2
1939	30.6	28.0
1945	23.3	20.9
1949	20.8	19.3
1953	24.2	22.7
1958	26.9	21.7
1965	29.2	23.7
1969	24.9	19.9

Sources: Robert J. Lampman, *The Share of Top Wealth-Holders in National Wealth* (Princeton, N.J.: Princeton University Press, 1962), p. 24; and James D. Smith and Stephen D. Franklin, "New Dimensions of Economic Inequality: The Concentration of Personal Wealth, 1922–1969," *American Economic Review* 64, no. 2 (May 1974): 166.

Table 2–2 The Growth of the Great U.S. Family Fortunes (in Millions of Dollars)

	1924	1937	1956	1964
DuPonts	238	574	4,660	7,629
Mellons	450	391	3,769	4,768
Rockefellers	1,077	397	3,515	4,742

Source: Victor Perlo, *The Empire of High Finance* (New York: International Publishers, 1957), pp. 44–45; and Ferdinand Lundberg, *The Rich and the Super-Rich* (New York: Lyle Stuart, 1968), pp. 143, 151, 158.

tune the most economically potent in the United States even though their directly owned assets represent only the third largest family fortune.[4]

The source of the wealth and economic power of their fortunes lies in the

---

[4] It is the size of *family* rather than individual fortunes that is the important indicator of concentration of capitalist-class wealth, since the leading families usually manage their wealth as family units. The stock and bond ownership of each member of the family in an enterprise must, for most purposes, be considered together with that of his/her relatives, and the tightly held family trust funds, endowments, and foundations, as a part of one economic unit. For good discussions of the role of family fortunes in the United States, see Ferdinand Lundberg, *The Rich and the Super-Rich* (New York: Lyle Stuart, 1968), especially chapters 4 and 5; Philip H. Burch, *The Managerial Revolution Reassessed: Family Control in America's Large Corporations* (Lexington, Mass.: D. C. Heath, 1972); James Phelan and Robert Pozen, *The Company State: Ralph Nader's Study Group Report on DuPont in Delaware* (New York: Grossman Publishers, 1973); and James C. Knowles, "The Rockefeller Financial Group," in Ralph L. Andreano, *Superconcentration/Supercorporation* (Andover, Mass.: Warner Modular, 1973).

gigantic corporations that dominate the U.S. economy. The individual fortunes of the capitalist class were made and continue to be enriched by ownership and control of these corporations.[5]

The capitalist class owns most of the stock issued by corporations, votes most of the stock that is voted, holds large blocks of stock, and forms coalitions among each other. Its members are thus normally able to control the boards of directors and the top management of the corporations even when they are not in top management positions or on the boards. Because of the general dispersal of stock, it is commonly accepted that control of a corporation can be obtained by control of about 5 to 10 percent of the outstanding stock.[6] This allows the large blocks of stock owned by the very wealthy to dominate corporations even when they hold only a small proportion of the total stock outstanding.

Table 2—3 gives an indication of the immense economic power of these corporations. The largest corporations have assets that compare with the GNPs of the largest countries of the world. If the largest American corporation (American Telephone and Telegraph) were a country, it would rank roughly as the twelfth richest country in the world (assuming a rough comparability of corporate assets and GNP). The immense wealth of these corporations can be translated into considerable power when these corporations deal with the countries of Asia, Africa, and Latin America — or for that matter, the governments of the advanced capitalist countries.

Only a few of the giant corporations actually dominate the U.S. economy. In 1968 the largest 200 manufacturing corporations had 60.9 percent, and the largest 100 had 49.3 percent of the capital assets of all manufacturing corporations. This compares with 47.2 percent and 39.3 percent, respectively, in 1947 (see table 2—4). Although the largest 500 industrial corporations totaled only 0.25 percent of the 203,000 manufacturing corporations in the United States in 1969, 76 percent of all industrial workers were employed by them.[7]

---

[5] There has been considerable debate about the relative role of corporate managers, legal owners, and the banks in controlling the corporations. The interested reader is referred to the following works: Paul Baran and Paul Sweezy, *Monopoly Capital* (New York: Monthly Review Press, 1966), chapter 2; A. A. Berle and Gardiner Means, *The Modern Corporation and Private Property* (New York: Macmillan, 1932); A. A. Berle, *The 20th Century Capitalist Revolution* (New York: Harcourt, Brace and World, 1954); Domhoff, *Who Rules America?*, chapter 2; Robert Fitch and Mary Oppenheimer, "Who Rules the Corporations?," *Socialist Revolution* 1, no. 4, 1, no. 5, 1, no. 6 (July-August, September-October, November-December 1970); S. Menshikov, *Millionaires and Managers* (Moscow: Progress Publishers, 1969); James O'Connor, "Question: Who Rules the Corporations? Answer: The Ruling Class," *Socialist Revolution* 2, no. 1 (January-February 1971); and Victor Perlo, *The Empire of High Finance* (New York: International Publishers, 1957).

[6] See Perlo, *The Empire of High Finance*, p. 38.

[7] *Statistical Abstract of the United States, 1975*, U.S. Department of Commerce, Bureau of the Census, 1975, pp. 355, 498, and 500.

Table 2-3 A Comparison of the Size of U.S. Corporations with the GNP of Various Countries*, 1974   (in Billions of Dollars)

The Biggest 35 U.S. Corporations Ranked by Assets		Selected Countries of the World Ranked by GNP	
AT&T	74.0	USA	1440.0
Bank of America	60.4	Soviet Union	797.0
Citicorp	57.8	Japan	448.0
Chase	42.5	West Germany	385.0
Prudential	35.8	France	292.0
Metropolitan	32.7	China	223.0
Exxon	31.3	United Kingdom	192.0
J.P. Morgan	26.0	Canada	136.0
Manufacturers-Hanover Trust	25.7	India	79.0
		Poland	76.2
Chemical Bank	22.2	Spain	70.0
GM	20.5	Netherlands	67.1
Banker's Trust	20.4	East Germany	59.9
Continental Ill.	19.8	Mexico	56.9
First Chicago Co.	19.1	Switzerland	44.8
Western Bancorporation	18.7	Argentina	36.7
Equitable	17.6	Iran	30.9
Texaco	17.2	Denmark	30.7
Security Pacific	15.5	Indonesia	18.0
Ford	14.2	Greece	17.2
Mobil	14.1	Nigeria	16.6
IBM	14.0	South Korea	14.8
Aetna Casualty	13.9	Philippines	12.1
New York Life	13.0	Peru	10.6
Wells Fargo	12.7	Thailand	10.5
Marine Midland	12.7	Pakistan	9.4
Gulf	12.5	Chile	8.8
General Telephone and Electric	12.0	Ireland	7.3
John Hancock	11.8	Cuba	6.1
Standard, California	11.6	South Vietnam	3.4
Sears	11.3	Ghana	3.4
Charter New York Corp.	11.3	Syria	3.0
ITT	10.7	Guatemala	3.0
Crocker National	10.3	Burma	2.8
Mellon National Corp.	9.9	Dominican Republic	2.8
Travelers	9.8	Haiti	0.8

Source: *Fortune*, May 1975 and July 1975.

Source: U.S. Arms Control and Disarmament Agency, *World Military Expenditures and Arms Transfers 1965-1974*, 1975.

* A comparison of corporate assets with GNP is not strictly justifiable, since GNP and assets are different concepts. Another comparison might have been between government budgets and corporate profits. Assets and profits are the only two measures of a corporation's size that apply across the board to all types of corporations. Although not strictly valid, the comparison used here does give a general idea of the power of the corporations compared with that of various countries. The types of corporations listed among the top thirty-five should be noted. Twenty-two of the thirty-five are financial corporations. Five of the remaining thirteen are oil companies.

Table 2-4 The Share of Total Corporate Manufacturing Assets Held by the 100 and 200 Largest Corporations in the United States, 1925-1968

	100 Largest	200 Largest
1947	39.3%	47.2%
1950	39.8	47.7
1955	44.3	53.1
1960	46.4	56.3
1965	46.5	56.7
1968	49.3	60.9

Source: Hearings before the Subcommittee on Antitrust and Monopoly of the Committee on the Judiciary, United States Senate. Ninety-first Congress, 2nd session; *Economic Concentration*, part 8; *The Conglomerate Merger Problem, 1969* (Washington, D.C.: U.S. Government Printing Office, 1970), p. 4896.

The Capitalist Class as a Social Class

The capitalist class forms a distinctive social class with its own traditions, manners, and habits. Members of this class belong to similar upper-class institutions, are similarly educated at exclusive upper-class schools, interact with each other on regular and friendly terms, intermarry (and are thus related to each other) and share a common consciousness of belonging to the same class.[8] This class passes its economic power on from generation to generation, although it co-opts a few of the brightest and most successful members of other social classes into it as they demonstrate either extraordinary service to the old rich families or extraordinary entrepreneurial skills together with the generations-long process of acquiring the social approval of the old rich families.[9]

The distinctive differences of the upper-class life-style are systematically produced and reinforced at each stage in the life of the rich — during their early years, through their nurses, governesses, special dancing and riding classes, and tutoring in foreign languages; during adolescence, through attendance at elite boarding schools and colleges, exclusive summer camps, family summer resorts, and distinctive upper-class social events; during adulthood, through common leisure-time activities, such as charity events, sports and hobbies, club member-

---

[8] The work of G. William Domhoff is dedicated to demonstrating that the capitalist class in the United States is a socially cohesive ruling class. See his *Who Rules America?* (especially chapter 1), *The Higher Circles* (especially chapter 4), *The Bohemian Grove and Other Retreats* (New York: Harper and Row, 1974), and "Social Clubs, Policy-Planning Groups, and Corporations," *The Insurgent Sociologist* 5, no. 3 (Spring 1975). Other excellent sources on capitalist-class cohesiveness include: Baltzell, *Philadelphia Gentlemen*; Baltzell, *The Protestant Establishment*; Stephen Birmingham, *The Right People* (Boston: Little, Brown, 1968); and Cleveland Amory, *The Proper Bostonians* (New York: E. P. Dutton, 1947).

[9] See Domhoff, *Who Rules America?*, Introduction, chapters 1 and 2.

ships, common resorts, social intermingling with one's relatives in the highly interrelated upper class, and intermingling in the process of governing the economy.[10]

As researchers such as G. William Domhoff and E. Digby Baltzell have shown, the close social ties that members of the capitalist class acquire from their schooling, clubs, resorts, common membership on boards of directors, and kin networks mean that their common experience and interests are manifested in a high level of class consciousness — that is, in a strong sense of identity as a class and a rather sophisticated understanding of their collective interest on which they tend to act in a collective way.[11] That they dominate the schools, the mass media, and the other mechanisms of mental production means there is essential correspondence between their interests and experiences and the dominant ideology.[12] Because their personal experiences are reinforced by the ideas to which they are exposed in the media and schools, there are few obstacles to the full development of their class consciousness. As a consequence the capitalist class normally has a higher and more homogeneous class consciousness than any other class in society.

The unity of the upper class is stronger than the antagonisms within it. Moreover, upper-class unity has been growing over time. The structural basis of this increasing unity includes:

1. The increasingly diversified stock portfolios of upper-class families and financial institutions. While in the past there was a tendency for single upper-class families to own outright a number of businesses, today the typical upper-class family holds significant shares of stock in a wide variety of different corporations. The economic interests of each family or financial institution have become so diffused that they increasingly tend to represent the interests of the entire capitalist class rather than just a narrow sector of it.

2. Greater interrelations among the upper classes as more generations of intermarriage occur. Greater intermarriage acts to diffuse upper-class economic interests by creating blood ties among different sectors of the economy.

3. The increasing importance of corporate law firms and financial institutions that deal with a wide range of different corporations. These institutions tend to act in the interests of the upper class as a whole, or at least large segments of it.

4. The growing collaboration among the leading financial interests, which are becoming more interlocked with each other. Increasingly, different interests share controlling blocks of stock in, or otherwise jointly control, a corporation and run their joint interests on the basis of mutual respect.

5. A distinctive upper-class culture becoming more firmly consolidated over time. Particularly important is the role of business and law schools, which tend to create a more uniform consciousness among the upper class than that which existed in the days of self-made men.

---

[10] See Domhoff, *Bohemian Grove*; *The Higher Circles*; and *Who Rules America?*
[11] See Domhoff, *Who Rules America?*; Domhoff, *The Higher Circles*; Baltzell, *The Protestant Establishment*; and Baltzell, *Philadelphia Gentlemen*.
[12] For evidence of capitalist-class domination of the schools and media, see chapter 11.

6. The assimilation of Jews and Catholics into the social institutions of the upper class, which is doing away with the traditional ethnic antagonisms.

7. The "Cowboys" — those with new aerospace and electronics money — are being integrated into the upper class through intermarriage, social assimilation in the second generation (many of the new fortunes were accumulated during World War II and the immediate postwar period), and their growing dependence on the major financial interest groups for money to finance investment.[13]

The Political Conservatism of the Capitalist Class

The uniformity of capitalist-class experience, the high degree of intraclass interaction, and the privileged position of the upper class means that the capitalist class is the most conservative (that is, supportive of the status quo) of all classes. In Great Britain in the 1950s only 9 percent of top business people supported the Labour party, and in Norway only 3 percent. In France in 1952, and in Italy in 1958, only 1 percent of top business people supported the Communists (see table 1—1).

Although there is essential unity within the capitalist class on the basic questions of preserving and advancing the capitalist system at home and abroad, preserving private property, keeping the working class in line, and maintaining control over the state, there are differences within this class on exactly how to go about realizing these shared goals. These differences largely stem from the different economic interests within the upper class. These different intraclass interests within the capitalist class are at the locus of most of the political controversies that arise in the United States. In general, an issue becomes an issue when different segments of the ruling class, which have different interests, take different positions. Their internal conflicts are thus fought out in Congress, in the executive branch of the government, in the regulatory agencies, in the courts, and in the media. It cannot be stressed too highly, however, that when faced with *inter*class issues (as opposed to *intra*class issues) the upper class is normally united.

Political Differences within the Capitalist Class by Type of Industry

One factor that determines the specific politics of industrial capitalists is the amount of their wealth and the size of the corporations with which they are connected. The wealthier and the more powerful they are, the more conservative they tend to be.

Table 2—5 shows that in the United States in 1955 the executives of firms employing more than 10,000 workers were 84 percent Republican and only 6

[13] See O'Connor, "Question: Who Rules the Corporations?"

Table 2-5 The Relationship Between the Size of a Firm and the Political Affiliation of Company Executives, 1955

Size of Firm	Republican	Democratic	Independent
More than 10,000 workers	84%	6%	10%
1,000 to 9,999	80	8	12
100 to 999	69	12	19

Source: Juan Linz and Seymour Martin Lipset, "The Social Bases of Diversity in Western Democracies," Center for Advanced Study in the Behavioral Sciences, Stanford, California, mimeographed, 1956, chapter 8, p. 5.

percent Democratic, while executives of firms employing between 100 and 999 workers were 69 percent Republican and 12 percent Democratic. Thus if Democratic and Republican preference can be taken as acceptable indicators of relative conservatism, the larger their firm the more conservative are business people. Unfortunately, data broken down by region of the country could not be obtained for this measure. Thus it is possible that at least some of this demonstrated relationship might be a product of the fact that Southern industrialists tend to be conservative Democrats and associated with somewhat smaller firms than are their Northern cousins. However, there are two reasons to feel that this effect is minor: (1) The results reported in table 2-4 are consistent with data from other countries;[14] and (2) from table 2-6 we can see that the textile industry, which is heavily concentrated in the South, is very heavily Republican.

Another cleavage among capitalists is that between the industries which produce consumer goods (goods that average people normally buy through retail outlets) and those which produce production goods (goods bought by other industries for use in producing consumer goods). Some examples of light consumer industries are the big retail and mail order corporations such as Sears, Montgomery Ward, Safeway, and A&P; food processing companies such as General Mills, Kraft, Borden, Campbell's Soup, and Armour; and large clothing manufacturers. Some leading producers of consumer durables (heavy consumer goods industries) include General Motors, Ford, General Electric, Westinghouse, and other manufacturers of goods which tend to last many years and be rather expensive. Steel, computers, and machine tools are among the leading production goods industries and are represented by such firms as U.S. Steel, IBM, and the Hughes Tool Company. Production goods industries tend to be more conservative than consumer goods industries. Production goods industries have high fixed costs and very heavy investments in fixed machinery which cannot be easily reduced when production falls off. Since heavy industry would find it difficult to make workers bear the costs of cutbacks through layoffs, it tends to advocate conservative wage policies and resist progressive income taxes that would work to its disadvantage. Many of these firms are armament producers, and others are among

[14] See Linz and Lipset, "Social Bases of Diversity," chapter 10.

the principal consumers of basic raw materials — much of which are imported at low cost from Third World countries. These firms thus tend to support imperial policies designed to subordinate Third World areas and to favor high levels of military spending.

Consumer industries are somewhat antagonistic to heavy industry because of their dependence on the latter to supply them with production goods, which they often must purchase at monopoly prices. They thus favor government policies designed to keep the cost of production goods down — for example, antitrust suits against the monopoly corporations and low tariffs on the importation of production goods. Consumer industries are less imperialistic and less in favor of heavy military spending, since they are not generally military contractors and have nothing to gain by aggressive foreign policies. In fact, they lose by heavy military spending, since it deprives the masses of disposable income to spend on consumer goods. The typically high labor intensity in consumer goods industries means that their fixed operating costs are significantly less than those of heavy industry. Consequently, it is easier for them to adjust to progressive wage and tax policies by laying off workers and retooling. Thus they tend to be more supportive of such liberal policies. Light industry favors full employment and moderate inflation, since both increase the spendable income of the working class, which spends a disproportionate amount of any increase in its income on consumer goods. Consumer industries also tend to favor governmental policies designed to encourage the unionization of heavy industry. The stronger the unions in basic industry, the more buying power the masses have, and thus the more profits consumer goods industries make from the additional consumption expenditures of the working class. Consumer goods industries, which sell directly to the consumer, are heavily dependent on the brand names they sell and on their public image to make profits. They are thus dependent on maintaining a good reputation with the masses of people. A shortsighted right-wing policy or frequent labor trouble may well result in consumer resistance to the purchase of their products.[15]

Table 2–6 illustrates the effect of the operation of the factors of consumer versus production goods on the politics of industries. The consumer-oriented industries such as clothing and accessories, real estate, publishing, wholesale and retail stores, and distilleries tend to be the most Democratic of industries, while the basic production goods industries such as timber, rubber, textiles, petroleum, glass, and chemicals tend to be the most Republican. While the relationship between consumer and production goods industries and politics is not perfect, a strong relationship can be observed.

Correlated with the difference between production goods and consumer goods industries (although by no means identical with it) is the difference between industries operating in monopolized markets and those in competitive markets. While production goods industries are more likely to be monopolized than consumption goods industries, the correlation is not perfect. As the examples of

---

[15] Daniel Guerin, *Fascism and Big Business* (New York: Monad Press, 1973), p. 25; and Linz and Lipset, "Social Bases of Diversity," chapter 10.

Table 2–6 The Percentage of the Total of Contributions of $10,000 or More Given to Democrats in the 1968 Elections by Industries

Clothing and accessories	82%
Factory and industrial components and equipment	60
Real estate	60
Investment banking and brokerage	59
Publishing and editing	59
Wholesale and retail stores	57
Distilleries	54
Electronics and computers	40
Mining	35
Automobile	34
Iron, steel, aluminum	33
Food processing and distribution	32
Consumer household products	32
Broadcasting	29
Banking and trust companies	18
Utilities	16
Transportation	16
Chemicals and pharmaceuticals	12
Glass	7
Petroleum	6
Textiles	0
Printing	0
Rubber	0
Timber	0
Restaurant and Motel	0

Source: Computed from data in Herbert Alexander, *Financing the 1968 Election* (Lexington, Mass.: D.C. Heath and Co., 1971), appendix G.

automobiles and many consumer durables bear out, consumption goods producers often operate in monopoly markets. Nondurable producers (for example, clothing), which require relatively low amounts of initial investment (and generally have high variable-to-constant capital ratios), are much more likely to be in competitive markets. Competitive industries tend to be small-scale producers for regional markets, while monopolized industries tend to be large-scale producers for national markets. Some of the more prominent examples of monopolized industries in the United States include automobiles, where General Motors, Ford, and Chrysler control almost all the market; electrical goods, where General Electric and Westinghouse predominate; computers, where IBM overshadows its competition; petroleum refining, distribution, and sales, where a handful of corporations such as Gulf, Mobil, Texaco, Shell, Exxon and the other Standard companies control the market.

The labor force in competitive industries is normally nonunionized, or if a union is present (outside of the construction industry) it tends to be weak and company-dominated. It is also disproportionately composed of national minorities, youth, and women, who are low paid and often employed seasonally or irregularly. The pressure of competition in such industries forces wages down and requires that the competitive sector capitalists oppose militant unions (which demand high wages and resist production speed-ups), welfare plans, high levels of military spending, and all other government projects that would increase their taxes and hence take a big bite out of their rather small profit margins.

Monopolized industries, however, tend to be unionized, employ white men, and offer rather stable employment and high wages. Because monopoly firms are able to determine their own prices (by implicit collusion), they are able to pass on wage increases and taxes to the buyers of their products. Consequently, they tend to favor unions and are less resistant to costly welfare and warfare policies than are competitive sector firms.[16]

The unions in the monopoly sector have worked out an arrangement with management whereby they will discipline the labor force (preventing work stoppages and other disruptions), ensure high levels of productivity, and support technological innovations in exchange for high wages and secure job tenure.

Export-oriented industries naturally favor governmental policies that facilitate acceptance of their wares in foreign lands. They almost all favor low domestic tariffs as a bargaining tool to get other countries to lower their tariffs against industrial imports from the United States. Some sectors of export industries support imperialist policies designed to secure guaranteed overseas markets for industrial goods. This is especially the case in those industries that specialize in producing goods sold primarily in Asia, Africa, and Latin America, where privileged access to markets is the source of great profits. However, those segments of the export industry that specialize in exports to the advanced capitalist countries and to the socialist countries often favor less imperialist policies designed to pacify opponents of aggressive U.S. policies in these countries. By following accommodation policies this sector of export industry hopes to reduce resistance to expanding U.S. trade. This is especially the case with those interested in trade with China and the Soviet Union, countries which are reluctant to expand trade while the United States is engaging in overseas adventures.

Companies that produce mainly for the domestic market and whose overseas competitors have lower costs (especially the labor-intensive industries such as textiles and shoes) favor high tariffs to protect the home markets they would otherwise lose. They also tend to be against protracted and expensive overseas wars from which they obtain no benefit. In fact, such businesses actually lose from such adventures because of the support given by the United States to overseas competitors (such as the textile and clothing producers of East Asia), who are able to use the extremely cheap labor guaranteed by the dictatorial regimes supported by the United States to penetrate U.S. markets in spite of its high tariff barriers.

All raw material importers (and corporations that own factories and overseas

---

[16] James O'Connor, *The Fiscal Crisis of the State* (New York: St. Martin's Press, 1973), chapter 1.

sources of raw material which they import into the United States) tend to be against high tariffs. Those whose interests are primarily in Asia, Africa, and Latin America (continents where U.S. interests are threatened by nationalization) tend to favor high levels of military spending and imperialistic foreign policies designed to maintain cheap and secure raw materials and a cheap and disciplined local labor supply. Conversely, corporations whose investments are primarily in industrial production in Canada and Europe are less supportive of imperialist policies and high levels of military spending. Not generally facing the threat of nationalization, their profit possibilities are hurt by the drain on the U.S. balance of payments and the consequent necessity to devaluate the dollar, which makes buying into foreign enterprises more expensive for them and makes it easier for foreigners to buy out U.S. enterprises. They are also hurt by the hostility that U.S. militaristic policies often provoke in other countries, which produces pressure to put restrictions on U.S. businesses and their operations.

In the post–World War II period most of the major export interests have tended to be somewhat less imperialistic than they had been before the 1930s (probably because a greater share of U.S. exports has been going to the technologically advanced countries). However, the major petroleum, copper, and other raw material industries with very heavy investments in Asia, Africa, and Latin America have been especially imperialistic. Note that two-thirds of Exxon's profits in the 1960s came from its overseas operations (mostly in Asia and Latin America). Exxon thus has every reason to support imperialist policies.

Table 2–6 reflects the attitudes of business on wage, regulatory, and welfare policies, where the Republicans and Democrats have had traditional differences (with the Republicans being more conservative), and on foreign policy and high levels of military spending, where the two parties' policies have been more or less identical. That this is the case can be seen in the position of electronics and computers, one of the industries most reliant on military orders. Forty percent of its money went to the Democrats. Textiles, an industry heavily dependent on the domestic market (and thus favoring high tariffs), gave no money to the Democrats. However, clothing and accessories, another industry heavily dependent on the domestic market and traditionally isolationist, gave 82 percent of its money to the Democrats. The political difference between textiles and clothing and accessories is found in the fact that the former sells cloth to the latter, which sells finished products (often with brand names) to the public. The latter is more liberal apparently because it is a consumer industry dependent on a good public image and high levels of welfare and wages.

A Look at the Politics of Some Specific Industries

Aerospace firms such as Boeing, Grumman Aircraft, McDonnell Douglas, and Lockheed produce aircraft and space-related equipment for the U.S. military and space program. Since most of this industry's business lies in providing military goods to the U.S. government and allied foreign governments, these companies are the leading proponents of militarism. In former years, before the rise of air power and rocketry, this role was reserved for the traditional munitions makers — that is, the manufacturers of battleships, tanks, cannon, shells, rifles, gunpowder, etc. Because such industries are highly capital-intensive, and because they generally work on the basis of cost-plus contracting in a monopoly market, they have no reason to oppose unions (providing they are not radical), high wages, or welfare. The ideal presidential candidate of this sector of the upper class is a man like Senator Henry Jackson, who is a strong advocate of both the AFL—CIO and militaristic policies.[17]

Somewhat less militaristic is the electronics industry (even though it is generally the next most important war contractor in this age of the automated battlefield). It is heavily involved in the production of consumer durables (especially household appliances). However, certain companies such as GE, RCA, and IBM have tended to be more militaristic than the average for the industry because of their high level of military contracts.

In the past (for example, during World War I when explosives were the major category of munitions) the chemical industry was among the most imperialist industrial sectors; however, it is now more dependent on supplying the consumption goods industry with raw materials (for example, plastics, fertilizers, drugs and artificial fabrics). But the competition with foreign imports of these materials has made this sector among the strongest proponents of high tariffs. That it is a production goods industry has tended to give it rather conservative politics on welfare and union matters. The DuPont family (whose wealth is based on chemicals) continues to be among the most right wing in the U.S. upper class. In the 1930s it was at the forefront of antiunion and anti–New Deal efforts and was a major financial supporter of various U.S. fascist groups. In the post–World War II period its traditional rightism has been somewhat mitigated.

The automobile industry at one time tended to be more militaristic than it is today because of the changes in the relative role of motorized ground and advanced electronic and aerospace equipment in warfare. The auto industry traditionally favored low tariffs to induce foreigners to allow the importation of U.S. cars. However, in recent years the auto industry has changed its position on the question of tariffs as foreign car imports have taken a greater share of the domestic U.S. market. Along with textiles and chemicals, this industry is now among the leading proponents of high tariffs. The auto industry tends to favor high wages, high levels of employment, and welfare policies, which give workers the income necessary to purchase cars. In times of recession one of the first ways people cut back is by putting off the purchase of a new car; therefore, profits suffer disproportionately in the auto industry. Consequently, this industry is in the forefront of those insisting on full employment and moderately inflationary

[17] See Perlo, *The Empire of High Finance*, part II, and *Militarism and Industry* (New York: International Publishers, 1963) for discussions of the politics of these industries.

policies. Its continued concern with exports, together with its interest in decreasing the tax burden of the masses, tends to make this industry rather less imperialist than the average. It is more interested in exporting cars around the world and in selling them at home than it is in securing sources of cheap raw materials.

The declining export position of the United States (caused by the rapidly increasing productivity of the other leading capitalist and socialist countries) has profoundly affected this industry.[18] The allocation of the best scientists, engineers, resources, and technology to military production for over a generation has meant that the durable goods industries such as automobiles have increased their productivity much more slowly than have their competitors in those countries that have not given priority to military development. Consequently, such industries, especially those primarily oriented to export (but also those which face foreign competition within the United States), are increasingly favorable to governmental policies designed to decrease the emphasis on the military. Instead they tend to pressure the state to facilitate exports as well as to emphasize increasing domestic productivity by subsidizing industrial research and training.

Shipping interests, raw material exporters such as the Northwest timber industry, and the growers, processors, and distributors of the basic grains tend to be somewhat antimilitaristic and supportive of governmental policies that facilitate exports — for example, the recognition of China and the normalization of trade relations with the socialist countries tended to be supported by West Coast lumber and shipping interests (who supported Congress members such as Wayne Morse). Needless to say, such interests also favor low U.S. tariffs to encourage other countries to lower their tariffs against U.S. exports.[19]

Bankers, unlike industrialists, have traditionally favored high interest rates and limited deficit spending by the government to prevent inflation. Inflation leads to the de facto canceling of part of the debt owed to them by industrial corporations and the general population (through the paying back of debts with money worth less than the value of the money originally lent). Banking interests thus tend to favor monetary and fiscal conservatism more than do most industries. The monopoly sector of industry would be happy to see deficit spending and inflation, providing it were caused by high levels of government spending on its products. However, with the increasing marriage of finance and industrial capital, the difference between bankers and industrialists on inflation is becoming less important.

Banking, because of its ties with many different types of industries, tends to be against favoritism to any special interests within the capitalist class (with the exception, of course, of itself). The banking industry, more than any other seg-

---

[18] For a discussion of the causes and effects of the declining export position of the United States, see Frank Ackerman and Arthur MacEwan, "Inflation, Recession, and Crisis: Or Would You Buy a New Car from This Man," *Review of Radical Political Economics* 4, no. 4 (August 1972).

[19] Perlo, *Militarism and Industry*, chapter 11.

ment of the corporate world (except perhaps the corporate law firms), is able to speak for the class as a whole. Its large resources, furthermore, give it a power base from which to speak definitively. Banks thus tend to be about average in their degree of support for imperial and militaristic policies. Variations within the banking community tend to reflect the composition of interests with which each bank is involved.

During World War I, the Morgan-associated financial groups (led by the Morgan Guarantee Trust Company and Morgan-Stanely and Company) were a major force behind militarism. The Morgan banks had granted France and England large loans that were in danger of being defaulted if the United States did not enter the war. Morgan-related munitions industries also stood to gain considerably by U.S. participation. In the post-World War II period the Morgan interests have tended to be somewhat less militaristic than the Rockefeller's. They are heavily involved in industrial investment in Western Europe but not so much in raw material extraction in Third World countries. They thus tend to favor more moderate foreign policies and the facilitation of industrial investment overseas, even if this means the liquidation of Vietnam-type adventures. Morgan interests traditionally have stressed fiscal and monetary "responsibility" and moderate reductions in government spending.[20]

The Rockefeller financial interest grouping is heavily committed to overseas investments in Third World countries wherever oil is to be found — especially in the Middle East and Latin America. They also have heavy investments in the aerospace industry. As a consequence this grouping tends to be more imperialistic and promilitary spending than the capitalist-class average. Rockefeller men, who have dominated the state department since World War II, consistently pursue imperialist and militaristic policies regardless of whether Democrats or Republicans are in office.[21]

New Money Versus Old Money

New money is generally more right wing than old money. Self-made men and women usually have not yet internalized the general upper-class consciousness, which includes the corporate liberal ideology of the necessity to assume social responsibility to guarantee upper-class rule — for example, to support moderate unions, welfare policies, and regulation of the economy by the state in the interest of the entire capitalist class. New fortunes are usually accumulated because of aggressive self-seeking attitudes, and thus their owners tend not to understand the necessity of class responsibility. Their natural rightism is enhanced by their resentment against the "Eastern banks" and the "Wall Street establishment" to which

---

[20] Perlo, *The Empire of High Finance*, chapters 16 and 17, and *Militarism and Industry*, chapter 10.

[21] Perlo, *Militarism and Industry*, p. 144f.

they are forced to turn for financial assistance (and to whom they must make concessions to get it), and against the "Washington bureaucrats" who regulate their activities in the interests of the major financial groups and the largest corporations.[22]

Most of the large fortunes made since the end of the Great Depression have been based in either petroleum production (predominantly in Texas and Southern California) or in the war industries, mainly aerospace and electronics (also concentrated in the Southwest). New money in these fields has been referred to as "Cowboy money" to distinguish it from the "Yankee money" of inherited wealth based in the older corporations and financial interest groups centered in the Northeast. The struggle between the "Yankees" and the much weaker "Cowboys" centers on whether the new millionaires can keep control of the industries they founded or must lose them to the established old line financial interests organized by the major banks. Multimillionaires such as Howard Hughes, H. L. Hunt, and W. Clement Stone illustrate the political rightism of much of the capitalist class in this region. The economic and social differences and consequently the consistency of the political conflict between the "Yankees" and the "Cowboys" has probably been exaggerated by some authors.[23]

Since the political differences within this class concern which segment of the upper class will benefit the most, these differences and the political struggles which they produce often have little effect on the lives of most working-class and petty bourgeois people. The outcomes of many other political conflicts within the capitalist class can, however, make a difference to people outside of this class. Whether unions are encouraged or repressed, whether health care is provided free, whether working people are drafted to fight in Third World countries, and whether workers in the textile industries have to change jobs and locations because of reduced tariffs can all result from the resolution of differences within the capitalist class.

Protestants, Catholics, and Jews

Members of minority ethnic groups who make it economically into the upper class, but who because of their ethnic backgrounds are socially excluded from the social institutions of that class (and hence from the real levels of power), develop a

---

[22] See Domhoff, *Who Rules America?*, p. 28f; Lundberg, *The Rich and the Super-Rich*, pp. 47-48; and Linz and Lipset, "Social Bases of Diversity," chapter 10, p. 28f.

[23] See Carl Ogelsby, "Contradictions," *Ramparts*, October, November 1971; and Kirkpatrick Sale, *The Power Shift* (New York: Random House, 1975) for the argument that the capitalist class in the United States is split between "Yankees" and "Cowboys." For an attempted refutation of this argument, see Stephen Johnson, "How the West Was Won: Last Shootout for the Yankee-Cowboy Theory," *Insurgent Sociologist* 6, no. 2 (Winter 1976). See also G. William Domhoff, *Fat Cats and Democrats* (Englewood Cliffs, N.J.: Prentice-Hall, 1972), chapter 2.

special hostility to the mainstream of the upper class. Unlike the Protestant new rich, the Catholic and Jewish upper class (and the handful of black and Latin rich) tend to be more liberal (rather than more rightist) than the mainstream. The Protestant upper class associates them with the lower-class members of their religions, with whom they in turn, because of discrimination, tend to identify (hence the propensity to be more liberal than the upper-class average).

Jewish and Catholic money also tends to be disproportionately liberal because of its concentration in nondurable consumer goods industries and other fields that require more liberal politics.[24] (The Kennedy family is an example of this.) It has traditionally been the Jewish and the Catholic wealthy that have financed the Democratic party.

Liberals Versus Conservatives

Partly because of the material factors already discussed and partly because of "accidents" of upbringing or individual orientation, the upper class is divided among the rightists, who were predominant before 1933 and are still influential, the corporate liberals, who have been dominant since 1933, and the upper-class progressives, who are the least influential of the three. The hegemonic corporate liberal tendency within the upper class is represented by the Council on Foreign Relations (CFR), the Committee for Economic Development (CED), the Business Council, and the major foundations and research institutions.[25] They control the leading universities and the executive branch of the U.S. government. Rooted in the major financial interest groups (especially the Morgan and Rockefeller interests, which are centered in New York), they are the proponents of the New Deal policies that have guided the United States since 1933. They approve of moderate trade unions. They support integration of minorities, moderate welfare programs, heavy state involvement in the economy, foreign aid, and the major international organizations such as the United Nations, the International Monetary Fund, and the World Bank.

The corporate liberals normally dominate both the Republican *and* the Democratic parties. Only once since 1936 have they lost control of the Republican party. That was in 1964, when the right wing of the upper class got the nomination for Goldwater over the candidate of the corporate liberals — Rockefeller. And only once during this period did they lose control of the Democratic party, when in 1972 McGovern won the nomination over Muskie and Humphrey, the corporate liberal candidates. The Republican party encompasses both the upper-class corporate liberals and the right wing of the upper and upper-middle classes.

[24] Domhoff, *Fat Cats and Democrats*, chapter 2.
[25] See chapter 10 for a discussion of the Council on Foreign Relations and other influential institutions controlled by the corporate liberal center of the capitalist class.

The oldest Protestant money outside of the South, together with the Protestant new rich (who are mostly right wing), tends to support this party, whose program is slightly to the right of center. The Democratic party includes both the upper-class corporate liberals and the left-liberals of the upper and upper-middle classes.

The ethnic rich (Jewish, Catholic, Latin, and black) tend to support the Democrats. In addition, there are many other corporate liberals who give money to, and work closely with, both the Republican and Democratic parties to ensure that regardless of which party wins an election, they will be the rulers. The corporate liberal ideology and corporate liberal policies prevail regardless of which party is in office. The corporate liberals in both parties are able to subordinate their minority tendencies — that is, the right in the Republican party, and the left *and* the Southern conservatives among Democrats. Note that if it were not for the conservative Southern forces in it, the Democratic party would be evenly balanced between the corporate liberals and the left-liberals of the McGovern stripe. Their presence in the Democratic party is thus very important for maintaining corporate liberal hegemony within the political system.[26]

The more right-wing segment of the upper class retains the pre–New Deal antagonism of much of the upper class to trade unions, welfare, free trade, foreign aid, internationalism, guaranteed rights for minorities, and much of the government's role in regulating the economy. It is opposed to the corporate liberal program implemented since 1933 through the efforts of such upper-class institutions as the CED, the CFR, the Business Council, and the major foundations. It has considerable animosity toward these organizations, as well as to the leading Wall Street financial institutions (particularly the Rockefeller and Morgan interests). The major organizations that normally articulate the view of this segment of the upper class are the National Association of Manufacturers and the Chambers of Commerce. These organizations are based on a coalition of the more conservative upper-class members with the smaller and regional businesses. These smaller businesses have a structural antagonism with both the corporate liberal-dominated state and the Wall Street financial interests that dominate the national economy. Old line upper-class families associated with the upper-class right include the DuPonts, the Pews (of Sun Oil), the Millikens, and the Milbanks.[27]

It must be emphasized that the politics of the upper-class right wing do not differ fundamentally from those of the dominant corporate liberals. Differences between the two tendencies center on the question of whose approach best maximizes profits and secures the necessary conditions for upper-class rule. The corporate liberals are merely more sophisticated than the less cosmopolitan right. The upper-class right wing should not be confused with right-wing extremists such as

---

[26] See Domhoff, *Fat Cats and Democrats*, chapter 3, for a discussion of the role of Southern Democrats.
[27] For an analysis of the capitalist-class right wing, see Domhoff, *Fat Cats and Democrats*, chapters 2 and 3.

the John Birch Society, the American Nazi party, and the like. These latter groups are far too extremist to gain the support of the upper class in times of relative social stability. The right-wing edges of "legitimate" politics are defined by the leading spokesmen of the upper-class right (for example, Barry Goldwater), thus isolating everything further right as illegitimate "extremism."

Although not as big and influential as the right, the upper-class left wing is nevertheless significant. In coalition with progressive upper-middle-class people, it managed to gain the Democratic party's nomination for George McGovern in 1972. Like the right and the corporate liberal center, the left-liberals have their own "think tanks," foundations, and journals. Political organizations that represent this upper-class tendency include the Southern Regional Council, the Americans for Democratic Action (ADA), Common Cause and the National Committee for an Effective Congress. These organizations give support to various liberal causes, especially to the moderate civil rights movement, campaigns for reductions in military spending, expanded welfare programs, and environmental cleanup campaigns.[28]

The left-liberals of the upper class function as both the innovators and the guardians of the ruling class. They often come up with new proposals to stabilize capitalism that are eventually adopted by the corporate liberal center. They also define the left boundary of respectable politics. Anything to the left of this group is considered beyond the pale and dismissed as illegitimate. They can remove their support from anyone who suggests tampering with the basics of corporate institutions, thus normally branding them as disreputable extremists. They oppose the formation of third parties on the left and defend a big business–oriented foreign policy (euphemistically called "internationalism"). A classic illustration of the role of the left-liberal upper class is their role in the establishment of the Americans for Democratic Action in 1948 to combat the third party effort of Henry Wallace. Wallace's Progressive party opposed the United States assuming a hostile stance toward the USSR. The ADA was viciously anti-Communist domestically and internationally. The ADA split the left-liberal forces and undermined progressive support for the Wallace candidacy. In the 1960s the left-liberal segment of the upper class worked to channel the black movement off the streets and into registering blacks to vote. The left-liberal foundations financed the Student Nonviolent Coordinating Committee's voter registration drives and the Mississippi Summer of 1964. In 1968 they set up the National Urban Coalition as a consensus-seeking and policy-forming organization that would include blacks, labor leaders, local officials, and leading upper-class liberals. One of the best publicized efforts of the left-liberal upper class to emerge in the 1970s was John Gardner's Common Cause, which grew out of the National Urban Coalition. The main goals of this group include "putting the country back together again" and making the Congress "more responsive to the social welfare of the people."

[28] For an analysis of the capitalist-class left wing, see Domhoff, *Fat Cats and Democrats*, chapter 4.

Summary and Conclusion

In this chapter the nature of the capitalist class in the United States was examined. It was seen that there is considerable concentration of wealth and economic power in the hands of the small number of people who own most of the corporate stock, sit on the boards of directors, and hold leading managerial positions. Ownership and control of the giant corporations serve as the basis for the formation of a social class of capitalists who share a similar upbringing and belong to a wide range of exclusive upper-class institutions, which creates a common social and political milieu in which they act. Although the capitalist class is more socially and politically homogeneous than any other class, there are nevertheless considerable political differences within it. Such differences, as long as the capitalist class as a whole is not under a serious threat from other classes, tend to be the basis of most day-to-day political issues in American society. The effect of amount of income, type of industry, age of money, ethnicity, religion, and political philosophy have been examined to discover the reasons for political differences within the upper class.

In general, most of the political issues and debate in the national and state legislatures, much of the litigation in the higher levels of the court system, and almost all the debate within the federal administrative and regulatory agencies are manifestations of the different economic (and to a lesser degree philosophical) interests within the corporate ruling class. Although the rhetoric attached to such legislation and litigation often cites the interests of the people or nation, differences *within* the capitalist class primarily underlie the verbiage. The internal class differences discussed in this chapter must be understood as secondary. It must be emphasized that the capitalist class is the most unified politically of any class in society.

The unity of the U.S. upper class was probably never greater than it was during the 1950s and 1960s. If it should break down in the future, it may well be because of differences among the left-liberals and corporate liberals on how best to handle a growing economic, social, and political crisis in the United States and the world — not because of sharp economic difference within the class. One major political difference emerging from different economic interests could be over U.S. foreign policy. The war-related industries — those with heavy investments in the Third World countries, and those especially dependent on cheap and secure raw materials obtainable primarily from Third World countries — would favor the continuation of the imperial policies of the post-World War II period, while those corporations heavily reliant on the production of consumer goods, the major exporters, and much of the production goods industry would favor reconciliation with the USSR and China *and* the rollback of U.S. imperial policies. Another major political difference could be over how far to expand the welfare state and federal regulation of the economy. Consumer-oriented interests would possibly favor a fuller development of such policies, while the war-related and production goods industries would probably resist them.

3

Political Differences within the Working Class

This chapter explores those social structural and economic factors that produce political *differences* within the working class. The effect of income and skill differences, unemployment experiences, intergenerational and rural-to-urban mobility, and membership in trade unions are examined. The differences among industrial, "white-collar," and agricultural labor are also examined. The ideological factors that affect political differences in the working class — that is, religious belief, level of education, and patriotism — as well as the demographic factors — race, sex, age, and generation — are discussed in separate chapters (chapters 11 and 5, respectively).[1]

Income Level and Politics

There is no consistent relation between income and political attitudes among manual workers. Greater poverty means greater frustration with the system and hence a greater likelihood of supporting those parties and movements seeking to eliminate inequality. But poverty also tends to repress concern for basic changes, as it forces people to deal exclusively with day-to-day concerns and it produces demoralization.[2] Increasing income often liberates individuals from their psy-

---

[1] For an excellent discussion of the structure of the U.S. working class and the effect of economic structures on the degree of leftism of the various segments of this class, see Judah Hill, *Class Analysis: United States in the 1970's* (P.O. Box 8494, Emeryville, California, 1975).

[2] Seymour Martin Lipset, *Agrarian Socialism* (Berkeley: University of California Press, 1967), p. 176; and Hamilton, *Affluence and the French Worker*, p. 186.

chological chains to day-to-day anxieties, gives them hope for further improvements, and creates the expectation of change. All this predisposes the individual to political radicalism as long as his/her condition remains basically oppressive. In some countries a positive relationship exists between levels of income and leftist politics (the better-off workers are more leftist), and in others a negative relationship exists (the poorer workers are more leftist) — see table 3-1.

It thus appears that the relationship in any given country between income and politics is a result of factors other than income, such as the role of left parties and unions and the strength of traditional values. Often when the influence of a Marxist party is especially strong in the working class, as it is in France and Italy, and the poorest segments of the working class consequently have access to a leftist analysis, then the poorest are the most likely to be supporters of the revolutionary left. In those situations where Marxist parties are weak the poor consequently do not have access to revolutionary ideas. Here it is those workers who are the most widely read and cosmopolitan in their interests (the better-off strata) who are the most likely to support the revolutionary left. This can be seen in the support for Communist parties illustrated in table 3-1. The better-off workers are also better able to relate to the moderate programs of the Social Democratic parties than are the poorer segments of the working class, who do not find sufficient attraction in their programs to pull them away from the more traditionalist ideologies. The poor tend to be rather conservative in normal times when the revolutionary movement is weak. But once they go into motion as part of a large mass movement, they tend to be the most radical segment of the working class.

The so-called phenomenon of "embourgeoisment" (the adoption of middle-class values and politics by workers) is a result of isolation from typically proletarian forces and exposure to middle-class institutions and values, not of relatively high wages. A growing conservativism follows increases in income for some. When involvement in their job decreases, when ties to union and workmates decrease, and when they live in areas socially isolated from people in a similar class situation, the better paid workers are likely to adopt the values and political attitudes of people with whom they now associate.[3]

Lenin, in his *Imperialism: The Highest Stage of Capitalism*, suggested that the reason the better paid British workers in the pre-World War I period were not revolutionary was their relatively high wages — which could only be paid to the workers because of the exploitation of the developed countries:

> ... *out of such enormous super profits ... it is possible to bribe the labour leaders and the upper stratum of the labour aristocracy. And the capitalists of the "advanced" countries are bribing them; they bribe them in a thousand different ways, direct and indirect, overt and covert.*

[3] See David Lockwood, "Sources of Variation in Working Class Images of Society," *Sociological Review* 14, no. 1 (November 1966): 246ff. See also John Goldthorpe et al., *The Affluent Worker: Political Attitudes and Behavior* (Cambridge, England: Cambridge University Press, 1967-1968; and John Goldthorpe et al., "The Affluent Worker and the Thesis of Embourgeoisment," *Sociology* 1, no. 1 (January 1967).

Table 3–1 The Relationship Between Level of Income and Support of the Left within the Manual Working Class

	West Germany[1] 1967 (S)[a]	Cuba[2] 1962 (C)[a]	Norway[3] 1949 (L)[a]		Sweden[4] 1946 (S)[a]		Australia[5] 1969 (L)[a]	France[6] 1955 (SU)[a]		USA (non-South)[7] 1964 (D)[a]
			(L)[a]	(C)[a]	(S)[a]	(C)[a]		(SU)[a]	(SI)[a]	
High wage[b]	55%	30%	73%	12%	56%	27%	36%	35%	76%	68%
Medium wage	51	33	82	9	74	14	61	41	75	70
Low wage	38	34	64	8	70	10	64	47	86	77

Sources:
1. Rose, *Electoral Behavior*, p. 152.
2. Zeitlin, *Revolutionary Politics and the Cuban Working Class*, p. 63. These data are for worker's attitude toward the CP before 1959.
3. Allen Barton, "Sociological and Pyschological Implication of Economic Planning in Norway," cited in Linz, "The Social Bases of West German Politics," p. 327.
4. Linz, "The Social Bases of West German Politics," p. 327.
5. Rose, *Electoral Behavior*, p. 455.
6. Hamilton, *Affluence and the French Worker*, p. 137.
7. Hamilton, *Class and Politics in the United States*, p. 324.

[a] Key to abbreviations:
S: support of the Social Democratic party
C: support of Communist party
L: support of Labor party
D: support of Democratic party
SU: support of the Soviet Union
SI: those sensing much injustice in society

[b] The definitions of high, medium, and low wage, of course, vary from study to study.

> *This stratum of bourgeoisified workers, or the "labour aristocracy," who are quite philistine in their mode of life, in the size of their earnings and in their entire outlook, is the principal prop of the Second International, and in our days, the principal social . . . prop of the bourgeoisie. For they are the real agents of the bourgeoisie in the working-class movement, the labour lieutenants of the capitalist class, real channels of reformism and chauvinism.*[4]

Lenin's thesis must be questioned. The effect of more money is often more than counterbalanced by the fact that workers making more money are located in larger plants, live in more homogeneous working-class areas, and belong to more leftist unions — all of which (as is seen later in this chapter) reinforce leftism.[5]

[4] Lenin, *"Imperialism": The Highest Stage of Capitalism* in *Selected Works*, vol. I, p. 717.
[5] See also Hamilton, *Affluence and the French Worker*, pp. 130-131, for a discussion of this point.

Skill Level and Politics

A major determinant of the political attitudes and behavior of workers is the distinctive characteristics of their occupations and skill level. The more unsatisfying is one's labor, the more prone one is to be leftist. Arbitrary and petty discipline, close supervision by others, minutely segmented and routine tasks with little opportunity to interest oneself in one's work or to exercise one's creative abilities, and the low regard in which one's labor is held by others creates on-the-job resentment. This resentment tends to be transformed into leftism.[6] The boring routine and degradation that one is subject to because of one's occupation is a major force producing leftism.

The frustrations of unskilled or semiskilled labor are captured by Paul Romano, a young factory worker:

> *The worker has to work. There is no alternative but to produce in order to provide even the bare necessities of life. The greater part of his waking hours are spent in the factory. It is here that he, as a worker, must think and act. No matter what the conditions of life are in the factory, he has got to make a living. . . .*
>
> *The worker is compelled on the job to perform a task which can only make him rebel: the monotony; the getting up every morning; the day by day drudgery which takes its toll. He labors under forced conditions. Not only that, but there is the fact that he compels himself to accept these conditions. Home, family, economics make him a slave to this routine.*
>
> *. . . a worker spends most of his waking hours in the plant or at his labor. His life, therefore, revolves around this activity. His subconscious becomes overwhelmed with facts and thoughts concerning machines, workers, bosses, regularity of work hours, and incessant repetition. When not at the shop, he breathes a little more like a man. His home is more like the expression of his life. When the break occurs in the work and he has his week-end, for a fleeting moment he has loosened himself from the effects of the shop. Then crash! He must reorient himself back on Monday to the same old routine. The mental strain at many times is immense.*
>
> *The life of a worker is transformed into working time. He does not know how to play. After working hours, in the company of other workers, the conversation invariably returns to the shop. It is like a drug that will not release his mind. The worker thinks of payday and the end of the week.*[7]

---

[6] Lipset, *Political Man*, chapter 7.

[7] Paul Romano "Life on the Job," in Tom Christoffel, David Finkelhor, and Dan Gilbarg, eds., *Up Against the American Myth* (New York: Holt, Reinhart, and Winston, 1970), pp. 189, 193, 194. For other good descriptions of the work-life of unskilled or semiskilled workers, see Elinor Langer, "Inside the New York Telephone Company," reprinted in William L. O'Neill, ed., *Women at Work* (Chicago: Quadrangle Books, 1972); Kenneth Lasson, *The Workers* (New York: Bantam, 1971); Upton Sinclair, *The Jungle* (New York: Signet, 1960); Studs Terkel, *Working* (New York: Avon, 1975).

The lack of respect with which workers are treated by office personnel, sales people, clerks, supervisors, professionals, and managers as well as by members of the capitalist class, and these people's failure to recognize the economic contribution and individual abilities of working people also produce considerable hostility.[8] This hostility can become the basis of leftist politics.

Jobs vary greatly in terms of both how boring and menial they are *and* the extent to which humiliations and degradations are experienced. Some jobs are automated, involve much paper work, are performed under well-lighted and clean conditions, allow for significant autonomy and creativity, and involve contact on a basis of mutual respect with engineers and supervisors, while others are physically difficult, unpleasant, routine, and involve generally unpleasant relations with superiors and staff people.[9]

A number of studies of assembly line workers vividly describe the oppressive conditions of their labor and trace their propensity to radicalism from this source. These workers view their jobs with anger and resignation. They feel powerless to control the speed of the line, and they feel considerable hostility to their supervisors. The least-skilled assembly line workers are the most likely to see society manipulated by business and to express a class-conscious attitude.[10]

Generally, the least-skilled workers are the most leftist (see table 3-2). These workers suffer the greatest humiliations and find their work the least satisfying. Note that in those countries with two major leftist parties, unskilled workers are much more likely to support the Communists than are skilled workers. Where there is free choice unskilled workers tend to choose the most radical of the left parties because their oppression is the greatest. This is not the case, however, where there is no significant Marxist alternative. In such countries less-skilled workers are likely to be demoralized and apolitical, as they have not yet been politically mobilized. Thus in Norway, Sweden, and Germany a positive relationship between the support of the moderate Social Democratic and the small Communist parties and skill level exists.[11] When the extreme left is weak, its appeal is mainly to the better-educated workers, but once it establishes a mass base the major component of its support changes to the least skilled, to whom Communism now gives a realistic hope for liberation.

A factor that contributes to the greater support of the left by the most-

---

[8] Richard Sennett and Jonathan Cobb, *The Hidden Inquiries of Class* (New York: Vintage Books, 1973), especially chapters 1 and 2.

[9] Jobs vary considerably by how much workers would rather not be doing them. See Robert Blauner, *Alienation and Freedom* (Chicago: The University of Chicago Press, 1964).

[10] For example, see Arthur Kornhauser, *When Labor Votes: A Study of Auto Workers* (New York: University Books, 1956); Blauner, *Alienation and Freedom*; Ely Chinoy, *Automobile Workers and the American Dream* (New York: Random House, 1955); Lewis Lipsitz, "Work Life and Political Attitudes," *American Political Science Review* 58, no. 4 (December 1964); and Goldthorpe et al., *The Affluent Worker*.

[11] See Hamilton, *Affluence and the French Worker*, chapter 6; Zeitlin, *Revolutionary Politics and the Cuban Working Class*, chapter 4; and Lipset, *Political Man*, chapter 7.

Table 3–2 The Relations Between Skill Level and Support of the Left within the Manual Working Class

	Italy[1] 1953 (C)[a]	France[2] 1954 (C)[a]	France[2] 1954 (S)[a]	West Germany, 1953[3] (S)[a] Medium Income	West Germany, 1953[3] (S)[a] Low Income
Skilled workers	16%	18%	41%	68%	51%
Unskilled workers	26	45	21	58	35

Sources:
1. Linz and Lipset, "The Social Bases of Diversity," chapter 6, p. 6.
2. Idem.
3. Linz, *The Social Bases of West German Politics*, p. 332, 333 (male employed workers only).

[a] For key to abbreviations see notes to table 3–1.

skilled workers in some countries is the particularly strong humiliations suffered by workers regardless of their income level. In spite of their income being equivalent to that of white-collar people and many professionals, skilled workers are denied the respect accorded to those groups and tend to manifest their hurt in greater leftism. The psychic injuries of working-class life — the bitterness of not being considered fully human — can manifest itself in support for leftist causes and parties (perhaps even more among skilled workers, whose relatively good material life has created expectations of human treatment, than among demoralized unskilled workers).[12]

The Effect of Unemployment

The discontinuity and frustration introduced in the life of individuals by unemployment, as well as the fear and memory of such unemployment, are among the greatest stimuli to leftist politics in the working class. Job instability is one of the major strains on the working class in capitalist society. Joblessness threatens to wipe out savings, bring poverty, force relocation, radically disrupt one's life, and frustrate life plans.

Those workers in occupations which are characterized by irregular and seasonal employment and irregular income tend to be the more leftist. Fishermen, miners, lumbermen, agricultural workers, and construction workers are all subject to employment cycles that vary greatly by season and often from year to year as well. Their employment is dependent on wide fluctuations in the market for the commodities they produce.[13]

[12] See Lipset, *Political Man*, p. 253; and Zeitlin, *Revolutionary Politics and the Cuban Working Class*, p. 108.
[13] Lipset, *Political Man*, chapter 7; Clark Kerr and Abraham Siegal, "The Interindustry Propensity to Strike," in Clark Kerr, *Labor and Management in Industrial Society* (Garden City, N.Y.: Doubleday, 1964); and Zeitlin, *Revolutionary Politics and the Cuban Working Class*, chapter 2.

John Leggett's study of Detroit auto workers demonstrates a strong correlation between radical consciousness and experience with unemployment. Forty-six percent of the unemployed (compared with 31 percent of the employed workers in his study) were (by his definition) class conscious.[14] Workers who enter the work force in times of high unemployment (such as the 1930s) carry with them the scars of this experience throughout their lives. Such workers consequently are more class conscious than workers who entered the work force during periods of high employment and prosperity.

Maurice Zeitlin found similar results for Cuba. Among workers whose weekly wage was $40 or less before the revolution, 37 percent of those who were typically under- or unemployed (compared with 22 percent of those who were regularly employed) reported in 1962 that they were favorable to the Communist party before 1959. The comparable figures for those who averaged $40 a week or more before the revolution was 42 percent for the under- and unemployed and 29 percent for the regularly employed.[15]

Richard Hamilton analyzed both the impact of actual unemployment and the fear of future unemployment on the French working class. His study shows that those who had a history of unemployment and were afraid of being laid off were the most leftist, while those without a history of unemployment and who had no fear of being fired were the most conservative (see table 3-3).

The U.S. Communist party had considerable success in organizing among the unemployed during the 1930s. (But once its activists got regular jobs, they usually dropped out of the party so as not to risk the little they now had.)[16] In the

Table 3-3 Leftism and Unemployment in France, 1955

	Unemployment (in Months)		
	None	Less than three	Three to twelve
Percent pro-Soviet among those with:			
No fear of unemployment	26%	41%	44%
Much fear of unemployment	33	54	62
Percent who expect change through revolution among those with:			
No fear of unemployment	31	24	53
Much fear of unemployment	33	75	74

Source: Richard F. Hamilton, *Affluence and the French Worker in the Fourth Republic*, p. 194. Copyright © 1967 by Princeton University Press. Reprinted by permission of Princeton University Press.

[14] John Leggett, *Class, Race and Labor* (New York: Oxford University Press, 1968), p. 80.
[15] Zeitlin, *Revolutionary Politics and the Cuban Working Class*, p. 65.
[16] Nathan Glazer, *The Social Bases of American Communism* (New York: Harcourt, Brace and World, 1961), pp. 100-102.

1950s Communist support in the West German working class was greatest among those workers who felt the most insecure about their jobs.[17]

The effect of long-term unemployment is usually very different from that of cyclical and normal periods of unemployment. While the recently unemployed (and the once unemployed who are currently employed) tend to be more leftist because of their oppressive experiences, those who have been unemployed for years tend to become demoralized and apathetic rather than revolutionary.[18]

Intraclass Communication

The probability of developing leftist or class-conscious politics is a product of the degree of intra- and interclass communication among workers. The more they interact with people in a similar class situation, and the less they interact with people in different class situations, the more likely workers are to be radical. Good communication and close personal contacts among people with common problems tend to cause them to become aware of common problems (and their causes) and also give them some notion of how collective solutions can solve their problems. The less the worker is confused with conflicting analyses and solutions coming from classes with different social experiences and interests, the more likely he or she is to develop class-conscious positions. The development of a leftist politics is greatly facilitated by a tight class community of workers and the presence of militant trade unions, working-class political parties, and leaders who serve as catalysts in the process of the development of class consciousness.

The two major structural factors enhancing intraclass communication and hindering interclass communication are the natures of the workers' work and living situations. Certain jobs facilitate on the job discussion considerably. For example, before cigar making was mechanized, workers sat around large tables rolling cigars by hand. This process was noiseless, and it placed workers in very close proximity throughout the day. As a result the workers spent their time talking among themselves. Often they would also hire people to come in to read newspapers and books to them while they worked. Since they were an oppressed group, it was inevitable that their discussions would turn to their occupational oppression, its causes, possible solutions, and its interrelation with broader social questions. Consequently, in many countries the cigar makers were among the first to form trade unions and support the anarchist and Marxist parties.[19]

[17] Juan Linz, "The Social Bases of West German Politics," (Ph.D. dissertation, Columbia University, 1959), p. 421.

[18] For discussions of the effect of long-term unemployment on leftist politics, see Linz and Lipset, "Social Bases of Diversity," chapter 6, p. 27f; Hamilton, *Affluence and the French Worker*, p. 186; E. Wight Bakke, *The Unemployed Worker* (New Haven, Conn.: Yale University Press, 1940); and Marie Lazarsfeld et al., *Die Arbeitslosen von Marienthal* (Leipsig: S. Hitze, 1933).

[19] R. V. Burks, *The Dynamics of Communism in Eastern Europe* (Princeton, N.J.: Princeton University Press, 1961), pp. 54–56.

Other occupations such as those of sailor, miner, and logger require men and women to live together apart from most of society. They must form almost homogeneous occupational communities because their job requires them to be in a definite and isolated place. These communities develop their own traditions, standards, myths, heroes, and class organizations in isolation from the cross-pressures of other classes and, because of their homogeneity and resultant class solidarity, are able to resist ruling-class ideological hegemony. The workers' union and party in such situations often functions as a quasi-government that is involved in all aspects of the workers' lives. The leaders in such communities are likely to come from the same class as do the workers. Class antagonisms are often exacerbated in such situations because the owners of the basic industry in these areas are also likely to be the owners of the workers' houses, the stores in which they shop, and perhaps also of the subsidiary industries in which the men's wives work (canneries in the case of fishermen, longshoremen, or sailors).

Living and working in close personal contact and relative isolation from other classes enhances a group's conception of its economic and political power and develops in it the confidence that the social function it performs is vital to the ruling class.[20] Workers under such conditions are able to see their strength and are thus likely to engage in militant strikes and other class actions as well as to develop a socialist or Communist consciousness. Consequently, sailors, lumbermen, and especially miners throughout the world have been among the most militant and class-conscious segments of the working class.[21]

Two of the best indicators of the degree of homogeneity of working-class experience, and hence of intraclass communication, are the size of the work place and the size of the city in which workers live. In general, the larger the factory, the more workers interact with one another, and the less they interact with their superiors. The same correlation exists between the proportion of the population of an industrial town or city that is manually working class and the degree to which workers interact with each other and not with members of other classes during their leisure time. It is in the large towns and small cities, which usually have the highest percentage of industrial workers, where we would expect the most leftism among the workers. Table 3-4 illustrates the effect of plant size on a worker's class consciousness. Table 3-5 illustrates the effect of community size on a worker's political attitudes.

Workers who are not able to communicate with each other because of the structure of their jobs (spacing, noise, small size of plants, rules against talking,

---

[20] See Seymour Martin Lipset, Martin Trow, and James S. Coleman, *Union Democracy* (Garden City, N.Y.: Anchor, 1962), chapters 6 to 8, for one of the most thorough empirical studies of the effect of occupational community, shop size, and work organization on political attitudes. Also see Hamilton, *Affluence and the French Worker*, pp. 205-214, 246-251; Kerr and Siegal, "The Interindustry Propensity to Strike"; Linz and Lipset, "Social Bases of Diversity"; and James Petras and Maurice Zeitlin, "Miners and Agrarian Radicalism," in James Petras and Maurice Zeitlin, eds., *Latin America: Reform or Revolution* (New York: Fawcett Publications, 1968).

[21] See Kerr and Siegal, "The Interindustry Propensity to Strike."

Table 3—4 The Relationship Between Leftism and Size of Plant in the Manual Working Class

	W. Germany: 1953[1] (C+S)[a]	France: 1955[2] (S)[a]	Cuba: 1962[3] (C)[a]	Japan: 1961[4] (S)[a]
Small plants[b]	38%	21%	25%	57%[c]
Medium plants	52	29	35	
Large plants	53	33	46	76

Sources:
1. Linz, *The Social Bases of West German Politics*, p. 377.
2. Hamilton, *Affluence and the French Worker*, p. 221.
3. Zeitlin, *Revolutionary Politics and the Cuban Working Class*, p. 174. Data are for worker's attitude toward the CP before 1959.
4. Lipset and Rokkan, *Party Systems and Voter Alignments*, p. 452. Data are for Tokyo only.

[a] For key to abbreviations see notes to table 3—1.
[b] The definitions of plant size vary from study to study. In the Hamilton study of France small plants have 49 or fewer workers, medium plants 50—299, and large plants 300 or more.
[c] Small and medium plants combined.

Table 3—5 The Relationship Between Leftism and Size of Community in the Manual Working Class

	West Germany, 1953[1] (S)[a]	France, 1955[2] (SU)[a]	France, 1955[2] (SI)[a]	Britain[3] (L)[a]
Villages and small towns (< 5,000)	10%	36%	78%	50%
Large town (5,000—20,000)	13	49	75	50[b]
Small city (20,000—100,000)	12	39	82	
Medium city (100,000—500,000)	22	41	78	53[c]
Very large city (> 500,000)	14			

Sources:
1. Linz, *The Social Bases of West German Politics*, p. 216.
2. Hamilton, *Affluence and the French Worker*, p. 247.
3. Rose, *Electoral Behavior*, p. 512.

[a] For key to abbreviations see notes to table 3—1.
[b] Places of less than 50,000.
[c] Cities of more than 50,000.

and so on) or who interact frequently with their managers or members of other classes are the least likely to be class conscious. Traditionally, workers in utilities (for example, water, gas, electricity), government, domestic service, and clerical and sales positions tend to live in multiindustry or at least multiclass communities and associate with people of quite different working experiences and class backgrounds. These workers are thus subjected to considerable pressure against developing class consciousness.[22] Textile and agricultural workers *do* become militant and class conscious when they form relatively homogeneous occupational

[22] Idem.

communities largely cut off from middle-class social pressures. Such was the case in the textile mill towns that gave birth to some of the most militant strikes in U.S. history such as Lawrence, Massachusetts and Gastonia, North Carolina, and the bitter strikes in California agriculture in the 1930s and the late 1960s and early 1970s.[23]

In small shops and towns the workers are likely to consider the bosses, with whom they interact on a personal basis, to be their friends. Further, because of the lack of sharp life-style and background differences, these workers entertain the hope that they, or at least their children, will become a boss — a position which, after all, "he achieved by his own effort."[24] In larger plants direct and personal contact with the boss disappears, as does the hope that they or their children, by their individual efforts, could ever become a boss, who now appears to have power because of class background rather than ability. This factor thus works in the same direction as the greater degree of intraclass communication in such situations to increase class hostility and promote leftism in the larger, impersonal work situations.[25]

Another factor producing leftism in larger plants and communities is the ease with which radical organizations can operate in these environments. The impersonality and distance between the bosses and the workers provide radicals with space and protection in which to work undetected until they succeed in establishing a firm base. Where the Socialist and Communist parties are strong, they often create a wide range of organizations to integrate all aspects of the worker's life. Cultural activities, sport clubs, women's groups, youth associations, and paramilitary groups are coordinated by the party. Workers read the party and union press and pamphlets and attend party- and union-organized study groups, lectures, and classes. A class culture is consequently created and reinforced by continuing association with other class-conscious workers.[26]

Recent changes in the economy have been producing increasing class homogeneity, whereas other changes have resulted in more class heterogeneity. The virtual disappearance of domestic work and its replacement by socialized service work has been destroying the traditional personal relationships between workers and the boss. The migration of rural groups from their heterogeneous rural environment to homogeneous working-class living areas and the evolution of white-collar work from providing mostly personal services to the boss to becoming structurally closer to factory labor facilitate the development of working-class con-

---

[23] See Melvyn Dubofsky, *We Shall Be All* (Chicago: Quadrangle Books, 1969), chapters 10 and 11, for descriptions of the Lawrence, Massachusetts, and Patterson, New Jersey, textile strikes of 1912 and 1913. See Liston Pope, *Millhands and Preachers* (New Haven, Conn.: Yale University Press, 1942), for a description of the textile strike in Gastonia, North Carolina in 1928. See Carey McWilliams, *Factories in the Field* (Santa Barbara, Calif.: Peregrine Publishing, 1971), for perhaps the best treatment of class conflict in California agriculture.

[24] Zeitlin, *Revolutionary Politics and the Cuban Working Class*, p. 176.

[25] Hamilton, *Affluence and the French Worker*, pp. 205, 227.

[26] See Lipset, *Political Man*, chapter 6.

sciousness.[27] Then again, the development of cheap mass transportation has somewhat undermined the traditional class homogeneous working-class living areas and leisure-time activities. The impact of modern transportation has been limited, however, by the common income situation, friendship patterns, and job-induced proclivities of the working class. Working-class neighborhoods survive, even if transplanted to the suburbs.[28] Similarly, class-related leisure-time activities continue to predominate. Activities such as hunting, baseball, bowling, and fishing bring working-class people together and separate them from the petty bourgeoisie and capitalist classes. These latter classes tend to participate in such activities as tennis and golf, and when they do engage in hunting, fishing, and socializing, do so with their personal friends — that is, people in a similar class situation. Thus, all in all, the factors tending to increase class homogenization may well override the factors working against it.

Mobility

As it developed over the last 200 years, capitalist industrialization promoted considerable social as well as geographical mobility. Whereas in feudal times people usually lived in the same village and often had the same occupation and status as their parents and grandparents, in capitalist society people tend to migrate from one town to the next in search of employment and to have a better chance of having a different (either higher or lower) class than their ancestors.

There are three manifestations of mobility on the development of leftist attitudes: (1) the actual amount of movement into and out of the working class from and to the petty bourgeoisie; (2) the belief that it is possible for one or one's children to enter into the petty bourgeoisie; and (3) the movement from rural areas into the urban working class. The effect of each is discussed in turn.

Class consciousness is inversely related to the degree of individual mobility — either upward *or* downward. Individuals whose parents were petty bourgeois or who began life in petty bourgeois occupations, but who are forced into the manual working class, generally hope (and expect) to return to the higher class and, hence, are likely to retain petty bourgeois values and political beliefs. They are thus less likely to join unions and support working-class political parties, and they are generally more conservative than the rest of the class.[29] Downwardly mobile workers tend to undermine class solidarity, which causes the entire working class

---

[27] From a discussion with Goran Therborn on the political effect of these social changes.
[28] See Bennett Berger, *Working Class Suburb* (Berkeley: University of California Press, 1960); and Herbert Gans, *The Levittowners: Ways of Life and Politics in a New Suburban Community* (New York: Vintage Books, 1969).
[29] See Seymour Martin Lipset and Hans Zetterberg, "Social Mobility in Industrial Societies," in Seymour Martin Lipset and Reinhard Bendix, eds., *Social Mobility in Industrial Society* (Berkeley: University of California Press, 1959), pp. 69-71; and Leggett, *Class, Race and Labor*, pp. 91-94.

to be susceptible to reactionary and obscurantist ideas.[30] The downwardly mobile also are usually subject to the cross-pressures of their background pushing them to conservatism while their contemporary situation pushes them left. As a result, their political attitudes and behavior are generally intermediary between the two classes.[31] Sometimes, however — especially in times of crisis — the downwardly mobile workers can form a large part of the basis for fascist strength in the working class, since the fascist appeal for a "third solution" between labor and capital resonates well with their own conflicting life experience. On the other hand, workers whose parents were also workers are more likely to be class conscious because they learned class-conscious attitudes and leftist politics as children. Their present day-to-day experiences reinforce the values obtained in childhood.

Workers from petty bourgeois backgrounds are usually more conservative than workers from working-class backgrounds (see table 3-6). The more generations in the working class, the more likely a worker is to be leftist. In West Germany in 1953, 56 percent of manual workers whose fathers and both grandfathers were in the manual working class (compared with 51 percent of those who had at most one grandparent but whose fathers were in the working class) voted for the Socialists or the Communists.[32]

A second important factor is the belief in the possibility of (*not* the actual) upward mobility out of the manual working class. If the opportunity for upward mobility — that is, an individual solution to oppression — *seems* to exist, there is consequently a reduction in *collective* effort toward social change. The more the values held by workers maintain that one can get ahead by one's own individual efforts, that the petty bourgeois and capitalist classes got where they are through hard work, and that the poor are poor because they are lazy or insufficiently educated, the less class conscious will be these workers, the weaker will be their unions, and the less influential will be the Marxist parties.[33]

The United States does *not* have a higher rate of individual mobility than other advanced capitalist countries.[34] The difference between the United States and other countries with regard to upward mobility is only in the differences in the workers' beliefs about the possibility of upward mobility. In fact, since 1950 the rapid industrial growth of most of the other advanced capitalist countries, together with the use of imported laborers in the least desirable jobs, has produced a greater rate of upward mobility in these countries than in the United States.

The actual differences in the rate of upward mobility by occupations, countries, and historical eras — although they are not as important as the differences in the beliefs about mobility — do have an effect on consciousness. If

---

[30] Zeitlin, *Revolutionary Politics and the Cuban Working Class*, p. 132.
[31] Lipset, *Political Man*, p. 220f.
[32] Linz, "The Social Bases of West German Politics," p. 441.
[33] See Lipset, *Political Man*, chapter 7; and Linz and Lipset, "Social Bases of Diversity," chapter 6, for discussions of the effect of the belief in social mobility.
[34] See Lipset and Bendix, *Social Mobility in Industrial Society*, chapter 2.

Table 3-6 The Effect of Intergenerational Mobility on the Leftism of Manual Workers

Father's Occupation	West Germany[1] 1953 (S+C)[a]	Sweden[2] 1964 (S+C)[a]	Finland[3] 1966 (S+C)[a]	Cuba[4] 1962 (C)[a]	United States (Detroit)[5] 1960 (CC)[a]
Middle class, professional, business person, salaried employee, manager, etc.	43%	81%	62%	24%	16% (including rural)
Manual working class	53	90	88	28	36
Farm	35	70	68	24	—

Sources:
1. Linz, *The Social Bases of West German Politics*, p. 441.
2. Rose, *Electoral Behavior*, p. 397.
3. Rose, *Electoral Behavior*, p. 299.
4. Zeitlin, *Revolutionary Politics and the Cuban Working Class*, p. 155.
5. Leggett, *Race, Class and Labor*, 1968, p. 92.

[a] (CC) = Class Consciousness. For key to other abbreviations see notes to table 3-1.

all the opportunities for upward mobility are blocked by economic stagnation or the successful efforts of petty bourgeois and upper-class parents to ensure good careers for their children, it would be very difficult to maintain successfully the myth of upward mobility for very long. As long as a number of individuals do "make it" into the middle class, the myths that hard work results in success and that the poor are responsible for their own lot gain credibility. In fact, the possibilities for upward mobility during the period of rapid industrial growth of the United States between the Civil War and World War I did fuel the myth of the possibility of individual advancement, which consequently greatly hindered the development of class consciousness in the United States working class.[35]

The effect of movement from farm occupations to the urban manual working class is complex. The effect of being uprooted from a traditional background and suddenly placed in an alien, impersonal, and oppressive industrial and urban environment is to embitter people and make them prone to being mobilized to resist their new situation. This type of reaction is facilitated by the fact that new migrants to industrial working-class jobs, who generally leave the rural areas with high expectations of what life will be like in the cities, usually find these expectations to be cruelly frustrated. New migrants are thus especially prone to rioting, spontaneous strikes, and other forms of unorganized resistance; however, they also are less likely to join unions and leftist parties, to engage in sustained and organized struggle, or to adopt sophisticated leftist ideologies. The disorganization produced by the move to the city and the new industrial life, combined often with some degree of gratitude for the improvements, however small, in one's life, and the simple inertia of rural non-class-conscious values and undisciplined forms of

[35] See Jackson Turner, *The Frontier in American History* (New York: Henry Holt, 1921); and Linz and Lipset, "Social Bases of Diversity," chapter 6, p. 50f.

behavior (it takes time for the discipline of working-class life and the understanding of the power of working-class solidarity to permeate the culture of new migrants) mitigates against the development of class consciousness.

The new migrants probably go through the following sequence of responses to their new environment. At first the migrant might feel demoralized and isolated from working-class culture. But after a period of getting his/her bearings, a period of militant resistance and bitterness usually ensues. Gradually, bitterness and spontaneous resistance become transformed into genuine class consciousness. This process seems normally to take two generations to run its full course. Studies of the effect of rural-to-urban migration often produce contradictory results. These conflicting findings seem to come from studying migrants in different stages of integration into the working class and from confusing the facts of resentment and spontaneous resistance with true class consciousness.

Studies that focus more on attitudes of bitterness and spontaneous behavior show that those born in rural areas are *more* militant than those born in urban areas. For example, John Leggett found that in Detroit in 1960, 52 percent of workers who grew up in rural areas (compared with only 22 percent of those who grew up in industrial areas) said that they would participate in a demonstration against a landlord who was charging high rents for poor housing. The relationship is just as strong when only blacks are examined. Fifty-eight percent of black workers from rural areas (compared with 35 percent of black workers from urban areas) would support such a demonstration.[36]

Studies that focus more on the attitudes of general class solidarity show that workers born in cities have more class-conscious attitudes than those born on farms. For example, Richard Hamilton found that in the United States in 1964, 49 percent of married manual workers outside of the South who were both reared and presently living in a large city approved of a federally guaranteed living standard, in comparison with 39 percent of large-city workers and 21 percent of small-town workers who grew up in small towns.[37]

The leftism of those uprooted from rural backgrounds in part stems from the fact that they are more readily exploited than workers who have been in a place for some time. They have the least job security, are the most susceptible to unemployment, are the least likely to be upwardly mobile, and are the most likely to be denied rudimentary rights.

Whether militant unions and working-class parties and movements are present is another factor determining the role of the more recent migrants. In their absence, the responses of demoralization and spontaneous resistance are likely to take hold and persist. In their presence, the disorientation and bitterness of the recent migrants can be rather easily mobilized into class consciousness and organized leftist behavior. Consequently, in the presence of active class organizations recent migrants from rural areas, who are not likely to have developed

[36] Leggett, *Class, Race and Labor*, p. 64.
[37] Hamilton, *Class and Politics in the United States*, p. 256.

individual defenses against the oppression and exploitation of manual working-class life and whose oppression is the most severe, are likely to respond in a most class-conscious manner.[38]

The effect of rural migration into the working class is also very much a product of the political consciousness of the migrants. Certain rural regions, because of their distinctive tenure pattern, predominant crops, and political history, tend to be radical; others, because of distinctively different conditions, tend to be conservative.[39] Consequently, the rural migrants from radical areas are carriers of revolutionary ideas into the working class rather than obstacles to their development. This apparently is a major factor in the radicalism of the French and Cuban working classes, and the relative conservatism of the West German working class.[40]

The Effect of Trade Unions

Whether the dominant trade unions in the working class are responsive to the rank and file and are leftist, or are bureaucratic and conservative, plays a very important role in determining the politics of the working class. When the unions are led by Marxists or other revolutionaries, they play a major role in educating the working class and facilitating the development of class consciousness. When the unions are run by labor bureaucrats who consider their job not to be one of raising class consciousness and leading the working-class struggle, but one of securing somewhat better terms for the sale of the commodity labor power, thereby enhancing their own positions, the presence of a union mitigates *against* working-class leftism. In such situations the more leftist and militant workers tend to lose their jobs and be isolated by the unions that act to suppress rather than to encourage militant class-conscious activity.

In countries in which a Communist or other revolutionary party leads the larger unions, the active presence of a union in a plant is one of the leading factors contributing to the radicalism of the workers. This is true whether or not the worker is a member of the union. The presence of union activity educates the workers and draws class lessons (for example, that the capitalist system rather than

[38] It has been reported that during the Russian revolutions of 1905 and February 1917, which were largely spontaneous outbreaks, the workers from rural backgrounds played a disproportionately large role. During the period of their very rapid growth during the spring and summer of 1917, the Bolsheviks recruited heavily from the uprooted workers. See Leggett, *Class, Race and Labor*, chapter 4.

[39] One of the reasons that many new migrants from rural areas tend at first to be more conservative than other workers is their adherence to the traditional religions (see chapter 11). Then again, migrants from areas which have been dechristianized tend to be radical (see Hamilton, *Affluence and the French Worker*, chapter 11).

[40] See Hamilton, *Affluence and the French Worker*, chapter 11; and Zeitlin, *Revolutionary Politics and the Cuban Working Class*, chapter 6.

bad bosses is the cause of their problems) that have a tremendous effect on the level of class consciousness (see table 3-7).

Where the leadership of unions is not closely tied to radical working-class parties, and where it is not held closely responsible to the rank-and-file workers, there exists a strong tendency for the union leaders — regardless of their class background and original intentions — to transform themselves into business executives whose job is the smooth and orderly sale of labor power at a "fair" price. Such union bureaucrats lose all concern for broader class questions. The bureaucrats, who initially obtained considerable powers from the rank and file to successfully lead the class struggle, come to think of their powers as their private preserve once they are entrenched in positions of leadership. They pay themselves salaries much higher than the average worker's and monopolize the internal channels of union communication, thus strangling internal union democracy so that they need not fear the rank and file. Unless such tendencies are neutralized, union bureaucrats come to think and act like any other business person, and the unions themselves become thoroughly integrated into the structure of capitalism as mere extensions of the labor relations departments of the corporations. Such unions negotiate and implement detailed contracts that establish the conditions of

Table 3-7 The Relationship Between Labor Union Membership and Support of the Left in the Manual Working Class

	West Germany[1] 1967 (S)[a]	Netherlands[2] 1956 (S)[a]	Sweden[3] 1968 (S+C)[a]	Britain[4] 1970 (L)[a]	Finland[5] 1966 (S+C)[a]	Australia[6] 1969 (L)[a]	United States[7] 1964 (D)[a]	France[8] 1955 (SU)[a] (SI)[a]
Member of major union federation	65%	90%	83%	60%		71%	84%	74% 89%
Member of minor union federation *not* associated with largest left party	b	9	b	b	88%	b	b	18 75
Not a union member	40	33	61	44	75	53	57	28 73

Sources:
1. Rose, *Electoral Behavior*, p. 153.
2. Rose, *Electoral Behavior*, pp. 243, 256.
3. Rose, *Electoral Behavior*, p. 407.
4. Rose, *Electoral Behavior*, p. 507.
5. Rose, *Electoral Behavior*, p. 303.
6. Rose, *Electoral Behavior*, p. 468.
7. Hamilton, *Class and Politics in the United States*, p. 321.
8. Hamilton, *Affluence and the French Worker*, p. 230.

[a] For key to abbreviations see notes to table 3-1.
[b] Only one labor union federation of consequence in the country.

the sale of labor power and typically limit the right to strike and engage in other forms of the class struggle. The union hierarchy, who by law must enforce its contracts, supplements management in regulating and oppressing the working class. All the demands of the class struggle are transformed by the union bureaucrats into demands for "reasonable" wage increases. Thus, the multifaceted oppression of workers and their tendency to fight back gets "cooled out" by the very organizations which originally arose to advance the interests of the working class.[41]

In general, where the working-class organizations (both the unions and the working-class political parties) are integrated into capitalist society and have agreed to play by its rules (rather than to oppose bourgeois legality and press for revolution), the politics of working-class people tend to be considerably less class-conscious than where the organizations play a revolutionary role. In those countries in which the franchise was extended to the working class *before* the rise of mass unions and working-class parties, these organizations, when they developed, tended to play by the rules of bourgeois legality and never adopted revolutionary Marxism. Where the working class had to fight for the franchise, the working-class organizations born in militant class struggle tended to become Marxist. The formative experiences of the unions and working-class parties continue to affect the degree of working-class radicalism. Once firmly rooted in the working class, Marxism *or* reformism is hard to uproot. The importance of "who got there first," which is determined by early historical conditions, is thus of great importance in understanding contemporary working-class politics.

Another factor which influences contemporary working-class consciousness is the deliberate decisions of Marxist organizations to organize certain industries or locations and not others. One of the reasons that certain industries, like auto and steel, are typically more leftist than others is the deliberate decision of Communists to organize the "basic industries."[42]

Also of importance is the history of attempts (successful and unsuccessful) of repressing Marxist organization. The leftism of lumber workers, dock workers, miners, and construction workers very much in evidence elsewhere is not generally manifested in the United States because of the systematic uprooting and sometimes violent repression of working-class anarchists, Wobblies, Socialists, and Communists, who either in the pre-World War I period or during the 1930s and 1940s had considerable influence in these trades.[43] One of the most effective repressions of Marxism in the working class was orchestrated by Adolf Hitler,

[41] See Andre Gorz, *Towards a Strategy for Labor* (Boston: Beacon Press, 1967); Michels, *Political Parties*; and Stanley Aronowitz, *False Promises: The Shaping of American Working Class Consciousness* (New York: McGraw-Hill, 1973) for discussions of this process.

[42] Linz and Lipset, "Social Bases of Diversity," chapter 6.

[43] For discussions of the role of repression in the uprooting of revolutionary ideas from the U.S. working class, see Robert Tyler, *Rebels of the Woods* (Eugene: University of Oregon Press, 1967); James Weinstein, *The Decline of Socialism in the United States* (New York: Monthly Review, 1967); Glazer, *The Social Bases of American Communism*; and Dubofsky, *We Shall Be All*, part IV.

who over a twelve-year period arrested and executed as many Communist militants as he could. The result of his repression, of course, is the relative conservatism of the West German working class since 1945, in spite of its long tradition as being among the most militant and class conscious in the world. And in the post–World War II period the U.S. government, either through the CIA or in collaboration with the bureaucratic unions in the United States, also attempted to prevent Communists from consolidating hegemony over European and Third World union movements.[44]

These attempts to disrupt the organization of workers and the development of class consciousness notwithstanding, the radicalization of unions continues in much of Europe and the Third World. The educational programs, the practical lessons taught through experience, and the struggles led by the unions are major determinants of working-class consciousness.

The Politics of White-Collar Workers

White-collar workers work in offices and salesrooms rather than in production. For the most part they do not need to exert physical strength on the job, nor do they normally dirty themselves in their labor. They tend to wear the same type of clothes to work as the owners and managers — hence the designation "white collar." Although there are differences between manual and white-collar workers, both sell their labor power to those who own the means of production, neither own nor control the tools with which they work, and neither control the labor power of others; hence both are part of the working class. White-collar workers must not be confused with others who wear "white collars" — professionals, managers, and business owners, who are in a quite different class.

White-collar workers labor under conditions that are becoming more identical to those of manual workers. The offices and salesrooms are becoming larger, more impersonal, and homogeneous, with banks of typists, file clerks, key punch operators, or sales people in close proximity and removed from direct contact with the bosses. Office work is becoming indistinguishable from most industrial labor. In both types of labor, workers predominantly manipulate powered and often automated machinery that does both the heavy work *and* the heavy thinking.

The politics of white-collar workers have traditionally been intermediate between those of the manual working class and the petty bourgeoisie (see table 1–1). Wherever there are large Communist, Socialist, or Labor parties, white-collar workers are found in the middle in their degree of leftism between these latter two groups. In the United States, however, Richard Hamilton has shown that at least in large cities white-collar workers are almost as Democratic as are manual workers and much less Republican than the upper middle class.[45]

[44] See Domhoff, *The Higher Circles*, p. 261f; William Morris, *CIA and American Labor* (New York: International Publishers, 1967); and Ronald Radosh, *American Labor and United States Foreign Policy* (New York: Vintage Books, 1969).
[45] Hamilton, *Class and Politics in the United States*, p. 258.

The intermediate character of white-collar politics reflects the intermediate character of the nature of their work. They generally perform the functions that the bourgeoisie did when it consisted primarily of small business people. They keep the records, do the calculations and billing, sell goods, and generally perform the labor of coordination, supervision, and sales. Because of their objective tasks, their generally closer physical proximity to the upper class, the somewhat less alienating conditions of their labor, the blockage of *intra*class communication because of the physical presence of higher class personnel, and the tradition in this group of identifying with the higher classes, white-collar workers have a tendency to adopt the political attitudes and behavior of the upper middle and business classes.

Salaried employees have traditionally obtained prestige from working in offices. They have tended to share psychologically in the authority and reputation of the capitalist class for which they worked. They dressed as much as possible like their bosses, and in general tended to adopt their life-style. The type of leisure-time activities this group has traditionally pursued is as likely to be that of the smaller capitalists as of the manual workers. Their on-the-job experience does not as readily lend itself to the feelings of solidarity which generate militant unions and class-conscious political action as does that of manual workers. The office and salesroom have been traditionally individualized and divided up in small groups with differential privileges and access to the boss. The traditional social separation between white-collar and manual workers was eloquently described in Upton Sinclair's *The Jungle*:

> *A poor devil of a bookkeeper who had been working in Durham's for twenty years at a salary of six dollars a week, and might work there for twenty more and do no better, would yet consider himself a gentleman, as far removed as the poles from the most skilled worker on the killing beds; he would dress differently, and live in another part of the town, and come to work at a different hour of the day, and in every way make sure that he never rubbed elbows with a laboring man. Perhaps this was due to the repulsiveness of the work; at any rate, the people who worked with their hands were a class apart, and were made to feel it.*[46]

However, the trend is toward physically removing from the front office much of white-collar labor, such as that of data processing, thus producing as much distance between the top managers and the white-collar workers as between the managers and the manual workers (as well as larger and more specialized work places).[47] These trends have greatly reduced the chance for personal influence by, and emulation of, top executives. While the old office and sales-room provided a setting that encouraged deference, the new factory-like office and salesroom facilitate the development of class consciousness. As the traditional per-

---

[46] Sinclair, *The Jungle*, p. 105.
[47] Hamilton, *Classical Politics in the United States*, p. 351.

sonal contact with bosses is replaced by increasing layers of bureaucracy and physical distance, the unique social position of white-collar people disappears.[48]

Their changing job situation, together with the increasing social influence of manual working-class people over them, tend to make this group more leftist. White-collar people (as do marginal business people) tend to be from manual working-class families, have close relatives and friends who are of the manual working class, and, in the case of many sales people, associate predominantly on the job with manual working-class people.[49] Of special importance is that white-collar work is now about three-fourths female and becoming even more women's work all the time. White-collar women tend to be married to manual working-class husbands and thus subject to considerable political influence stemming from their mate's occupational situation. These latter factors make the politics of white-collar workers increasingly like those of manual workers.[50]

There is considerable variation in political consciousness among white-collar workers, just as there is among blue-collar workers. White-collar employees in small firms and cities tend to identify more with owners, and hence be the most conservative, whereas white-collar employees in large businesses and cities tend to identify more with the manual working class and hence be the most leftist. Employment in smaller establishments enhances the white-collar worker's sense of status, produces closer personal interaction with the boss, and promotes identification with her/his affairs and interests. It also generally means less monotonous work and more job authority, which reduces feelings of alienation. The smallness of such operations also encourages the belief that it is possible for the worker himself to become an independent entrepreneur. None of these factors operates in the large firm, where the conditions of labor become increasingly proletarianized.

The larger the firm in which white-collar workers are employed, the more leftist they are. Juan Linz found that in 1953, 21 percent of white-collar men and 17 percent of white-collar women working in firms of under ten workers supported the Social Democrats; whereas in firms of more than one-hundred, 35 percent of men and 26 percent of women supported this party.[51]

City size has an effect similar to that of size of firm. In the larger cities

---

[48] See Lewis Corey, *The Crises of the Middle Class* (New York: Covici & Friede, 1935); C. Wright Mills, *White Collar* (New York: Oxford University Press, 1951); Linz and Lipset, "Social Bases of Diversity," chapters 8 and 9; and Harry Braverman, *Labor and Monopoly Capital* (New York: Monthly Review Press, 1974), chapter 15.

[49] See Hamilton, *Class and Politics*, pp. 349-352. White-collar workers with manual working-class parents tend to be more leftist than those with white-collar or professional parents. Juan Linz found that 35 percent of white-collar men and 23 percent of white-collar women with manual working-class parents supported the Social Democrats in 1953, while only 17 percent of men and 16 percent of white-collar women who had white-collar parents supported this party. See Linz, "The Social Bases of West German Politics," p. 531.

[50] See Albert Szymanski, "The Socialization of Women's Oppression," *The Insurgent Sociologist* 6, no. 2 (Winter 1976).

[51] Linz, "The Social Bases of West German Politics," p. 539.

white-collar employees are much more likely to live in either class homogeneous neighborhoods or in manual working-class neighborhoods than in the small towns where the classes are physically more closely associated.[52] Moreover, the network of after-hours leisure-time associations in larger cities encourages class-conscious or leftist politics.

In West Germany in 1953, 38 percent of white-collar men in cities of over 20,000 and 29 percent of white-collar men in cities of less than 20,000 supported either the Communists or the Social Democrats.[53] In the United States in 1964, 60 percent of lower middle-class (that is, white-collar) Protestant, married non-Southern workers in large cities supported the Democratic party compared with 42 percent of those living in small towns. In the large cities the lower middle class was almost as Democratic as the manual working class; but in the small towns they were much closer to the upper middle class than to the manual working class in their politics.[54]

The Politics of Rural Wage Laborers

Agriculture in capitalist society is increasingly turning to wage labor as the predominant relation of rural production. With the development of modern agricultural technology, farm units have become larger, utilizing up-to-date mechanized equipment and scientific techniques. There are four principal subtypes within this system:

1. The plantation system, used in the production of labor-intensive crops generally requiring several years for maturation;
2. The migrant worker system, used in fruit and vegetable areas where there is a seasonal succession of planting and harvesting requiring large numbers of laborers for very short periods;
3. The agricultural factories, which employ a small number of laborers full time to run a highly capital-intensive agricultural plant — for example, large dairying and grain production;
4. The ranch, where a relatively small number of workers is needed to look after animals roaming over wide areas of land (for example, cattle, sheep).

Crops such as rubber, coffee, sugar, and some tree fruits tend to be produced by the plantation system. These crops are labor intensive and usually require con-

---

[52] White-collar workers living in proletarian districts are considerably more leftist than those living in middle-class districts. In Berlin in 1927, 30 percent of white-collar workers living in proletarian districts (but only 15 percent of those living in middle-class districts) supported the Social Democratic party. See Linz and Lipset, "Social Bases of Diversity," chapter 9, p. 22f.
[53] Linz and Lipset, "Social Bases of Diversity," chapter 9, p. 21f.
[54] Hamilton, *Class and Politics in the United States*, p. 258.

siderable capital investment in the best land and equipment (thus making their cultivation by tenants or family farmers virtually impossible). The nature of the crops also dictates that a labor supply must be available for a long period of time, but not the full year. This system thus produces a labor force which is available to work when its labor is needed and is poorly paid, unskilled, and uneducated. An especially privileged owning class, which often has aristocratic pretensions, is also produced by this system.

Plantation workers normally are not politically active, again for reasons similar to the political inactivity of peasants and unfree laborers. The system lends itself to relatively stable domination by the landowning class. But, as is also the case with poor peasants and slaves, once they become politically mobilized, they tend to become very militant and lend substantial support to revolutionary forces (for example, the Cuban sugar workers and the Indochinese rubber plantation workers).[55]

Ranch workers are inclined to political leftism because of their relative freedom from close supervision, the ease of intraclass communication, and their geographical mobility. Because relatively few workers are needed in this system, there is no need actively to recruit and repress a large labor force. The labor forces of ranches thus tend to be more mobile and as a result rather undisciplined and inclined to take pride in macho behavior. These factors contribute to their propensity to leftism.[56]

Migrant workers, like plantation workers, usually are especially oppressed. The vegetable and fruit crops they tend need to have large numbers of workers harvest (and to a lesser extent plant) them for several weeks each year. Because growing seasons vary by climate and various crops have different growing and harvesting seasons, a mobile class of workers is required to move South to North and back with the natural crop cycle. They work crops that are labor intensive and have not yet developed efficient mechanized techniques for harvesting. As the production of fruits and vegetables becomes increasingly mechanized, this group diminishes in importance (as do, for the same reason, plantation workers). Migrant workers tend to be more political than plantation workers because their constant movement gives them a broader understanding of social conditions, relative freedom from close supervision by their bosses, and considerable mobility of radical cadre (which puts them in touch with many people).

The workers in the agricultural factories, such as those that produce the basic grains in the capitalist countries, are coming to be typical of all rural proletarians and rural cultivators. This system is used where all aspects of handling the crops can be mechanized, and consequently only a relatively small number of workers is necessary to work large areas of land. The workers in such capital-intensive, large-scale agriculture usually are year-round, full-time employees

---

[55] Arthur Stinchcombe, "Agricultural Enterprise and Rural Class Relations," in Reinhard Bendix and Seymour Martin Lipset, eds., *Class, Status and Power*, 2nd ed. (New York: The Free Press, 1966), pp. 188–189.
[56] Ibid., p. 189.

whose job, like that of any industrial workers, is simply to tend machines, leaving the supervision and coordination of the agricultural enterprise to the agricultural corporations for which they work. Consequently, the politics of these workers are similar to those of any other industrial workers.

In countries where the Left is strong, farm laborers are (or are almost) as leftist as urban manual workers. For example in Finland in 1966, 70 percent of farm workers (compared with 80 percent of urban manual workers) supported the Communists or Socialists; in France in 1956, 29 percent of farm workers and 49 percent of urban manual workers supported the Communists; and in Italy in 1958, 77 percent of farm workers (compared with only 62 percent of the manual urban workers) supported the Communists or Marxist Socialists. Among Communist supporters in France in 1952, 75 percent of farm laborers (but only 48 percent of the manual urban workers) thought their situation would benefit from social revolution.[57] This suggests that once rural workers are mobilized by the Left, they become as militant as urban workers.

Tobacco cultivation requires delicate care, continuous attention, intensive cultivation, and steady and careful work on the part of the agricultural laborers. Consequently, the cultivation of this crop produces a better-off and rather skilled class of rural workers and farmers who tend to cultivate relatively small units (since there is little advantage in capital-intensive machinery). Quite often in tobacco-growing areas there is considerable politicalization and leftism among the tobacco workers and small farmers. Tobacco workers have traditionally been among the very first to become class conscious.[58]

Conversely, sugar production requires extensive cultivation, intermittent jobs for many, and strength instead of skill. These requirements produce a large class of especially oppressed seasonal laborers who work on plantations. Sugar produces a reactionary owning class and a generally apathetic rural proletariat. However, when the rural proletariat is mobilized — either spontaneously or through the efforts of bourgeois or proletarian forces — their reactions can be extremely militant. Note that the great slave insurrections occurred in sugar cane-growing areas of the Caribbean, and that sugar workers were among the most militant supporters of the Cuban Revolution.[59]

Summary

In this chapter a number of structural differences within the working class have been examined and the effect of these structural factors on workers' political

---

[57] Linz, "The Social Bases of West German Politics," p. 743.
[58] See Ramiro Guerra y Sanchez, *Sugar and Society in the Caribbean* (New Haven, Conn.: Yale University Press, 1964); Burks, *The Dynamics of Communism in Eastern Europe*; and Fernando Ortiz, *Cuban Counterpoint: Tobacco and Sugar* (New York: Vintage Books, 1970).
[59] See C. L. R. James, *The Black Jacobins* (New York: Vintage Books, 1963); Zeitlin,

attitudes analyzed. The differences in the nature of work of white-collar, urban manual, and rural workers have been shown to produce different propensities to support the Left. As the nature of work in these three types of occupations becomes more alike, the traditional political differences decrease over time. The two factors that are often said to play the most important role in determining support of the Left among manual workers — income level and skill — have been shown to have *no* clear and consistent effect on the degree of leftism of the manual working class. The higher paid and most-skilled workers are *not* necessarily the most conservative.

The degree of intraclass communication or the homogeneity of working-class job and living environments was shown to have a consistent effect on class consciousness within the working class — the greater the intraclass communication, the more leftist a particular group within the working class. Similarly, social mobility was shown to have a clear effect. Both upward and downward social mobility were shown to have a conservatizing effect on working-class people. Geographical mobility has a mixed effect. Migration from rural to urban areas apparently promotes spontaneous resistance, whereas long-term residence in urban areas apparently tends to promote leftist political attitudes.

Perhaps the two factors that were shown to have the greatest effect on leftism within the manual working class are the experience and fear of unemployment and membership in leftist-led trade unions. Lengthy past experience with unemployment and the expectation that one might lose one's job have a considerable effect in generating leftism (however, it should be noted that prolonged unemployment tends to demoralize and hence depoliticize). Membership in a leftist-led trade union translates discontent into conscious support of the leftist political parties, while membership in conservative unions defuses discontent.

In summary, the two types of factors that generate the greatest propensity to leftism or conservatism among manual workers are: (1) major changes or traumatic experiences in one's life, such as unemployment or social mobility; and (2) the integration into either leftist- or conservative-led trade unions or political parties that greatly influence a worker's world view. A worker's wage level, or the inherent rewards or oppressions of the job, do not generally have a direct effect on a worker's politics. The effects of these factors are mediated by structural factors such as life experience, class homogeneity, degree of intraclass communication, and integration into a working-class milieu dominated by either leftist organizations or a conservative subculture. This last factor — integration into a working-class social milieu and working-class organizations — seems to be the most important determinant of working-class politics. However, it should not be taken as the final explanation of workers' politics. The presence and persistence of a leftist or conservative subculture and working-class organizations must in turn be explained through historical and social structural analysis.

Revolutionary Politics and the Cuban Working Class; Guerra y Sanchez, *Sugar and Society*; and Ortiz, *Cuban Counterpoint.*

4

The Politics of the Petty Bourgeoisie

The petty bourgeoisie lies between the capitalist class and the working class. Unlike proletarians, members of this class either do not sell their labor power — or if they do, they have authority over the work process. Neither do they receive most of their income from the exploitation of those whom they employ, as do capitalists.

The petty bourgeoisie consists of three types of people: independent business people (including family farmers), who own their own means of production but who employ no, or only a very few, workers; professionals, whether self-employed or working for the state or private business (professionals normally have a college degree, considerable job autonomy, relatively high remuneration, and creative work), and lower- and middle-level managerial personnel (those employees who have authority over the labor of others, but who do not have ultimate decision-making power or great privilege). The rural petty bourgeoisie consists of the small landowners or independent farmers who work their own land. The petty bourgeoisie is thus highly diverse. Some are self-employed, some work for others; some have creative jobs, others have routine jobs; some work for the state, others for private enterprise; some have authority over others, others do not. As a consequence there are many diverse and contradictory political tendencies within this group.[1]

This class is truly a "middle class." It shares with the upper class either

---

[1] For excellent summary descriptions and analyses of the petty bourgeoisie, see Hill, *Class Analysis: United States in the 1970's*, pp. 9–22; Corey, *The Crises of the Middle Class*, especially chapters 6 to 14; and Mills, *White Collar*, especially chapters 1, 2, 3, 5, 6, 7, 13, and 15.

ownership or control of the means of production or authority over the labor of others, and, generally, autonomous work. But class members share with the manual working class and white-collar employees a fundamental lack of control over their lives and society, as well as a basic subordination to the authority of others on the job or to the uncontrollable forces of the market. The income of the members of this class, and consequently the quality of their lives, is intermediate (except for the marginal small-business people and farmers, whose income is of the order of, if not less than, that of the manual working class) between that of the two major social classes.

At one time the petty bourgeoisie was the leading proponent of democratic and progressive reforms. It provided much of the leadership and impetus for the English, American, and French revolutions. The petty bourgeoisie fought for a new social order incorporating the ideas of liberty, equality, democracy, and progress. This class consistently fought the arbitrary domination and special privileges of the nobility, church, and king (powers with which the wealthy merchant class had long since learned to compromise). It opposed feudal rights, the nonaccountability of the state bureaucracy, and the state-guaranteed economic monopolies of the merchant class. It was the petty bourgeoisie, not the wealthy merchants, financiers, and industrial monopolists, that proved to be the fighters for liberty and democracy. This was the case in England, where this class gave birth to Cromwell's New Model Army and the Puritan Revolution; in America, where it became the major fighting force in the American War of Independence; and in France, where its representatives, the Jacobins, became the leading force for liberty and equality.[2]

In Europe the last great independent upsurge of this class in the name of democratic ideals occurred in the revolutions of 1848. In America it occurred with the Populist party — a party composed of small farmers that advocated nationalization or the breaking up of the big corporations and banks — in the 1890s. In the twentieth century this class generally ceased to be a leading progressive force. It now frequently fights to avoid being swallowed up by the capitalists and the working class, often grasping at romantic straws as it becomes an even less important historical force.

Normally today this class does not act as a major independent political force. Rather, it equivocates between the working class and the capitalist class. It typically demonstrates politics intermediate between those of the two great social classes. It favors state actions against both the big corporations and the unions. The small independent farmers in its ranks often are both strongly against agrobusiness *and* strongly against agricultural workers' unions, since they are being pressured from both sides. The petty bourgeoisie, when it does act as an independent class (as tends to happen in times of crisis), moves toward fascism or other forms of reactionary authoritarianism. This class, for example, provided the social basis for Mussolini and Hitler (see chapter 12). The fascist program is the

[2] Corey, *The Crisis of the Middle Class*.

realization of the middle-class ideal — smash the unions, put the workers in their place, break up big business, return to the land, put women back in the home, control the bankers — in sum, roll back the tide of history *by any means necessary*. The ideals it now puts forth are typically reactionary — that is, going back to Jeffersonian Democracy or the folk life of medieval or pre-Roman Europe. It is not, however, inevitable that the petty bourgeoisie will take the fascist road when under great pressure. It *can* be mobilized by the working class and its parties in a united front against the capitalist class. The greatest sources of cleavage in the petty bourgeoisie are those based on relative income and authority. The upper reaches of this class tend to identify closely with the upper class and its politics, while the lower reaches tend to share the attitudes and politics of the manual working class. The various segments of this class thus tend to adopt the politics of that major social class with which it is most similar and in contact.[3]

That the politics of the petty bourgeoisie lie between those of the capitalist and working classes can be seen from both tables 1-1 and 4-1. This class is not as conservative as big business, nor is it as leftist as the working class. Within the petty bourgeoisie, the higher income segments are considerably more conservative than the lower income segments. In the United States in 1968, 41 percent of non-Southern, medium-income, independent business people and 62 percent of low-income business people supported the Democratic party. Among managers and officials, 38 percent of those with medium incomes and 60 percent of those with low incomes supported the Democrats. We can see that low-income managers, officials, and business people were almost as Democratic as the manual working class. Although in Britain the low-income business people, managers, and officials are much less in favor of the Labour party than the manual workers, their support of this party is considerably greater than that of the medium-income business people, managers, and officials. In both countries the independent professionals (primarily doctors and lawyers) are the least leftist group within the petty bourgeoisie. In the United States salaried professionals (teachers, engineers, etc.) are in the middle of the petty bourgeoisie in their politics, whereas in Britain they are the most leftist of their class.

The Politics of Small Business

By small-business people are meant those individuals who own their own place of business, do much of the manual, sales, and clerical work of the operation themselves, and employ only members of their immediate family or a handful of others (often only part time).

Many small-business people are individuals who were once a part of the manual working class and whose immediate friends and relatives are part of that class. Their parents and earlier job experience are, more often than not, also

[3] Hamilton, *Class and Politics in the United States*, chapter 5.

Table 4-1 Political Differences within the Urban Petty Bourgeoisie

	United States Percent Democratic in 1968 (non-South)[1]	Great Britain[a] Percent Labour in 1951[2]
(Top business)	(6%)[3]	(8%)
Medium income independent business people (more than 15,000 year)	41	10
Medium income managers and officials	38	19
Independent professionals	25	6
Salaried professionals	43	24
Low income independent business people	62	15
Low income managers and officials	60	b
(Manual workers)	(70)	(51)

Sources:
1. Hamilton, *Restraining Myths*, pp. 47, 65. The data are for married, economically active respondents.
2. John Bonham, *The Middle Class Vote* (London: Faber and Faber, 1954), pp. 129, 168.
3. This figure of 6 percent is from Linz and Lipset, "Social Bases of Diversity," chapter 8, p. 5. It is for executives of firms employing more than 10,000 workers in 1955 (in the United States).

[a] The categories used by Bonham are not exactly compatible with those of Hamilton, which are used as the row headings. Thus the numbers reported here should be taken as only general indicators of the relative position of the various groups. The boundary between medium and low income in the U.S. data is $15,000 a year.
[b] Combined with medium-income managers and officials.

manual working class. Quite typically, marginal small-business people such as restaurant and gas station owners and managers are only temporarily out of the working class. Their frame of reference and their political socialization are thus essentially the same as that of manual working-class people. Conversely, the better-off petty bourgeoisie is generally isolated from close social relationships with the manual working class. Most aspire to upper-class status and generally identify with this class.[4]

Smaller-business people (both the marginal business people and the employers of small numbers of clerks) generally are considerably more left than the upper class. This group, particularly outside of small towns, is objectively powerless and subject to domination by the markets structured by the giant chain stores and monopolies. In smaller towns, as contrasted with cities, the local small-

[4] Ibid., chapter 9.

business people become something of an elite, are influential in local politics, and are consequently inclined toward conservatism.[5] The presence of large businesses competing for his/her business generally drives the small-business person to develop politics hostile to big business and to turn to the state for support. Such business people are often sympathetic to the anti–big business attacks of the left. They can be, and often have been, organized to support the working-class parties.[6] In the absence of a strong left-wing working-class party or an effective united front policy on the part of the Left, the small-business person can well become the social basis of fascism or other right-wing anti–big business movements (for example, George Wallace, Joseph McCarthy). Such movements have a distinctively middle-class, anti–big business, anti–working class, pro-"little-guy" appeal, although they are always manipulated by big business for its own ends (see chapter 12).

Small-business people who employ few if any workers, have no reason to be anti-union. To the contrary, strong unions in the big businesses in their markets mean: (1) higher prices for the commodities produced by big business; and (2) more spending power for the customers of small business. Other factors operating to move small-business people to the left include the social and economic influence of their working-class clients. Since their clients spend more money when they are working or receiving high levels of welfare (the smallest-business people are not burdened with social security payments), small business tends to favor governmental guarantees of full employment and social security, although this is mitigated where welfare programs are financed by property taxes (which typically hit small businesses especially hard).

The high degree of social interaction between small proprietors and working-class people in predominantly working-class neighborhoods and shopping areas tends to move small-business people to the Left while isolating them from the social pressures of bigger-business people and the conservative segments of the better-off middle class.[7]

The higher the income of small-business people, the more conservative they are. Juan Linz found that in West Germany in 1953, 42 percent of the poorer small-business people (those making under 250 DM) supported the Social Democratic party, while only 12 percent of the better-off business people (those making over 400 DM) did so. He also found that West German business people who were not employers were considerably more leftist than those who were. While 57 percent of nonemployers supported the Social Democrats, only 15 percent of those who employed one to five workers, and only 6 percent of those who employed more than five did so.[8]

---

[5] See Linz and Lipset, "Social Bases of Diversity," chapter 10; and Hamilton, *Class and Politics in the United States*, chapters 5 and 9, and *Restraining Myths*, chapter 2.
[6] See Linz and Lipset, "Social Bases of Diversity," chapter 8.
[7] Ibid., chapter 8.
[8] Linz, "The Social Bases of West German Politics," pp. 614-615.

The Politics of Professionals

Professionals, such as doctors, lawyers, teachers, scientists, engineers, social workers, and artists — especially those who are salaried — have contradictory forces operating on them. Professionals are among the most privileged groups in society. They generally have high income and high prestige. Their work is rather creative and is performed under more or less autonomous conditions. They generally express a high level of contentment with their jobs. Studies show that almost all would choose the same career if they had to do it over again. The nature of professional work usually brings professionals into closer contact with the upper middle and upper classes than with the manual working class. All these factors operate to make this group conservative.

Then again, there are considerable social forces operating on most categories of professionals to bring them closer to the manual working class. Such factors as the lack of fundamental job control, the prostitution of creativity and autonomy, the ideology of the professions, the nature of the clientele, the skills required by professional work, and the trend of objective proletarianization of large segments of this group have a radicalizing effect.

Considerable diversity exists among professionals. One of the most important sources of this diversity lies in the nature of their employers. Many professionals work for the state, others for private business, and still others for themselves.

The proportion of all professional and technical people that sells its labor power to others has been rising since 1900. In 1900, employed professionals represented 74 percent of all professionals; in 1970, 89 percent. The old independent professions such as law and medicine have been rapidly outdistanced by the rapid growth of such occupations as teaching, engineering, nursing, scientific research, and various forms of technical work. However high their pay, members of this group do not control the conditions of their labor. By all indications, their on-the-job autonomy is declining as an increasing percentage of the labor force performs professional functions. There is simply a limited number of jobs which can profitably be allowed the relatively wide-ranging autonomy of a research physicist or a full professor. Most teachers, nurses, engineers, technicians, and the like now have their work schedules set up for them and are supervised relatively closely. The proportion of all professionals and technicals in the labor force grew from 4.3 percent of the total in 1900 to 8.6 percent in 1950 to 14.4 percent in 1970. Note that the average salary of employed professionals has since 1947 fluctuated around 50 percent more than that of semiskilled workers.[9] It is not surprising, then, that salaried professionals are as a rule considerably more left than independent professionals.

Doctors and lawyers are the most conservative of all professionals. Most

---

[9] Albert Szymanski, "Trends in the U.S. Class Structure," *Socialist Revolution* no. 10 (July-August, 1972).

lawyers typically spend a large proportion of their energies defending the interests of the business classes in the courts. They thus assimilate the positions of those they work for, and their salaries and patterns of communication encourage the development of conservative politics. For lawyers to associate with the Left would damage their chances of being retained by business interests (where most of their income originates). A further factor leading lawyers to conservatism is the nature of law itself. Law is rooted in notions of precedent, tradition, and order — concepts drilled into every law student and reinforced every day in the courts.[10]

Medicine also brings its practitioners great monetary and prestige rewards as well as job autonomy and creative work, and thus tends to be a very conservative profession. However, doctors, although basically conservative, are often slightly more liberal than lawyers because of the nature of their work and clients.[11] Many doctors spend a high percentage of their time in contact with people of the lower classes. They are thus more likely to develop sympathy for their sufferings as well as be influenced by their ideas and attitudes. The scientific training of doctors (unlike the scholastic training of lawyers) predisposes them to be slightly more critical and analytical, thereby somewhat opening them to the Left. Occasionally, doctors take the medical ideology — that curing the sick is the primary purpose of medicine — seriously, and thus may come to advance the health and general well-being of the masses of people even at the expense of their own interests.

There is a considerable range of political proclivities within science. Biologists and chemists are generally the most conservative, whereas physicists and mathematicians are the most leftist — probably because physics and mathematics are the most theoretical and analytical of the sciences. Their practitioners are thus predisposed to carefully and analytically examine issues and come to rational conclusions. Theoretical elegance and simplicity are learned as scientific values. All of these traits influence the attitudes mathematicians and physicists have about society. Marxism (and other rational and critical approaches to society) thus have a certain appeal to these segments.

Conversely, the more empirical and less analytical sciences such as chemistry and biology reinforce the values of respect for concrete and immediate empirical reality, rather than for theoretical understanding and the power of reason. Their analysis of society reveals a respect for what is currently observable, rather than a critical understanding of the underlying social reality and the potential forces of change as is characteristic of the rationalistic sciences. Not surprisingly, the more analytical and the more empirical sciences attract rather different types of people as well as reinforce different proclivities. The more analytical (and hence

---

[10] Linz and Lipset, "Social Bases of Diversity," chapter 11, p. 51f. This chapter of the Linz and Lipset manuscript contains one of the best general treatments of the politics of professionals anywhere. Unfortunately, the treatment of intellectuals in Lipset's *Political Man* (chapter 10), which is based on this manuscript, is only a partial and abbreviated treatment of this topic. My treatment of professionals relies very heavily on Linz and Lipset.

[11] Linz and Lipset, "Social Bases of Diversity," chapter 11, p. 57f.

radically inclined) tend to go into mathematics and physics while the more empirically inclined (and hence conservative) into biology and chemistry.[12]

Artists can have relatively leftist politics — at least in times of high politicalization. Sometimes they are inclined to be apolitical. The political attitudes of artists are largely a result of the inevitable conflict between the values and interests of the business classes and those of creativity. Many artists view their work independently of its market value. They see it either in terms of its inherent value or its contribution to a movement with which they identify. Market relationships (in which artists must participate to live) are frequently considered degrading to artists. Those artists who adjust their style and production to appeal to the commercial market often are considered by other artists (and by themselves) to have degraded their talent — and themselves. The subject matter and sensitivities of many artists, especially poets and authors, put many of them in close touch with the feelings and hopes of the people. This also can be a radicalizing influence.[13]

Professionals who work for the state, especially social service workers, tend to be rather leftist. For example, the Communist Party had the highest ratio of members to workers in any occupation among the social workers of New York City in the 1930s and 1940s.[14] Because of the nature of their work, social workers are generally more sensitive to the inequities and oppressions of capitalist society. The needs of state clients are so pressing that it is difficult (given the nature of their professional education and ideology) not to identify with them to one degree or another. Of course, their close contact with state clients also familiarizes them with the political orientations of these groups. They are faced with the contradiction between adequately dealing with the needs of the state clients and the requirements imposed on them through the state bureaucracy to serve the interests of capital and the perpetuation of the class sytem. These factors act to develop leftism in this strata.

Other factors that encourage the militancy and leftism of civil servants in general are (1) the fact that since they are working for the government, they see nothing inherently wrong with expanding state services at the expense of private ownership; (2) the increasing bureaucratization and general proletarianization of the lower level of civil service work; (3) the financial pressure the state is under to reduce costs (and thereby both salaries and social services); and (4) the illegality of strikes in the public sector. The illegality of strikes forces civil servants to undertake political action and seek allies among the working class and among their clients to win their struggle against the state. Note that unions of state-sector workers *do not* generally share the function of unions in private enterprise of maintaining labor discipline, since the basis of wage increases is increased taxes, not expanded output and profits (as it is in good part in the private sector). That wage increases can generally come only from increased taxation makes the state more reluctant than corporate employers to grant wage increases (hence the need

---

[12] Lipset, *Political Man*, p. 342f.

[13] Linz and Lipset, "Social Bases of Diversity," chapter 11, p. 68f.

[14] Glazer, *The Social Bases of American Communism*, p. 143.

for more militant tactics). Moreover, a proposed wage increase for public-sector workers becomes a source of antagonism with private-sector workers, who must pay any increased taxes.[15] In recent years in the United States the most rapidly growing unions and many of the most militantly fought strikes have been in the public sector.

Middle-level state bureaucrats generally have different politics from social service workers, who are in direct contact with state clients. The politics of these groups tend to be moderate and supportive of whatever (non-radical) party happens to be in power. Extreme political views of either the right or the left are rather dysfunctional when one's career hinges largely on the policies of the party in power and the goodwill of the top administrators it appoints. There are, however, definite limits to the flexibility of this group. When a radical party assumes control of the state, the middle- and top-level civil servants tend to resist the government and undermine revolutionary policies.[16]

The Politics of College Students

The political attitudes and behavior of college students must be understood to result from their peculiar status, their family backgrounds, and the professions for which they are being trained. Specifically, the politics of students stem from:

1. The nature of the professions for which they are training (this includes both the content of the subject matter and the conditions of labor within the profession);
2. The job opportunities (or lack thereof) that will be available upon graduation — as a rule, the more abysmal the job prospects, the more radical the students;
3. The oppressive and impersonal conditions of learning and the inferior status of students;
4. The easy intragroup communication and population concentration among students (especially at the larger schools) that make them rather easy to mobilize;
5. The general propensity of youth to be more critical, principled, and adventuresome than their elders;
6. The tendency to reject socialization into roles that many come to realize are oppressive both of their own potentialities and for the people they would deal with as professionals;
7. The relatively great freedom, lack of responsibilities, isolation from

---

[15] See Linz and Lipset, "Social Bases of Diversity," chapter 9, p. 25f, and chapter 11, p. 32f; and O'Connor, *The Fiscal Crisis of the State*, chapter 1.
[16] Linz and Lipset, "Social Bases of Diversity," chapter 9, p. 25f; and Hamilton, *Affluence and the French Worker*, p. 44.

pressures to conform ("the freedom to sow wild oats"), and the prolonged period of uncertainty about the future inherent in student life;

8. The family background of students (students from liberal professional parents tend to be among the most leftist, while upwardly mobile students of petty bourgeois parents tend to be among the most conservative).[17]

These eight factors often make students significantly more leftist (but sometimes more rightist) than either the petty bourgeoisie where most are headed, or the population as a whole.

Students have traditionally been among the most politicized groups in society. The predominant politics of students, however, has as often been nationalist as Marxist. In the countries of the Third World, where students have the greatest social impact, these two ideologies converge. Student movements in Europe before the 1930s were predominantly nationalist — progressive nationalist movements in such countries as Poland, Ireland, and Italy before their modern reconstitution; but reactionary movements in countries such as Germany, where the nationalist and fascist youth dominated the German student movement until the defeat of Hitler.

The student movement usually is a bellwether of social movements. When right-wing movements appeal to students, it is the precursor of massive right-wing movements in the society. When left-wing movements, such as those of the late 1960s, appeal to them, it is the first step in the radicalization of society. Students, because of their special characteristics (for example, freedom, concern with principle, and audacity) are more responsive to new social currents than any other group in society.[18] In many respects students' politics reflect their essentially petty bourgeois position. Their movements tend to put forth the traditional demands of this class: liberty, equality, democracy, and nationalism.

Students often play a major role in stimulating social unrest and fostering social changes. The Russian Social-Democratic party, the Chinese Communist party, the Cuban 26th of July movement, and most of the national liberation movements of Third World countries were founded primarily by students or people who had recently come to their politics as students. The typical course of the development of revolutionary movements in the twentieth century is for the universities to serve as seedbeds in which some youth come to an understanding of oppression and adopt, or develop, revolutionary alternatives and forms of struggle. These students and young intellectuals generally drop out of school (before or

---

[17] Some of the best studies of the causes of student radicalism include: Richard Flacks, *Youth and Social Change* (Chicago: Markham, 1971); Seymour Martin Lipset and Sheldon S. Wolin, *The Berkeley Student Revolt* (Garden City, N. Y.: Doubleday, 1965); Seymour Martin Lipset, *Rebellion in the Universities* (Boston: Little, Brown, 1971); and Kenneth Keniston, *Young Radicals* (New York: Harcourt, Brace and World, 1968). For a good summary of many of the factors that produce radicalism among students, see Scott McNall, *The Sociological Experience*, rev. 3rd ed. (Boston: Little, Brown, 1974), chapter 13.

[18] Lipset, *Rebellion in the Universities*, chapter 1.

after receiving their university degrees), form revolutionary organizations, and go to the peasants and workers, mobilizing them for a revolution. The role of students as catalysts of social upheaval is especially important when, unable to find professional jobs, large numbers of students take working-class jobs instead, and transmit their radicalism, fueled by personal resentment, to workers who have never been to college.

In the United States, students from professional and white-collar families are the most leftist, while students from independent petty bourgeois (farmer or proprietor families) are the least. Children of manual working-class backgrounds fall somewhere in between in the degree of their radicalism. A 1970 national survey of students showed that students from professional and white-collar family backgrounds were the most likely to identify themselves as radicals and participate in student demonstrations, while students from rural and business backgrounds were the least likely to do so. This same study also showed that in general the *higher* one's family income, the more likely one was to be a radical.[19]

It appears, then, that students from families that have already "made it" by the criteria of status and income, but that are not actually fully integrated into the business elite, are the most leftist. These students go to college with an inclination to find themselves and to learn — not to be upwardly mobile and get ahead, as typically do the children of small-business people and the skilled manual working class. Students from families that are close to poverty, or whose parents are pushing them to go to school to avoid the sweatshop or the dead end of a small family business, are much more likely to resent demonstrations and to view education as a way to "make it." Then again, students from more comfortable backgrounds often become disillusioned with the rewards of "making it" and have more difficulty taking the "rat race" seriously. The relative conservatism of less well-off students must be viewed as a manifestation of the conservatizing influence of upward mobility.

The students at the "better" schools (that is, those with the highest admissions standards) and students with the highest college board scores and grade-point averages are disproportionately leftist.[20] Most of the largest and most violent student outbreaks of the 1960s occurred at the elite institutions of the United States: for example, Berkeley, Harvard, Wisconsin, Columbia, and Santa Barbara (San Francisco State is a notable exception).

Student activists' majors usually correspond to what we would expect from the nature of the various professions and the people they draw. The humanities and social sciences are the most radical, while the sciences (especially chemistry and biology), business, and engineering are the least.[21]

---

[19] Ibid., pp. 86, 92, 93.

[20] See Lipset, *Rebellion in the Universities*, p. 92; and Lipset and Wolin, *The Berkeley Student Revolt*.

[21] See, for example: Camila Auger, Allen Barton, and Raymond Maurice, "The Nature of the Student Movement and Radical Proposals for Change at Columbia University" in *The Human Factor* (Fall 1969): 36.

The Politics of Independent Farmers

The politics of landholding farmers are a function of the size and productivity of the land held, the prevailing system of tenure, and the principal crop grown, as well as of the standard factors which influence the urban petty bourgeoisie (such as level of income and patterns of communication). In general, larger farm owners and managers are as conservative as the rest of the upper petty bourgeoisie, while small farm owners have politics similar to those of marginal business people. The wealthier the farmer, the less leftist he is. This can be demonstrated with data from West Germany, France, Italy, and the United States, where support for the more leftist of the major parties is greater among the marginal farmers (see table 4-2).

The effect of tenure systems

In the capitalist world system there have been five basic types of rural tenure systems:

1. Peasantry, based on more or less self-sufficient producers with some rights to the land but who must turn over their surplus to the dominant classes that market it;
2. Unfree or semifree rural laborers (serfs in Eastern Europe and slaves in the Caribbean region of the Americas) controlled by the commercial landed classes that sell their production on the market (both from the sixteenth to the nineteenth centuries);

Table 4-2 Wealth and Politics of Independent Farmers

	West Germany 1953[1] (S)[a]	Italy 1958[2] (C+LS)[a]	France 1954[3] (C)[a]	United States 1952[3] (D)[a]
Better-off farmers[b]	4%	0%	4%	29%
Average farmers	6	3	27	
Poor farmers	2	12	42	41
Tenant farmers		74		

Sources:
1. Linz, "The Social Bases of West German Politics," p. 777.
2. Lipset and Rokkan, *Party Systems and Voter Alignments*, p. 158.
3. Linz and Lipset, "Social Bases of Diversity," chapter 12, pp. 8, 9.

[a] Key to abbreviations:

(S) = Support of Social Democrats
(LS) = Support of left Socialists
(C) = Support of Communists
(D) = Support of Democratic party

[b] The definitions of "better off," "average" and "poor" vary from study to study, thus these figures should be taken as indicating order of magnitude only.

3. Small-scale landownership by family farmers who are not self-sufficient and who themselves sell most of their production in the market;

4. Family-size tenancy, where the land is, in one way or another, rented to family farmers who are required to turn over a share of their production or a cash payment to the landowners;

5. Rural wage labor in the fully capitalist agricultural enterprise.

In this latter system agricultural capitalists hire wage labor on the same terms as industrial capitalists do in manufacturing or mining. Such a labor force has no rights to the land, nor do the capitalists have any rights to their bodies.[22] This is the only fully capitalist system of agricultural relations. In all the others, residual feudal, slave, or petty bourgeois relations of production are used to produce an economic surplus that is appropriated by those who control the land, who then sell it in markets created by industrial capitalists whose locus is in the cities. All the remnants of earlier forms are being undermined and replaced by full-fledged capitalist agriculture as capital accumulation proceeds and the factory system becomes universal in the fields.

The more primitive capitalist tenure systems utilizing slaves and peasants to generate surplus value produced dominant classes that were highly class conscious and very conservative, and underclasses that were normally politically inactive (although occasionally they rebelled).[23]

Family Farming The defining characteristics of family farming are that the land is owned by those who work it and that production is for markets. Family farming usually is labor intensive, since all family members work the land. This factor, together with the prohibitive costs of purchasing modern equipment and the impracticality of using modern agricultural technology on small units, means that the system is rather inefficient.

Family farmers are highly political, normally with distinctively petty bourgeois or intermediate politics, but in times of crisis radical (either socialist or fascist). Family farmers are directly affected by fluctuating markets for their commodities, credit conditions, and the price of land. All these factors are highly unstable in a commercial economy, and consequently the farmer is led to political mobilization as the solution to his problems. Farmers' movements tend to be

---

[22] See Eric Wolf, *Peasants* (Englewood Cliffs, N.J.: Prentice-Hall, 1969); and Arthur Stinchcombe, "Agricultural Enterprise and Rural Class Relations," in Bendix and Lipset, *Class, Status and Power*.

[23] For discussions of the politics of such groups, see: Stinchcombe, "Agricultural Enterprise"; Barrington Moore, *The Social Origins of Dictatorship and Democracy* (Boston: Beacon Press, 1966), chapter 6; Eric Wolf, *Peasant Wars of the Twentieth Century* (New York: Harper and Row, 1968); Eugene Genovese, *The Political Economy of Slavery* (New York: Vintage Books, 1967); Herbert Aptheker, *Negro Slave Revolts in the United States* (New York: International Publishers, 1943); and James, *The Black Jacobins*.

directed at the maintenance of prices, the availability of cheap credit and auxiliary services (crop storage facilities and reliable and inexpensive transportation), and the reduction of taxes.[24]

Family farmers in the United States have a long history of militance, including the Revolutionary War against Britain, opposition to the Federalist Constitution, Shays' Rebellion, the Pennsylvania Whiskey Rebellion, the Populist movement in the 1880s and 1890s, the Farmer-Labor movements of the 1920s, and the radical farmer movements of the 1930s.

Areas where the land is distributed relatively equally are typically the most radical rural areas. Such was the case in the English, French, and Chinese revolutions. Such has been the case in Indochina and the North American Great Plains.[25] It is in such regions that the farmers have the greatest internal control over their own affairs, the highest degree of intraclass communication, the greatest isolation from penetration by upper-class forces, a certain amount of security to fight for a larger share (they cannot be evicted, they can grow their own food), and the greatest probability of developing revolutionary leaders.[26] Such farmers also believe things can change because of their efforts, since they have already gained something. Conversely, complete poverty normally produces demoralization.

Abuses removed throw into relief those which remain. It is thus the relatively better-off or *middle* farmers (and tenants and peasants as well) who tend to be the most radical in times of crisis, especially in the most homogeneous areas. The very poorest *and* the relatively better-off land holders (and peasants and tenants) are less likely to be radical *except* when a strong external force challenges the existing social structure and presents these strata with the necessity of making a choice — for example, the Communist Party of China in the 1940s. Factors inciting the poorer and middle farmers to rebellion include their tendency to predominate in more marginal areas relatively free of landlord control. The poor and middle land holders also are the most vulnerable to changes caused by commercialism. They are most affected by falling prices and more difficult credit. Because of their precarious position on the land, they tend to send their children to the towns to work as manual laborers. Often they themselves have done manual work in the towns. Consequently, these land holders have a direct link with the radicalism of the urban working class.[27]

Family-Size Tenancy   In this system the family unit works the land owned

---

[24] Stinchcombe, "Agricultural Enterprise," p. 187f; Linz and Lipset, "Social Bases of Diversity," chapter 12.

[25] Edward Mitchell, *Land Tenure and Rebellion: A Statistical Analysis of Factors Affecting Government Control in South Vietnam* (Santa Monica, Calif.: The Rand Corporation, 1967); Eric Wolf, *Peasant Wars of the 20th Century*, p. 290f; and Lipset, *Agrarian Socialism*, chapter 8.

[26] Eric Wolf, *Peasant Wars of the 20th Century*, Conclusion.

[27] Ibid., p. 292.

by the landlord class, and the result of their labor (either in the form of money or the product) is divided between the two classes. The cultivator does not seek self-sufficiency, and the product of the land ends up in the market. Formal title to the land might actually be held by the cultivator, but the system of mortgages and heavy debt works to ensure that the farmer functions objectively as a tenant. This tenure system occurs when the land is very productive and expensive, the crop is highly labor intensive, mechanization is not developed, no appreciable economics of scale exist (that is, no incentive to move to rural wage labor on large units), and the period of production of the crops is one year or less.

Family tenants usually are the most radical of independent farmers during normal times. Sometimes this radicalism is manifested in radical nationalism, and other times in support for the Marxist parties. Agrarian radicalism was especially strong in areas having this kind of tenure system during the French Revolution, the post-World War I rural movements in Eastern Europe, the rural uprisings in Ireland over the centuries, the twentieth-century agrarian insurrections in the Philippines, the medieval peasant rebellions in southeastern England, and the early years of the Communist movement in rural China.[28]

Conflict is built into the tenancy system. There is a perpetual struggle between the landowners and the cultivators over the share going to each, the time and conditions of the harvest, responsibility for mistakes and crop failures, the types of crops, and the conditions of their cultivation.[29] Conflict is aggravated by the fact that the landowners are usually absentee landlords who both lack knowledge of the techniques of cultivation and have a very different life-style and values from the cultivators. The lack of social contact between the classes, and its corollary of a high degree of intraclass communication in the underclass, facilitates the development of class consciousness. Since the producers have the technical knowledge of production, they could raise and sell their crops just as well if the landlord did not exist. The landlord's parasitical nature is thus transparent. The landlord class appears as being alien, superfluous, and exploitative, and hence becomes the object of bitter hostility. Family tenants are especially prone to radical movements in times of declining prices or increasing exploitation that had been preceded by periods of improvements in living standards.[30]

The effect of the type of crops

The politics of rural groups are also very much a product of the numbers and types of crops they tend. Single-crop farmers are more susceptible to price fluctuations and accidents of nature. Consequently they tend to be the most likely to make demands on the state to seek redress. They are typically the *most* political and the *most* leftist when there are crop failures and low prices. During times of rural prosperity they are less politically active and become more conservative. U.S.

---

[28] Stinchcombe, "Agricultural Enterprise," p. 186.
[29] Ibid., pp. 186-187; and Hamilton, *Affluence and the French Worker*, p. 129.
[30] Stinchcombe, "Agricultural Enterprise," pp. 186-187.

wheat farmers in the Midwest (especially in its western section where annual rainfall is slight and erratic) have traditionally been the most radical farmers in the United States. The wide fluctuations in the price of wheat combined with the frequency of crop failure (caused by the variation in the level of rainfall) made this group, along with the marginal cotton farmers of the South, the basis of the Populist movement in the United States in the 1880s and 1890s. A detailed study of Nebraska Populism demonstrated that the vote for the People's Party in this wheat-growing state varied inversely with the average annual rainfall, and that the big surge of Populism in the late 1880s in this state coincided with a number of years of below-average rainfall.[31] The collapse of Populism in this area in the mid-1890s coincided with the return of economic prosperity in the wheat-growing areas. Many of the more marginal wheat farmers who had previously been populists joined the Socialist party after 1900.[32] The radicalism of wheat farmers exploded again in the 1930s and periodically continues to manifest itself whenever economic conditions deteriorate.

Produce farmers who grow a variety of crops and utilize irrigation are well isolated from crop failures and the effect of wide price fluctuations, since even if one crop should fail or if it should bring a low price, there will be compensation in other crops. Such farmers are traditionally much more conservative than are single-crop farmers operating in nonirrigated areas. Truck farms are typically more labor intensive than the single-crop grain farms, and thus are considerably more dependent on cheap, plentiful, and docile seasonal labor to plant, tend, and especially harvest their crops. The necessity for short-term seasonal exploitation of a large pool of labor power in truck farming and fruit growing tends to produce a right-wing anti–working class mentality among such farmers.

Summary

The study of the petty bourgeoisie — those who are intermediate in income, power, prestige, job control, and control over the labor power of others — shows that their politics typically lie between those of the two major social classes in capitalist society (although in times of crisis they tend to be the major impetus for fascist-type movements). Small-business people, professionals, and independent farmers all have considerable conflicting forces acting on them that pressure them to have the same politics as the working class, and yet also pressure them to adopt the politics of the capitalist class. Together with big-business people, they typically either own or control their work place; but together with the working class, they typically do not have fundamental control over the conditions of their employment. Unlike the case in the manual working class, there appears to be a clear and consistent relation between income level or size of one's business and political

---

[31] John D. Hicks, *The Populist Revolt* (Lincoln: The University of Nebraska Press, 1961).
[32] See Weinstein, *The Decline of American Socialism*, chapter 1.

attitudes. The larger their income or the bigger their business, the more conservative are the members of the petty bourgeoisie. This is a result of the inherent rewards of superior economic position and, perhaps more importantly, the social distance from the working class which a higher income brings about. While the more marginal business people, professionals, and farmers tend to live in working-class neighborhoods, have working-class backgrounds, relatives, and friends, and often, consequently, working-class life-styles, the more prosperous members of the petty bourgeoisie live in fancy suburbs, associate with the relatively well to do, are less likely to have working-class relatives, and consequently are very likely to have distinctively petty-bourgeois life-styles and rather conservative politics. Thus, as with the working class, we can see the mediating effect that social structural factors have between income and political attitudes.

5

The Politics of Sex, Race, and Age

Other social factors besides class structure people's life experiences and the social groups of which they are a part, and hence produce systematic political differences among people of the same class. Three of the most important of these are sex, race, and age.

The Politics of Sex

Most available evidence indicates that women are generally more conservative than men. Evidence supporting this observation from France, Italy, Norway, Ireland, the Netherlands, Great Britain, West Germany, Finland, Australia, Argentina, and Cuba is reported in table 5-1. Similar empirical findings have been established for most countries of the world in most time periods for as long as there have been elections.[1]

The ruling class has systematically taken advantage of the traditional conservatism of women. The franchise was extended to women largely to dampen the effect of the growth of radicalism in the working class after World War I. Remember that the Nineteenth Amendment granting women the vote in the United States was passed by Congress in 1919 and ratified by the states in 1920 (all in the middle of the postwar Red scare). Communists and their allies would have won elections in Chile in 1958, and in Italy in 1948, if men only had voted. The percentage of women who voted for the Right in Germany during the 1920s

---

[1] Zeitlin, *Revolutionary Politics and the Cuban Working Class*, p. 120; and Maurice Duverger, *The Political Role of Women* (Paris: UNESCO, 1955).

Table 5–1 Differential Support of the Left by Sex

	France[1] 1952 (C)[a]	Italy[2] 1958 (LS+C)[a]	Norway[3] 1949 (C+S+L)[a]	Ireland[4] 1969 (L)[a]	Netherlands[5] 1968 (S)[a]	Britain[6] 1969 (L)[a]	West Germany[7] 1967 (S)[a]	Finland[8] 1966 (S+C)[a]	Australia[9] 1967 (L)[a]	Argentina[10] 1965 (S+P)[a]	Cuba[11] 1962 (C)[a]
All men	31%	47%	58%	—	33%	—	—	53%	—	44%	—
All women	22	27	50	—	26	—	—	51	—	39	—
Working-class men	—	—	—	31	—	56	56	83	64	—	33
Working-class women	—	—	—	25	—	48	41	77	54	—	25

Sources:
1. Lipset and Rokkan, *Party Systems and Voter Allignments*, p. 161.
2. Idem.
3. Duverger, *The Political Role of Women*, p. 50.
4. Rose, *Electoral Behavior*, p. 639.
5. Rose, *Electoral Behavior*, p. 255.
6. Rose, *Electoral Behavior*, p. 522.
7. Rose, *Electoral Behavior*, p. 156.
8. Rose, *Electoral Behavior*, p. 307.
9. Rose, *Electoral Behavior*, p. 458.
10. P. H. Lewis, "The Female Vote in Argentina," *Comparative Political Studies* III, no. 4 (January 1971): 432. Reprinted by permission of the publisher, Sage Publications, Inc.
11. Zeitlin, *Revolutionary Politics and the Cuban Working Class*, p. 127.

[a] Key to abbreviations:

(C) = Support of the Communist party
(LS) = Support of the left Socialists
(L) = Support of the Labour party
(S) = Support of the Social Democratic party
(P) = Support of the Peronists

and early 1930s was higher than the percentage of men, even though the nationalists' women's program was summed up by the slogan: "children, kitchen and church."[2] Wherever there are Socialist and Communist parties competing with religious and nationalist parties for the loyalty of the masses, women have disproportionately supported the religious and nationalist, rather than the Marxist and leftist parties even though these latter parties typically hold out programs of full equality with men.

Data from the Gallup poll indicate that women in the United States are still slightly more conservative (as defined by class issues) than men.[3] In 1976, 33 percent of all men compared with 30 percent of all women defined themselves as left of center, while 49 percent of all women compared with 47 percent of all men defined themselves as right of center. In 1974, 18 percent of all men compared with 15 percent of all women thought that business was primarily responsible for inflation. Forty percent of men compared with 37 percent of women were in favor of the government taking over and running the railroads (1973), and 49 percent of men compared with 45 percent of women supported the right of sanitation workers to strike (1976). On most issues that directly reflect class questions, men are more left than women in the United States.

On issues not directly related to class questions, however, women in the United States are generally more "progressive" than men, especially on issues that reflect the traditional "female" traits of compassion, gentleness, and support — for example, issues of harshness on criminals, war, amnesty, welfare, civil rights, and the like. In 1974, 41 percent of all women opposed reinstituting the death penalty compared with 31 percent of all men; and 44 percent compared with 38 percent of all men supported amnesty for Vietnam War resisters. In 1973, 61 percent of women opposed the bombing of Laos compared with 52 percent of men, and 45 percent of women compared with 40 percent of men favored cutting off funding to Vietnam. Sixty-eight percent of women compared with 63 percent of men opposed reducing federal social spending in 1974, while in 1975, 48 percent of women compared with 43 percent of men thought the federal government ought to spend more to create employment. In 1974, 36 percent of women compared with 33 percent of men favored busing to achieve better racial balance in the schools. These differences between the sexes in their support for positions on these two types of questions probably reflect both their different socialization and their different work experiences. Women are taught to be "humanitarian," while men are taught to be "tough." Men's experience in socialized labor outside of the home teaches class consciousness, while women's isolation in the home insulates them from class pressures.

Men are more supportive of women's rights than are women. In 1976, 59

---

[2] Duverger, *The Political Role of Women*, p. 56.
[3] All the Gallup poll data on the United States from 1973 to 1976 are taken from the following issues of *The Gallup Public Opinion Index*: December 1972; February, March, and May 1973; September and November 1974; August and October 1975; and February, March, April, and June 1976.

percent of men compared with 55 percent of women supported the Equal Rights Amendment (ERA) to the U.S. Constitution, while 75 percent of men compared with 71 percent of women said they would vote for a qualified woman candidate for the presidency of the United States. This seems to indicate the degree to which women in the United States have internalized feelings of inferiority.

There was no appreciable difference between men and women in support of either McGovern in 1972 (37 percent versus 38 percent) or Reagan in 1976 (33 percent versus 32 percent). However, there was an appreciable difference between the sexes on support for Wallace. In 1975, 21 percent of men compared with 15 percent of women said they would vote for Wallace in a three-way race that included Ford and Kennedy. In the case of McGovern and Reagan support, the relative effects of the class and the humanitarian factors worked against each other to neutralize themselves and produce no significant difference between the two sexes. But in the case of Wallace support, this candidate's explicit appeal to the "little guy" and his antiestablishment rhetoric coupled with his toughness on welfare and militarism worked in the *same* direction to exert a double appeal for men and a double repulsion for women.

Single women in the working class seem to be significantly more conservative than married women. For example, among manual working-class people between the ages of 21 and 49 in Great Britain in the early 1950s, 76 percent of married and 68 percent of single women supported the Labour party. In West Germany in 1953, 50 percent of married working-class women between the ages of 18 and 30 supported the Socialists or Communists, but only 30 percent of the single working-class women did so.[4] In West Germany 48 percent of the married women, 30 percent of the single women, 25 percent of the widows, and 64 percent of divorced women within the working class supported the Socialists or the Communists.[5] Thus although marriage acts as a radicalizing force within the working class, divorced women are significantly more radical than either married women or women who have never been married.

Housewives are pressured to adopt the politics of their husbands. Duverger found that married women vote the same way as their husbands about 90 percent of the time. This tendency seems to be stronger in the manual working class than in most other groups.[6] Within the working class, married women are more likely to vote for leftist parties than single women, not only because they have closer attachments to working-class men with leftist views, but also because their closer integration into working-class communities and their greater family responsibilities make the economic burden of being a worker more salient for them than it is for single women.[7] Support for this observation can be found in the explanation for the greater leftism of the divorced woman. To get a divorce in the first place

[4] Linz, "The Social Bases of West German Politics," p. 243.
[5] Ibid., p. 236.
[6] Duverger, *The Political Role of Women*, p. 46.
[7] See Lipset, *Political Man*, pp. 216–217; and Zeitlin, *Revolutionary Politics and the Cuban Working Class*, p. 130.

requires her to be somewhat independent of traditionalism. But no matter how independent she is, divorce places a great burden on women of her class, who typically have to support their children and themselves.

The traditional conservatism of women in the face of their greater oppression is analogous to the traditional conservatism of economically backward areas or the rural poor. The majority of women in capitalist society have typically been housekeepers and mothers — occupations which isolate them from people in similar class positions and which consequently generate parochialism. Spending the day communicating with children and being exposed to the values broadcast by television and radio is a definite conservatizing experience. Socializing with a variety of social strata in leisure and work activities centering on the mother-wife role does not facilitate the development of working-class consciousness. The relative isolation from others in a similar social position, together with the special oppression of being treated as the personal servants of men rather than as their equals, cause working-class women to have a propensity to become religious, to be superstitious, and to support charismatic *male* leaders. A further factor influencing their political attitudes is their social conditioning. From childhood they were subjected to pressures by their parents and teachers to be submissive, supportive, uncritical of authority, and, in general, "feminine" in preparation for their future roles as housewives. The consequence of such socialization is their tendency to adopt "feminine" (that is, nonradical) attitudes in politics — attitudes which are manipulated by the ruling class to support their policies.

Because of their isolation in the home from experiences of socialized production, which encourages mystification, and because of the inculcation of religious values in them when young, women tend to be more religious as adults than men. Women's religiosity is an important factor in the formulation of their political attitudes. The established churches, which are typically opposed to communism and socialism, manipulate women's religious sentiments to gain their vote for religious or other conservative parties. In France in 1952 among workers who reported that they never attend church, 57 percent of the women and 44 percent of the men expressed support of the Communist party.[8] In West Germany in 1967, 43 percent of the nonchurch-going women compared with 50 percent of the nonchurch-going men supported the Social Democrats; while 26 percent of the church-going men and 20 percent of the church-going women supported this party.[9] In Belgium 47 percent of the nonreligious women and 51 percent of the nonreligious men, but only 13 percent of the religious men and 11 percent of the religious women supported the Socialists.[10] These figures suggest that a part of, but not all of women's greater conservatism must be attributed to their greater religiosity. Since even nonreligious women are generally more conservative than nonreligious men, this suggests that the isolation of housework operates independently of religion as a conservatizing force.

[8] Linz, "The Social Bases of West German Politics," p. 256.
[9] Rose, *Electoral Behavior*, p. 157.
[10] Ibid., p. 93.

Once women break through the socialization and isolation preventing them from developing class consciousness, they might well be more radical than men. In fact, as the logic of capitalism breaks down their traditional isolation, and as traditional sex roles are shattered, there is evidence that this is becoming the case. The mechanization of housework and the socialization of child care is freeing women from *having* to be full-time housewives. Moreover, the rapidly expanding needs of the corporations for increasing numbers of white-collar and sales personnel are helping to radicalize women. Women's primary economic role in capitalist society is switching from housewife-mother to white-collar-service worker who must sell her labor power.[11] As a result all the factors which operate on working people under socialized conditions of labor (see chapter 3) are increasingly operating on women to produce their politicalization (both the development of relative class-conscious politics and the development of feminist politics). The transformation of the economic role of women is bringing with it the rise of a massive movement for women's liberation, and the demands of that movement for the elimination of sexual barriers. It is the women who are the *least* isolated from one another who are in the forefront of that struggle: young white-collar and professional women in the larger cities who see much of each other both on and off the job and whose oppression as women is especially acute (because they are treated as sex objects or not taken seriously by their professional colleagues, and because they suffer the most from competition with men).[12]

The undermining of the parochializing effect of housework and the politicizing effect of working outside the home is also manifested in the increasing leftism of women.

The women's movement in the United States

Women have had a long history of organizing themselves against sexual discrimination and for equality with men. In the history of the United States (and Western Europe) this movement has been strong during two periods — the last half of the nineteenth and early years of the twentieth centuries, and again since the mid-1960s. Although much of the early women's movement was concerned with the general condition of women, the focus of its energies was on gaining women the right to vote. The latter-day movement has focused on the equality of women in general.[13]

---

[11] For a discussion of the changing economic position of women, see Albert Szymanski, "The Socialization of Women's Oppression," *The Insurgent Sociologist* VI, no. 2 (Winter 1976).

[12] Marlene Dixon, "Why Women's Liberation — 2," in Roberta Salper, ed., *Female Liberation* (New York: Alfred A. Knopf, 1972).

[13] For the history of the women's movement in the United States, see Barbara Deckard, *The Women's Movement: Political, Socioeconomic, and Psychological Issues* (New York: Harper and Row, 1975); Eleanor Flexner, *Century of Struggle* (New York: Atheneum, 1970); Aileen S. Kraditor, ed., *Up From the Pedestal* (Chicago: Quadrangle Books, 1968); Aileen S. Kraditor, *The Ideas of the Woman Suffrage Movement, 1890-1929*

In the United States the early women's movement grew out of the struggle against slavery. Women such as Lucretia Mott, Elizabeth Cady Stanton, Susan B. Anthony, and Lucy Stone were activists in the abolitionist movement who saw similarities between their own condition and that of black slaves (the similarities were considerable — no right to vote or to own property, virtual ownership by fathers and husbands, etc.). In 1848 these women called a national convention at Seneca Falls, New York, which resolved to fight for equality in marriage, wages, property rights, education, and politics. A very loose national steering committee was set up to pursue propaganda and agitation for these goals. The defeat of the South in the Civil War, the abolition of black slavery, and the enfranchisement of blacks raised the hopes of the early women's movement that women also would be granted full civil rights. The frustration of these hopes produced both anger and new organizational forms.

In 1869 two new women's organizations were established. The National Woman Suffrage Association (NWSA), organized by Elizabeth Cady Stanton and Susan B. Anthony, and the American Woman Suffrage Association (AWSA), organized by Lucy Stone and Henry Ward Beecher. While the first group admitted only women as members and was a multiissue organization concerned with all aspects of women's lives, the second admitted both men and women and focused its concern only on gaining the vote. This latter group issued no critique of religion, marriage law, and customs, and made no attempt to organize working women. They each published periodicals: *Revolution* by the NWSA, and *The Woman's Journal* by the AWSA. In 1890 the two organizations merged, adopting the name National American Woman Suffrage Association (NAWSA), with Elizabeth Cady Stanton as president. The politics of the NAWSA were essentially those of the old NWSA, focusing almost entirely on gaining woman suffrage primarily by working for changes in state, as opposed to federal, laws. The conservatization of the women's movement, which became increasingly manifested in the anti-working class, antiimmigrant, and anti-Socialist rhetoric of most of its leaders after the mid-1880s, must be attributed to the fact that virtually all of its activists and leaders were upper middle- and upper-class women who shared their class's contempt for, and fear of, the rapidly growing and largely foreign-born industrial working class. This fear was greatly enhanced by the national anti-Red hysteria that swept the country after the Haymarket Massacre in May of 1886. One of the principal arguments used by the women's movement as a reason for giving women the vote was that the women's vote would counteract the pernicious influence of the alien working class.

A minority of women activists continued to be concerned about the position of working-class women, however. In 1903 the National Women's Trade Union

---

(Garden City, N.Y.: Doubleday, 1971); William O'Neill, ed., *The Woman Movement* (Chicago: Quadrangle Books, 1969); Sheila Rowbotham, *Women, Resistance and Revolution* (New York: Vintage Books, 1974); Sheila Rowbotham, *Hidden From History* (New York: Vintage Books, 1976); and Salper, *Female Liberation*.

was formed, composed primarily of settlement workers and other professionals, with only slight ties to the mainstream of the suffrage movement. This organization, as well as the National Consumer League, did give some support to the struggles of working women, especially during the great strikes in the New York garment district in 1909.

During its first twenty years, the NAWSA — in spite of its concerted efforts — was unable to win the franchise for women in a single state. All the referenda that it succeeded in putting on the ballot in the various states went down to defeat. The ineffectiveness and conservatism of this organization led a number of more militant younger women to break away and set up more disciplined and militant groups — for example, the Equity League of Self-Supporting Women (which later became the Women's Political Union), established in 1907 (its most famous figure was Charlotte Perkins Gilman).

In 1914 the Congressional Union of Woman's Suffrage (CUWS), under the leadership of Alice Paul, was founded. Unlike the NAWSA, this organization limited itself only to highly committed women and was the first women's group to employ the militant tactics of hunger strikes, sit-ins, parades, and picketing. In addition to focusing on obtaining an amendment to the *federal* Constitution enfranchising women, it also pressured for the passage of an equal rights amendment that would guarantee women full civil equality with men. In 1917 the CUWS formed the Woman's party, which escalated the level of militancy to the point of mass arrests for picketing the White House during World War I. According to many, the militance of the Woman's party played a decisive role in finally getting the Congress to pass the Nineteenth Amendment in mid-1919 and getting the states to complete ratification in the summer of 1920. The general Red scare combined with the argument advanced by most of the women's movement that their vote would offset that of the radically inclined immigrant working class was also a decisive factor in the passage of the women's suffrage amendment at this time.

The women's movement collapsed immediately after enfranchisement. The prediction by many suffrage leaders that women would use the vote to obtain general equality — that is, that suffrage was the precondition for further gains — was not borne out. That most of the suffrage movement had for so long sacrificed all other issues and concerns to the end of achieving the franchise bore fruit in the dissipation of energy with the achievement of this goal. Although the Left, especially the Communist Party, continued to raise the issue of women's equality during the 1930s and 1940s, there was little or nothing in the way of either a separate women's movement or concerted women's politics until the revival of the feminist movement in the mid- and late 1960s.

Once again in the 1960s, the women's movement arose out of women's involvement in the struggle for the civil rights of black people. Beginning around 1964 women active in the Student Nonviolent Coordinating Committee and the Students for a Democratic Society began agitating for equality within these organizations, and shortly thereafter to make the issue of women's equality a major focus of the Left. Soon many women had severed their ties with the "male-dominated" civil rights and student movements to establish their own autonomous feminist organizations, which once again took up the historical struggle of women for equality. Other women remained in the same political organizations as men, but insisted that these organizations take up the struggle for sexual equality in a serious way.

The women's movement soon became divided into three basic tendencies: the liberals, the radical feminists, and the Marxists. In 1966 the National Organization of Women (NOW) was organized under the leadership of Betty Friedan. The focus of NOW has been to achieve full equality with men through a gradual process of education, lobbying for new legislation such as the Equal Rights Amendment and adjudication in the courts. NOW is willing to work in a friendly way with men who support its cause. The membership and appeal of NOW is almost exclusively to middle-class and professional women. In many ways NOW is the legitimate heir of the old NAWSA.

Radical feminism directs its appeal only to women and tends to insist that achieving women's equality is the first political priority of the country. This tendency typically expresses considerable hostility to men, takes separatist forms of organization (including complete separation from men among some women, as with the radical lesbians), strongly emphasizes the unity of "the personal and the political" — that is, the understanding that all interaction with men is political (and thus that struggle against male domination should take place on a daily basis) — and is willing to use militant tactics in pursuit of its goals.

The third principal tendency within the women's movement, Marxism (or increasingly Marxism-Leninism), does not advocate the separate organization of women but rather focuses on organizing within the working class, paying special attention to the problems of working-class women. The Marxist tendency, unlike either the liberal or radical feminist trends, maintains that working-class women have more in common with working-class men than with upper- and middle-class women. This tendency argues that only the abolition of the capitalist system can produce the full liberation of women. The Marxist tendency is thus the legitimate heir of such early women activists as Ella Reeve Bloor, Mother Jones, and Emma Goldman, who, outside of the mainstream of the suffrage movement around the turn of the century, devoted their lives to organizing working-class women. Although in the United States most adherents of this tendency had the same social origins as many of the radical feminists, its social basis is increasingly diverging as these women take working-class jobs and as they succeed in winning over working-class women with whom they come in contact. In Europe, where the Marxist tradition is strong in the working class, this tendency has its greatest appeal in this class. The social basis of radical feminism seems to be remaining among younger women students and professionals, who suffer from intense competition with male students and professionals and from white-collar workers in large firms in large cities — especially younger single women who feel oppressed by their personal dealings with men.

The Politics of Minorities

The primary factor driving people to adopt leftist politics is the humiliation and degradation they suffer in social relations in their work life and outside of it. Leftism is an indication of the striving for dignity through the demand for self-determination and equality. National, ethnic, religious, and cultural minorities within a class are thus normally more leftist than the class norm. Minorities bear the double burden of their class oppression and their national, religious, ethnic, or cultural oppression. In addition, because of their common situation, which is usually manifested in working and living in close contact with other members of their minority group (largely a togetherness forced by discrimination), their double oppression is easily translated into a common leftist consciousness. The propensity to leftism among minorities is also enhanced by their relative isolation from the ideological hegemony of the ruling class. The overt racism of the dominant culture acts as a prophylactic against the legitimating ideologies of patriotism, universal suffrage, economic prosperity, and so on. By their close association with racist ideas, such legitimating ideologies tend to be discredited in the eyes of minorities.

The leftism of ethnic minorities in the twentieth century has tended to take one of two basic forms: (1) "nationalism," or the demand for separation from the majority group or self-determination for all members of the minority group *regardless* of their class (typically under the leadership of the better-off segments of the minority community). Class is here considered to be of secondary importance to the overriding common racial, religious, or cultural features unifying the group; and (2) Marxism, which is shared with much of the working class. This latter tendency stresses the need for radical or revolutionary change to transform the social order that is oppressing *both* the majority *and* the minority groups in the working class, and is further responsible for the *additional* special oppression of the minority group. Both programs for achieving equality for the subordinant minority groups are generally leftist. Both are hostile to the existing state power, to the government's overseas adventures, to economic inequalities that are disproportionately suffered by the minorities, and so on.

The probability of ethnic minorities taking one path or the other is largely determined by the predominant tendencies within the *majority* community. In the 1930s Jews and blacks gravitated toward Marxism. In the 1920s blacks were attracted to nationalism at the same time the KKK was at the peak of its strength, and again in the 1960s at the height of pro-Wallace sentiments in the working class. Since the Nazi experience, Zionism, rather than Marxism, has had the upper hand in the Jewish community. Whenever the working-class left is strong and dynamic, its influence permeates minority groups (their intermediate classes as well as their working classes). But when it is weak and divided, "nationalism" (for example, Zionism or black cultural nationalism) becomes the dominant force.

John Leggett's study of Detroit workers found that black workers tended to be considerably more class conscious than white workers. He found 59 percent of the blacks, as opposed to only 22 percent of the whites, to be what he termed "militant."[14] This relationship held up when he controlled for union membership, employment status, and income. For example, among those with high incomes 61 percent of the blacks but only 19 percent of the whites were "militant."[15] Thus race appears to override income as the primary determinant of class consciousness among black workers.

Maurice Zeitlin's study of Cuba found that black workers were more likely than whites to support the revolution. He found that among skilled workers 50 percent of the blacks and 42 percent of the whites were pro-Communist before the revolution, while among the unskilled 29 percent of the blacks and 27 percent of the whites were pro-Communist.[16]

On almost all dimensions the Gallup poll data indicate that nonwhites (most nonwhites in the United States are blacks) in the United States are more leftist (as defined by their attitude to class) as well as more "progressive," than are whites.[17] In 1976, 40 percent of nonwhites compared with 32 percent of whites defined themselves as left of center, while in 1974, 41 percent of whites compared with 20 percent of nonwhites defined themselves as conservative. Fifty-six percent of nonwhites compared with 45 percent of whites supported the right of sanitation workers to go out on strike, and 46 percent (versus 37 percent of whites) favored the nationalization of the railroads.

Nonwhites are considerably more likely to oppose the death penalty (50 percent versus 34 percent), support amnesty for Vietnam War resisters (54 percent versus 39 percent), oppose reductions in federal social spending (70 percent versus 65 percent), and support more governmental spending to create jobs (58 percent versus 44 percent). Sixty-eight percent of nonwhites compared with 56 percent of whites opposed bombing Laos in 1973, 54 percent (versus 41 percent of whites) favored cutting off aid to Vietnam in 1973, and 44 percent (versus 36 percent of whites) thought that less money ought to be spent on defense. Nonwhites are also more supportive of equality for women than are whites. In 1976, 60 percent of nonwhites compared with 56 percent of whites favored the ERA, while 81 percent of nonwhites (versus 72 percent of whites) said they would vote for a qualified woman candidate for president of the United States.

The one type of question on which whites demonstrate a greater degree of leftism than nonwhites is that relating to attitudes toward big business. In 1973, 31 percent of whites compared with 21 percent of nonwhites said they had no confidence in big business, and in 1974 only 10 percent of nonwhites compared with 17 percent of whites thought big business was responsible for inflation.

Minority group workers are often among the first segments of the working class to adopt socialist politics. Again this is because of their special oppression and

[14] Leggett, *Class, Race and Labor*, p. 80.
[15] Ibid., p. 100.
[16] Zeitlin, *Revolutionary Politics and the Cuban Working Class*, p. 88.
[17] All data from the Gallup poll are taken from the following issues of the *Gallup Public Opinion Index*: December 1972; February, March, May, and July 1973; May and November 1974; October 1975; and February, March, April, and June 1976.

their relative isolation from the majority group which discriminates against them, thus enhancing their *intra*group communication and feelings of strength and solidarity. Such was the case in the period before 1900 in the United States, when the Socialist movement was composed primarily of European immigrants, most of whom were radicalized *after* they arrived in the United States because of the oppressive conditions and disappointments they faced.[18] A similar phenomenon occurred in the 1960s with the development of class consciousness in segments of the U.S. ethnic minority working class. This was manifested in the growth of the League of Revolutionary Black Workers and the popularity of the Black Panthers, both of which groups adopted explicitly Marxist-Leninist politics. These developments among black workers have been followed by similar trends among Spanish-speaking workers (for example, the Puerto Rican Socialist Party, CASA, and the August 29th Movement).

Even the petty bourgeois segments of ethnic minorities tend to be leftist, certainly much more leftist than the rest of the petty bourgeoisie. Jews are perhaps the best-known case in point. Overseas, Chinese throughout Southeast Asia are another. The leftism of the petty bourgeois segments of minority communities is principally caused by the discrimination against them by the rest of the petty bourgeoisie and the resultant bitterness that the lack of dignified treatment creates.

The black movement in the United States

Black people, by far the largest ethnic minority in the United States today, have had a long history of struggle against racist oppression.[19] In the post-Reconstruction period (after the mid-1870s) there have been numerous political tendencies among black people. After the suppression of the post-Civil War Reconstruction governments of the South, in which black people played a major role, the predominant organized tendency among blacks for a generation was represented by Booker T. Washington, head of the Tuskegee Normal and Industrial Institute in Alabama. Washington's program for black people, which was endorsed by most of the white upper class of the time, consisted of teaching blacks crafts, encouraging black businesses, working hard, getting an education, and saving money, and *not* fighting Jim Crow laws, demanding the right to vote, or otherwise challenging the organized system of oppression against blacks. Wash-

---

[18] See John Laslett, *Labor and the Left* (New York: Basic Books, 1970); and Weinstein, *The Decline of Socialism in America*, chapter 1.

[19] For the history of the black movement in the United States, see Phillip Foner, ed., *The Black Panthers Speak* (Philadelphia: J. B. Lippincott, 1970); William Z. Foster, *The Negro People in American History* (New York: International Publishers, 1954); Dan Georgakas and Marvin Surkin, *Detroit: I Do Mind Dying* (New York: St. Martin's Press, 1975); Joanne Grant, ed., *Black Protest* (New York: Fawcett World Library, 1968); Theodore G. Vincent, *Black Power and the Garvey Movement* (Berkeley, Calif.: Ramparts Press, n.d.); Daniel Wynn, *The Black Protest Movement* (New York: Philosophical Library, 1974); and Howard Zinn, *SNCC: The New Abolitionists* (Boston: Beacon Press, 1964).

ington was antiunion and anti-Socialist and looked to the white upper class for support in very gradually improving the condition of blacks.

In 1905 black people who were in opposition to the Booker T. Washington tendency of accommodation, the best known of whom was W. E. B. DuBois, held the Niagara Movement Conference, which endorsed a struggle against Jim Crow laws and lynching (which were used to terrorize blacks). In 1910 the tendency which grew out of the Niagara conference consolidated itself in the National Association for the Advancement of Colored People (NAACP). By 1915 the NAACP had about 9,000 members in fifty-four branches around the country. The NAACP has always worked to realize its goals of full integration into American society by lobbying for legislation, fighting in the courts, and conducting educational campaigns. Throughout its life it has been based primarily in the better-off strata and classes among black people.

In 1911, probably largely as a response to the formation of the NAACP, the Booker T. Washington trend, together with upper-class white supporters, founded the National Urban League which eschewed politics and dedicated itself to providing social services for blacks. This organization was antiunion and often acted to provide black scabs in prolonged strikes of white workers against major corporations in Northern industrial cities.

The first major nationalist movement among black people in the United States grew up in the immediate World War I period among the recently urbanized black immigrants from the South in the Northern cities. Marcus Garvey's Universal Negro Improvement Association (which had been founded in Jamaica) had a million members (predominantly in the United States but also in forty other countries around the world by 1921). Garvey, like Booker T. Washington, was antiunion and anti-Socialist (he saw unions and Socialists as instruments of white working-class oppression of black people). Instead, he advocated separation of blacks from whites (rejecting the integrationist goal shared by both the Washingtonites and the NAACP), the building up of black businesses in the United States (the most famous of these being Garvey's *Black Star Lines*), and, increasingly after 1921, the return of all black people to Africa. This movement's earlier struggles against Jim Crow laws were set aside after 1921 as Garvey tried to reach an accommodation with white racists (he had a well-publicized meeting with members of the KKK) to facilitate the back-to-Africa movement. By 1920 Garvey's weekly, the *Negro World*, had the largest circulation of any black weekly in the United States. Garvey's movement, in its demand for the business and political development of blacks, in its hostility to solidarity with white working people, and in its rejection of union organization for black working people, seems to have reflected the interests of the emerging petty bourgeois class among blacks who desired a guaranteed clientele, as well as clear leadership of blacks (almost all of whom were working class or share croppers). Garvey was arrested in 1923 for mail fraud, sentenced to five years in jail, and expelled from the country in 1927. The repression of the Garveyite movement, together with the utopian nature of its program, led to its decline and virtual disappearance by the end of the 1920s.

Beginning around 1910 — the peak of the strength of the Socialist party in the United States — Marxism began to win adherents among blacks. In 1920 the Socialist party won 25 percent of the vote in Harlem. A. Philip Randolph, who had joined the Socialist party in 1911, emerged as a leading organizer of black workers in the 1920s (in 1925 he founded the Brotherhood of Sleeping Car Porters). The African Blood Brotherhood, a post–World War I militant nationalist group (with about 4,000 members) organized to defend black communities against invasion by white mobs (there had been many major antiblack riots in 1919), moved close to Marxism. In the mid-1920s many of its leaders joined the new Communist Party.

In 1925 the American Negro Labor Congress was organized by the Communist Party (many of its leaders had been members of the African Blood Brotherhood). In 1930 this organization merged into the League of Struggle for Negro People, which in turn merged into the National Negro Congress (NNC) in 1936. The NNC was a broad-based organization which included many Socialists and Progressives, as well as those sympathetic to the Communist Party. It involved itself in the struggles against Jim Crow and lynching, supported CIO organizing activities, relief for the unemployed, and integration in the trade unions. The NNC, which was dissolved in 1947, was perhaps the most effective black organization in the late 1930s.

The Communist Party gained much support among blacks (in the late 1930s it had 10,000 black members) because of its involvement in the national campaign to save the "Scottsboro boys" from execution for allegedly raping two white women in Alabama. The Communist Party had considerable support in the black ghettos of the North until the early 1950s. Benjamin Davis, a black Communist, was elected to multiple terms on the New York City council from Harlem in the 1940s. W. E. B. DuBois, the leading figure in the NAACP during its early years and perhaps the most prominent black leader of the first half of the twentieth century, joined the Communist Party in 1945. Paul Robeson, perhaps the most accomplished black artist of the twentieth century, was also a member of the Communist Party and a leader of its antiracism campaigns. During the 1930s and 1940s the Communist Party was perhaps the leading force in the United States fighting for black equality. Its appeal, unlike the NAACP, was predominantly to working-class blacks, although it also attracted many black intellectuals and professionals. The party's program for blacks during this period consisted of three basic parts: (1) integration and equality for blacks in the North; (2) self-determination for blacks in those counties of the South where blacks were a majority (this *might* have implied secession and formation of a Negro state); and (3) unionization and improvement in the conditions of the working class (employed and unemployed), of which almost all blacks outside of the rural South were a part.

With the suppression of the Communist Party in the late 1940s and early 1950s, the black movement reached a low point. It essentially had to start from scratch when spontaneous actions against the Jim Crow system began breaking out in the South in the mid-1950s. The event that precipitated the revival of the black movement was Mrs. Rosa Parks's refusal to give her seat to a white man on a

Montgomery bus in 1955. This incident sparked a boycott of all Montgomery buses by blacks until the city finally agreed to integrate seating. Martin Luther King, Jr., who became involved in the boycott movement, was instrumental in calling together a number of Southern black leaders to form the Southern Christian Leadership Conference (SCLC) in 1957. The SCLC was dedicated to nonviolence and peaceful civil disobedience to achieve full integration. It also ran voter registration campaigns and sponsored frequent demonstrations, which often ended in massive arrests — which evoked considerable national sympathy for the plight of blacks in the South. A new phase of the Southern movement began in 1960 when black students in Greensboro, North Carolina, sat in at the local Woolworth's lunch counter demanding that they be served. (The Jim Crow system in the South forbade blacks from eating at lunch counters with whites.) This action precipitated a wave of sit-ins by young black and white students throughout the South. Out of this movement grew a new organization, the Student Nonviolent Coordinating Committee (SNCC). This group (like the SCLC, to which it was linked during its first years) was dedicated to nonviolence and militant mass tactics designed to achieve integration as soon as possible. Both the SCLC and the early SNCC had both black and white members.

In the mid-1960s the SNCC underwent a fundamental transformation. In 1965 it expelled all its white members and renounced principled adherence to nonviolence. It soon became a leading force for black nationalism, with Stokely Carmichael the leading spokesman for its position. It temporarily merged with the Black Panther Party in 1968, and after severing its ties with the Black Panther Party because of the latter group's opposition to cultural nationalism, faded away.

In the late 1960s black nationalism (as it had been in the post–World War I period) once again became the dominant tendency within the black movement. The nation of Islam (the "Black Muslims"), whose roots dated to the World War I period and the Garveyite movement, and who in 1960 had about 100,000 members, achieved considerable national notoriety in the mid-1960s with its advocacy of Garveyite programs of building black businesses, and its advocacy of complete separation from whites. The social basis of the Muslims was the younger lower-class blacks of the urban ghettos. In the early 1960s the most prominent spokesman for the Muslims was Malcolm X, who broke with the organization in 1964 because of its antiwhite positions. Announcing his adherence to Marxism, he formed a new organization, the Organization of African American Unity, which, because of his assassination in 1965, never really got off the ground. Other black nationalist organizations were formed during the mid- and late 1960s, including such groups as Ron Karenga's US., Robert Williams's Republic of New Africa, and Amiri Baraka's (LeRoi Jones's) Congress of Afrikan Peoples. The appeal of most of these latter groups was largely to young black intellectuals and students, but also included many lower-class blacks in the Northern black ghettos.

In the late 1960s and early 1970s many blacks once again turned to Marxism-Leninism. The most significant early movement in this direction was the formation of the Black Panther Party, formed in Oakland, California in 1966 by Bobby Seale and Huey P. Newton. Inspired at first by Malcolm X and Frantz

Fanon, and shortly thereafter by Mao Tse-tung, Fidel Castro, the Viet Cong, and various other Third World Marxist revolutionaries, the Black Panther Party was organized as an all-black revolutionary group adhering to Marxism-Leninism. Its early work focused on protecting poor ghetto blacks from police harassment (the Panthers, armed with guns and law books, would follow police cars to intervene in defense of people being pushed around by the police). They engaged in a wide range of activities in the black ghettos, including protesting rent evictions, fighting for traffic lights, holding classes in black culture and history, and organizing free breakfast programs for school children. They achieved national notoriety in 1967 when they held an armed protest action at the California state legislature. Within two years the Panthers were the most prominent black organization in the United States, with chapters throughout the country. Its supporters tended primarily to be young black students and intellectuals and the unemployed or semiemployed black youth in the ghetto. The militant tactics and even more militant rhetoric of the organization combined with their very rapid growth provoked a quick and overwhelming campaign of repression against them, which resulted in most of their leadership being assassinated, jailed, or driven into exile by 1970. The organization, except in Oakland, was destroyed by the state almost as quickly as it arose. The struggles between the Marxist-Leninist Panthers and the various cultural nationalist groups were sharp. They all left a residue within the black community. The philosophy advocated by the Panthers was to be picked up on by their successors.

One of the most interesting developments in the black movement was the growth of the League for Revolutionary Black Workers in Detroit in the late 1960s. In 1968 there was an all-black wildcat strike at the main Dodge assembly plant in Detroit. Out of this action grew an organization called the Dodge Revolutionary Union Movement (DRUM), which was soon imitated in numerous plants throughout the Detroit area. A weekly newspaper, the *Inner City Voice* (edited by John Watson), articulated the Marxist philosophy of the revolutionary union movement among black workers. In 1969 the various RUM organizations that had grown up spontaneously in Detroit merged into the League of Revolutionary Black Workers. In 1971 the league split between those who, like Watson, wanted to put most of their energy into organizing a national black worker's organization, and those who wanted to continue to focus primarily on Detroit. The former group, together with James Forman (formerly of SNCC), organized the Black Worker's Congress, while the latter, after having a change of heart about the need for a national organization, merged into the Communist League (a Marxist-Leninist group) in 1972. Both groups soon came to play a role in the Marxist-Leninist movement in the United States. But within a few years (except for the Communist League in Detroit) both virtually disappeared.

Meanwhile a number of other former black nationalists turned to Marxism-Leninism in the mid-1970s. For example, Amiri Baraka's Congress of Afrikan Peoples, which built roots in the Newark black working class, came to endorse Marxism-Leninism, and in 1976 changed its name to the Revolutionary Communist League. Thus the black movement has twice gone through the same historical cycle. From the turn of the century to the 1930s, its primary thrust evolved from accommodation, to militant integration, to black nationalism, to Marxism. The same process was repeated in an even shorter time period from the mid-1950s through the early 1970s.

The Politics of Age

It is argued that the young are more leftist than the old and that older people are more radical than youth. Factors cited as reasons why one should expect greater conservatism among older people include the allegation that the older one gets, the higher one's income and status, the more family responsibilities one has, and the more likely one is to move to the suburbs for the sake of one's children (putting oneself into a relatively conservative environment). It also is argued that people better appreciate authority once they become parents, that older people gradually lose their idealism and come to accept the dominant values of society, that they lose their will to fight, and that they merely become wiser. Then again, factors that perhaps produce *greater* radicalism as one grows older include the disillusionment with the myth of individual mobility as it becomes increasingly clear that the best hope for improvement is through class action, the increased responsibility of having a family and children to support and hence the greater personally felt necessity for leftist action, fuller integration into the working class as one builds stronger ties in a working-class community with age, greater fear of unemployment as one acquires a family, and the greater costs of being fired, quitting, or having to move. Other important factors influencing manual workers after their mid-forties are the difficulty of finding employment because of one's age, and the lack of increase in real income and status because of the gradual slowdown of one's physical powers. Younger workers are preferred as manual laborers because they will work harder for less pay. Consequently, the insecurity of older workers tends to enhance their leftism.[20]

The propensity for youth to become more conservative with age apparently occurs only where the dominant culture of the working class is not radical; hence greater responsibility and integration into that class drives the young worker away from radicalism. However, where the working class is radical, the same force works to increase radicalism with age. In either case the effect of *aging* appears to be greatly exaggerated. Age in itself plays a relatively small role in determining one's politics.

American attitudes toward the war in Vietnam in the late 1960s were *not* correlated with age. In 1968, 42 percent of those between the ages of 21 and 29 considered themselves doves, as opposed to 38 percent of those between 30 and 49, and 43 percent of those over the age of 50.[21]

In some countries young people seem to be more left at a given time than

---

[20] Lipset, *Political Man*, pp. 283–286.
[21] George Gallup, *The Gallup Poll* (New York: Random House, 1972), p. 2125.

old people. In Italy in 1968, 22 percent of manual workers under 40, but only about 15 percent of those over 40 reported that they supported the Communists.[22] In Japan in 1960, 37 percent of everyone under 30 supported the Socialists, but only about 18 percent of those over 40 did so.[23] In Britain 83 percent of workers under 44 with below-average incomes supported the Labour party, while 63 percent of those over 44 did so.[24]

In some other countries at a given time older people support the Left more than younger people. In Belgium in 1968, 23 percent of people under 40 and 30 percent of people 40 and over supported the Socialist party.[25] Similar results were found for the Netherlands in 1968, and for Australia during the 1950s.[26]

In still other countries there appears to be no significant difference in support of leftism by age. For example, in Finland in 1966, 28 percent of those below 28 and 31 percent of those above 50 in the working class supported the Communists.[27] In Norway in 1949, 52 percent of male workers under 40 and 48 percent of those over 40 supported the Socialists or Communists.[28] In West Germany in 1967 about 49 percent of workers under 35 and about 48 percent of workers 35 or older supported the Social Democrats.[29] Similar results were found for Sweden.[30]

In summary, there appears to be no consistent relationship between age per se and politics. In some places at some times older people are more leftist; in other places at other times younger people are. No consistent relationship between chronological age and leftism can be established.

More important than the effect of *aging* on the politics of different age groups is the experiences each age *cohort* had when it was entering the labor force and forming its political ideas. The effect of the economic and political experiences of workers from their mid-teens to their mid-twenties is to fix political attitudes that last for their lifetimes. In general, the generations that enter the labor force in times of great unemployment and depression, or during times of massive radical movements and social upheaval tend to adopt especially leftist politics which stay with them throughout their lives. Those workers who enter the labor force in times of great prosperity (especially when immediately preceded by serious depression) or during times of social order and the relative passivity of radical politics tend to

---

[22] Rose, *Electoral Behavior*, p. 193.

[23] Seymour Martin Lipset and Stein Rokkan, eds., *Party Systems and Voter Alignments* (New York: The Free Press, 1967), p. 449.

[24] Ibid., p. 119.

[25] Rose, *Electoral Behavior*, p. 91.

[26] Lipset and Rokkan, *Party Systems and Voter Alignments*, p. 83; and Rose, *Electoral Behavior*, p. 253.

[27] Rose, *Electoral Behavior*, p. 307.

[28] Allen Barton, "Sociological and Psychological Implications of Economic Planning in Norway," (Ph.D. dissertation, Columbia University, 1954), p. 323; cited in Linz, "The Social Bases of West German Politics," p. 866.

[29] Rose, *Electoral Behavior*, p. 158.

[30] Ibid., p. 428.

adopt relatively conservative politics which last throughout their lives.[31] Leggett found that 31 percent of Polish Detroit workers who entered the labor force during the depression, but only 21 percent of those who entered during times of prosperity were militant.[32] Zeitlin found that the most pro-Communist workers in Cuba were those who entered the labor force during the periods of economic crisis and political upheaval.[33] Thus, to understand why sometimes the older and sometimes the younger workers are radical, it is more important to consider the political climate during their formative years than their chronological age.

Movements of the elderly

While never of the significance of the youth movements (especially of students), old people's movements have periodically occurred. Old people's movements, unlike student movements, tend to limit themselves to specific problems of the elderly. In the United States old people's movements have been especially strong in the state of California.[34]

The most famous and influential of all the movements of the elderly in U.S. history was the Townsend movement of the 1930s. Dr. Francis Townsend, a California doctor, developed a program to provide every person in the United States above the age of 60 with $200 a month. According to the Townsend plan, the $200 would have to be spent immediately to generate demand for products and thus create jobs, thereby (allegedly) generating the funds to pay for the plan. The Townsend movement won many adherents in California and also across the country. In 1935 the *Townsend National Weekly* had a circulation of 300,000. In 1936 there were 1,200 Townsend clubs in California alone. In 1938, 20,000 people attended the Townsend convention. The appeal of the movement was mostly to the elderly, who joined the Townsend clubs in great numbers, participated in its massive rallies, distributed its literature, and periodically engaged in initiative and referendum campaigns to secure a generous pension from the state of California. The last time the Townsend movement was able to get an initiative measure on the California ballot was in 1944, when its deflated proposal for $60 a month was defeated.

The late 1930s also saw the development of the Ham and Eggs movement, whose principle figure was Robert Noble. The *National Ham and Eggs* paper

---

[31] See Karl Mannheim, "The Sociological Problem of Generations," in Paul Kecskemet, ed., *Essays on the Sociology of Knowledge* (New York: Oxford University Press, 1952); and Lipset, *Political Man*, pp. 279-283.
[32] Leggett, *Class, Race and Labor*, p. 116.
[33] Zeitlin, *Revolutionary Politics and the Cuban Working Class*, chapter 9.
[34] For the history of old people's movements, see Carol Offen, "Profile of a Gray Panther," *Retirement Living* 12, no. 12 (December 1972): 32-37; Jackson Putnam, *Old Age Politics in California* (Stanford, Calif.: Stanford University Press, 1970); and Frank A. Pinner, Paul Jacobs, and Philip Selznick, *Old Age and Political Behavior* (Berkeley: University of California Press, 1959).

achieved a national circulation of 80,000. The basic idea of this movement was to provide $30 a week to everyone over 50. Even more than the Townsend movement, it focused its efforts on placing initiatives on the California ballot. But similar to the Townsend movement, it always failed to win referendum elections even when it was able to get the 400,000 signatures necessary to hold a special election.

The elderly people's movement in California continued through the 1940s and 1950s. Its principal form in these years was George McLain's California Institute of Social Welfare (the institute has been known by several different names). In 1948 the institute had about 70,000 supporters, mostly among the elderly. It was able to place popular referenda on the California ballot to liberalize old age pension laws in 1948, 1952, and 1954. Unlike its predecessors, one of its initiatives actually won (by the narrowest of margins), only to be rescinded in another special election a year later.

In the early 1970s a small but vocal organization, the Gray Panthers, was founded to agitate for the interests of the elderly. Founded by a sixty-seven-year-old former social worker, Maggie Kuhn, and several of her friends, the Gray Panthers have been funded in part by various Protestant churches. Without organized chapters, the movement consists of several hundred people in loose touch with one another, predominantly on the East Coast. The focus of the organization is on combating "ageism." The movement works to reduce fares on public transportation for the elderly, change the social security laws to allow old people to work more, increase Medicare, etc. It argues against segregated housing for old people, and for the continued involvement of the elderly in productive labor.

Summary

In this chapter we have examined three of the principal social structural factors other than class that influence political attitudes and behavior and on which political movements have been based: minority status, sex, and age. Ideological factors that reflect exposure to schools, religion, the media, and so on, rather than social structural differences are examined later in this book.

While important social movements have been based on the specific interests of all three types of groups (the more influential movements based on minority groups, the least on age groups), the three factors have different effects on the politics of people. Minority status generally has a radicalizing effect because of the special oppressions of economic discrimination and concentration in the lower classes along with the effect of being forced together with others of the same minority status, which facilitates intragroup communication with the consequence of promoting common consciousness and action. While women also bear a special oppression, the social structure of the sexes has exactly the opposite effect from that of minority groups. Women live together with men and are disproportionately isolated from one another in the home. Thus unlike minorities, and in spite of their greater oppression than that experienced by men of the same class, women are generally more conservative than men. This difference between minorities and women illustrates the very important effect of the social structure (independent of the degree of oppression) in determining political consciousness and behavior.

Unlike either sex or minority status, age has no consistent effect on political attitudes or behavior. While the young are at times more left than the old, at other times the old are more left than the young. The only consistent effect of age is not a product of physical aging, but rather a product of the special experiences of one's age cohort at the time when it was first entering the labor force. Experiences of unemployment and political upheavals in one's early years generally make one more radical during one's entire lifetime than those who grew up amid order and prosperity.

6

Elections and Political Parties

Although the manner in which people vote tells us much about the social structural factors which shape their political attitudes and behavior, it does not tell us much about the forces operating to determine state policies. The leading myth of parliamentary democratic forms, whether in Europe or America, is that voting is the principle determinant of state policies. Most of the remaining chapters in this book attempt to demonstrate that this is not the case.

The Role of Elections

The general belief in the sovereignty of the masses as exercised through voting is an effective tool for securing the sovereignty of the capitalist class — which is all the more secure by being founded on the consent of the governed. The act of voting every several years acts to legitimate the rule of the capitalist class as firmly as did the coronation of emperors by popes in the past. In neither case does the act of legitimation mean that those who grant the authority have power. Because the act of voting is an act of conferring legitimacy, a decline in the percentage of the eligible population that votes can thus be interpreted to mean a decline in the legitimacy of the society (such a phenomenon has been occurring in the United States since the beginning of the 1960s).

The electoral contest in capitalist societies is partly a show — that is, to create the illusion that there actually is a struggle for governmental office in which the people decide who their rulers will be. In fact, it is usually the liberal center of the capitalist class that dominates (through supporting its favorite candidates) the nomination and the selection processes as well as the formulation of government policy. This is shown by the fact that since 1933 there have been no significant domestic or foreign policy discontinuities between Democratic and Republican administrations. Throughout this period liberal corporate policies as formulated by such groups as the Council on Foreign Relations (CFR), the Council for Economic Development (CED), and the Business Council have prevailed, while elections have served chiefly as a plebiscite acting to affirm the legitimacy of corporate rule — in a manner fully analogous to the plebiscites of Napoleon or Hitler. It is also shown by the basic continuity in recent years in West Germany and Britain between the Conservative and Christian Democratic administrations, and the Labour and Social Democratic parties. (Chapters 10 and 11 attempt to demonstrate that the capitalist class controls the U.S. state, while chapters 8 and 9 outline the ways in which the state serves capitalism.)

The universal franchise was a device consciously used by upper-class leaders in the nineteenth century (notably Bismarck in Germany and Disraeli and Gladstone in England) to prevent the radicalization of the working class. The extension of the franchise has come to be a normal ploy of the powerful whenever opposition to its rule grows. It was coyly used to defuse the working class's propensity to use violence to secure change (a means which, if adopted by them, would result in their victory) and to channel this class into electoral politics — an arena within which the upper class normally has mastery. The upper class understands the techniques of mass manipulation and thus will always try to shift the field of contest away from the streets and into electoral politics, where its strengths can be given the fullest play. The franchise was granted to women in that period when Socialist strength peaked in the working class (so that the more conservative women's vote would neutralize the effect of the more radical men's vote). In 1971, the eighteen-year-old vote was instituted in the United States at the time the student movement peaked. This was done with the intent of taking students out of the streets (where they were having a considerable effect on the country's policy) and diffusing their strength by channeling it into party politics, where it would inevitably be neutralized and made ineffective.

The ruling class has adopted the most advanced Madison Avenue techniques to befuddle the people and win elections. Nixon was a master of the use of advertising technique. Throughout his political career he relied primarily on experienced advertising firms that had mastered the art of selling commodities without reference to their substance to run his campaigns. His campaigns were structured around the use of selling techniques to create the correct public image. This Madison Avenue electoral philosophy emphasizes the use of television to elicit nonrational emotional responses from the viewing audience based on the candidate's makeup, facial mannerisms, tone of voice, mastery of demagogic skills, and the meticulous use of editing. Madison Avenue selling techniques are based on the ability to use prejudices to achieve desired buying behavior. These firms apply the same principles to selling soap and cars as they do to selling politicians.[1]

Political parties that base their appeal on nonclass factors are the corollary of

---

[1] See Joe McGinnis, *The Selling of the President* (New York: Trident Press, 1969); Edward Bernays, *The Engineering of Consent* (Norman, Okla.: The University of Okla-

the universal franchise. Organizations such as the Republican and Democratic parties in the United States and the Christian Democratic parties of Europe were developed to channel the political sentiments of people in ways harmless to the rule of the capitalist class. By doing small favors for the working class, the urban party machines secured their loyalty and ensured the unchallenged rule of the upper class in the United States. The religious parties of Europe did the same by the use of religious values.

Nationalistic and conservative parties controlled directly by the ruling class also have been able to secure massive popular support by playing up patriotic and racist themes, introducing pseudo-left programs (such as the expropriation of Jewish businesses, attacks on intellectuals, opposition to foreign migration, and restrictions on unpopular minorities such as blacks), and by using electrifying strongmen who gain the personal allegiance of the masses. Conservative parties use such issues as immigration, religion, anti-Catholicism, anti-Semitism, racism, and hostility against urban or rural areas to secure the votes of working people, thus neutralizing the appeal of the parties attempting to mobilize them on the basis of their class interest.[2] If the upper class is unable to mobilize the masses on the basis of such appeals, it must abandon the electoral system.

Allowing parties and candidates of all persuasions to run for office under conditions where it is normally impossible for them to win because of the capitalist parties' virtual monopoly on the media and money, as well as because of the ideological hegemony of capitalist values, gives the illusion that the society is free and that the electoral results are the authentic representation of the people's will. If Communists, Socialists, and radicals of all kinds can legally publish their papers, print and distribute their leaflets, and be on the ballot, but nevertheless receive less than 1 percent of the people's vote, this is a sure sign that the people have found the capitalist parties to be in their best interest. To forbid Communist and Socialist propaganda, to prohibit the candidacy of their members, and to expel them from legislative bodies is to give credence to the idea taught by the Left that the state is a "dictatorship of the bourgeoisie" as well as to discredit the myth of voting (that is, that the people *freely* choose their own representatives) — and hence to delegitimate bourgeois society. Such prohibitions, bans, and expulsions are normally used only as a last resort.

However, if and when the capitalist class can no longer rule effectively with the political participation of the Left (because of the strength of these forces and the danger that they are becoming a majority), the capitalist class supports military coups d'états or fascist dictators who suppress elections, abolish legislatures, and rule by decree. The resultant capitalist dictatorship must rely on other means of legitimation than the myth of elections. In such periods the democratic myth is replaced by greatly intensified appeals to nationalism, economic prosperity,

---

homa Press, 1955); and George Thayer, *Who Shakes the Money Tree?* (New York: Simon and Schuster, 1973), p. 264ff.
[2] Linz and Lipset, "The Social Bases of Diversity," chapter 5, p. 2f.

and the charismatic qualities of popular leaders (for example, Hitler and Mussolini) to buttress capitalist-class rule. Such appeals are liberally supplemented with systematic violence and the massive use of police terror against leftist opponents of the regime. Concentration camps, assassinations, executions, persecutions of all kinds, and the banning or castration of labor unions and leftist political organizations become part of the strategy for maintaining upper-class rule.

Another important function of elections in capitalist society is their role as "barometers" of the political state of the masses. When the ideological hegemony of the capitalist class is secure, this will be reflected in large numbers of votes for the upper-class-controlled parties. Conversely, the rise of radical and Communist parties among the oppressed classes indicates that something must be done to reinforce upper-class rule. The electoral trends over time, the relative strength of various leftist parties, the geographical distribution of leftist support as well as the total number of votes for the Left provide important information to the upper class for formulating strategies to defend its rule.

People will vote for opposition parties before they are willing to engage in direct action to bring about a revolution. Elections are thus early warning systems for the bourgeoisie. When the leftist or other radical or antisystem vote is significant, there is still time to take measures to prevent a social revolution or other social disruption. These measures might be characterized by maintaining a tone of conciliation and compromise while making highly publicized but nonsubstantial concessions. They also might involve providing the opposition movement's leaders with well-paying and high-status positions (including seats in the national legislature), thereby "cooling out" the movement and buying off its leaders. Alternatively, they might include adopting a repressive strategy, including the banning of leftist parties and organizations and the persecution, jailing, assassination, and driving into exile of leftist leaders.

The role of elections in informing the ruling class about the political tendencies of the masses has been diminished considerably since the development of scientific public opinion polling (for example, the Gallup and Harris polls). These polls are able to judge the pulse of the people far more frequently and in a much more precise and systematic manner than do elections. Polls give the upper class exact information on the support of certain parties and candidates before elections, thereby enabling them to counter that support with appropriate campaign methods. Such information might include a measure of the working class's support of various specific issues (so that the upper class can make intelligent decisions about what kinds of concessions are necessary to grant), explanations for their support of the Left (to be better able to split the masses from their leaders), and demographic profiles of the types of people who support various aspects of the Left's program. Unlike electoral data, opinion poll data are broken down by sex, race, age, education, and occupation, and thus can be used to target different groups with different appeals calculated to counter the Left in each.

Other functions of elections include resolving differences within the capitalist class and guaranteeing the rule of law. (These functions are discussed in chapter 8.)

The Effect of Electoral Systems

Various types of electoral systems are institutionalized in different countries at different times largely to prevent the growth or diminish the influence of radical political parties. The uses of proportional representation (where each party receives a number of legislative representatives proportional to its popular vote), the single-district, single-ballot systems (where the candidate with a plurality takes all) as well as a wide variety of intermediate systems must be understood in these terms. While it cannot significantly affect the basic underlying forces producing or preventing the development of class consciousness in the working class, the electoral system can and has served to brake or accelerate that process through inhibiting or facilitating the growth of leftist political parties.

Proportional representation encourages a large number of parties representing a wide range of political positions. This system simply reflects political differences rather than exaggerating or diminishing them. All significant political positions among the people are represented. Consequently, the growth of mass support for the positions of small parties is facilitated because the parties can use their parliamentary strength to win people over. One does not "waste one's vote" by supporting a radical party under such systems. Once people start to vote for a small radical party, they become susceptible to supporting it more actively. Proportional representation also encourages parties to split into smaller groups, since each smaller group is still able to maintain its representation. Proportional representation thus encourages ideological clarity (rather than the mystification required to patch up principled differences to maintain the coalitions necessary for electoral victory in the plurality-takes-all system).

Proportional representation is very sensitive to sudden and major developments in public opinion, which result in the formation of new parties that are immediately able to express themselves in Parliament. Conversely, it is rather insensitive to moderate and slow changes in public opinion that produce slight gains or losses for the various parties and parliamentary coalitions rather than the substitution of one party by another (as often happens under a plurality-takes-all system); hence, violent changes in parties are dampened rather than accelerated.[3] The upper class usually favors single-district, single-ballot, plurality-takes-all systems where it is able to control the two major parties, which are buttressed by such a system. But once one of the two major contenders becomes a Socialist or Communist working-class party that they cannot control, the ruling class tends to push for a switch to proportional representation. Proportional representation was introduced in Europe when the Socialist parties became the second largest in several countries and thereby represented actual threats to winning an election.[4]

Single-district, single-ballot, plurality-takes-all systems (such as those found in the United States, Great Britain, and Canada) dampen the support for third

---

[3] The argument in this section of the chapter relies very heavily on Maurice Duverger, *Political Parties* (New York: John Wiley and Sons, 1963).
[4] See Duverger, *Political Parties*, p. 303, for data on the Netherlands.

parties, but exaggerate it for the two major parties. For example, a Marxist party that averaged 20 percent of the vote against two major capitalist parties, which split the remaining 80 percent, could secure no parliamentary representatives at all, or at best only a handful from those areas of particular Marxist strength. Marxist parliamentary strength and thus their opportunities to use Parliament to educate the people or to heighten the periodic crises of capitalism is thus greatly diminished by such systems. Conversely once a Marxist party is able to win about 40 percent of the vote, with the remainder divided equally between two capitalist parties, it is able to achieve an overwhelming majority in Parliament even though it does not receive the support of a majority of the population. This happens because the Marxists are able to achieve a plurality in most electoral districts, since the other two parties split the non-Marxist vote. Under such conditions, the single-district, single-ballot, plurality-takes-all system *increases* the strength of the Marxists.

Recall that under identical conditions in a country using a proportional representation system, the two capitalist parties would be able to rule in coalition, in spite of the fact that the Marxists were the single largest party. For example if Italy and France, where the Communists are the second largest parties, had electoral systems identical to that in the United States, the strength of the Communist Party in Parliament, and hence their influence over Italian and French political life, would be considerably enhanced. Under such an arrangement, the electorate would be faced with the clear choice of voting Gaullist/Christian Democrat *or* voting Communist, the other alternatives being generally regarded as wasted votes (since third parties are grossly underrepresented in such systems). Under this condition many socialists, independent leftists, and others opposed to Gaullism and Christian Democracy would vote for the Communists or for small third parties with no chance of achieving a plurality, and thus perhaps create a social crisis through an electoral victory for the Communists. Consequently, in both France and Italy the upper classes do not resort to the same electoral techniques as they do in the English-speaking capitalist countries. To prevent the Communist parties from growing, they rely either on proportional representation as in Italy, or on the single-district, two-ballot system as in France since 1958.

The single-district, two-ballot system has the benefits of both proportional representation *and* the single-ballot, plurality-takes-all systems in limiting the influence of the Left and preserving the unity of the conservative forces. Under this system, each party fields candidates on a district-by-district basis in the first round of elections. In the second round the first-round candidates form coalitions around the two candidates who got the most votes the first time. Since they do not often finish first or second, small parties (the more leftist or extreme rightist) are not able to influence the electoral majorities to any significant degree. This has the advantage of diminishing leftist strength (which is the strong point of single-district, single-ballot, plurality-takes-all systems), while not exaggerating the strength of the powerful left-wing parties who, even when they are able to dominate electoral coalitions in the second round, cannot win an election unless they gain a majority of the vote (rather than the plurality sufficient in the United

States–British system). It also has the advantage of preserving the strength of the major conservative party and undermining the support of extreme right-wing groups not under the domination of the upper class. Thus this system has the same advantage as proportional representation in preventing a left-wing electoral victory while avoiding the possibility (existing in the latter system) that conservative strength could be dissipated. Historically, the upper class has moved from support of single-district, single-ballot, plurality-takes-all systems to support of proportional representation and the two-ballot system as the Socialist and Communist parties become major forces.

Single-ballot, single-district, plurality-takes-all systems similar to that of the United States strongly encourage *two*, and no more than two, parties. New parties are discouraged until such time as a new party can, in spite of the hindrance of this electoral system, establish strength equal to that of the older two parties. Once this happens, one of the old parties usually drops away,[5] its decline greatly accelerated by the system that previously preserved its strength. Such was the history of the Liberal party in Great Britain in the early twentieth century, when it was displaced by the Labour party as the chief opposition to the Conservatives.

New York City was one of the few areas in the United States to use proportional representation. In the mid- and late 1940s the Communist Party used this system to elect members to the New York City Council. To counteract this threat to the ruling class's hegemony, the electoral rules were changed to restore the single-district, single-ballot system that would, of course, be dominated by the Republicans and Democrats. Wherever Socialist or other leftist parties, such as the Communists or Populists, have been able to gain pluralities in a given district (for example, Milwaukee during the early twentieth century), the Democrats and Republicans normally oppose the Left with a single candidate to prevent its plurality from being turned into an electoral victory by the properties of the single-district, single-ballot, plurality-takes-all system.

The one-party system of the U.S. South functions in a similar manner. Twice in the history of the post–Civil War South, the upper-class control of the Southern states was challenged, once by the Republican party during reconstruction, and again in the 1890s by the Populists. Each time the party challenging the upper class's slate of candidates achieved considerable electoral gains and threatened its hegemony. In reaction, the upper class resolved to settle any internal differences it had, select the individuals to run for office through the Democratic party primary, and then unify behind its candidate in the regular elections. This made it very difficult for a non-Southern upper-class-controlled party, such as the post–Civil War Republicans or the Populists, to win elections — since to do so they would have had to obtain 51 percent of the vote, which they would not have had to do if they were a third party contending against two capitalist parties. That the challenges to the rule of the Southern upper class have been more serious than to that of any other segment of the U.S. upper class has required it to close ranks to preserve its power. Consequently, the Southern upper class developed the

[5] Ibid., chapter 11.

American version of the French single-district, two-ballot system to facilitate this effort.

In summary, the effective manipulation of electoral systems to minimize the strength of the Left helps the upper class to maintain parliamentary forms and avoid the necessity of turning to fascist or military alternatives to formal democracy.

The Role of Political Parties

Political parties in capitalist societies function to select the candidates for legislative and top administrative positions. Party struggles produce the candidates who are finally selected for office. The parties nominate candidates and then work to have them elected to governmental office. They thus act as the gatekeepers of the political system.

Furthermore, parties contribute to policy formation and the mobilization of working and petty bourgeois support for state policies. While the various parties in the capitalist countries vary considerably in the extent to which they contribute to policy formation, almost all perform this function to some degree. Although they go through the motions of working out a program and selecting candidates on the basis of their stands on issues, the two major political parties in the United States in fact give very little weight to either of these processes. Probably more than in any other leading capitalist country, policy formation in the United States occurs almost exclusively outside of the political parties. In the United States this occurs through such organizations as the CED, CFR, the Business Council (discussed in chapter 10), and the leading foundations and universities, *and* with the assistance of lobbying and the personal influence process in the executive branch. In the European capitalist countries that have more internally cohesive political parties, the upper class operates more through the parties which it dominates and finances than it does in the United States.

Capitalist political parties vary considerably in the extent to which they are used as mechanisms to mobilize the population behind the policies of the ruling class. In the United States they are not as important as the schools and media in this regard, but they do play some role in convincing people to support capitalist-class policies. This role is less important than it was in the past, since fewer Americans identify with either major party. But to the extent that people are led to identify themselves as Republicans and Democrats ("the party of the common man"), they tend to support the policies of the elected officials for whom they vote. Some working people believe that since the officials they vote for are members of "their" party, they must be representing "their" interests. Party affiliations can thus tend to obscure the political process.

Parties also vary in the extent to which they are interested in the short-term process of candidate selection. The major parties in the United States are almost *solely* interested in the immediate winning of elections. They are essentially coalitions for placing individuals with acceptable politics in top governmental jobs.[6] Conversely, revolutionary (and other) parties with visions of transforming society consider working to get their own people elected to office (at least in the short run) to be incidental to their primary work of popular education and mobilization behind the party's program. Running candidates in elections serves to educate and mobilize people for these parties. Party members often envision coming to power as a long-term goal that might well occur primarily outside of the electoral process — for example, through intensive and widespread popular support and mass action. The Communist parties have traditionally been at the forefront of political activity of this kind.

Because the upper class and its various sectors are interested in placing candidates favorable to their interests in governmental office and (where parties play an important role in the processes of policy formation and popular mobilization) because they are interested in dominating these processes, they attempt to control all of the non-anticapitalist parties. It is normal in a capitalist party system for big business to finance all the parties from the extreme right, such as the fascists, nationalists, and monarchists, through the centrist liberals, to the Christian Democrats and right-wing socialists. Often the same individuals or families will finance several parties or individuals competing for the same office. Since the parties and individuals they support are primarily concerned with obtaining office, and only secondarily with minor policy differences, they can normally be easily persuaded to support the particular business interests that finance them. Thus, it makes sense for business people to finance all the nonleftist candidates for the same office — at least when there is a real challenge from the Left — since no matter who wins the election, business policies of one variety or another will be implemented and popular participation in the candidate selection process short-circuited.

Variations in Party Structure

Parties vary in their internal cohesion and in the emphasis they put on programs rather than in how they get individuals into office. They range from the very loose electoral machines of the Democratic and Republican parties in the United States to the traditionally tight and dedicated Communist organizations. In England modern capitalist political parties appeared after the extension of the franchise to the masses in the 1830s. Before that time parties were merely caucuses within Parliament. Before the 1830s a member of Parliament represented an average of only about 330 people. Since only a very few people could vote, the process of selecting candidates could be handled on an informal basis. In the United States the earliest parties (the Federalists and the Democratic-Republicans) were also

---

[6] Domhoff, *Fat Cats and Democrats*, chapter 5. Here Domhoff discusses the role of U.S. parties.

very loose organizations run on an informal and personal basis. In England the extension of the franchise to the masses required more of a stress on mobilizing the electorate to vote for the two parties, as did the increasing popular participation in the United States. While in Britain the Conservative and Liberal parties have maintained their rather loose structure and function primarily as election machines, they are somewhat more disciplined and guided by principles than are the Democratic and Republican parties in the United States. These U.S. parties exert almost no pressure on their elected officials in the presidency, governorships, or legislatures to adhere to a common party policy or to support one another. The basis of their unity lies almost solely in giving each other support as individuals to get elected — not in the desire to implement any common policy.

Parties such as the two American parties, or the somewhat more rigorous British Conservative and Liberal parties, are essentially electoral organizations (normally) dominated by the upper class. A small number of individuals control what there is of party organization. These individuals are typically the leading figures in the legislature or the executive branch. They are not at all interested in enrolling members or in nonelectoral popular programs such as mass rallies, demonstrations, or popular education. These parties come alive only during election campaigns, and then only for the purpose of getting individuals (normally those favored by one or another section of the rich) elected to office. They thus function principally to manipulate popular opinion to secure votes. Struggles within such parties are a combination of struggles for personal power among various individuals, and struggles among different segments of the capitalist class and among the organized sectors of the middle class for a voice in the candidate selection process. These struggles are, however, presented to the people as struggles over general principles or party programs to mobilize support behind the various contending individual interests and class forces.[7]

A second common form of party in the developed capitalist countries is what has been referred to as the *branch party*. Such parties, unlike the electoral coalitions discussed earlier, *are* interested in obtaining many members. They take their programs somewhat seriously and engage in political actions and education at times other than during election campaigns. Most of their financing comes not in the form of several large contributions, but from the dues of their members. The Social Democratic parties of the advanced capitalist countries are the best example of this type.

These parties have general programs that are taken seriously by their elected representatives. They also have considerable internal discipline, enforced by expulsion if necessary. Members are expected to meet certain minimum requirements, often no more than paying regular dues and endorsing a few broad principles of party unity. These parties, however, have very little control over the activities of

---

[7] Duverger, *Political Parties*, book 1, chapter I; Charles Merriam and Harold Gosnell, *The American Party System* (New York: Macmillan, 1950); and M. Ostrogoski, *Democracy and the Organization of Political Parties*, vol. II (Garden City, N.Y.: Doubleday, 1902, 1964).

their members, and allow the full range of participation from inactive to full-time militant. Local party policies are discussed and formulated at regular meetings normally held on the neighborhood level. Such party branches are the basic units of the organization. Because of the loose membership requirements of branch parties, there is typically a low level of participation at the base level and, consequently, a few individuals are able to dominate the internal life of the party. The actual power in such parties is usually located in the party bureaucracy, and not necessarily in the leading elected figures (except when the leading party officials are elected to office). Political struggles in such parties normally combine struggles over political principles with struggles among ambitious individuals.

There are several types of capitalist parties that are intermediate between the branch-type parties (such as the Social Democrats) and the electoral coalitions (such as the Democrats and Republicans in the United States and the Conservatives and Liberals in Great Britain) — that is, the Christian Democratic, labor, and agrarian parties of Europe. These parties have somewhat more popular participation than do the electoral coalition parties, but somewhat less than the branch parties. Usually they are considerably more dependent than are the branch parties on financial contributions by rich individuals rather than on dues. They engage in less political education and political activity between elections than do the branch parties, but more than the electoral coalitions. They have general party programs that carry some weight but are not the principal consideration guiding elected officials. A small amount of party discipline exists, and leading members can be, but are infrequently, expelled. In practice, very wide variations in political perspectives are allowed. Leadership of these parties is centered in their leading elected officials and not in a separate party bureaucracy. The rank-and-file members of such organizations exercise relatively little control over party policies. This is more the case with the Christian Democratic parties, where control is in the hands of business people and the church, and less the case with the labor parties, where the unions exercise considerable power, and the agrarian parties, where the various constituent farmer organizations often exercise considerable influence.[8]

The long-term tendency in capitalist society is for political parties to evolve from electoral coalitions to branch parties. This has been made necessary by increasing popular participation in politics and the increasing difficulty of manipulating people. To secure the popular vote for ruling-class candidates, the masses of people have had to become more involved in the political process. With increasing levels of political concern and competence, people are less content with voting for an individual because of his/her personal qualities. Increasingly, as class consciousness awakens in the working classes, working people tend to support candidates because of the program they put forth. Politics thus becomes more a struggle of class interests and less a struggle of individuals contending for office.

In Europe, the growth of the mass working-class Socialist parties in the latter part of the nineteenth century brought the masses actively into politics and raised the specter of working-class revolutionary regimes throughout the conti-

[8] Duverger, *Political Parties*, book 1, chapter 1.

nent. To counter the growth of these parties, the ruling class had to adopt many of their tactics. The ruling-class parties also had to begin stressing programs and utilizing mass mobilization. They had to build parties the masses of people could take seriously so that these masses could be effectively mobilized behind upper-class interests, and not lost to the Socialists.

The Christian Democrats and the nationalists are the clearest examples of the upper-class-controlled parties adopting much of the organization and techniques of the working-class Socialist parties. These latter parties used Christian or patriotic doctrine instead of Marxism to mobilize the working and lower middle classes. The Christian Democratic parties are especially effective in preventing the masses from supporting the left parties. In periods when fascism and extreme nationalism have been made unpopular (such as the immediate postwar period in Europe), Christian Democracy has stepped into the gap with humane welfare-oriented programs and appeals for Christ and against Godless atheism to undermine the class appeal of the Left. The Christian Democrats, and more often the nationalists, create popular images for their programs and sponsor activities for the masses, but they are both closely controlled from the top down. Mass participation in such organizations is more of a farce than it is in the true branch parties such as the Social Democrats.

Communist Party Organization

A new type of party emerged from the Russian Revolution — one that required a much higher level of commitment and discipline than did the Social Democratic parties. The success not only of the Bolshevik Revolution in Russia in 1917 but also that of Chinese and Vietnamese Communists, waged against the greatest odds, must be largely attributed to this form of political organization. The Vietnamese were able to win against the most advanced military power the world has ever known only because of their organizational form.

The technical superiority of the Communist organizational form has been demonstrated whenever it has been in fair competition with Social Democratic or anarchist organizations for hegemony in the working class. While Social Democrats and anarchists tend to establish their organizational forms on the basis of how they think organization *ought* to work, the Bolsheviks, through a process of trial and error, seem to have discovered the laws of maximal organizational efficiency. Generally, only revolutionary movements that have adopted Communist organizational forms have been able to make successful anticapitalist revolutions in the twentieth century. If we want to understand the reasons for their success as well as the source of the growing strength of Communists not only in Southeast Asia and Africa but throughout most of the world, we must understand the strengths of their organization as conceived of by the people who have made it work to change the course of history. The validity of this viewpoint must be judged by their results. This, of course, does not mean that all groups which claim to be Communist *are* organized according to all of these principles — only that (1) those who are the most successful approximate these forms, and (2) all typically expound such principles to their membership.[9]

Leninist parties are organized on the basis of small units (once called "cells") composed normally of three to fifteen members who whenever possible share a common workplace. Leninist parties do not try to recruit just anyone. They attempt instead to recruit as many as possible of the "natural leaders," or the most respected, "class-conscious," hardest working, and most informed members of the oppressed classes (especially of the working class). Perhaps only one in ten meets these criteria — even in a group where almost everyone supports the program and goals of the Communists. Communist parties differ radically in this regard from virtually all other parties that are content to allow almost anyone who verbally supports their program to join. Bolshevik parties can be joined by invitation only, although individuals might apply for membership. According to Lenin, the party must be an organization of "professional revolutionaries" — that is, people whose lives are committed to the struggle to overthrow capitalism. Once the party recruits such people, it attempts to reinforce their inclinations. According to Lenin, "We must train people who will devote the whole of their lives, not only their spare evenings, to the revolution."[10]

The strength of the Bolshevik organization does not depend on secrecy. Its strength lies instead in its ability to coordinate and energize its members, and to inspire confidence and respect in the masses of nonparty people whom the party aspires to lead. Police agents are able to infiltrate Bolshevik organizations and to report to their superiors all the plans of these organizations. But to maintain themselves in positions of trust, they must act like "good Bolsheviks" — that is, they must work very hard for the party, thus typically contributing more than the harm they do. The Russian Communist Party was itself infiltrated at its highest levels in the period from 1912 to 1917.[11]

Collective and voluntary discipline is the strength of the Leninist party. The power of Leninism lies in its ability to fully coordinate the energies of its members. The discipline that such coordination and undivided effort requires can only be a self-discipline. The basic policies, analyses, strategies, and tactics of such a party must be thoroughly understood by its members if it is to be successful.

---

[9] The discussion of the characteristics of Bolshevik organization relies mainly on Lenin, *Selected Works*, especially "What Is to Be Done," "The State and Revolution," and "Left-Wing Communism: An Infantile Disorder"; Frank Meyer, *The Moulding of Communists* (New York: Harcourt Brace Jovanovich, 1961); Phillip Selznick, *The Organizational Weapon: A Study of Bolshevik Strategy and Tactics* (New York: McGraw-Hill, 1952); Joseph Stalin, *The Foundations of Leninism* in Bruce Franklin, ed., *The Essential Stalin* (Garden City, N.Y.: Doubleday, 1972); Mao Tse-tung, *Selected Works in Four Volumes* (Peking: Foreign Languages Publishing House, 1965); and *The Party Organizer*, an internal publication of the Communist Party of the United States which appeared during the late 1920s and most of the 1930s.

[10] Lenin, "What Is to Be Done" in *Selected Works*, vol. I, p. 121.

[11] Lenin, "Left-Wing Communism: An Infantile Disorder" in *Selected Works*, vol. III, p. 396.

Party cadres, if they are to be effective, must be able to make decisions independently when called upon to do so. The ability to merely follow orders is not a desirable characteristic in potentially successful Leninist organizations.

When operating properly, Bolshevik organizations can be both highly centralized *and* highly democratic. The principles on which this democratic centralism operates are the subordination of the minority to the majority, the subordination of the various party organizations to the central decision-making body, and the subordination of the lower party units to higher party organizations. For the most rational strategy to be adopted, it is necessary that free and wide-ranging debate based on the widest possible experiences and the deepest theoretical and historical knowledge take place. But once a thorough internal discussion has taken place and a policy is formulated, the minority as well as the majority in the internal debate must fully and without reservation do their best to carry out the party policy. After a period of practice, there is a period of reevaluation of the "party line." During this period the opponents of the policy again are able to raise their objections in view of what was learned from the previous attempt to put "the line" into practice. Depending on how successful the policy was, it may be continued, scuttled, or modified. But as long as it is party policy, the principle of the subordination of the minority to the majority continues to apply. The Bolshevik party is thus structured both to give a *single* will to millions and to formulate that will in the most intelligent way possible.

The small size of the basic unit of the Leninist party facilitates a critical discussion of the merits of the party's policies, which allows for a give-and-take discussion where all sides of the question can be articulated under conditions where all members can fully participate. Once a unit makes a decision, it informs its representatives to the next highest level of the party organization of its decision. After a discussion at this higher level a decision is reached, and representatives to meetings at still higher levels are informed of *its* decision, and so on. This principle, however, has often been severely compromised within many Communist parties in favor of top-down decision making — usually with serious long-term consequences for the implementation of revolutionary policies.

Although intense struggle over policies is encouraged for individuals within the party's units, the formation of ongoing factions that meet separately, publish their own publications, or systematically work in a coordinated way within the party is prohibited. Such activities would destroy the unity of command in the organization, dissipate the energies of cadres in internal squabbling, sow distrust of leaders and comrades, and, consequently, demoralize those who are committed to carrying out the party line.

The formal democracy of the properly functioning Leninist party is supplemented by the fact that membership in a Communist organization is voluntary. Members join and participate because they believe that the Communist organization is best suited to guide the struggle for the liberation of the oppressed. If members believe that decisions are being made against the interests of the working classes, against the will of the rank and file, or are arbitrary and lacking in factual or theoretical soundness, they are likely to become alienated from the party leadership and eventually leave the organization. Thus, the mechanisms of formal party democracy are reinforced by this informal process, which compels the leadership to be responsive to the knowledge and will of the rank and file and to follow policies that in the best judgment of the rank and file are best for the working class.

Bolshevik organizations understand the extremely important role of good leadership. Therefore, every means is used to promote the people who show the most promise to leadership positions. Good leadership cannot be arbitrary. Above all else, leadership ability is the capacity to inspire confidence in those who are led. Continuity of leadership is regarded as essential. People who have accumulated experience and skills are not usually wasted. Leaders are not generally replaced except for reasons of demonstrated inadequacies, adherence to bad politics, or tendencies to become bureaucrats. As long as it pursues a "revolutionary line," respect for leadership is encouraged. But if leaders should betray the faith placed in them by the rank and file, respect is soon transformed into resentment.

This discussion of the principles of Bolshevik organization has been from the viewpoint of activists within such organizations. It must be taken seriously because of the great successes of such organizations in the twentieth century. Nevertheless, there is a tendency among Communists to romanticize and idealize these principles in ways that serve as an ideological cover for often undemocratic and ineffective policies and organizational forms. However, the greatest successes of the Communist form of organization seem to occur when these principles are the most closely adhered to (for example, in Russia in 1917, China from 1937 to 1949, and Vietnam from the 1940s to 1975), and the failures and stagnation occur in those times and places when they are subverted (for example, in Western Europe since the late 1940s). But in any event we cannot understand the growth of Communism without understanding how it is organized.

Summary

Voting does not determine state policies so much as it confers legitimacy on those who actually run the state. It also gives the state advance warning that the common people are discontented so that the state can institute appropriate measures (that is, reforms or repression). The illusion of popular rule created by popular elections makes rule by the capitalist class all the more effective.

Different electoral systems have different effects on the strength and rate of growth of political parties. Proportional representation facilitates the growth of small parties, but inhibits large parties from winning elections. Conversely, single-district, single-ballot, plurality-takes-all systems, such as those which exist in the Anglo-Saxon countries, inhibit the growth of small parties while facilitating electoral victories by large parties. The varying effects of the different forms of electoral systems are often used to limit the effect of radical political parties.

Political parties serve three basic social functions in capitalist society: (1) the selection of candidates for political office, (2) the mobilization of the common people to support one or another candidate and party, and (3) the formulation of public policies. Some parties primarily emphasize the first two of these, others the last two. Parties such as the Democrats and Republicans in the United States are concerned almost exclusively with winning the *next* election for their candidates and care little about policies. Other parties such as the traditional Communist parties care primarily about realizing their program and relatively little about winning office per se.

Political parties also differ considerably in how much commitment and discipline they require of their members. Parties vary from being election machines of the Democratic and Republican types that come alive only at election time, to being of the Communist type, consuming the major part of their members' time and energy during the entire year.

The preceding chapters focused on the social structural determinants of the political attitudes of people in capitalist society. The following chapters concentrate on analyzing the nature of power in capitalist society and understanding the actual role played by the state.

The Origins of the Capitalist State

The state is a relatively new development in the history of human society. The first states did not arise until around the fourth millennium B.C. Thus states have existed for only about 6,000 years. All human societies before that time and most human societies since (that is, primitive hunting and gathering and simple horticultural societies) have been without states. Those societies that have never known states have very different solutions to the problems of maintaining order, resolving conflicts, collective decision making, and the implementation of the collective will than do state societies. Primitive societies are organized along lines of kinship, rather than along lines of class, state power, or territory. Crimes and warfare are handled within that kinship framework through such institutions as blood vengeance (where the relatives of the offended party seek retribution for offenses) and a popular militia system where all adult males serve during times of war, but no one is a full-time soldier.

The most primitive social forms are far more democratic and equalitarian than anything class societies have ever known. These societies have no powerful chiefs or strong leaders of any kind. What leadership there is is based on voluntary consent to *proved* leadership abilities. Real decision-making power rests in assemblies of the whole tribe, and within these leadership is exercised through persuasion.[1]

A considerable amount of data on a thousand different (mostly primitive)

---

[1] For good descriptions of primitive democracy, see Morton Fried, *The Evolution of Political Society* (New York: Random House, 1967), chapter 3; Krader, *The Formation of the State*, chapter 2; Gerhard Lenski, *Power and Privilege* (New York: McGraw-Hill, 1966), chapters 5 and 6; Eleanor Leacock, Introduction to Engels, *The Origin*; and Lewis Morgan, *Ancient Society* (Cambridge, Mass.: Belknap Press, 1964).

societies studied by anthropologists have been brought together by George Murdock and published as the *Ethnographic Atlas*. The systematic codification of the various traits of each society allows researchers to correlate the frequency of one type of trait with that of any other type. Thus we can determine what proportion of a certain kind of society has one or another institution.

Hunting and gathering societies are the most primitive type of society. Food is secured in essentially the same manner as all other mammals secure theirs — through capturing animals and collecting roots, berries, and fruits. Before 10,000 years ago *all* societies of Homo sapiens were at this stage of development. Until a few hundred years ago most societies on earth were still of this type. A few hunting and gathering societies still exist in the remote areas of the Amazon Basin, Southeast Asia, and Central Africa. There is no record of any anthropologist having discovered such a society with a chief who had substantial power. Only about 36 percent of such societies had a leader with moderate power.[2]

Horticultural societies are those that secure most of their food from working the land with hoes or digging sticks. Simple horticultural societies do not have metallurgy and thus use only wooden sticks to work the land, whereas advanced horticultural societies, having metallurgy, use metal hoes, shovels, rakes, and other hand tools to work the land. Thirty-eight percent of all simple horticultural societies (about which data have been collected in the *Ethnographic Atlas*) and 63 percent of all advanced horticultural societies had chiefs with substantial power (compared with 0 percent of the hunters and gatherers). Virtually all agricultural societies (those that use the plow, typically harnessed to a beast of burden, to secure food) have leaders with substantial power.[3] Thus it is clear that the more developed a society (the more advanced its technology and the wealthier it is), the greater the differences in political power.

The state developed as a social institution in response to the growth of classes — that is, the development of a division of labor between those who produced goods and services and those who supervised and benefited from the production of them. While all societies probably differentiate among people on the basis of prestige (for example, the older or the better hunters have a somewhat higher status), only a few in the history of humankind have had classes. The development of class lines among people (which were not only maintained throughout people's lifetimes but were also hereditary) required qualitative changes in the democratic political institutions that hunting and gathering societies had employed from time immemorial to make decisions, adjudicate disputes, and ensure social order.

The division of society into rich and poor, which supplanted the old kin-based organization, meant that the institutions of blood vengeance and the popular militia ceased to function properly in their task of maintaining social order. When the poor of one clan or family stole from the rich of another, the poor members of the latter clan or family did not have the motivation to avenge their

[2] Gerhard Lenski, *Human Societies* (New York: McGraw-Hill, 1970), p. 138.
[3] Idem.

rich relatives. Instead, they were likely to sympathize with the poor criminals, even though they were not their kin. A professional police, army, and criminal justice system therefore had to be developed to secure the wealth of the minority. Similarly, the maintenance of the privileges of the wealthy required the replacement of the tribal councils by undemocratic mechanisms of decision making. Unless the democratic assemblies were subverted, nothing would stand in the way of the overwhelming majority of the poor from limiting the privileges, or even confiscating the wealth of the rich.[4]

The breakdown of primitive equalitarian and communal economic institutions that precipitated the collapse of the primitive democratic institutions can be documented from data reported in Murdock's *Ethnographic Atlas*. Using his definition of class, about 2 percent of all hunting and gathering societies and 17 percent of simple horticultural societies studied by anthropologists have been found to have a class system. This compares with 54 percent of advanced horticultural and 71 percent of agricultural societies.[5] Anthropologists have found only a few hunting and gathering societies with private ownership of land. In 14 percent of simple horticultural societies and in 47 percent of advanced horticultural societies, however, private ownership of land is the rule.[6] And in agricultural societies, private ownership of land is even more common. That even 2 percent of hunting and gathering societies had class systems and that a small percentage had any private property rights to land at all is almost certainly a result of extended contact with class societies through trade and political domination, which induced the development of these institutions in what otherwise would have been fully equalitarian and communal social orders.[7] Anthropological data clearly indicate that the more advanced a society is, the more likely it is to have considerable economic inequality as well as private ownership of wealth.

After the development of the state only a minority continued to have the right to exercise legitimate force (that is, the full-time police and soldiers). The process of decision making ceased to be the prerogative of all adults (or all adult

---

[4] According to Engels, the invention of a mechanism was needed by the newly wealthy and privileged that

> ... would not only safeguard the newly-acquired property of private individuals against the communistic traditions of the gentile order, would not only sanctify private property, formerly held in such light esteem, and pronounce this sanctification the highest purpose of human society, but would also stamp the gradually developing new forms of acquiring property, and consequently, of constantly accelerating increase in wealth, with the seal of general public recognition; an institution that would perpetuate, not only the newly-rising class division of society, but also the right of the possessing class to exploit the non-possessing classes and the rule of the former over the latter.
>
> And this institution arrived. The *state* was invented.

From Engels, *The Origin*, p. 263.

[5] Ibid., p. 137.

[6] Ibid., p. 139.

[7] See Leacock, Introduction to Engels, *The Origin*.

males) and was now vested in the hands of the economically hegemonic class. The process of the implementation of those decisions was no longer voluntary or based on group social pressure, but now came to be dependent on the ultimate sanction of physical force exercised by the police and soldiers who were paid by, and commanded by, the full-time decision makers and administrators in the state bureaucracy.[8]

Primitive democracy broke down gradually without people being aware that it was occurring. The transformation occurred along with basic changes in the techniques of production, the consequent great increase in wealth, and the rise of social classes. The possibility for classes and the state to exist arose with the development of a technology sufficiently productive to produce an economic surplus large enough to allow the dominant economic class *and* state officials, full-time soldiers, and police to exist without themselves having to work. The realization of this possibility was a product first of the functionally necessary and socially rational allocation of resources, and then, increasingly, of the self-interest of those entrusted to manage the common affairs.

The first differentials in authority and privilege were established democratically because of the increases in efficiency that were foreseen would result from a division of labor. The initial functionally necessary differences, although rather small, were enough to allow for the operation of the forces of self-interest (forces which could no longer be effectively controlled by popular social pressure). The rich increasingly exercised influence over the public officials when they themselves did not hold the public offices. The self-interest of the originally democratically selected public trustees converged with that of the rich, either because public office was used to accumulate wealth or wealth was used to obtain office — or because the two strata simply merged. The accumulation of private property in the hands of the wealthy and political prerogatives in the hands of public trustees was greatly limited by the traditions and institutions of the primitive democracy that acted as a fetter on the excessive concentration of wealth and personal power. To eliminate the barrier caused by popular control, the traditional institutions had to be abrogated and a state substituted for them.[9]

---

[8] For good analyses and descriptions of the breakdown of primitive society and the rise of the state, see: Engels, *The Origin*; Krader, *The Formation of the State*, chapters 3 and 4; Fried, *The Evolution of Political Society*, chapters 5 and 6; Lenski, *Power and Privilege*, chapter 7; and Karl Polanyi et al., eds., *Trade and Market in the Early Empires* (Glencoe, Ill.: Free Press, 1957).

[9] Engels insists that the origins of the state must be understood in terms of the functions it performed:

> In each such community there were from the beginning certain common interests the safeguarding of which had to be handed over to individuals, true, under the control of the community as a whole: adjudication of disputes; repression of abuse of authority by individuals; control of water supplies, especially in hot countries; and finally, when conditions were still absolutely primitive, religious functions. Such offices are found in aboriginal communities of every period — in the oldest German marks and even today in India. They are naturally endowed with a certain measure

The growth of trade is one important process that undermines the kin-based communal organization of primitive society. While almost all societies engage in some trade, the most primitive — the hunters and gatherers and the simple horticultural peoples — tend to be self-sufficient and thus engage in relatively little trade. But as the means of production develop their traditional self-sufficiency is increasingly difficult to maintain and trade becomes increasingly important.[10] This is the case because groups become stationary and can no longer acquire all the things they could when they were nomadic, and because their increasingly complex technology means that more materials are needed. As it develops a tribe tends to specialize in the supply or production of one or another item, depending on its geographical location near a source of a certain metal, salt, or a certain kind of food. This tribal specialization results in the creation of specialists within a tribe, who collect, produce, and transport the trade goods. As trade becomes more important for a tribe, these groups — particularly those that control the actual trading process — use their position to increase and consolidate their privileges and wealth. External trade thus induces internal differentiation, and consequently internal trade among those who are specialized in the process of maintaining external trade. Trade within the tribe greatly accelerates the process of destruction of the traditional communal ties as well as the creation of a rich and a poor that cuts across the old kinship ties.

Political differentiation can arise in another way. As population and population density increase within a society, the need for the coordination of economic activities to obtain more food from a given territory grows. Hence the political leaders whose social responsibility (a responsibility initially democratically delegated to it) is to coordinate economic projects — especially to control flooding and maintain irrigation — become increasingly important. These leaders (like traders) tend to use their entrusted authority to consolidate and augment their advantage, thus betraying the initial delegation.

This latter process appears to be the way the state developed in the Nile River valley, Mesopotamia, and other river valleys where the precondition of

---

of authority and are the beginnings of state power. The productive forces gradually increase; the increasing density of the population creates at one point common interests, at another conflicting interests, between the separate communities, whose grouping into larger units brings about in turn a new division of labour, the setting up of organs to safeguard common interests and combat conflicting interests....

Here we are only concerned with establishing the fact that the exercise of a social function was everywhere the basis of political supremacy; and further that political supremacy has existed for any length of time only when it discharged its social functions. However great the number of despotisms which rose and fell in Persia and India, each was fully aware that above all it was the entrepreneur responsible for the collective maintenance of irrigation throughout the river valleys, without which no agriculture was possible there.

From Engels, *Anti-Duhring*, pp. 247-248.

[10] See Polanyi, *Trade and Market*.

dense population settlement was the control of flooding and irrigation works. In areas of regular rainfall where water control projects were not the precondition of dense settlement — and especially in areas around the fringes of the great states established in the river valleys (in areas where trade with the river states was facilitated) — the first process of state formation described earlier appears to have been predominant (for example, in ancient Greece and Rome).

It has also been argued that political differentiation occurred through military conquest and through the leadership of priests. The military conquest theory argues that one tribe conquered another and forced those it conquered to work for the conquerors, thus establishing class society. The priest theory argues that the developing class of priests convinced the tribal members to excuse them from physical labor, give them a luxurious standard of living, and defer to their authority. While it is possible that the state could have originated by either of these routes, these processes are more likely to have merely accelerated the development of the state already occurring by means of one of the first two processes discussed earlier. Military conquest as a way to establish class society is only viable if the conquered society is already producing a considerable economic surplus beyond its own basic needs.[11] If it were producing such a surplus, it is likely that either a class of merchants or state officials had already developed, or was at least well on the way to developing, and thus that the conquest merely substituted one group of rulers for another, rather than actually creating a state out of nothing. Similarly, if a group of priests is able to talk its way into becoming a ruling class of a new state, it is highly likely that the priests are also performing an essential economic function, such as the construction and maintenance of waterworks, and are using religious ideology to justify and consolidate their new privileges.

The consolidation of a ruling class that has a virtual monopoly of power, wealth, and privilege can be a result of any of these processes. The different composition of various ruling classes in earlier societies is a function of the relative importance of one or another of these. In some early class societies the core of the ruling class was the merchants, in others the controllers of the state apparatus, and in others the war leaders. But quite naturally, whatever may have been the predominant way in which a group consolidated its power, once it becomes a ruling class it uses its power base to gain or attempt to gain a monopoly of power in all areas. Thus, a group that may have achieved a strong position through its monopoly on trade can use its wealth to capture control of the political apparatus, the military structure, and the popular ideology as well as to secure for itself the ownership of the land and the productive apparatus of the society. Similarly, leaders whose power is initially based on the control of the political apparatus or military conquest can consolidate their position through gaining control over the economy.

The crystallization of class society occurred with the introduction of the plow. By greatly facilitating weed control and the maintenance of soil fertility, it significantly increased the available economic surplus, and hence the oppor-

[11] See Engels, *Anti-Duhring*, part II, chapters 2 to 4.

The intense competition among the feudal lords for dominance meant that the bourgeoisie of the towns were courted by all sides. The struggling lords needed goods, especially military goods, to fight their wars. It was the bourgeoisie that could both supply the goods and loan the money to buy them. The bourgeoisie tended to favor the centralizing forces because the profitability of commerce and the prosperity of the towns depended on increased political centralization to facilitate trade and to eliminate the feudal restrictions on commerce and trade (for example, local customs duties, monetary systems, and measurement units). The bourgeoisie wanted an end to the perpetual wars that disrupted trade as well as an end to the great barriers to growing trade thrown up by the decentralized political units.

The tendency for a strong centralized state to develop under conditions of increasing commercialism almost reached its culmination in the sixteenth to eighteenth centuries in Europe. During this period very strong absolutist monarchies developed. In these absolutisms the ruler was virtually all powerful, and the central state became the coordinating institution in society and the dominant force in the economy. Although most actual production took place in units owned by the landlords, the guilds, or private individuals, the state played a major economic role through economic regulation and state monopolies.

As powerful as they were, the monarchs never succeeded in subordinating the merchant class, which was able to maintain its autonomy. The merchants were simply too important to the kings to subordinate totally to royal control. The protracted and intense competition among the relatively small nation-states of Europe, together with the struggles between the nobility and the centralizing monarchs within each state, meant that the bourgeoisie, wooed by all sides, was protected. The bourgeoisie's mastery of technology and control over trade was a very valuable asset to all the competing forces. Thus, the bourgeoisie increased their power and wealth until finally they became more powerful than the feudal lords and centralizing monarchs that gave them birth. They acquired the ability to force a dissolution of the absolutist state and establish republics — either formal republics, such as France and Switzerland, or constitutional monarchies, such as England and Holland. The developing bourgeoisie was able to overcome the tendencies attempting to consolidate the modern despotic state and eventually was able to achieve power in almost all the European countries.

The major function of the early capitalist state established by the bourgeoisie was to guarantee the class rule of the capitalists. State functions during the early phase of industrial capitalism (for example, the nineteenth century in Britain or America) tended to be restricted to preserving law and order (that is, keeping the masses in line); guaranteeing private property at home and overseas; collecting

---

cannot be examined in depth in this book. Good analyses of the breakdown of feudalism and the birth of capitalism are contained in Paul Sweezy et al., *The Transition from Feudalism to Capitalism* (New York: Science and Society, 1967); and Maurice Dobb, *Studies in the Development of Capitalism* (New York: International Publishers, 1947), chapters 2 to 4.

tunities for those with more power and privilege to expand and consolidate their social position. The state reached its full development with the consolidation of absolute power by the ruling class and the creation of the great empires of antiquity.

The state attained very different forms and came to serve very different interests over the centuries. In some societies, such as the ancient empires, the state was very powerful — so powerful in fact as to totally dominate society in the interests of the state officials, who came to own the land and other means of production.[12] In other societies, the central state was so weak as to be without significant powers to dominate developments in the countryside. In such weak states, political power was concentrated in local officials/landowners, who came to control very small areas.[13] Such was the situation in feudal Europe before the rise of capitalism and the development of the strong central states of the immediate precapitalist period.

The Development of the Capitalist State

Like primitive society before it, feudal society was a noncommercial society largely divided into self-sufficient local units. And like primitive society, it also was gradually dissolved by expanding commerce. Increased population density was one of the main forces encouraging innovations, a growing division of labor, and the migration of peasants from the land and into the towns. The creation of towns was encouraged by the feudal lords who wanted to secure the goods they were capable of producing or securing from afar. The competition among lords for more and better goods for use in warfare and for conspicuous consumption was another important factor encouraging the growth of towns and, hence, the unanticipated dissolution of feudalism. A class of rich merchants and the institution of the guilds grew up early in the history of the towns as a result of the growing demand for economic services. In the lords' struggle among themselves for hegemony it became increasingly important for them to cultivate the favor of the towns and their chief merchants, money lenders, and guild masters. The struggle among the lords for dominance grew more serious as the means became available for the creation of strong central states.[14]

---

[12] For analyses of such states, see Karl Wittfogel, *Oriental Despotism* (New Haven, Conn.: Yale University Press, 1957); Lenski, *Power and Privilege*, chapters 8 and 9; Karl Marx, *Pre-Capitalist Economic Formations* (New York: International Publishers, 1965); and Eric Hobsbawm, Introduction to Marx, *Pre-Capitalist Economic Formations*.
[13] See Marc Bloch, *Feudal Society* (Chicago: University of Chicago Press, 1961); Henri Pirenne, *Economic and Social History of Medieval Europe* (New York: Harcourt, Brace, 1937); and Lenski, *Power and Privilege*, chapters 8 and 9.
[14] Unfortunately, the social structure of feudal Europe and the contradictions of feudal society that gave rise to the formation of strong states in the immediate precapitalist period

taxes; recording births, deaths, and income for purposes of taxation and raising armies; guaranteeing contracts; providing the infrastructure (railroads, canals, communications) for the new industries; facilitating the growth of private industry; mediating among the various wealthy interests; and securing a cheap and disciplined labor force for private enterprise. The new bare-bones state of early capitalism had only a small bureaucracy, made few social payments, and (in England and America at least) had a small standing army. Consequently, taxes were greatly reduced and collected indirectly (largely through tariffs on imports). Balanced state budgets became the rule and the state debt was radically reduced. In the capitalist states that industrialized after Great Britain and the United States, there was a strong tendency for the state to directly involve itself in capitalist development to a much greater extent than in these two countries. Once Great Britain had shown the way and demonstrated that military and economic power come with industrialization, the powerful state bureaucracies and landed classes in other countries (for example, Germany and Japan) consciously adopted policies of strong state support for capitalist development up to and including the actual founding and running of productive enterprises by the state until such point as they could be turned over to private capital to be run at a profit.[15] In such countries the British model of the laissez-faire state never was tried. In countries such as Germany and Japan, the capitalist state was from the beginning heavily involved in the direct management of the economy.

Perhaps the principal task of the early capitalist state in Europe was creating and disciplining the labor force of industrial capitalism. The state collaborated closely with the commercial agricultural interests that wanted the peasants off the land so it could be turned over to such commercial uses as sheep grazing. The state abrogated the traditional rights of the peasantry, such as the use of common grazing land for their animals; common woodland for firewood, building materials, and hunting; rights to the water of streams; and so on. It also collaborated with the agricultural interests to deprive the peasants of legal title to their land. As a result many peasants were forced to migrate under pain of starvation to the towns. The forcibly displaced peasants resisted the degrading and tedious labor of the mills, which demanded twelve to sixteen hours a day six or seven days a week under the most miserable conditions for a wage that barely allowed one to keep one's family alive. Therefore the state again stepped in to ensure that the new migrants would overcome their initial resistance and take such jobs. It resorted to a wide range of draconian measures to force people into the mills. Begging was outlawed and made punishable by the chopping off of one's hands. Petty theft (including the mere stealing of bread) was made a capital offense. (During this period in Great Britain there were over 200 separate offenses for which the death

---

[15] See Paul Baran, *The Political Economy of Growth* (New York: Monthly Review, 1957), chapter 5; Dobb, *Studies in the Development of Capitalism*; John Clapham, *The Economic Development of France and Germany* (Cambridge: The University Press, 1948); Barrington Moore, *Social Origins of Dictatorship and Democracy*; and Thorstein Veblen, *Imperial Germany* (New York: Macmillan, 1915).

penalty could be exacted.) Vagrancy (having no visible means of support) was made a crime and punishable by deportation to the colonies. Welfare of any kind was given only under conditions that were even more degrading and humiliating than mill labor. The poorhouse system was instituted, which forced people to work under such oppressive conditions that the mills were paradise by comparison. The state broke the resistance of the former peasants and played the key role in the creation of a working class.[16]

The state in both Europe and America prohibited as conspiracies against property unions, strikes, or collective actions of any kind against employers on the part of workers. Such actions, together with working-class riots, demonstrations, radical agitation and propaganda, were systematically and harshly repressed. The laissez-faire nature of the state had only to do with letting the capitalists enrich themselves. The state showed nothing but a strong hand to the working class, against whom the repressive state apparatus was consistently used.[17]

The economic contradictions of early competitive capitalism soon forced the state — even in Great Britain and America — to assume a more active role in directing the economy. The rapidly growing working class, which came to present an increasing danger to the social order, forced the state to mitigate its earlier purely repressive policies and resort to expanded social welfare, legally supported collective bargaining, compulsory education, and patriotism, which became the principal mechanisms for keeping the working class in line. The violent economic cycles of unemployment, trade, profit, and production forced the state to intervene to regulate the business cycle, the banking system, the stock market, and foreign trade in the interests of guaranteeing reasonable prosperity. The abuses of the new unregulated monopolies — especially those in transportation, communications, and power — forced the state to regulate these sectors to ensure that these basic services were provided on a reliable basis for a reasonable fee to all capitalists, while preserving the capitalist character of their industries. In Europe, essential enterprises such as railroads, steel, coal mining, and airlines that private enterprise was unwilling or unable to operate at a profit were developed or nationalized by the state to ensure the profitability of the private sector in general. The vast growth in the state bureaucracy that these expanded functions required created a need for large sums to finance social service payments (unemployment benefits, disability benefits, old age pensions, and medical care) and a large standing army (needed because of the rivalry among states for overseas markets and to ensure against domestic insurrection). This in turn required the

---

[16] For descriptions of the role of the state in the creation of the British working class, see Eric Hobsbawm, *The Age of Revolution* (New York: New American Library, 1964); E. P. Thompson, *The Making of the English Working Class* (New York: Vintage Books, 1966); G. D. H. Cole, *The Common People: 1746–1938* (London: Methuen, 1938); and *A Short History of the British Working Class Movement: 1789–1947* (London: G. Allen and Unwin, 1948).

[17] See Thompson, *The Making of the English Working Class;* Louis Hacker, *The Triumph of American Capitalism* (New York: McGraw-Hill, 1940, 1965); and Hobsbawm, *The Age of Revolution.*

reinstituting of direct taxation, deficit financing, and the growth of massive state debts (which also proved very profitable to the bankers who collected the interest).[18]

The Historical Development of Parliamentary Forms

As the commercial class became the dominant class in society, it established republican and parliamentary forms as the instruments of its rule. These forms are best suited to articulate the diverse interests within this class and work out a common class will. The wealthy classes selected representatives of their various diverse interests to sit in a common body, where they worked out compromises among these interests and made state policies in the interest of the wealthy as a whole.

In a precapitalist-class society most upper-class people (as well as most villagers) share similar interests. But in a capitalist society there is a wide diversity of economic interests among the commercial classes. There are merchants, financiers, industrialists, and agricultural capitalists — all of whom share conflicting economic interests. Among the industrialist interests are importers, exporters, producers for the domestic markets, capital goods producers, consumer goods producers, new wealth, old wealth, governmental contractors, nongovernmental contractors, transportation, energy and communications companies, durable and nondurable goods producers, overseas investors, domestic investors, and so on. Because of this immense diversity of economic, and hence political interests, the commercial classes have encouraged the development of parliamentary and republican forms of government to work out compromises and a common will that benefits the maximum number of divergent interests within the class.

Another important reason for the prevalence of parliamentary and republican forms in commercial societies is the special need in such economies for the rule of law. Such economies are highly fragile. They involve a wide range of contracts, and require forecasts of future wages, prices, interest rates, availability of materials, market conditions, and the like. Consequently, businesses must have assurances from the state that it will not arbitrarily interfere with the system of contracts and expectations. The best guarantee of moderation and lack of arbitrariness on the part of the state is the parliamentary form, where the commercial elite governs itself in a manner that requires compromise and mutual respect. Another generally desirable property is the inertia of the parliamentary policy-making process, where committees hold hearings, make reports, and conduct floor debates with pressures applied and compromises made at all stages.

---

[18] See Gabriel Kolko, *The Triumph of Conservatism* (Chicago: Quadrangle Books, 1967); James Weinstein, *The Corporate Ideal in the Liberal State 1900–1918* (Boston: Beacon Press, 1968); Harold Faulkner, *The Decline of Laissez Faire 1897–1917* (New York: Rinehart, 1951); and Carlton Hayes, *A Generation of Materialism, 1871–1900* (New York: Harper and Row, 1941).

In contrast to parliamentary forms, strongman rule brings with it arbitrary and unpredictable interference in the economy. The commercial upper class abrogates such forms only under the most extreme duress. It turns to overt dictatorship and military strongman or fascist rule only when there appears to be no other way to ensure its own rule. Dictatorial methods are especially necessary when the rule of the commercial class is first instituted (before it has been able to consolidate its position) and in the periods of its decline and crisis (when its rule is threatened by the rise of new social classes — see chapter 12). Whenever possible, the bourgeoisie does its best to restore parliamentary forms as quickly as possible after a strongman takeover.

The commercially dominant states of the ancient world, such as Athens, tended to be republican. The ancient traditions of primitive democracy had almost withered away in ancient Greece, but were restored after the growth of the commercial power of the city-states — not on the old basis, where all tribal members were full participants, but on a new basis of all *citizens* (perhaps only about 10 to 15 percent of the population). Within its ruling class, Athens enjoyed a democracy as thorough as any in the ancient world. With the conquest of the small, predominantly commercial societies by the giant despotic states, such as late Rome, republican and parliamentary forms disappeared.

It was not until the revival of commerce in the thirteenth century that republican and parliamentary forms reappeared in the leading commercial areas of Western Europe. These were areas in which the rising cities, because of the extreme decentralization of the feudal society, had been able to secure considerable political autonomy. Thus many of the medieval cities of Italy (Venice being the best known) whose business was foreign trade emerged as parliamentary republics. The development of republican city-states in Italy was paralleled by similar developments throughout the loosely organized Holy Roman Empire. North of the Alps, the Hanseatic league cities emerged on a similar basis as the Italian city-states. In areas of greater central state control, such as Spain, Holland, England, and France, the commercial classes pressured the centralized monarchy for greater institutionalization of republican and parliamentary forms.

As a result of such pressure from the thirteenth to the fifteenth centuries in Spain, the cities and their ruling commercial classes were granted increasing powers. The Cortes (Spanish Parliament) became an important institution for the commercial class's participation in the state. Because of the king's dependence on the commercial classes for financial support, he was forced to grant increasing powers to this body. During the fourteenth century, France developed a powerful Estates General led by the commercial classes. Again it was the king's need of financial support that led him to grant the emerging parliament greater powers.

In both Spain and France, however, from the fifteenth century on, the power of the emerging parliaments (which had never been fully consolidated) withered away under attack by the increasingly powerful state bureaucracies. The withering away of the power of the commercial classes coincided with the general depression of world trade during this period as well as with the birth of a new absolutism. The basis of political power was control over the state machinery, just as it had been in the Roman Empire or any of the classical despotisms. Such rule was itself never fully consolidated, however, since the bureaucratic upper class remained dependent on the commercial classes. The internal struggle for power between the various lords and the external struggle among the various nation-states forced the state bureaucrats to encourage the bourgeoisie and to continue to grant privileges and concessions to the cities. Although ascendant from the fifteenth to the eighteenth centuries in Western Europe, the new absolutist states eventually collapsed under the onslaught of the commercial classes, which successfully demanded the abolition of despotic forms and feudal remnants as well as the reinstitution and full development of republican and parliamentary forms. The conflict between the declining bureaucratic and feudal forms and the rising bourgeois interests was decided largely through violent revolution, military struggle, and civil war (for example, the rebellion of Holland against Spain, the English Revolution of the seventeenth century, and the French Revolution).[19]

Unlike what happened in France and Spain, the developing parliamentary forms were not defeated in the most commercial states, Holland and England, where the commercial forces proved stronger than the state bureaucratic forces. The commercial classes became a power in the British state just as the commercial classes in France and Spain were becoming an influence in their countries. In the thirteenth century the House of Commons obtained the right to tell the king how much money it was willing to grant him to meet his military or personal expenses. In exchange for being granted money for war and personal expenses, the king had to grant the general petitions of the towns and agree to institutionalize and increase the power of Parliament. Beginning in the fourteenth century, Parliament met regularly once a year. The concessions granted earlier by the king were turned into rights. Parliament gradually became the source of governmental legitimacy, and in the fifteenth century the House of Commons made good its claim to initiate all money bills and to regulate elections.

The sixteenth and early seventeenth centuries saw English kings attempt to imitate their brothers on the Continent and consolidate absolutist rule in England. They attempted to bring the British commercial classes to heel and eliminate the power of Parliament. The effort to establish absolutist forms in Britain was frustrated by the English Revolution. With the execution of Charles I in 1649, Parliament became the center of state power. Until the Restoration after Cromwell's death, the commercial classes were able to dominate the British state. More than just beating back the attempt of the kings to establish absolutist forms, they went on the offensive and assumed state power on their own.[20]

After the restoration of the monarchy, Parliament continued to play the

---

[19] For an account of early parliamentary forms in Europe, see Edward Cheney, *The Dawn of a New Era 1250–1453* (New York: Harper and Row, 1936), chapters 2 and 3.

[20] See Christopher Hill, *Puritanism and Revolution* (London: Secker and Warburg, 1958), and *The Century of Revolution* (Edinburgh: T. Nelson, 1961).

dominant role. The attempt to establish absolutist forms in Britain had been completely defeated. The struggle among mercantile capital, industrial capital, and landed property (which had long since been commercialized, serfdom having been largely abolished by the fourteenth century) for dominance in the English state continued until the 1830s, when the industrial capitalists established hegemony over the other segments of the commercial classes. Parliamentary forms developed further and consolidated themselves earlier in England because England was always a major and eventually *the* leading commercial power in the world. The development and triumph of parliamentarianism in the British Isles must be understood as a natural result of the early development and consolidation of commercial, and later industrial capitalist forms in that country.

In the early bourgeois republics political participation was limited to property holders — at first only to the most wealthy, and later, as the influence of the petty bourgeoisie increased, to all the owners of property. Beginning with the French Revolution, all classes in Europe became politically mobilized. France was the first major country to extend the franchise to all adult males. France was also the first to draft all adults (of all classes) into the army. The other countries of Europe were forced to follow suit on both counts to compete militarily. In feudal Europe the masses of the peasantry were not used in the military. In fact, it was a crime for peasants to even possess arms. The prohibition on the use of peasant armies was for good reasons. Armed peasants were likely to turn their weapons against their own lords. The development of mass armies throughout Europe in the nineteenth century was thus a major factor in the expansion of the franchise.[21] The rise in popular agitation and the growth of Socialist movements in the working class also made it expedient to extend the franchise to all, thus meeting in a formal way the demands of the masses for political participation.

The corollary of the universal franchise was necessarily the development of mechanisms to guarantee that the franchise was not exercised by the masses to disturb the rule of property. It was imperative that the masses believe that *they* were controlling the state, when in fact they were being manipulated to support the upper-class interests. The incorporation of the masses into politics required the implementation of several other mechanisms for ensuring their loyalty. Expanded welfare services (unemployment, old age pensions, disability insurance, compensation for injuries, and medical and child support); universal compulsory education (with emphasis on political indoctrination in civics, history, geography, and religion); the creation of urban political machines to harvest the workers' votes and of mass political parties that could use demagogic appeals to patriotism, religion, and racism to befuddle the masses; the recognition and co-optation of trade unions and their transformation from instruments of class struggle into mechanisms for the management of labor conflict; the development of mass media (popular sensationalist newspapers, magazines, paperbacks, and, eventually, radio and television) to permeate the working classes with the ideology of the upper class; the encouragement of religious revivals among the masses; the development

---

[21] See Alfred Vagts, *A History of Militarism* (New York: The Free Press, 1967).

of mass observer sports into which the masses could channel their aggressions; and the repression of radicals were all necessary corollaries of permitting the masses to vote.[22]

The Development of the Capitalist State in the United States

As an example of the process of capitalist state formation, it is useful to look at the foundation and development of the American state. Parallel processes occurred in other capitalist countries. But because it is the most powerful state in the history of the world, and because most of the readers of this book are probably more familiar with its history than with that of any other state, it serves as a case study illustrating the general process.

The war for national liberation fought by the Americans against the British involved two different struggles: (1) the struggle of the small farmers, merchants, and artisans against the privileges and prerogatives of monopoly and wealth, both British and American; and (2) the struggle of the wealthy planters and merchants against the restrictions placed on their profit-making opportunities by the British state, over which they had little influence. The vast majority of whites in the colonies (small independent farmers) wanted the universal franchise (in many of the colonies only a minority of the adult males held sufficient property to be allowed to vote), equal representation for all in the legislatures (no multiple votes for certain classes, areas, or institutions), and the abolition of feudalistic privileges and restrictions governing the sale of land, property ownership, or practicing certain occupations. They wanted an end to arbitrary state decrees, judicial proceedings, and taxes. In short, they demanded equal treatment for all, thoroughly democratic institutions, and the guarantee of the basic rights of the people — that is, equality, democracy, and liberty. This class found its chief proponent in Tom Paine, whose book, *Common Sense*, inflamed the colonies against British autocracy.

The wealthy classes of slave owners and big merchants had several serious conflicts with the British, whose state was controlled by commercial and agricultural interests operating from the West Indies and the British Isles. The British state, working to defend the economic interests of those who controlled it, acted to prohibit industrial manufacture in the colonies, thus forcing the colonists to purchase all their manufactured goods from British capitalists. It prohibited the importation of raw materials from anywhere but British possessions, thus guaranteeing higher priced British commodities (especially sugar) a secure market even though considerably cheaper commodities were available from the French, Portuguese, Spanish, and Dutch. The British forbade settlement to the west of the Appalachian Mountains to secure the area for British fur-trading interests. This was devastating for the slave-holding plantation lords of the South, who required

---

[22] See Hayes, *A Generation of Materialism 1871−1900*, chapter 5.

new land in the West to keep the slave system profitable. The conflict of interests between American wealth and those who controlled the British state became so fundamental that the American upper class was forced to attempt to establish independence from Britain or suffer irreparable economic losses. The two struggles — that of the wealthy and that of the lower middle class — merged into the successful War of Independence.

The movement for independence emerged gradually. There had been at least two major uprisings against British rule prior to the 1770s — that of Nathaniel Bacon in Virginia in 1676, and that of Jacob Leisler in New York in 1689 to 1691. Both had been put down by the British and their leaders hanged. Resentment against the British smoldered and flared up again in the 1760s when the British attempted to increase their control over the colonial governments and increase the taxes extracted from the colonial economy. In 1765 an organization called the Sons of Liberty was established. It was mostly composed of lower middle-class individuals and engaged primarily in discussion and propaganda about British oppression. In 1772, through the new Committees of Correspondence, the focus of oppositional activities shifted to mass action and political agitation. It was this organization that organized the famous Boston Tea Party, the embargos against British goods, and the first Continental Congress. In 1775 the organization was transformed into the Committees of Safety, whose primary function was the organization of a popular militia and army to engage in revolutionary war against British rule. (The Committees of Safety could be said to be "the political arm" of the Revolutionary Army.)[23]

The War of Independence was not only a war against the British state, it was also a civil war. Approximately one-third of the colonists remained loyal to Britain and fought on the "other side." As in all civil wars, the internecine struggle got nasty. Concentration camps were set up, houses were burned, property confiscated, and "tories" tortured, killed, and driven out of certain areas. The Revolutionary War created 100,000 refugees who were forced to settle in Canada and the West Indies. The Committees of Safety set up dictatorships in the various colonies without the benefit of elections (which could not be held in the middle of a civil war), raised money, collected weapons and supplies for the troops, and carried on the administration of civil affairs until regular legislatures could be convened. The war was bitterly fought and was won by the Americans only with substantial support (troops and materials) from the Dutch, the Spanish, and especially the French.[24]

Although very strong at the outset of the Revolutionary War, the radical petty bourgeoisie emerged from the war in a subordinate position to the wealthy upper classes. Despite the fact that many of the demands of the petty bourgeoisie were realized with the elimination of feudal restrictions and the expansion of democratic institutions and liberties, the wealthy remained in control of the states and held their economic privileges intact. A depression in 1785 to 1786, which

[23] Hacker, *The Triumph of American Capitalism*, part II.
[24] Ibid., chapters 12 and 13.

hit the small farmers particularly hard, resulted, however, in the revival of popular radical agitation against the privileges of wealth. When there were large numbers of mortgage foreclosures during this period, the state legislatures which were predominantly influenced by small farmers tended to stay mortgage payments, abolish imprisonment for debt, and encourage inflation through accelerated printing of paper money to lessen the burden of debt repayment. It was an actual farmers' uprising in central Massachusetts that worried the wealthy the most. In 1786 a group of farmers led by Daniel Shays took over the town of Springfield and burned the courthouse mortgage records. This insurrection had to be put down by the militia sent in from Boston.[25]

State power after the War of Independence resided in each of the thirteen states. The central government that was set up under the Articles of Confederation had neither the power to tax nor to raise an army without the consent of the individual states. It was so weak as to be virtually irrelevant. This political situation — especially with the revival of radical agitation in 1785 — became increasingly disagreeable to the wealthy merchant and planter interests. The moneyed interests did not like the states issuing paper money, since it was causing an inflation which meant that they as creditors were being paid back in money worth less than that originally loaned out. The slave-owning plantation lords of the South were increasingly fearful of slave rebellions incited by either successful insurrections in the nearby Caribbean or by white farmer revolts in the North. No individual state government felt confident that its own small militia would by itself be able to put down either a massive slave uprising or a revolt of small farmers. The rich trading interests of the Northern cities were being hurt by the absence of a navy to protect their shipping (American flag ships were easy prey for pirates, who didn't have to worry about retaliation); by the lack of consistent tariffs against European manufactured goods (to create a guaranteed market for higher priced American goods); and by the existence of internal tariffs restricting trade among the various states, which hindered the development of sufficiently large domestic markets. The rich land speculators and fur interests of the West were having considerable trouble because they were unable to control the Indians in the absence of a strong army. Large numbers of the wealthy had bought up most of the paper money issued by the Continental Congress during the Revolutionary War to finance the fighting. This paper money soon became worthless because the central "state" did not have the power to tax. Since the money could not buy anything, its original holders happily parted with it for from 5 to 20 percent of its face value to those who chose to speculate that someday the central state would be in a position to make the money good. Most of their paper accumulated in the hands of a relatively few wealthy individuals.[26]

---

[25] For discussions of the revival of radical agitation among small farmers in the 1780s, see Hacker, *The Triumph of American Capitalism*, chapter 14; and Charles Beard, *An Economic Interpretation of the Constitution of the United States* (New York: Macmillan, 1913, 1962), chapter 2.

[26] Beard, *An Economic Interpretation*, chapters 2, 3, and 4.

As a result of their unhappiness over the absence of a strong central government to serve their collective interests, the wealthy merchants and plantation lords agitated and organized for the establishment of a new strong central state. After failing in their attempt to get the established governmental institutions to transform themselves through legal channels, they stepped outside of existing constitutional arrangements and simply issued a call for a new constitutional convention (ignoring the old confederate structure). The delegates to the constitutional convention were chosen by state legislatures that had *not* been elected on the issue of revising the state structure. In addition, women, blacks, indentured servants, and one-third of all free adult white males were not allowed to vote for legislative representatives. The legislatures, not always knowing exactly what was happening, responded to the call to select people to go to Philadelphia by generally appointing the people who seemed the most interested in the idea. As a result the delegates were virtually unanimously in favor of a strong central government organized to secure the rule of large property. Not one delegate of the fifty-five was a small farmer or mechanic. Five-sixths had a direct material interest in seeing a strong central state that would guarantee large property. Forty of the delegates held the paper money issued by the Continental Congress to finance the Revolutionary War, fourteen held land west of the Appalachian Mountains, twenty-four were creditors and mortgage holders, eleven were merchants or manufacturers, and fifteen were slave owners. These delegates knew their interests and were well aware of the impact of the document they wrote.[27]

The deliberations of the Constitutional Convention were held in complete secrecy, since it was important that the public not understand the true nature of the document being written and the motives for those responsible for it. Nevertheless, the position papers (*The Federalist Papers*) issued in defense of the document and the later memoirs of participants made it clear that the two overriding concerns of the writers of the American Constitution were the protection of the privileges of private property and guarantees against the force of majority rule.

Since they were operating outside of the existing legal structure, the delegates to the Constitutional Convention arbitrarily established the rules by which it would be activated. They simply said that once nine of the thirteen states ratified the document in special ratifying conventions elected for the purpose the document would go into effect and the strong federal state would come into being.

In many states the vote for the delegates to the ratifying conventions was rushed through without adequate chance for public debate. The farmers in the back country had very little chance to debate the issue or find out the significance of what was happening (after all, the proceedings of the convention had been secret). Conversely, the moneyed interests concentrated in the larger coastal towns were well informed, conscious of their interests, and well organized. They knew in advance what was at stake. They were able to marshall their forces quickly and effectively. Wealth, talent, and professional skills were on the side of the federalist forces. Since they did not understand the gravity of what was about to happen, the

[27] Ibid., chapter 5.

majority of the eligible voters took little interest in the issue of ratification and did not vote in the elections. Only about 160,000 people (approximately 20 to 25 percent of the adult white male population) voted in the ratifying elections, suggesting a rather low level of public concern (even off-year congressional elections in the United States get twice this proportion of the eligible vote). Of course, blacks, women, and many propertyless white men had no input into the process of ratification, as they were not eligible to vote.

In six of the states, including the three most populous (New York, Virginia, and Massachusetts), the delegates elected to the ratifying convention were initially either opposed to ratification or very evenly divided between the pro- and anti-ratification forces. The backcountry small farmers sent mostly anticonstitution delegates to the ratifying convention, while the more urban coastal areas almost unanimously sent proconstitution representatives. In the course of the deliberations of the ratifying conventions, majorities for ratification were eventually obtained in all but two states (North Carolina and Rhode Island). Although these two states refused to ratify it, the Constitution did become effective in the other eleven states. North Carolina and Rhode Island were eventually forced to join the new federal state under threat of economic sanctions from the new government. The proconstitution forces were able to secure majorities in the key states only by the promise of adding ten *amendments* to the basic document guaranteeing the basic rights and liberties of the small farmers (the Bill of Rights). Since the original document was concerned exclusively with the protection of private property and the establishment of constraints on popular rule, it made no reference to such radical issues as the rights of free speech, religion, trial by jury, and the right to bear arms.[28]

It is difficult to maintain that the Constitution was a deliberate expression of the will of the people. Rather, it was a class document, revealing the class nature of the American state. Many of the major provisions of the Constitution are guarantees of private property. States were forbidden to issue money (to restrict inflation to benefit creditors at the expense of debtors). The federal and state governments were forbidden to impair the obligations of business and labor contracts. The federal government was given the exclusive right to regulate interstate and international commerce. The federal government was given the power to regulate bankruptcy proceedings and to protect patents. The federal government was given the right to dispose of the lands west of the Appalachians. The federal government was mandated to maintain an army and navy and to "ensure a republican form of government" in each state. The provision for the establishment of an army and the guarantee of a republican form of government were instituted primarily to protect against domestic insurrection on the part of black slaves, small white farmers, and Indians. The federal government was given the authority to suppress such insurrections wherever they were to occur. The federal government was mandated to take over and pay at 100 percent of face value the Revolutionary War debts not only of the Continental Congress, but also of each individual state. This resulted in a bonanza for the wealthy money speculators

---

[28] Ibid., chapters 8, 9, and 10.

who had bought this paper from the poor soldiers and small suppliers of the troops for from 5 to 20 percent of face value.

Those articles of the Constitution that do not deal with guaranteeing private property have to do with frustrating the popular will. The convention considered the establishment of a constitutional monarchy with George Washington as king, but decided that antiroyalist sentiment was too strong among the masses to gain popular assent to such a system. Popular representative forms were too dear to the people who had just fought a seven-year war for equality, liberty, and democracy. The drafters of the Constitution, however, designed a system that would function like a constitutional monarchy in greatly constricting the rule of popular majorities, while using democratic forms. There would be two "houses" of Congress, the representatives to only one of which would be elected by the people (a parallel to the British House of Commons). Since there was no hereditary aristocracy, representatives to the other house would be selected by the state legislatures (a parallel to the British House of Lords). No legislation could be enacted without the concurrence of both houses, the democratic House of Representatives (designed to be the voice of the people) and the aristocratic Senate (the voice of the notables). To insulate the Senators from popular pressures exerted indirectly through the state legislatures, their terms were established at six years, one-third of the body being *appointed* every two years.

As further guarantees against popular majorities infringing on the rights of property through the legislature, the president (the equivalent of the constitutional monarch) was given the power to veto any legislation passed by both legislative bodies. Such a veto could only be overridden by a two-thirds vote of each legislature voting separately. To isolate the president from popular pressures, his office was filled through a process participated in only by local notables (the electors) who were in turn "appointed" in a manner determined by the state legislatures. There are no stipulations in the U.S. Constitution for either the direct *or* the indirect election of the president by the people. The president was given very strong powers appropriate to a constitutional monarch. During his fixed term of office he cannot be recalled by either the people or the legislature (except because of extreme misbehavior). He appoints the heads of governmental agencies, the commanders of the military, the judges of the federal courts, and foreign ambassadors. His appointments of judges, administrators, and ambassadors were made subject to approval of the Senate (the body designed to consist of the American equivalent of an aristocracy), but *not* of the House of Representatives (the body designed to be the voice of the people). This was to guarantee that the president's appointees would not offend any important sectors of the upper class. It also would ensure their isolation from the control of the people. Not only were federal judges made appointive (thereby isolated from popular influence), but they were given life tenure. Once appointed by the president and approved by the Senate, judges can only be removed for extreme misconduct. It was important that the judicial system, which was designed to defend the interests of property against the common people, be isolated from pressures from those people. Note that the Senate was also given the *exclusive* right to try all impeachments and to approve all treaties (both requiring a two-thirds vote). To ensure that popular majorities could not democratize the basic document, it was made very difficult to amend. A majority of both branches of Congress plus three-fourths of the state legislatures must approve changes in the basic document. In sum, the Constitution was a set of rules for stabilizing the rule of the wealthy against the common people. It established a state that appeared democratic enough to be legitimate in the eyes of the people, while it allowed for the propertied upper classes to run things pretty much as they pleased.

The state established by the Constitution was dominated by a coalition of Southern slave owners and rich Northern merchants until the 1850s. A balance was maintained for a considerable time by having the Senate consist of 50 percent Southern representatives of the slave lords and 50 percent representatives of the Northern commercial interests. From the 1840s on, however, the rising class of industrial capitalists in the North became increasingly powerful as these states industrialized.

The ascendancy of industrial over merchant capital in the North led to a growing and fundamental conflict of interests between the wealthy classes in the North and those in the South. The commercial interests in the North that dominated the cotton trade (acting as the intermediary between England and the industrialists of the North) profited considerably from credit, shipping, buying and selling, and insurance, and thus were not antagonistic toward the slave system. This was not the case with the Northern industrialists, however. They fought for high tariffs on imported European manufactured goods to guarantee a secure market for their own, more expensive products in the South. The South, which wanted to purchase the cheapest possible goods wherever they could be found, fought for the reduction or elimination of tariffs. The South wanted to make the settlement of the western lands difficult for small farmers to create a favorable environment for the introduction and growth of large plantations utilizing slave labor. Conversely, the northern commercial and industrial forces saw more profit in encouraging the rapid development of small family farming and the production of grains by free labor as well as a political advantage in securing a basis for political support for the industrial interests. The Northern interests wanted to facilitate the development of the West by having the state develop canals and railways that would tie the West closely to the Northeast (the river system of the West naturally tied this area with the South). Thus, the South strongly opposed public support for East–West canals and railways. The only railway to the West Coast it supported was one that was to run through Texas to southern California — that is, one that would encourage the expansion of the slave system. The South also opposed the encouragement of European migration to the industrial cities of the North (since this would increase the economic power of the developing capitalist class) and subsidies to U.S. shipping (why should Southerners pay taxes only to have their shipping charges increased?). Then again, the Southern planters favored allowing what amounted to again allowing the states to issue paper money (because of the inflation and consequent relief of the planters' debt to the North this would entail). The cotton-producing slave states (unlike the slave-breeding states of the upper South whose profits depended on a protected market) wanted to reopen the slave trade to reduce the costs of labor. The resulting conflict between the two segments of the upper class was so sharp that neither system (neither the slave economy of the South nor the capitalist economy of the North) was able to thrive because of the constraints that the other put on its development through its veto power in the U.S. state.[29]

The U.S. state was essentially paralyzed until 1860, when the new Republican party won the presidential election. The Republican party was organized in the 1850s as a coalition between the rising class of industrial capitalists and the small farmers (especially those in the West). The older Democratic party was left in the hands of the big merchants of the North and the slaveholders of the South. The Republican party, while far from being radical, took considerably stronger positions on the principal economic issues of the day than did the Democratic party. The Republicans' program offered support to both the small farmers and industrial capitalists. Note that the Republican party did not call for the abolition of slavery, but rather for its containment in the areas where it already existed, thereby leaving the settlement of the remainder of the West to the small farmers and big railroads. Lincoln's presidential victory, however, gave the signal to the South that the U.S. state had tilted to the North. Since they no longer had any reasonable hope of dominating the central state, they had little choice but to attempt to secede from the federal union created seventy years before. Upon secession they set up a new state that was the clear and consistent instrument of the slave-owning class. The Civil War thus became the second of two prolonged and violent civil conflicts that have torn America apart in its short 200-year history.

The superior economic basis of the North inevitably enabled it to militarily conquer the South, thereby bringing about the collapse of the slave lords' state. After a short period of struggle among the victors that took place between the moderate and radical wings of the Republican party — a contest that almost culminated in the removal of President Johnson (Lincoln's man) — the industrial capitalist class emerged as the master of the U.S. state. In the first years of their undisputed rule, marked by the overwhelming victory of the radical Republicans in the 1866 elections, they quickly enacted the Thirteenth, Fourteenth, and Fifteenth Amendments to the Constitution freeing the slaves and promising full political rights to blacks. They also began the implementation of a policy of reconstruction for the South. This policy was designed to undermine the social basis of the political power of the old slave lords by creating a firm alliance between the black freedmen and the poor white farmers of the South within the Republican party. The loyalty of the blacks was virtually automatic, since this party had waged the Civil War, granted emancipation, and promised full equality. The loyalty of the poor white farmers was to be expected since the program of the

---

[29] The account of the causes of the Civil War is taken largely from Hacker, *The Triumph of American Capitalism*, part III; Moore, *The Social Origins of Dictatorship and Democracy*, chapter 3; and Genovese, *The Political Economy of Slavery*.

Republicans (which was successful among the small farmers of the West) was designed in the interests of this class. With the creation of a solid basis for Republicanism in the South, these states could eventually enter the Union, sending representatives to the national legislature who would be fully supportive of the policies of the industrial capitalists. The actual program instituted in the South under the protection of the Union army of occupation included the abolition of property qualifications for voting, which traditionally had disenfranchised many poor whites in the South, the abolition of property qualifications for holding office, free education, the abolition of imprisonment for debt, the establishment of social services, the decentralization of local and town governments, and a more equitable tax structure.[30]

The Republican strategy for winning the South, however, failed. It did not go far enough in creating the economic basis for a Republican majority. Although the proposal was seriously debated in Congress, the necessary step of expropriating the plantations of the old slave lords and the redistribution of the land to the freedmen *and* poor whites along with sufficient capital to work the land ("forty acres and a mule") was rejected as setting too dangerous a precedent.

Consequently, because its economic position remained largely intact, the Southern ruling class was able to reassert its hegemony within its region. Blacks were intimidated because, although they were formally free, they were forced to become sharecroppers for their old slave lords to survive. Many of the poor whites, resenting the defeat of the South in the Civil War and the presence of the Union army of occupation, resisted the Republican attempts to win their support for the Reconstruction governments even though the Republicans' economic policies were favorable to them. The futility of trying to establish Republicanism in the South was apparent by the mid-1870s, and in 1877 the Union army of occupation was withdrawn from the South and the attempt at reconstruction ended. The industrial capitalists were able to give up on the attempt to establish Republicanism in the South because the social basis of their rule had by 1877 been firmly established in the West. The Republican party had built up a firm foundation of support among the small farmers of the rapidly growing western states. Many of these states had been admitted into the Union in the postwar period. Thus even without the Southern states, the Republican party (the party of industrial capital) was able to hold the presidency in all but eight years until 1912.

The abandonment of Reconstruction also crystallized a new alignment of classes in the United States. The period in which the primary contest for state power in the United States was between the industrial capitalists and the slave lords (1840s to 1865) gave way to one in which the primary struggle was between industrial capital (and its auxiliary agricultural and textile capitalists of the South — the transformed slave lords) and the small farmers and rising industrial working class.

The emerging primary contradiction was demonstrated in the growing threat to property from these classes, which was manifested in the example of the

---

[30] Hacker, *The Triumph of American Capitalism*, part III.

Paris Commune of 1871 (a workers' uprising in Paris), the rapidly growing urban industrial slums, and the increasing incidents of rioting and strikes by the working class in the United States. The fear of the new working class peaked in the summer of 1877, when widespread and violent rioting erupted in the working-class areas of most major industrial cities. In these riots hundreds of people were killed and the authorities lost control over large areas of the cities for weeks.[31] The capitalist class also had to cope with the rising militancy of the farmers in both the South and the West, which was to culminate in the 1890s in the People's party and its demand for the nationalization of the railroads and banks.

Growing discontent among the small farmers and the workers forced the Northern and Southern upper classes together under the overall hegemony of industrial capital. The Southern wealthy accepted their defeat in the Civil War and their secondary place in the U.S. economy and state in exchange for the reestablishment of their hegemony within the states of the old Confederacy and their integration into the industrial capitalist system.

The rule of industrial capital has not been seriously challenged since the defeat of the slave lords in the 1860s. The capitalist class turned the state completely into its instrument. The state heavily subsidized the building of the railways and internal improvements. High protective tariffs were established. Immigration of laborers was encouraged. Free land was given to the farmers and the railroads. The working class was kept in line and prevented from organizing. In every way the state facilitated the rapid and unimpeded advance of industrial capital.

During the generation after the Civil War, the state played a laissez-faire role in the economy. It guaranteed the conditions in which private business could prosper without attempting to direct, regulate, or manage the economy. Gradually, however, as the contradictions of capitalism matured and the monopolies secured firm control in industry after industry, the state's role in the management of the economy began to increase. The first large increase in the state's economic role occurred in the two decades after 1900 (the so-called "Progressive era"), and the second during Franklin Roosevelt's presidency (the New Deal and World War II). During these two periods, the monopoly capitalist state reached its mature form. In both phases of its development the impetus for its expansion came from the giant corporations.

After a period of mergers and corporate formation, by 1900 it became apparent that the new corporate interests required the elimination of the cutthroat competition among themselves, the control of the erratic fluctuations in the economy, and the ability to plan for the future.[32] The inability of the corporations

---

[31] See Robert Bruce, *1877: Year of Violence* (Chicago: Quadrangle Books, 1970); and Richard Boyer and Herbert Morais, *Labor's Untold Story* (New York: United Electrical, Radio and Machine Workers of America, 1955).

[32] See Kolko, *The Triumph of Conservatism*; Weinstein, *The Corporate Ideal in the Liberal States*; Karl Polanyi, *The Great Transformation* (Boston: Beacon Press, 1944, 1957); and Faulkner, *The Decline of Laissez Faire*.

and banks to rationalize and stabilize the corporate economy led them to turn to the state for assistance. Only state regulation could solve their problems. A number of regulatory agencies were set up to control the sectors of the economy that the corporations wanted regulated. Each of these regulatory commissions was essentially controlled by the "regulated" industries themselves.

The expansion of state activities not only provided for the self-regulation of business and ensured economic stability and predictability for the corporations, but it also served as a safety valve for democratic and radical ferment. For example, popular demands for nationalization of the railways and banks such as those put forth by the Populists in the 1890s were defused as the corporations were able to claim that federal "control" had ended the abuses of the system.

The programs begun during the Progressive era were extended during the Franklin Roosevelt administration. During the worst depression the country has ever known (and the potential of massive disruption that it raised), a series of governmental programs were instituted that were designed to increase the stability of the system by ameliorating some of the harshest aspects of capitalism, integrating the most active segments of the working class into the system, and providing enough buying power in the economy to keep employment and profits at respectable levels. Social security was instituted to provide subsistence income to the special victims of the system (the unemployed, the disabled, the aged, and mothers with dependent children), trade unions and collective bargaining were encouraged, and a massive program of public works, and eventually military spending, was launched.[33]

The heavy involvement of the state in the capitalist economy was consolidated during World War II. It was the unprecedented military spending of that period that in fact ended the Great Depression. The upper class learned the lesson that to ensure prosperity (while at the same time exerting U.S. world hegemony and cooling out the domestic class struggle with jingoism), the state would have to sustain the economy with a very heavy and continuing infusion of military spending. In 1946 the U.S. state's responsibility to ensure economic prosperity was incorporated into law with the passage of a full employment act establishing the Council of Economic Advisers, the Economic Report of the President, and the legitimacy of the state's role in moderating economic cycles and ensuring sufficient economic demand. Since 1946 the state's involvement in the U.S. economy has gradually increased as the state comes to manage ever more of the economy and spend an ever increasing percentage of the GNP.

Summary

The state is a rather new form of political decision making and administration. States have existed for only about 1 percent of the time that humans have lived together in societies. Primitive classless societies operated without states, but with

---

[33] See Domhoff, *The Higher Circles*, chapter 6.

democratic assemblies of all adults (or at least all adult males). States and the rule of the masses of common people by a small ruling class developed at the same time that societies became differentiated by classes. States developed to consolidate and preserve the domination of the newly developed privileged classes.

The redevelopment of strong central states in Europe occurred because of an alliance between the rich merchants and the centralizing monarchs, who had a common interest in suppressing the power of the feudal lords. The victory and consolidation of unshared rule by the capitalist class often occurred only after a process of violent revolution and civil war. The capitalist state developed in Europe in the period between the seventeenth and nineteenth centuries to advance the interest of the rising capitalist class against the other classes in society and to coordinate the affairs of the bourgeoisie as a whole.

Parliamentary forms tend to occur together with commercial societies because of the complexity of the structure of interests in such social forms and because of the special need for predictability and stability. Parliamentary forms became dominant in many Western European countries long before anyone but the richest landowners and merchants were allowed to vote. The franchise was not generally extended to the masses of the common people until after the middle of the nineteenth century. This was done largely to generate legitimacy for the system and to co-opt seething discontent in such a way as not to surrender any appreciable amount of actual power to the masses.

The capitalist state in the United States has grown up within the framework established by the U.S. Constitution, a document written by and for the alliance of Northern merchants and Southern slave lords in the late 1780s. The ascendant industrial capitalist class, after fighting a bloody civil war against the declining slave owners of the South, won full control of the state in 1865. It implemented laissez-faire politics until the early years of the twentieth century, when various reforms were implemented to facilitate the growth and consolidation of monopoly capitalist institutions and defuse discontent. Chapters 8 and 9 analyze the function of the capitalist state during the mid- and late twentieth century.

8

The Functions of the Capitalist State

**Part One:
Implementing and Tempering the
Capitalist-Class Will, Funding the State,
Preserving Law and Order, and Maintaining
Legitimacy**

The modern capitalist state performs a wide range of functions necessary for the survival and advance of the capitalist mode of production. These functions can be divided into three fundamental categories:

1. The formation and tempering (or moderating) of the capitalist-class will;
2. The implementation of the tempered capitalist-class will in realizing the social and economic conditions for the prospering of capitalist enterprise;
3. The maintenance of the state itself.

The second set of functions consists of three basic "outputs" or external functions of the state: securing the legitimacy of class society and the state (for example, the "America, Love It or Leave It!" attitude), preserving existing social relationships (through force when necessary), and facilitating the process of capital accumulation and maximizing the profitability of private business. A capitalist-class-oriented political directorate is necessary to coordinate and execute effective capitalist-class policies. The capitalist state is that instrument. In the words of Marx and Engels, the state is the executive committee of the capitalist class.

This chapter discusses the first and third types of functions and the first two subsets of "output" functions. First the state bureaucracy and state finance are considered, followed by a discussion of the role of the state in helping shape and temper the capitalist-class will. Finally the role of the capitalist state in legitimizing and reproducing existing social relationships is analyzed. (Chapter 9 discusses the state's role in guaranteeing profitability and ensuring the capital accumulation functions, as well as the contradictions among the various functions.)

The State Bureaucracy and the Financing of the Capitalist State

To accomplish its central and continually expanding functions, the capitalist state employs an enormous and ever-growing number of workers to administer its various programs. In 1974 the U.S. government (all levels) employed 16.4 million workers. This represented 17.6 percent of all wage and salaried workers, up from 13.8 percent in 1950 (see table 8–1). The expansion of the governmental sector has had a large impact on the overall employment market in the period 1960 to 1974. Thirty percent of all new jobs created in the American economy during this period were in the governmental sector.

The largest concentrations of U.S. state employees are in education and the military. However, during the early 1970s the majority of governmental workers were in neither of these fields. The long-run trend is clearly for nonmilitary workers to increase as a percentage of all governmental workers (see table 8–2).

After education and the military, the leading areas of U.S. government employment are health and hospitals, the postal service, highways, and police, in that order (see table 8–3).

State financing

The state has three ways of raising revenue to support its activities: (1) taxes, both direct and indirect (which includes the indirect tax of simply printing money); (2) borrowing money to cover current expenses (deficit financing); and (3) obtaining income from state enterprises and monopolies whose profits go to the

Table 8–1 The Number of State Workers in the United States (All Levels of Government)

	Number of State Workers	*As Percentage of All Workers*
1950	8,383	13.8
1955	9,801	15.0
1960	10,847	15.9
1965	12,931	16.7
1970	15,435	17.9
1974	16,425	17.6

Source: U.S. Department of Commerce, *Statistical Abstract of the United States*, 1975, pp. 323, 344, 357; and U.S. Department of Commerce, *Historical Statistics of the United States*, 1960, p. 709.

Table 8-2 U.S. State Workers in the Education and Military Sectors (Including Civilian Personnel)

	Education[b]		Military	
1950	1,723	(20.6%)[a]	3,345	(37.1%)[a]
1955	1,935	(19.7%)	4,034	(41.6%)
1960	2,525	(23.3%)	3,526	(35.4%)
1965	3,337	(25.8%)	3,915	(30.1%)
1970	4,258	(27.6%)	4,068	(26.4%)
1974	4,931	(30.0%)	3,183	(19.4%)

Source: U.S. Department of Commerce, *Statistical Abstract of the United States*, 1975, pp. 272, 323, 357; and U.S. Department of Commerce, *Historical Statistics of the United States*, 1960, p. 709.

[a] As a percentage of the total.
[b] Excluding federal personnel.

Table 8-3 U.S. State Workers (All Levels) in 1972

Function	Number of Employees	Percentage of All State Workers
Education[a]	5,922	36.2%
Military and international relations	3,255	19.9
Health and hospitals	1,375	8.4
Postal service	692	4.2
Police	616	3.8
Highways	604	3.7
Natural resources	413	2.5
Financial administration	381	2.3
Fire protection	299	1.8
Sanitation and sewage	206	1.3
Parks and recreation	191	1.2
All other	2,387	14.6
Total	16,339	100

Source: U.S. Department of Commerce, *Statistical Abstract of the United States*, 1974, p. 265.

[a] Including federal personnel.

state. A large part of the income of the early states came directly from the lands owned by the king, emperor, or state, and state monopolies, such as that of salt production or other vital materials. Part of the state's revenue often was obtained by leasing the rights to exploit the state monopolies to private individuals and corporations. The modern capitalist state is greatly limited in its abilities to obtain monies from this latter source, since the capitalists who dominate it do not want competition from the state, and thus prevent it from engaging in productive enterprises. They usually allow the state to run only those enterprises which are not profitable (thereby reserving the profit-making opportunities for themselves).

Therefore, the capitalist state relies primarily on taxation to finance its activities and to accomplish the purposes of those who dominate it.

Consequently, taxation of the people is one of the principal functions of the capitalist state. Historically, taxation and military conscription have required that the state keep records of the population within its territory. The state thus requires registration of births, marriages, deaths, changes of name, property ownership, transfers of ownership of property, and typically takes censuses of its population and its population's basic characteristics. Without such information, it is difficult for the state to tax its people or raise armies.

During the period of the formation of the modern state, taxation existed to support the armies of the king. Taxation tended to be irregular and geared to the special requirements of the king's wars. It was the need to secure funding for military adventures that forced the kings to call parliaments and grant them special prerogatives in exchange for granting taxes. Later on, as the centralized state bureaucracies consolidated their power, they increasingly imposed taxes without asking for general consent (England and several other countries were exceptions). Such funds quickly came to be used to support the state bureaucracies and the social and political policies of the kings.

After the transformation of the imperial state bureaucracies into purely capitalist states in the nineteenth century, state expenses were greatly reduced. The capitalists who controlled the state generally reduced its interference in the economy (often after an initial period of heavy subsidization of industry). They typically insisted that the state not engage in deficit financing — that is, that it keep its budget balanced and resort to loans only in exceptional circumstances (mainly during a war). Taxation during the early period of the capitalist state was primarily indirect to conceal the social effect of taxes and prevent the state from encroaching on private interests by making inquiries into personal wealth (which potentially could become controls over income and wealth).[1]

These classic principles of state financing have been generally negated in the period of monopoly capitalism and replaced by the principles of heavy and rising state expenditures, deficit financing, increasing state debt, and increased financing through direct taxation (made necessary by the rapidly expanding state budget). Table 8–4 illustrates the process of increasing reliance by the U.S. federal government on direct taxation (especially on direct taxation of individuals).

Deficit spending has become a normal part of state financing in monopoly capitalist society. In the period 1970 to 1974 the U.S. federal government ran an average deficit of $13.6 billion a year, which had to be financed through the sale of governmental bonds, mostly through private banks. This represented 5.9 percent of federal outlays. At the end of 1972 the U.S. federal debt was $437 billion. This represented about 2.5 times the level of federal expenditures (excluding transfer payments, such as social security). However the state has not come to rely increasingly on deficit spending. In the period 1950 to 1954 the average federal deficit was $3.3 billion a year (equal to 5.7 percent of federal out-

---

See O'Connor, *The Fiscal Crisis of the State*, pp. 70–72.

Table 8–4 Trends in the Forms of Income of the U.S. Federal Government[a] (as Percent of the Total)

	1900	1916	1930	1950	1973
Individual and employment taxes	0	9.4	31.6	43.6	53.9
Corporate income taxes	0	7.9	34.8	27.6	18.9
Estate and gift taxes	0.5	0	1.8	1.8	2.6
Excise taxes (indirect taxes)	53.6	52.3	15.6	19.3	8.3
Customs duties	44.1	29.3	16.2	1.1	1.7

Source: U.S. Department of Commerce, *Statistical Abstract of the United States*, 1974, p. 222; U.S. Department of Commerce, *Historical Statistics of United States*, 1960, p. 713.

[a] The percentages are computed on the basis of all internal revenue collections plus customs receipts (certain minor receipts, such as income from sale of public lands, are not included in the basic figure).

lays).[2] The ratio of debt to federal expenditures rose from 1900 to the end of World War II and has shrunk since. The ratio of federal debt to federal expenditures was the same in 1900 as it was in 1972 (see table 8–5).

While the governmental debt rises, it does not do so as rapidly as governmental expenditures. Excessive borrowing to finance current expenses is frowned on by the big financial institutions that buy and resell governmental bonds. These financial interests regard massive deficit financing as inflationary and fiscally unsound. Consequently, they are reluctant to see the state's debt rise more rapidly than the state's expenditures (except in times of crisis, when other goals become primary); hence, the capitalist state must look primarily to taxation, rather than to borrowing, to finance itself.

There are limits to the ability of the state to tax. People will tolerate being taxed only to a certain level as long as they are allowed to vote. The ability of the state to tax is thus restricted by the imperatives of a formally democratic system. The capitalist state's ability to tax is also limited by the problems of inflation and rising wages. If state expenditures are too large and grow too rapidly, considerable impetus is added to the demand for workers, goods, and money in the monopoly sector, thereby allowing it to raise prices very rapidly, while workers throughout the economy are able to obtain large pay increases (because of the shortage of labor). To contain inflation and combat the tendency of wages to rise, the state must follow policies designed to create unemployment (that is, promote high interest rates and low governmental spending) — policies difficult to pursue while increasing spending.

It has been estimated that that limit in the United States in the early 1970s was not much over 30 percent of the country's GNP.[3] If state projects require

---

[2] U.S. Department of Commerce, *Statistical Abstract of the United States*, 1974; U.S. Department of Commerce, *Historical Statistics of the United States*, 1960.

[3] See O'Connor, *The Fiscal Crisis of the State*, p. 234; also Baran, *Political Economy of Growth*, pp. 125–127.

Table 8-5 The Ratio of Federal Debt to Federal Expenditures (Excluding Transfer Payments)

1900	2.5
1920	3.8
1940	4.8
1950	6.5
1960	3.9
1970	2.4
1974	2.4

Source: U.S. Department of Commerce, *Statistical Abstract of the United States*, 1974, p. 221; U.S. Department of Commerce, *Historical Statistics of the United States*, 1960, p. 720, 721.

much more than this amount, the state must resort to other measures to finance them. Since deficit spending beyond a certain point and profit-making state-owned enterprises are both ruled out, the state may have to resort to increased subsidization of, and cooperation with the monopoly sector of the economy. This is designed to increase its rate of growth and hence the tax base available to the state.[4]

To obtain the needed revenue, the state thus must increasingly encourage private accumulation. But even this course is limited by the rather slow rate of growth and productivity in this sector.

The redistributive effect of taxation

Popular mythology has it that the effect of the taxation system together with state welfare policies is to redistribute income from the wealthy to the poor in capitalist societies. But in reality state financing involves the redistribution of income from the working class and small-business people to the large monopoly corporations. As is shown in the next chapter, the corporations gain most of the benefit from state expenditures. But it is the people who must pay most of the taxes to finance the state. The taxes of the small-business people and working people go primarily to subsidize directly the corporations; to military contracts given to the largest corporations; to foreign aid that ends up in the hands of the large corporations; to infrastructure expenses such as highways, airports, navigational, and communications aids that serve the corporations, and so on. The redistributive effect of taxation (from the poor to the rich) permits the monopoly capital sector to expand in income and wealth and to secure the stability it needs to prosper at the expense of the rest of society. The tax system in capitalist society is thus an indirect mechanism of exploitation of the working class and small business by the monopoly corporations.

Although the federal income tax is mildly progressive up to incomes of about $100,000, state and local taxes are heavily regressive. About one-half of state tax revenues come from sales taxes. While about one-half of the expenditures of the very poor are subject to sales taxes, only one-third of the expenditures

[4] See O'Connor, *The Fiscal Crisis of the State*, pp. 46–48.

of those earning over $10,000 are subject to such taxation. Local governments rely heavily on property taxes that fall mainly on the working class and the petty bourgeoisie, which either pay them directly or indirectly (through higher rents). It has been estimated that business people and landlords are able to shift about 75 percent of their property taxes onto their customers and tenants.[5] Leaving the actual amount of property taxes paid aside, the higher one's income the less the percentage of one's income must be paid directly in state and local taxes. For example in 1958 those making less than $2,000 a year paid 11 percent in taxes, those making between $2,000 and $6,000 paid 9 percent, and those making over $15,000 paid 6 percent.[6] Further, the rich are able to avoid paying most of the federal income taxes they technically are supposed to pay. Table 8—6 reports the discrepancy between the formal and the actual federal income tax rates.

Few members of the upper class pay more than 35 percent of their reported income to the federal government. Those few superrich individuals making over $5 million a year in 1960 paid an average of only 24.6 percent in federal income taxes. The bite of federal taxation on the very rich (over $500,000 a year) was less than that for the less wealthy ($100,000 to $500,000).

Some individuals and corporations have mastered the legal techniques of avoiding taxes to the extent of paying no, or virtually no, federal taxes at all. In 1969 there were 761 individuals who reported an income of over $100,000 but who paid no federal income tax. There were 52 who reported an income above $1 million and who paid nothing.[7] In 1973 after the reform of the tax laws (passed in 1969), 24 people who made over $1 million and 54 who made between $500,000 and $1,000,000 paid no federal income tax.[8]

In 1971 Alcoa Aluminum, McDonnell-Douglas, and Gulf and Western paid no federal income taxes in spite of considerable profits and dividends. In the same year Standard Oil of California paid 1.6 percent of its reported net income in federal corporation taxes, Gulf paid 2.3 percent, Texaco paid 2.3 percent, and ITT paid 5.0 percent.[9] In 1974 eight major corporations with considerable positive net incomes paid no federal tax at all. These included the Ford Motor Company, Lockheed, Honeywell, American Airlines, and Eastern Airlines. Numerous other corporations paid less than 10 percent of their profits in taxes in 1973. These included Chase Manhattan, Texaco, Mobil, American Motors, Bank of America, and McDonnell-Douglas.[10]

There are numerous gimmicks by which the very rich avoid paying taxes on their huge incomes and wealth. Income from capital gains is one of the most

---

[5] Ibid., chapter 8, p. 207.
[6] Gabriel Kolko, *Wealth and Power in America* (New York: Praeger Publishers, 1962), p. 37.
[7] Philip Stern, *The Rape of the Taxpayer* (New York: Vintage Books, 1972), chapter 1; and Howard Tuckman, *The Economics of the Rich* (New York: Random House, 1973), chapter 6.
[8] *The Oregonian*, September 11, 1975, p. A7.
[9] Stern, *The Rape of the Taxpayer*, pp. 17, 18.
[10] *The Oregonian*, October 8, 1975, p. B3.

Table 8-6 Federal Income Taxes as Percentage of Income, 1960

Income Group	Due per Rate Schedule	Actually Paid
Under $5,000	20.7%	9.0%
$5,000 to $9,999	23.7	11.0
$10,000 to $19,999	29.4	14.8
$20,000 to $49,999	44.1	21.8
$50,000 to $99,999	60.8	31.1
$100,000 to $150,000	73.6	34.6
$200,000 to $499,999	84.1	33.3
$500,000 to $1,000,000	88.6	31.1
$1,000,000 and over	90.1	32.3
$5,000,000 and over	90.7	24.6

Source: Philip Stern, *The Great Treasury Raid* (New York: Random House, 1962), p. 6.

important ways of avoiding high taxes. Capital gains originate from the sale of property or stocks that have increased in value since their purchase. Corporate executives are able to obtain a large part of their salaries in the form of capital gains through the mechanism of stock options. They are offered a part of their salaries in options to buy stock at a future time at a relatively low set price. When they exercise their options and sell the stock, they must pay only the 25 percent capital gains tax on their profit. The wealthy invest in tax-exempt municipal bonds and thus receive a significant proportion of their income in this tax-free form.

Oil and other raw material investments allow such extraordinary deductions from one's taxes that profits from such investments become almost tax free. From the 1920s until 1969, such investors were allowed to deduct 27.5 percent of their *gross* income (not net income or profits) from their taxes. (However, the Tax Reform Act of 1969 reduced the oil depletion allowance to 22.5 percent.) The wealthy charge travel, entertainment, transportation, and meals to expense accounts. Since the rich receive most of their income in forms other than wages and salaries, they also can underreport their income. According to the federal government, in the 1950s while only 3 percent of wage and salary income went unreported, 27 percent of entrepreneurial profits, 14 percent of dividends, and 58 percent of income from interest was not reported.[11]

The rich are also able to avoid paying inheritance taxes and hence keep their fortunes under family control by use of such mechanisms as the creation of foundations allegedly set up for charitable purposes. Contributions to such foundations are tax deductible. As nonprofit enterprises, their earnings are not subject to the corporate income tax. Large gifts to such foundations can make a family's fortune immune to inheritance taxes. The theoretically confiscatory inheritance tax of up to 77 percent on estates of more than $10 million can also be circumvented by using several other mechanisms. A married man can divide his estate so that one-half is taxed upon his death and the other half on his wife's death. This allows the

[11] Kolko, *Wealth and Power in America*, p. 21.

fortune to be taxed at the lower rate that applies to each half taken separately. Gifts made by the wealthy during their lifetimes are taxed at a rate much lower than the inheritance tax. Therefore the rich transfer much of their wealth to relatives long before their deaths, often in ways that specify how such gifts must be used. The rich also establish trust funds for their descendants. This postpones the payment of inheritance taxes for generations after the death of a wealthy individual as well as divides the family fortune, for taxation purposes, into smaller units subject to much lower inheritance tax rates. Wealth involved in trusts is fully under the control of those who established the trusts and were assigned control over them, thus preserving them intact.[12]

When the indirect burden of taxation is also considered — that is, the ability of the monopoly corporations to raise their prices when their taxes are increased, thereby making the working people who buy their goods bear much of the real burden of increased taxes — the actual amount of the tax burden shouldered by the people is revealed. It has been estimated that the corporations are able to shift one-third to one-half of their tax onto consumers. Leon Keyserling, who chaired Harry Truman's Council of Economic Advisers, estimated that in 1960 those earning less than $5,000 a year actually paid about 40 percent of their income in taxes directly or indirectly (through the shifting of taxes onto them by the corporations), while those making over $10,000 a year paid only 32 percent.[13] Although there have been some modest reforms in the federal income tax system since the 1950s (most notably the Tax Reform Act of 1969), the evidence (such as the continuing existence of high income persons and corporations who pay no or almost no federal income taxes) suggests that these reforms have made little or no difference in the redistributive effect of taxation.

In spite of widely held myths, the system of taxation — far from redistributing income to the poorer classes from the rich — has acted to make the rich richer and the poor poorer. The allocation of state funds must be considered along with the incidence of taxation in determining the redistributive effect of state financing. For example, in 1958 those making less than $4,000 a year paid *directly* about $6 billion dollars in federal taxes. But in that same year total federal payments for welfare amounted to only about $4.5 billion.[14] As is demonstrated in chapter 9, an overwhelming share of the federal budget is allocated to payments that directly support the corporations. But it is the working class that must bear most of the burden of financing such support.

The Formation and Tempering of the Capitalist-Class Will

The capitalist class dominates the state in capitalist society (this point is demonstrated in chapters 10 and 11). This section examines the ways in which the state

[12] Ibid., chapter 2.
[13] Domhoff, *Who Rules America?*, p. 42.
[14] Kolko, *Wealth and Power in America*, p. 39.

operates to form the common will of the capitalist class and to temper that will with the interests of other classes. As was noted in chapter 2, the upper class in capitalist society is highly diversified in its economic interests and, consequently, has considerable internal political differences. Pluralism of a sort does exist in capitalist society, but it is largely a pluralism among the various and diverse interests within the capitalist class.

The various divergent interests within the class are partly worked out through compromise outside of state bodies. This compromise occurs in the basic consensus-seeking private organizations of the capitalist class, such as the Council on Foreign Relations (CFR) and the Committee for Economic Development (CED). (These and other such upper-class, consensus-seeking, and policy-forming organizations are discussed in chapter 10.) However, a unified class will encompassing all of the capitalist class's interests is not generally obtained on all issues through these institutions. Consequently, conflicts within the capitalist class are manifested in struggles in the legislatures, the courts, the regulatory agencies and the top advisory and policymaking units of the administrative apparatus of the state. The compromise solutions that emerge from such struggles generally become the common will of the capitalist class. The procedures of the courts and governmental agencies, and the techniques of lobbying for legislation are normally considered legitimate by all segments of the capitalist class. Therefore, all typically agree to accept the outcome of such processes. General acceptance within the capitalist class of the compromises necessary to form a class will and the forms in which these compromises must be carried out are necessary conditions of effective class rule. Internecine interest-group struggles undermine the stability of the upper class and can result in the formation of alliances between various factions of the capitalist class and groups outside of their class. Such alliances could threaten the rule of that class.

There exists no simple and obvious upper-class will in capitalist society similar to that which exists in other forms of class society where the interests of the upper class are much more homogeneous. The great diversity of forms of capital in capitalist society means that almost any policy of the state will displease some segments of the capitalist community.

In an electoral system, those members of the upper class who are displeased with governmental policies can (1) support and attempt to install in office candidates favorable to their position in future elections, and (2) use the threat of doing so to prevent consistent action from being taken against their interests. Thus the presence of elections works to moderate the rule of those with special access to the capitalist state. It gives them a motive for never-ending compromise to suit the widest range of interests within the capitalist class. It discourages a rule that would favor some segments at the expense of others, and thus perhaps eventually lead to major disruption (perhaps even a revolution) by the alienated segments of the elite.

Herein is found one of the major reasons for the high correlation of commercial societies with parliamentary forms of government having highly developed legal systems (as the legitimate way to resolve disputes). The rule of autocratic (even if probusiness) dictators necessarily undermines the legitimate channels of compromise and the legal processes on which the highly complex and fragile economic interrelations of capitalism are built. Wherever such procedural forms do not exist in commercial societies, there is strong pressure for their creation.

The capitalist class is *not* able to have the state fully satisfy its will. The conditions of maintaining parliamentary and legal forms, as well as the condition of preserving law and order and preventing social upheavals, are that the capitalist-class will must first be tempered by the demands of the upper middle classes and their special interest groups (such as the American Medical Association [AMA]), and then further tempered to head off spontaneous and organized resistance from the working classes. Thus, although the capitalist class dominates the state, it has only limited policy options available to it — especially if it wants to continue its rule under conditions short of an *overt* class dictatorship (a situation that would have serious internal contradictions).

Much of the discussion and compromise that goes on both outside (in the CFR, CED, major universities, and foundations) and inside the government (especially in the legislatures and administrative agencies) is designed to perform the functions of tempering the capitalist-class will so that it assumes a form that can in fact *provide* effective guidance for the entire society.

The major forum for the upper middle classes and the regional and local business interests in the United States is Congress, especially the House of Representatives. In the early 1960s only 15 percent of the U.S. Senators and almost no members of the House of Representatives were from the upper class.[15] However, about two-thirds of the 435 House members had significant outside interests (either in ownership of private businesses or fees paid from them). Twenty percent had an interest in financial institutions (usually hometown banks), and about 10 percent had an interest in oil and gas companies. Many had interests in communications (fourteen held interests in local radio and TV stations), airlines, and railways.[16] The major impact of lobbying groups composed of large numbers of small businesses or professionals (for example, the AMA, the various dairy cooperatives, and farmers associations) is on Congress, and especially on the House of Representatives. Such groups can exercise considerable clout on the local level on which representatives are elected. The wider area represented by Senators tends to neutralize the impact of various local business and professional associations on the Senate, and thus it is much more under the influence of the upper class than the House. Consequently, when the House and Senate differ on legislation, it usually is because of a difference in interest between the upper class *and* smaller-business people.

The major power that Congress (and especially the House of Representatives, which has the exclusive power to initiate appropriations for governmental programs) has is its power to control governmental funding. To secure the support of the upper middle-class interests in Congress, concessions must be made

---

[15] Domhoff, *Who Rules America?*, p. 111.
[16] Morton Mintz and Jerry Cohen, *America, Inc.* (New York: Dell, 1972), p. 260.

to the parochial interests of the various local and upper middle-class groups. Typically, such interests are satisfied if they can obtain a high level of agricultural price supports (for the better-off farmers), military bases, dams, and other giveaway and pork-barrel programs benefiting local business interests. Congress members are anxious to secure such benefits for their hometown backers. They are generally happy to let the executive branch establish basic social, economic, and foreign policies in exchange for such programs. Congress technically has great powers to oversee economic, social, and foreign policies (through its control over the financing of programs in these areas). In fact, however, because of the bargain struck between the wealthier petty bourgeoisie and the upper classes, and because of the differential abilities and interests of the two classes in such policy questions, it rarely exercises its prerogatives. Generally, as long as the upper middle class and smaller regional business interests get what they need from the federal pork barrel, they accept the political and ideological hegemony of the corporate upper class. Unless the economic, social, and political policies of the upper class (implemented through the executive branch of the government) directly offend large segments of the local business interests, these latter groups will not oppose such policies.

The House of Representatives, however, is not a rubber stamp for the upper class on those issues that directly affect the interests of its local business and upper middle-class constituency. For example, the House usually is the most resistant to welfare legislation. This is because higher welfare costs mean higher taxes for the upper middle class and smaller businesses that are not able to pass on taxes through raising prices, as can the upper-class-controlled monopoly corporations. This is also because these interests would have to pay higher wages as a result of the rising minimum subsistence guaranteed to those who do not work. The big corporations pay considerably higher wages than do the competitive marginal businesses and are thus not adversely affected by such welfare legislation. The House also is usually the most hostile to legislation that increases the powers of unions. This is because it is the smaller, more marginal businesses that suffer the most from the increasing strength of unions. The larger corporations already pay high wages and have thoroughly integrated the unions into their system of controlling labor.

Furthermore, the House offers the greatest resistance to foreign aid and to overseas support programs of all kinds, as well as to reducing barriers to international trade. This is because the smaller, more marginal businesses have no foreign investments and are disproportionately involved in labor-intensive industries (for example, textiles and other nondurable goods), which suffer the greatest competition from imports. Hence, they oppose programs that do not aid their businesses but for which they must bear the burden. The large international corporations, on the other hand, advocate foreign aid as an instrument by which to secure favorable treatment for their overseas investments as well as tariff reductions to expand their overseas markets. The House is also the most enthusiastic about closing tax loopholes that aid the very wealthy, whereas the Senate traditionally resists tax reforms. In general, because of its social base, the House of Representatives is the least sympathetic branch of the U.S. federal government to the leading corporate interests *and* to the demands of the poor and working classes.

This is not to say that the upper class is without influence in the House. In fact, it is very powerful. The legislative struggles within the House, unlike those in the executive branch, are as much between the upper class and the upper middle class as they are among the various interests in the upper class or among the various interest groups in the upper middle class. The right wing of the upper class is especially strong in the House because of its ability to mobilize small-business people through such organizations as the National Association of Manufacturers (NAM), the Chambers of Commerce, and the Farm Bureau. The politics of most state legislatures also reflect the same types of struggles as those that go on in the House.[17] In neither arena does the upper class exercise the hegemony it has obtained in the executive branch of the federal government.

Since 1933 the executive branch, acting in concert with the leading upper-class consensus-seeking organizations such as the Business Council, the CED, the CFR, the Ford, Rockefeller, and Carnegie Foundations, and the Brookings Institution, has initiated the various programs designed to stabilize capitalism, prevent social disruptions, and maximize profits. During this period the executive branch has often had to act against the alliance of the right wing of the upper class (for example, NAM, the Chambers of Commerce, and the Farm Bureau) with large segments of the smaller business community and professional groups such as the AMA to implement these policies.

The capitalist-class will must also be tempered by the potential danger of social disruption and eventual revolution coming from the working classes. Welfare measures, such as unemployment insurance, workingman's compensation, old age insurance, disability benefits, aid to families with dependent children, minimum wages, government-enforced safety regulations, the provisions of collective bargaining guaranteed by law, and other governmental measures designed to take the edge off the most brutalizing features of the system, act to "cool out" working-class discontent. These "concessions," together with the repressive measures against revolutionaries and the pervasive ideological hegemony of the capitalist class, hinder the development of working-class consciousness and the social disruption that its emergence would entail. Especially in times of economic crisis and social upheaval (for example, the 1930s and the late 1960s), the upper class must expand the programs designed to buy off the disaffected and prevent general discontent from taking the form of revolutionary movements.

Thus, the lower classes *do* have an impact on state policy, especially when they begin to act as a class rather than passively accepting capitalist-class hegemony. But the ways in which that discontent is typically channeled in the

---

[17] See, for example, O'Connor, *Fiscal Crisis of the State*, pp. 82–91; and Domhoff, *Who Rules America?*, chapter 6.

United States are determined, *not* by representatives of the oppressed classes, but by the *ruling class*. The role of the AFL—CIO and various individual unions, as well as that of liberal civil rights groups such as the NAACP, CORE, and the National Urban League must be interpreted within this context. The political effect of all such organizations is to mitigate the abuses of the system for those segments of the working class and minorities that are most likely to be politically active, thus defusing their discontent and stabilizing the system. These organizations almost never challenge the legitimacy of capitalism or the hegemony of upper-class rule in the United States — they merely demand a "share of the action," offering the specter of social disruption on the part of their constituents if the moderate demands of these organizations are not met. These working-class and minority organizations have been thoroughly integrated into the general mosaic of upper middle-class, professional, and small-business special interest groups that permeate politics on the state and congressional levels — they are each just another "interest group," on par with any number of business associations (but never even remotely equal to the business associations taken together).

The Preservation of the Legitimacy of the System

In the United States few people ever challenge the fundamental assumptions of capitalism and the state structure. People usually accept the basic "rules of the game" and judge the system to be fundamentally just and legitimate even if they see many specific failings. Such a high level of voluntary acceptance of the system does not occur spontaneously. The state must work very hard to produce such sentiments and reinforce them once they are created. The capitalist state maintains the legitimacy of the capitalist system through propagating procapitalist values and attitudes in the schools and encouraging the cult of patriotism. These positive mechanisms are supplemented by repressive measures designed to check the spread of anticapitalist and antistate consciousness.

Legitimacy is also maintained by mitigating enough of the most oppressive aspects of the system for the groups most likely to cause trouble and by buying off smaller and regional businesses to keep discontent from breaking down the system's legitimacy. Unless such legitimacy is maintained, the role of the capitalist class would be jeopardized. In addition to massive welfare payments to the poor, the state must subsidize small business through such means as the programs of the Small Business Administration, the facade of antitrust legislation, enforcement of fair-trade legislation (which protects the profits of small-business people by prohibitions on competition), farm subsidies and price supports. The maintenance of legitimacy consequently is an expensive process.

The state's role in producing and reproducing the ideological hegemony of the capitalist class by utilizing the educational system is analyzed in chapter 11. Here one need only note that approximately 90 percent of all secondary and primary school students in the United States in 1974 were attending public schools (most of private school students were attending Catholic schools). Further, 75 percent of students enrolled in institutions of higher education were attending public colleges and universities. The federal government is able to exercise considerable control over the leading private universities through its various funding programs. In 1973, all governmental units in the United States spent a total of $70 billion on education (of which more than one-quarter went to colleges and universities). This represented 22 percent of all expenditures of all governmental units in the United States. The role of the state in education has been increasing. In 1950 only $9.6 billion was spent by all governmental units on education. This represented 16 percent of all governmental expenditures (of which 11 percent was for higher education).[18] The state's role in higher education is thus seen to be rising very rapidly.

The state also encourages the cult of patriotism. By promulgating public holidays and state rituals in the schools, media, and through public ceremonies and parades, it intensifies feelings of identification with the state which are then used to inspire the working class's loyalty to the very state policies that are designed to benefit the capitalist class.

Military training can be especially important in establishing the legitimacy of the system. The collective and romanticized memories of past struggles, and the regular celebration of past sacrifices and victories produces and reproduces a patriotic ethos, which in turn reinforces the legitimacy of capitalist institutions and obedience to the dictates of the state apparatus. The experience of military service can reinforce authoritarianism, submissiveness, and feelings of inadequacy in working people. It also gives them a sense of personal involvement in defending "their" country's interests. By reinforcing sentiments of patriotism that operate to increase working people's willingness to do its bidding, the capitalist class is thus better able to manipulate them. The effects of military indoctrination and military discipline, and the memories of collective solidarity and heroism are reinforced by participation in veterans' groups such as the American Legion and the Veterans of Foreign Wars (which are composed mostly of working-class veterans). Such organizations keep the military spirit alive, reproduce the sentiments of patriotism, and add to the authoritarianism of working-class people, thus enhancing their susceptibility to capitalist-class manipulation. In 1974 there were a total of 29.3 million veterans in the United States, representing 47 percent of the twenty-one and over male population.[19]

The experience of military service does not always reinforce the system's legitimacy in the eyes of soldiers and veterans, however. The more decisive the military victory and the lighter the casualties and suffering of the troops as well as the people back home, the greater the legitimization effect. Conversely, military

---

[18] U.S. Department of Commerce, *Statistical Abstract of the United States*, 1975, pp. 111, 112, 114, 140, 253, 254.
[19] Ibid., p. 6, 332.

defeats (or very costly "victories") — especially those that entail great suffering among the soldiers — tend to generate bitterness among the troops and often act to delegitimate the system that led them into battle. Both soldiers and veterans in such situations have played a major progressive and revolutionary role. This was the case in Russia in 1917, where soldiers and veterans supported the Bolsheviks in large numbers; in many of the Western European countries at the end of World War I (including Italy, France, and Germany); in China after World War II; and even to a degree in the United States in the aftermath of the Vietnam War.

Providing that the domestic suffering in terms of reduced standards of living and lives lost does not reach a critical point, overseas wars and adventures have traditionally produced popular identification with the capitalist class's imperialist policies. The frustrations and aggressiveness of the working and middle classes can be channeled into vicarious participation in the military victories of the ruling class. In times of domestic unrest, militarism and overseas adventures have often been encouraged by the upper class to distract the working classes from issues that would bring them into conflict with the social order. Such was the case with the rise of fascism in Italy and Germany during times of considerable domestic upheaval. Domestic opposition to the U.S. capitalist class was annihilated during the late 1940s and early 1950s largely as a byproduct of cold war hysteria, the rapid expansion of the U.S. military, and participation in the Korean War. The crusade-against-Communism atmosphere of the 1950s not only encouraged blind respect for the authority of the ruling class, but isolated domestic opposition by identifying it with an external "enemy." Militarism typically fosters the reactionary and irrational forces in society and builds docility and conformity at the expense of critical and class-conscious attitudes.

In addition to inculcating procapitalist and pro-state values and attitudes in the schools and the military, the state actively promotes the legitimacy of the system through giving "hand-outs" or mitigating some of the worst abuses of the system. This is done to produce gratitude among the most oppressed and those who are likely to become poignant critics of the system.

Welfare payments to the poor help preserve the legitimacy of the system. Historically, welfare programs (food stamps, aid to families with dependent children, aid to the unemployed, aid to the sick and disabled, housing subsidies, job-training programs, and community development projects) are expanded when social unrest fosters large-scale spontaneous or organized resistance to capitalism, and are contracted or abolished when political stability is restored. Welfare functions to restore order in periods of turmoil. The more militant and disruptive the underclass, the greater the level of welfare payments. The extension of welfare to the unemployed and poor working class in times of unrest gives the state a mechanism both to "cool out" discontent by making the masses grateful to the state and mitigating the worst abuses, *and* to control them by putting stipulations on obtaining relief. For example strikers or political activists are ineligible for benefits; recipients must actively pursue low-wage work; and recipients must be obsequious to welfare officials and adhere to petty regulations designed to humiliate and reproduce class divisions. Expanded welfare is especially important as a mechanism of control when the constraints that capitalists can impose on the worker (in the form of promotion and firing) are removed by unemployment.[20]

The Protection of Private Property and the Maintenance of Order

Under normal conditions most people usually obey the laws and accept the basic "rules of the game" voluntarily — at least in U.S. society. Some people never do; and occasionally the majority of the people will question or not accept the legitimacy of one or another capitalist institution or law and thus will not willingly respect them. Pervasive social crises could cause the legitimacy of the system to break down altogether. In some capitalist countries entire classes do not accept the legitimacy of capitalist values and institutions (for example, France and Italy). Consequently, physical force and the threat of its use by the police and army must be used to make people obey the laws and respect capitalist institutions.

Criminal justice

The police, criminal courts, and prisons in capitalist society are primarily designed to guarantee the private property of the capitalists. A sufficient level of "law and order" (that is, a low level of crime against persons and personal property) must exist for the economy to be able to function. Many kinds of crimes against private property are punished by the state — for example, burglary, larceny, theft, robbery, embezzlement, and trespass. However, the forms of taking people's property that are an integral part of the logic of the capitalist system, such as the banks' foreclosure of small-business loans and home mortgages, high interest rates, monopoly prices, and the expropriation of surplus value by capitalists, are *not* punished by the capitalist state as crimes.[21] The system works to sentence George Jackson, a lower-class black, to fifteen years in prison for stealing $75 from a business person, but to reward the Secretary of Agriculture with a high salary for implementing policies that raise the price of bread and thus cost the working people millions of extra dollars, which end up mostly in the hands of the corporations that grow wheat and produce bread. In 1974, approximately 90 percent of the crimes reported to the police in the United States were crimes against property.[22]

The criminal "justice" system is very much a class institution. Its principal

---

[20] See Frances Fox Piven and Richard A. Cloward, *Regulating the Poor* (New York: Vintage Books, 1972).

[21] See Herman and Julia Schwendinger, "Defenders of Order or Guardians of Human Rights," *Issues in Criminology* 5, no. 2 (Summer 1970); and Tony Platt, "Prospects for a Radical Criminology in the United States," *Crime and Social Justice* 1, no. 1 (Spring-Summer 1974).

[22] U.S. Department of Commerce, *Statistical Abstract of the United States*, 1975, p. 150.

function is to keep the working class in line. It operates to prevent members of that class from individually expropriating enough from the capitalists and the upper middle class to survive without having to sell their labor power to the capitalists. It also guarantees capitalist enterprises against disruption and ensures tranquility in upper-class and upper middle-class neighborhoods. It is primarily the poorer members of the working class, plus many lumpen proletarians (who must be controlled to keep them from disrupting the system as well as to deter the poorer segments of the working class from attempting to survive by becoming lumpen), who commit most crimes. This is true both for crimes against property (committed for survival or to supplement low incomes) and for crimes against persons (committed largely out of the frustration with the oppression of life at the bottom of society). Members of such classes fill the courts and prisons. In the early 1970s approximately 350,000 individuals were incarcerated in federal and state prisons and local jails.[23] Of these, over one-third were nonwhites. Of the 160,000 inmates of local jails in mid-1972, about 45 percent earned less than $2,000 a year and 85 percent earned less than $7,500 before their incarceration. Forty percent were unemployed at the time they were jailed, and 30 percent of the total had been jobless for at least a year. Of those who had been employed, 60 percent had worked only on a part-time basis.[24] Of all persons executed in the United States from 1930 to 1974, 54 percent were black.[25] The judges in the courts are largely from upper middle-class and upper-class backgrounds and are very much inclined to implement their class interests and values against the largely poor working-class and lumpen defendants they face, as are most juries. Those actually ending up in the prisons and jails are considerably more likely to be of working-class and lumpen backgrounds, than those actually arrested for crimes. The well-off who are accused of crimes are able to secure good legal help to make the best possible cases for them, and are also able to impress judges, juries, and probation officers who, because they share common class values and experiences, are much more likely to be lenient or to not convict. Not only do the poorer classes actually commit more crimes against property than those that own property, but they also are more likely to be arrested for crimes (even those they didn't commit) and to be convicted and harshly sentenced than are members of the better-off classes.

The courts (especially the civil courts) also play an essential role in resolving disputes among capitalists and in securing the enforcement of contracts between capitalists and the working class (who are thus made to pay their debts to the capitalists and otherwise honor obligations entered into on unequal terms). Private business can function successfully only in an environment which provides for peaceful adjustment of conflicts among capitalists, between capitalists and workers,

---

[23] U.S. Department of Commerce, *Statistical Abstract of the United States*, 1975, pp. 107, 168.

[24] Carl Rowan, Column in the *Oregonian*, September 25, 1974, section 1, p. 28. Taken from data from *Survey of Inmates of Local Jails*, by the Law Enforcement Assistance Administration (Washington, D.C.: U.S. Government Printing Office, 1973).

[25] U.S. Department of Commerce, *Statistical Abstract of the United States*, 1975, p. 171.

and between capitalists and the government. A developed and legitimate legal system is thus essential to the orderly conduct of business affairs.

Political repression

In addition to protecting private property and maintaining public order the state also functions to repress the movements of the oppressed that cannot be manipulated and those radical leaders that cannot be bought off. Movements such as the Industrial Workers of the World, the American Communist Party, and the Black Panthers were destroyed by such tactics. Mass arrests, frame-up trials on conspiracy, FBI harassment of individuals and organizations, public embarrassment by governmental investigatory committees, jailings for violating laws passed to eliminate radicals from unions and public life, and laws prohibiting radical publications from using the mails and radicals from holding public office have all been used successfully.

One of the principal tools available to the ruling class to preserve its rule is the repression of leftist groups and individuals. For example, in 1968 and 1969 the Black Panther Party probably suffered more than any other U.S. leftist organization. During that period the organization experienced eighteen police raids on and five bombings of its offices, three deportations, three gun fights with police, and twenty-one cases of individual harassment of members.[26] In this period 768 Panthers were arrested on a total of 1,003 charges, including 178 charges of possession of weapons, 96 charges of disorderly conduct and disturbing the peace, 92 charges of attempted murder, suspicion of murder, or conspiracy to murder, 38 charges of conspiracy to bomb, 36 charges of leafleting or selling newspapers, 16 charges of rioting or conspiracy to riot, 11 charges of unlawful assembly, and 1 of setting up an unlawful table.[27]

Periods of intensified repression have historically coincided with periods of social crisis and relative strength of the Left. Thus in the United States the last few years of the eighteenth century and the periods 1877 to 1890, 1916 to 1924, 1947 to 1953, and 1964 to 1971 have witnessed the greatest repressions in the country's history. The only period of general crisis and strength of the Left that did not witness a widespread repression was the 1930s. During this period the mainstream of the upper class resorted mostly to co-option and reform to deal with the crisis and growing discontent.[28]

Among the techniques used by the government to harass and demoralize the Left have been the use of legislative committees such as the House Un-American Activities Committee to expose and discredit leftist leaders, workers, and teachers; FBI harassment of radicals; and infiltration of organizations to spy on their activities, to organize internal factions to split them apart, to discredit their leaders with personal attacks, and to provoke them into adventuristic actions for which the police can break them up. In November of 1974 the FBI released a report on

[26] Alan Wolfe, *The Seamy Side of Democracy* (New York: David McKay, 1973), p. 50.
[27] Ibid., pp. 49–50.
[28] Ibid., p. 94.

its activities from 1956 to 1971 to disrupt and neutralize left-wing organizations. This report admitted FBI involvement in pressuring employers, landlords, and local governments to fire, evict, and harass leftists; leaking unfavorable information about leftists to the press; sending anonymous letters accusing radical leaders of being FBI agents to various groups to destroy their ability to lead, and anonymous reports to family members or the press alleging immoral activities on the part of radical leaders; informing credit bureaus and creditors of the political and moral activities of leftists; establishing sham organizations to disrupt movements; and using the citizen's band radio to disrupt demonstrations.[29]

Whenever the regular police are unable to preserve social order and whenever insurrections, revolutions, or even spontaneous riots break out, the military is used to suppress them, restore order, and preserve capitalist relationships.

In U.S. history the military has been called out innumerable times to quell domestic unrest. The National Guard was called up 147 times from 1919 to 1944 and 256 times from 1945 to 1969 to handle civil disturbances such as student rebellions, strikes, and rioting of lower-class people.[30] During the first period most of the call-ups were to deal with strikes, but during the second period the call-ups were predominantly to deal with "racial disorders." The increase in the use of the military to control civil disorders in the late 1960s against students, workers, and national minorities reflects the rise in militancy in those years. The military has always been used during such periods of upheaval.

Thus it can be seen that when legitimation breaks down and people no longer voluntarily respect private property, the state resorts to physical force to guarantee "law and order." Both the generation and reproduction of positive values about the capitalist system and the backup of the police and army are the instruments by which the capitalist state guarantees the capitalist system.

Summary

In this chapter four of the functions of the capitalist state for capitalist society were examined: the formation and tempering of the capitalist-class will; the generation and reproduction of the legitimacy of the capitalist system; the protection of private property and the maintenance of order; and the maintenance of the state bureaucracy itself. The state serves to reconcile various interests within the capitalist class to produce a general class policy, to create broad popular support for capitalist institutions, and to physically prevent those who do not respect capitalist institutions from violating the norms of private property. The accomplishment of these tasks (and those discussed in the next chapter) requires an enormous and growing bureaucratic apparatus and an increasing proportion of the society's Gross National Product. In the next chapter the multitudinous ways in which the state facilitates profit making and investment for business are analyzed.

[29] See Nelson Blackstock, *Cointelpro* (New York: Vintage Books, 1976).
[30] Wolf, *The Seamy Side of Democracy*, pp. 120–121.

9

The Functions of the Capitalist State

Part Two:
The Facilitation of Capital Accumulation

The most complex of the functions of the modern capitalist state is the facilitation of capital accumulation. The state can employ a variety of means to facilitate business profit making and the reinvestment of those profits in ways to ensure the making of still more profits. This chapter discusses seven ways in which the state facilitates the capital accumulation process:

1. The provision and regulation of a labor force for the corporations;
2. The facilitation of commerce;
3. The ensuring of sufficient buying power in the economy;
4. Engaging in countercyclical economic policies;
5. The subsidization of individual corporations;
6. The state-sanctioned self-regulation of corporations;
7. The advance of the overseas interests of the corporations through economic and military means.

The Provision and Regulation of the Labor Force

The essence of the capitalist state lies in its manipulation of the working class in the interest of capital. In addition to preserving the private property of the capitalists and preserving social order, this implies the regulation of wages, the maintenance of skills, the guarantee of sufficient numbers of able-bodied workers, the prevention of industrial disruption through the regulation and control of working-class mass organizations, and the guarantee that the working class will respond to the wage incentive and offer their labor power to the capitalists on terms which ensure high profits and work discipline.

Note that the general task of regulating the labor force is not unique to capitalist states. One of the major tasks of the state in slave society was to regulate and control the slaves, just as one of the major functions of the state in peasant and feudal societies was to control and manage the peasants and serfs. Even in authentically socialist societies, the state plays a central role in the allocation and training of the labor force. There are considerable differences, however, among these social formations in the ways in which the state recruits, channels, trains, and coordinates labor — differences that are a product of the very basic differences in the mode of production of each type of society. For example, the state's role in educating slaves, peasants, or serfs is restricted to religious or some other indoctrination, which is used to keep them passive, whereas in capitalist society education is greatly expanded to provide basic industrial skills and advanced training, creating a highly skilled working class that is suited for a wide range of occupations and employers. Although it is also oriented to giving working people the skills needed by the society, socialist education is equally concerned with developing the potentials of those it educates for their own sake, independent of the needs of industry.

Educational institutions serve two major functions in capitalist society. In addition to reproducing the legitimacy of the capitalist institutions, they also train the working class in the basic skills they need to perform the tasks required of them by the corporations. Manual workers are trained in the basic industrial skills (shop math, basic reading and writing, mechanical drawing, basic machine and carpentry skills), and even more importantly in work discipline, in punctuality, in obedience to rules and supervisors, and to respond to the material incentives of individualized grading (the analogue of the wage). White-collar workers are trained in the skills of office math, basic reading and writing (with stress on correct spelling and form rather than on creativity), typing and use of office machinery, and again, in work discipline, compliance, proper manners, dress, and to respond to material individual incentives through grades. The highly skilled professional workers are given special job training in colleges, where they learn advanced math and science, managerial skills, creative writing, and the various specific skills required by the professional occupations. Such training usually offers considerably more room for initiative and autonomy than does the training of the manual and white-collar proletariat, from whom discipline and obedience, rather than creativity and autonomy, are the requirements of capital.

In addition to basic education, the government is also involved in various manpower retraining and adult education programs designed to retrain the labor force, giving them skills which are currently demanded by the corporations. In 1972 the federal government alone spent $1.5 billion on manpower training programs. Because of the rapid changes in technology, the skills taught in the schools decades ago are now largely obsolete. The retraining programs, financed and run by the government, make an important contribution to the labor force of the corporations. The corporations are spared the cost, not only of the original training required of their labor force, but also the costs of the retraining of adult workers. Over time an increasing share of the burden of training the working class has come to be borne by the state, rather than by the corporations, through on-the-job and apprenticeship programs. The costs of training the labor force are also being socialized (that is, paid for by the working class itself through their taxes). Education is free only in form.

The government uses welfare programs (food stamps, aid to families with dependent children, and especially unemployment benefits) to maintain and regulate the labor force and guarantee that it will respond (as it is supposed to) to wage incentives. The state desires to keep the temporarily unemployed in a reasonably healthy condition during times of recession or periods between jobs so that when prosperity returns or new jobs are found they will be able to resume their labor. Under the slave system, in slow periods the slave masters had to feed and otherwise look after their slaves even though they were not producing. This was dictated by their great capital investment in them. Under capitalism the cost of the maintenance of the productive class, when it is not working, has been socialized, with the state picking up the tab of ensuring subsistence.

The level of welfare benefits usually is manipulated to control the labor force. In periods of high demand for unskilled cheap labor the welfare rolls are trimmed. People are required to accept any employment offered as the condition for the granting of relief. Conversely, in periods of low employment demand, conditions become lax and it becomes considerably easier to get welfare. For example, in many areas of the South of the United States the poor (especially the black poor) have traditionally been able to obtain relief only during the slack season in agriculture. Because the planters needed every hand they could get working for a few dollars a day during the cotton-picking season, relief was virtually unattainable during this time.[1]

State relief is offered only under conditions so degrading and humiliating to the recipients that they are discouraged in every way from accepting it and are given every incentive to seek work instead. Such treatment is necessary to ensure that the masses of the poor are willing to offer their labor power at a low wage to the capitalists. It is essential that welfare not be allowed to undermine work discipline by giving encouragement to those who might elect to quit work because of on-the-job humiliations and attempt to subsist on state-provided welfare. Welfare payments must be so low and given under such humiliating conditions that they will not threaten either the size of the labor pool competing for jobs or the level of wages. If welfare payments are higher than minimal subsistence, many will choose to live on welfare rather than take degrading jobs at the minimum wage. High welfare payments would then force the level of wages up and improve the conditions of labor by giving the most oppressed sections of the working class an alternative to selling their labor power.

Beginning in the 1930s the state encouraged the development of conservative trade unions and the process of collective bargaining. These two factors

---

[1] Piven and Cloward, *Regulating the Poor*.

have integrated the potentially most militant and disruptive sections of the U.S. working class into the corporate system. The passage of the National Labor Relations Act in 1937, after years of preliminary work by upper-class-controlled institutions such as the National Civic Federation and the American Association for Labor Legislation, guaranteed the workers' right to organize and bargain collectively — but, of course, under the overall supervision of the U.S. government. Later amendments to this act — especially the Taft-Hartley Act of 1947 — specified the conditions under which the unions' rights would be guaranteed. One of the most important of these was the prohibition on Communists holding union office — that is, a guarantee that the unions would not be used to upset the status quo. The essence of the new arrangement was that wages were to be increased and job conditions improved through the efforts of the unions, in exchange for which the unions were to act as adjuncts of the labor relations departments of the corporations. The unions were to enforce lengthy and detailed job requirements stipulated in the negotiated work contracts, and also put the lid on disruptions such as sabotage, slow downs, and wildcat strikes. The new state-supported unions have thus become just another business, whose product is the collective sale of labor power at a better price than workers could obtain individually. Today, the unions' major social functions are to discipline the labor force and prevent radical movements from emerging in the working class. Working-class upheavals are generally inhibited by the unions, who either repress them outright by encouraging the firing of malcontents and the suppression of wildcat strikes, work refusals, and other acts that violate contracts, or by simply organizing workers who are becoming militant, thereby channeling their frustrations and general discontent into demands for more pay.[2]

The government has a well-developed procedure for arbitrating and resolving labor disputes to prevent the disruption of the economy and the development of radical working-class movements. A complex and elaborate system of labor law and labor courts exists to resolve these disputes in a manner having the intended effect. Such institutions operate very slowly and require adherence to stultifying bureaucratic requirements. As a result the outbursts of working-class militancy that often occur spontaneously in response to one or another outrage are defused and eventually channeled harmlessly into another 40 or 50 cents an hour. State support of trade unions has been the quicksand of working-class militancy.

The government also regulates the economy so as to keep wages down, a plentiful labor supply available to the corporations, and, consequently, profits up. In times of very low unemployment rates, the absence of unemployed workers begging for work reduces the pressure on the workers who have employment. The employed thus can confidently demand higher wages under the threat of strikes or individual quitting. Under these conditions expansion of the number of workers working for a firm must largely come through inducing the workers already employed by someone else to quit and take a new job. This can normally be done only by offering significantly more money. The result of this process is that wages rise rapidly when unemployment is low.

[2] See Domhoff, *The Higher Circles*, p. 218ff. and Aronowitz, *False Promises*, chapter 4.

Consequently, the government is obliged to ensure that the rate of unemployment is high enough to keep wages down. Large numbers of unemployed mean that there are large numbers of workers willing to work for less than what many of the currently employed are getting. Such people seeking work apply pressure on the higher-paid workers, who therefore find it impossible to secure pay increases or better jobs. As a result of the surplus of labor, wages decline. The government usually articulates the problem of rising wages and declining profits as one of "inflation" and then proceeds to implement policies to "slow down the rate of inflation." These policies are designed, however, to increase the number of unemployed, thereby increasing the downward pressure on wages and the upward pressure on profits. One of the favorite ways of accomplishing this is by increasing the prime interest rate, thereby making new investment and consumer purchasing on time more difficult. Layoffs in the investment goods and durable consumer goods industries follow, as does a rise in the rate of unemployment. Another favorite means used to reduce wages is cutting back on governmental spending and increasing taxes, thereby reducing the demand for both production and consumer goods in the economy while again producing the layoffs that cause downward pressure on wages.

In addition to using unemployment to keep a large and relatively low-paid and disciplined labor force available for the corporations, the state also accomplishes this goal in two other ways: (1) by putting legal controls on wages, discouraging strikes and wage settlements that promise any significant improvement in the workers' actual wages, and training workers in those skills held by the best-paid workers to lower wages in these occupations; and (2) by encouraging and regulating massive immigration (permanent or temporary) of laborers from the poorer, more rural areas of the world to serve as a cheap and plentiful labor force.

In the history of industrial capitalism in the United States the major sources of such immigrants have been in turn the farms of the Northeast (in the early years of the nineteenth century), the Irish (in the mid-nineteenth century), Eastern and Southern Europeans (in the late nineteenth and early twentieth centuries), the blacks and poor whites from the South (from 1914 to the 1960s), and Latin Americans (since the 1960s). Each group in turn has moved into the most menial and low-paying occupations. Industrial capitalism in Europe has experienced a similar phenomenon. In the pre-World War I period there were massive population shifts from rural areas such as Ireland, Southern Italy, and Poland to the industrial areas of England, Northern Italy, Northern France, and Western Germany. Since World War II, the migration pattern in Europe has been from Portugal, Spain, Southern Italy, Greece, Turkey, and North Africa to France, Germany, and the other developed capitalist countries of Northwestern Europe. And for the British, it has been from India and the West Indies to England. The permanent and temporary migrations of workers have been facilitated and managed by the capitalist state to secure plentiful and cheap labor for the corporations.[3] In times of great labor shortage the state imposes few obstacles

---

[3] See Stephen Castes and Godula Kosack, *Immigrant Workers and Class Structure in Western Europe* (London: Oxford University Press, 1973).

on immigration (even legal restrictions are laxly enforced in such periods — for example, the nonenforcement of immigration laws against those who enter the Southwest of the United States from Mexico). Thus in the period between the U.S. Civil War and World War I, European migration to the United States was not only very easy legally, but was encouraged by the U.S. government. Information and propaganda campaigns in the source countries, subsidies for transportation, immigrant worker housing, and a range of welfare programs have been provided to the temporary immigrants from the Mediterranean basin to Northwestern Europe in the post-World War II period. When there is a labor surplus in the host countries, however, legal restrictions on immigrants are created, existing restrictions are more strictly enforced, and the various state programs designed to encourage and promote immigration are curtailed.

The Facilitation of Commerce

The capitalist state provides a wide range of supportive services to capitalist enterprise. Among these are the provision and regulation of money, the guarantee of weights and measures, statistical services, the protection of innovations, the regulation of capital markets, monitoring and reporting on weather conditions, suppression of fraud, governmental maintenance of natural resources for exploitation by the corporations, the guarantee of contracts, and the regulation of credit.

The capitalist state is responsible for the printing and coining of money (an essential condition of trade) and guaranteeing its integrity. It must prevent counterfeiting, ensure that the money is in fact acceptable to the entire domestic population and is convertible into other currencies (by backing it with gold or otherwise ensuring its acceptability), and avoid too rapid inflation (which by undermining contracts and expectations turns people away from paper money and back toward barter or precious metals). A sound currency is a necessary condition for exchange among corporations, the sale of commodities, the credit system, capital markets, and all types of contracts.

The state must maintain and guarantee the standardization of a system of weights and measures for use in exchanging commodities within its territory. Standard weights and measures are necessary for purchases and sales within a capitalist economy.

The modern capitalist state provides a wide variety of statistical services for the corporations. The capitalist state produces and distributes regular statistics on virtually everything imaginable that can be of use for the marketing and labor relations activities of corporations, and for state and private insitutions interested in social control. Detailed statistics are reported on wholesale and retail sales, consumption of durable goods, inventories, disposable income, money supply, construction, manufacturing orders, investment, capacity utilization, use of raw materials, use of various forms of transportation, power and communications, exports and imports, agricultural conditions and production, employment, profits, wages, housing starts and vacancies, labor turnover rates, workers' migration habits, educational and skill levels of the labor force, and so on.

The capitalist state guarantees the right to make profits from innovations. The exclusive right to a new process or invention is guaranteed by the U.S. Constitution itself. The state monitors, reports, and predicts the weather at no cost to private enterprise so that agricultural business, transportation companies (especially airlines and shipping), and other businesses directly affected by weather patterns are able to take appropriate measures in the face of adverse weather conditions. The U.S. state, through the Securities and Exchange Commission, regulates the stock market to facilitate the process of accumulating funds for capital investments and prevent unnecessary obstacles stemming from fraud, mistrust, or excessive speculation from obstructing the obtainment of funds through the stock market. It generally guards against blatant use of fraud by marginal businesses to maintain a general atmosphere of trust conducive to higher levels of trade (this is one of the functions of the regulatory commissions).

The state (largely the federal government) owns and manages approximately 40 percent of the land in the United States. Most of this land is undeveloped and is used for forests, grazing, and raw material exploitation. The greater part of federally owned and managed land is handled through the Bureau of Land Management of the U.S. Department of the Interior, which leases the land, or rights to the products of the land, to the lumber industry for tree harvesting, to livestock companies for grazing, and to raw material extracting companies for mineral exploitation. The land is also managed to maintain a water supply for business and industry and otherwise encourage the conservation of resources so that they can be exploited in a rational and sustained fashion by business. The government itself explores for raw materials and encourages the use of governmental lands by private business. In the first half of the 1970s the U.S. state has encouraged the energy corporations to exploit petroleum, oil shale, coal, uranium, and other potential sources of cheap energy on federal lands. The private corporations pay only nominal sums for the rights to exploit public lands.

The capitalist state, like states in many types of societies that have money markets, guarantees orderly credit markets. This entails guarding against excessive devaluation of the currency (which hinders lending because of the insecurity of not knowing how much of a loan and interest will actually be returned to creditors). It also entails governmental enforcement through civil and, when necessary, criminal proceedings of contracts, the regulation of banks and other lending institutions (to guard against fraud and other obstacles to orderly credit), and the regulation of interest rates and governmental guarantees on private loans (to provide sufficient credit to facilitate demand).

Ensuring Sufficient Buying Power in the Economy

The state in monopoly capitalist societies must counteract the tendency for monopoly capitalism to sink into permanent economic stagnation. This tendency to stagnate is due to corporations not paying sufficient wages to their workers to allow them to buy back from the corporations all the goods they are producing.

The attempt of the corporations to make huge profits tends to be frustrated by the fact that profit maximization requires wages to be as low and prices as high as possible. As monopolies consolidate their position in more sectors of the economy, and as fewer firms dominate the economy, monopoly power is strengthened. The corporations' ability to raise prices while resisting real wage increases grows. With it necessarily grows the tendency toward underconsumption.

The state must counter the economic effect of this tendency toward stagnation by stimulating the economy to counteract the effect of the private corporations trying to maximize their profits. The state can do this by stimulating private consumption beyond the point justified by rises in wages through encouraging a rapidly rising debt (which is done by implementing easy credit policies, such as low interest rates and federal loans and loan guarantees), and through heavy state spending to take up the slack in the economy — that is, through buying up what the working people do not have sufficient money to buy.[4]

The lesson learned by the corporate capitalist class during World War II was that only massive governmental spending could pull the economy out of extended depression. Policies based on this lesson (formulated by groups such as the Business Council and the Committee for Economic Development) guided the U.S. state in the postwar years. The government was given the responsibility for buying those goods the corporations would otherwise not be able to sell at a profit. It makes little difference what the government actually spends its money on in combating stagnation just as long as it increases its expenditures commensurate with growing stagnation. While all types of expenditures are equally good for simply creating enough buying power, all types are *not* equally effective in promoting a rapid rate of growth.[5] The realities of capitalist society dictate that the state must use its massive expenditures to support, not undermine, corporate profit making. Thus the state cannot spend money in ways that undermine the stability of the class structure, nor can it invest in projects that lower rents or profits, nor can it engage in enterprises that make profits for the state (thereby depriving private businesses of opportunities for profit making). Table 9—1 illustrates the rather rapid tendency for governmental expenditure to rise as a percentage of the GNP. This figure stood around 7 to 8 percent in 1902, 20.7 percent in 1938, 30.0 percent in 1960, and at 33.4 percent in 1973.

Most categories of governmental spending have increased considerably during this period; but some have increased more rapidly than others (see table 9—2).

Before the 1930s the greatest share of governmental expenditures was

---

[4] See Paul Baran and Paul Sweezy, *Monopoly Capital* (New York: Monthly Review Press, 1966), chapters 6 and 7; and Victor Perlo, *The Unstable Economy* (New York: International Publishers, 1973), chapter 9.

[5] See, for example, Albert Szymanski, "Military Spending and Economic Stagnation," *American Journal of Sociology* 79, no. 1 (July 1973): 1—14; Seymour Melman, *Our Depleted Society* (New York: Holt, Rinehart and Winston, 1965), and *The Permanent War Economy* (New York: Simon & Schuster, 1974); and Bruce Russett, "Who Pays for Defense," *American Political Science Review* 63, no. 2 (June 1969): 412—426.

Table 9-1 Local, State, and Federal Expenditures as a Percentage of U.S. GNP

1902	8%
1913	8
1927	11.7
1938	20.7
1950	24.7
1955	27.8
1960	30.0
1965	30.0
1970	34.0
1973	33.4

Source: U.S. Department of Commerce, *The Statistical Abstract of the United States*, 1975, pp. 253, 381; U.S. Department of Commerce, *Historical Statistics of the United States*, 1960, pp. 139, 723.

Table 9-2 The Major Components of U.S. Governmental Spending (Federal, State, and Local)

	Total Government Spending (billions of dollars)	Military and International Affairs as Percentage of		Social Expenditures as Percentage of[a]		Infrastructure Expenditures as Percentage of[b]	
		State Expenditures	GNP	State Expenditures	GNP	State Expenditures	GNP
1902	$ 1.7	9.9%	0.7%	19.6%	1.4%	35.1%	2.4%
1913	3.2	7.8	0.6	23.6	1.9	38.3	3.1
1922	9.3	9.4	1.2	24.6	3.1	34.7	4.4
1932	12.4	5.8	1.2	28.3	6.0	31.9	6.8
1938	17.7	5.9	1.2	38.4	7.7	27.6	5.5
1950	70.3	26.1	6.4	33.0	8.2	16.7	4.1
1960	151.3	33.9	10.2	31.5	9.5	15.6	4.7
1971	369.4	23.6	8.3	43.7	15.3	14.3	5.0

Source: U.S. Department of Commerce, *Historical Statistics of the United States*, 1960, p. 723; U.S. Department of Commerce, *The Statistical Abstract of the United States*, 1973, p. 414.

[a] Education, public welfare, social insurance, hospitals, health, and housing.
[b] Post office, space, highways, other transportation, police, fire, sanitation, and utilities.

allocated to the economic infrastructure necessary for profitable business operations. The state concentrated on ensuring that the transportation and communication systems of the country were in such shape that commerce would be facilitated — for example, it took care of the roads, delivered the mail, and subsidized the railways, canals, and the early airlines. It protected private property against crime and fire, provided, when necessary, basic sanitation services (public sewers and garbage collection), and provided public utilities (such as electricity and water) when private enterprises were unable to do it cheaply and profitably. While the state has continued to be deeply involved in providing such infrastructure to the corporations, such activities have shown no significant tendency to rise as a percentage of the GNP since World War I.

Military spending

What clearly made the difference between the Great Depression of the 1930s and the relative prosperity of the post-World War II years was military expenditures. As a percentage of all governmental budgets, it rose from 6 percent in the 1930s to around 30 percent during most of the 1950s and 1960s before declining significantly in the 1970s. As a percentage of the GNP, it increased from a little over 1 percent in the 1930s to around 10 percent during most of the 1960s. Social expenditures increased from around 7 to 8 percent of the GNP in the late 1930s to around 8 to 10 percent in the 1950s and early 1960s, while infrastructure expenditures as a percentage of the GNP decreased from the 1930s to the 1950s. Clearly, then, military spending, which increased its impact on the GNP by a factor of about seven to eight times from the 1930s to the 1950s, made the difference between economic stagnation and prosperity within this time period. Most of the heavy new involvement of the state in the economy in the immediate postwar years was in the form of military purchases from the corporations and military salaries. The great addition to buying power caused by military spending allowed the corporations to sell very profitably the goods they otherwise would not have been able to sell because of endemic underconsumption.

In 1975 the military spent $14.8 billion for the procurement of weapons, $8.7 billion for research and development of weapon systems, and $25.7 billion for the operation and maintenance of weapon systems. It spent $1.6 billion for military assistance (mostly in the form of weapons) to other countries. In addition, it spent $25.0 billion for the salaries and pensions of military personnel, and $2.6 billion for construction.[6] The military thus plays an enormously important role in the U.S. economy by encouraging capital accumulation and realizing the profits of the giant corporations.

In 1968 twenty-five corporations provided 45 percent of all military equipment purchased by the U.S. government and one-hundred corporations provided 67 percent.[7] There is considerable stability among these top contractors; eighteen of the top twenty-five military contractors in 1958 were also among the top twenty-five contractors in 1967.[8]

Profits are especially high among war contractors because of the system of cost-plus contracting (which adds on a predetermined profit rate to whatever the padded costs of production are for the corporations). It is standard practice to pad the costs attributable to governmental production by charging salaries, rents, royalties, and other payments that the corporations would have to make even if they did not have governmental contracts for the production of military hardware.

[6] U. S. Department of Commerce, *Statistical Abstract of the United States*, 1975, p. 316.
[7] Adam Yarmolinsky, *The Military Establishment* (New York: Harper & Row, 1971), p. 249.
[8] Ibid., p. 251.

The system of subcontracting also allows especially high profits to be made, since each subcontractor adds on a predetermined profit rate above his padded costs, which consequently appears as part of the "costs" of the prime contractors on which they add *their* profit. Since the Department of Defense is not a profit-making operation, and since many of the sales agreements are made between retired officers in industry and their still active cohorts in the military (many of whom will be looking for plush jobs with private corporations upon retirement, and who are thus very interested in creating good feelings in private industry), there is a strong tendency to allow private corporations to obtain highly profitable contracts.

Why was the infusion of funds into the economy during the immediate post-World War II period by the government mostly in military expenditures? First, it was the immense military expenditures of World War II that actually got the United States out of the depression. Also, the corporate ruling class had observed that the Nazis had brought Germany out of the depression during the mid-1930s through massive peacetime military expenditures. Since the Nazis proved that military spending could restore full employment, it was decided that the United States would continue massive peacetime military spending after the war to ensure prosperity. Military spending, of course, also has had additional advantages. Most military orders went to the very largest corporations and were placed on terms that guaranteed a high profit rate (through cost-plus contracting). Thus the very largest corporations made immense profits. The uses of the military were also of great importance to the corporations. Whereas before World War II the United States was content to protect U.S. business interests in Latin America and the Pacific, after the war the United States attempted to establish the hegemony of U.S. business throughout the world. Not only did it adopt a policy of protecting U.S. interests (as it did before the war), but it now insisted on the primacy of U.S. economic interests over those of all other countries, including the formerly hegemonic economic power, Great Britain, as well as the strong latecomers, Germany and Japan. U.S. military hegemony in the world became the best guarantee of the profitability of U.S. overseas investments, the security of cheap raw materials, and massive U.S. exports. In sum, heavy military spending greatly benefited the giant corporations in a number of ways, both in their domestic and international operations.

The gargantuan military expenses of the U.S. state have also been a product of the fact that corporations are reluctant to support a large expansion of governmental expenditures into fields that tend to undermine profit-making opportunities or the class structure.[9] The financial institutions that hold household and apartment building mortgages, together with the companies that own apartment complexes, make money only because of high rents. If the government were to create subsidized public housing on such a scale as to adequately answer the need for cheap, quality housing, the low rents available in publicly owned units would

---

[9] For a discussion of the barriers to public spending, see Baran and Sweezy, *Monopoly Capital*, chapter 6.

depress the rents of privately owned units, and hence the market value of all rental properties. This would deprive the home-owning and mortgage-holding companies not only of their high rents and mortgage payments, but also of a large part of the value of their capital investment. The banks and real estate interests therefore strongly oppose any significant involvement of the state in massive public housing. The private power companies are opposed to public power because, being sold more cheaply (since there is no need to add on a profit, and larger scale coordinated production is more efficient), it would drive private power companies out of business.

The amount of money that can be channeled into education is limited by the need to train three-fourths of the population for menial nonthinking labor such as manual, service, sales, and low-level office work. The schools attended by most working-class people must then be of sufficiently low quality to prevent the children of these classes from developing sufficient autonomy, enthusiasm, and ambition to become unsuited for such work. The state could never make quality college education a free and guaranteed right as it does with primary and secondary education. To do so would create the expectation in most working-class youth that they could be professionals. They would then be spoiled as menial laborers. Quality education must be limited to the minority for which the corporations hold out the relatively creative professional and managerial jobs. Thus education could not serve as a sufficient outlet for the money the government had to spend to keep the economy operating profitably.

Money provided as welfare (unemployment, disability, old age, and all other forms of aid to the poor and needy) must be limited in order not to undermine the material incentives for the working class to take low-paying menial jobs. If the government were to significantly expand welfare payments, the viability of wage labor would be threatened, since workers would then have the option of whether to sell their labor power.

Even though the United States has relatively poor levels of infant mortality and child and adult health, the government was blocked in the post-World War II period from financing quality medical care for all by the vested interests of the American Medical Association (AMA) and the private drug, hospital, and medical equipment industries with which it is integrated, all of whose income would be undermined by free, quality medical care. The AMA even goes so far as to spend large sums of money to lobby Congress *not* to give aid to medical schools and *not* to provide free medical care to those who need it.

There have been blocks, such as those described above, to virtually every form of nonmilitary governmental spending. The vested interests opposing any given measure would not normally be sufficient to prevent the government from initiating massive spending in an area were it not for upper-class solidarity. All segments of the capitalist class (and their allies in the petty bourgeoisie) in the immediate post-World War II period joined together to oppose massive governmental spending in any area that threatened the profit-making potential of any segment of the capitalist class.

The major exception to the obstacles to governmental spending has been projects that do not compete with private enterprise or undermine the class structure and that provide de facto subsidies to profit-making corporations. The military met these conditions admirably. Spending on highways and space also met these conditions, although these two outlets cannot approach that of the military in importance (because patriotism cannot be used in the same fashion to overcome public resistance to the taxation necessary to implement these policies, and because the possibilities for spending are in fact much more limited in these areas). In all three areas there is no competition with private enterprise. None of the three undermines the class structure or the incentives for the working class to work. All three imply large and extremely profitable purchases from the large corporations. The aerospace and electronics industries, plus large segments of other major industries, secure a very high proportion of their profits from military and space contracts and spending. The petroleum, automobile, glass, rubber, tire, steel, concrete, and construction industries derive a considerable profit from governmental spending on highways. Without the superhighways, people would turn to mass transit and away from the private automobile. Not only would the automobile industry then lose most of its profits, but the suppliers of that industry (steel, rubber, and glass) as well as those supplying fuel for the automobile would also lose immensely. This, incidentally, is the reason why these groups (and thus the entire capitalist class) have resisted massive public spending for cheap and efficient mass transit.[10]

Social expenditures and capital accumulation

In spite of the obstacles to increases in social spending and the encouragement of military, highway, and space spending, these items have been decreasing in overall importance in the governmental budget since the late 1950s. In the immediate postwar period, they were the major factors preventing stagnation. But the pressures for expanded social spending have resulted in a reversal of the relative roles of the two types of spending. In 1960 the total of military, space, and highway expenditures represented 41 percent of all governmental expenses, while the total of education, welfare, social insurance, public health, and housing expenditures represented 32 percent. But in 1971, military, space, and highways accounted for 30 percent of all governmental expenses, while education, welfare, social insurance, public health, and housing represented 44 percent — a clear reversal in primacy (see table 9–3).

The relative reversal of the roles of social and military expenditures can be seen in table 9–4, which shows the trends in the ratio of federal social expenditures to federal military expenditures.

There have been two reasons for the inexorable expansion of social spending and the relative contraction of military spending even against the barriers represented by vested interests. First, to maintain the legitimacy of capitalist institutions and the hegemony of the capitalist class, it has been necessary to spend

---

[10] For a discussion of the role of highway and space spending, see Baran and Sweezy, *Monopoly Capital*, chapter 6.

Table 9-3 U.S. Governmental Expenditures (All Levels) by Function (*Percentage Distribution*)

	1960	1971
Military, veterans, and international affairs	33.9%	23.6%
Public welfare and social insurance	14.6	21.2
Education	12.8	17.3
Interest on the public debt	6.1	5.9
Highways	6.3	5.0
Natural resources and parks	6.1	4.3
Hospital and health	3.4	4.0
Utilities	3.4	2.8
Postal service	2.4	2.4
General administration	1.9	1.9
Police	1.3	1.5
Housing	0.7	1.2
Sanitation	1.1	1.1
Space	0.3	0.9
Fire	0.7	0.6
Other	4.8	6.2
Total	100	100

Source: U.S. Department of Commerce, *Statistical Abstract of the United States*, 1973, p. 414.

Table 9-4 The Ratio of Total U.S. Federal Social Expenditures to Total Military Expenditures, 1960-1975[a]

1975	1.79
1974	1.56
1973	1.46
1972	1.26
1971	1.08
1970	0.85
1969	0.73
1968	0.66
1965	0.64
1960	0.45

Source: Computed from data in U.S. Department of Commerce, *The Statistical Abstract of the United States*, 1975, pp. 226, 253.

[a] The ratio is the sum of federal expenditures for community and regional development; education, manpower, and social services; and health and income security divided by expenditures for national defense.

more to satisfy the demands of the upper middle-, working-, and underclasses to prevent the transformation of their discontent into opposition to the system. Consequently, subsidies to small-business people and farmers have had to be maintained, while welfare for the poor and social benefits (such as free medicine) for the working class have had to be increasingly expanded. The cost of preventing the rise of oppositional movements within the framework of formally democratic institutions increases.

Second, conditions in the world market are forcing the U.S. corporations to trim costs wherever they can to maintain the international competitive position of U.S. products (both as exports and against foreign products within the United States), and are forcing the U.S. government to cut back on military expenditures. The rapid postwar recovery of Japan and Germany and the competition from these and the other advanced capitalist countries in the world market have driven the United States from the preeminent economic position it occupied in the 1950s. The tremendous military expenses of the United States over the postwar period have had serious negative consequences for the rate of growth of the economy — that is, in Marxist terms, the uses of military spending to preserve economic prosperity has been inherently self-contradictory. A number of studies have shown that military spending causes a slowdown in the rate of economic growth.[11] To maintain its position as the strongest military power in the world, the United States has had to channel not only about 10 percent of its GNP into nonproductive military uses, but also has had to channel a far higher percentage of its scientists, research laboratories, and most advanced industrial sectors to such uses. The development of military technology became the leading edge of the U.S. economy, whereas the development of productive technologies became the leading edge of the United States's competitors. Since military technology has only minimal spin-offs for increasing productivity and hence promoting economic growth, the United States fell increasingly behind West Germany and Japan and the other leading capitalist economies in the world market. As a consequence, state support has had to shift from emphasizing military to emphasizing social expenditures.

To produce quality goods as cheaply as its competitors, U.S. capital has turned to the U.S. state for the subsidization of research and development, training of its labor force, supplements to wages (thereby allowing take-home pay to be reduced), and other forms of direct and indirect subsidies, thereby allowing it to remain competitive while making considerable profit. The demands of the world market thus have forced the corporations to socialize their wage and operating costs as much as possible.[12] This requirement is increasingly overriding the forces predominant in the first two postwar decades that successfully blocked large-scale governmental subsidization during that period.

Massive governmental grants for basic and applied research (spin-offs from the government-financed space, military, and atomic energy programs as well as the traditional research, development, and educational program in agriculture and marketing) have socialized most of the costs of the research and development of

[11] See Szymanski, "Military Spending and Economic Stagnation"; Melman, *Our Depleted Society*, and *The Permanent War Economy*; and Russett, "Who Pays for Defense?"

[12] For a discussion of the growing tendency of the state to subsidize the wage and operating costs of the corporations, see the excellent discussion in O'Connor, *The Fiscal Crisis of the State*.

profit-making innovations. The state has become vitally concerned with increasing the productivity of the large corporations. In 1975 the federal government funded 53 percent of all research and development projects (including those in private industries and universities) in the United States. In comparison, private industry financed only 43 percent of the total.[13] The role of federally funded research and development has been expanding in the U.S. economy. In 1955 it represented 0.88 percent of the GNP; in 1971, 1.30 percent.[14]

In addition to subsidizing research and development, the government has socialized a large share of the wages of corporate employees through expanded social consumption. The state has stepped up subsidies to wages in the form of expanded health care, aid to basic and college education, subsidized mass transit, childcare for workers, and expanded social security for the retired, sick, disabled, and unemployed.[15] The expanded role of the government in these areas means that the working class can obtain the same standard of living with reduced personal wages, since more of what once was purchased individually is now provided by the state. Workers are partially relieved from having to save money for retirement, sickness, unemployment, and to spend large sums on transportation to and from work, and on medical care and education.

Consequently, the private corporations are relieved from the considerable and increasing burden of wage increases. Note that in the period 1965 to 1976, the actual take-home wages of industrial workers declined. This effected an immense savings in wages to the corporations that has increased the profits available to them for reinvestment in modern technology and has allowed them to reduce their prices in the international market to remain competitive. In 1960 wage subsidies by U.S. governmental units totalled 11 percent of all wages and salaries; in 1973, 19 percent. In 1973 the total amount of the wage subsidy (which includes all governmental expenditures on education, health, housing, and welfare) came to almost $130 billion, whereas in 1960 it was about $30 billion. The greatest increases over this period have been in health care and retirement programs.[16]

Wage subsidies thus seem to play a significantly greater role than governmental support for research and development in reducing corporate costs. Note that wage subsidies are rather rapidly increasing, whereas governmental funding of research and development, after a very rapid growth during the late 1950s and early 1960s, has tapered off.

Infrastructure expenditures

State expenditures for infrastructure — power, communications, transportation — for the corporations continue to play a major role. The U.S. government is deeply

---

[13] *The Statistical Abstract of the United States*, 1975, p. 548.

[14] Ibid., pp. 380 and 548.

[15] For a discussion of the increasing role of the capitalist state in subsidizing wages, see O'Connor, *The Fiscal Crisis of the State*, chapter 6.

[16] *The Statistical Abstract of the United States*, 1975, pp. 253, 360, 366.

involved in providing the linkages among, and basic services for, the corporations when private corporations find it unprofitable to do so. The state produces and distributes approximately 25 percent of the electrical energy produced in the United States. In addition to many locally owned and operated electric power facilities, the federal government operates the Tennessee Valley Authority, the Columbia and Colorado Rivers' power-producing facilities, and a number of other facilities. It also subsidizes electric power through the Rural Electrification Commission. The federal government has a legal monopoly on production and control of atomic fuels. The state builds and operates the highways, and operates part of the mass transit system (most of the intracity buses and subways, and almost all of the intercity railroad passenger traffic). It also builds and operates the airports, canals, and lighthouses, and provides other aids to water transportation, including the building and supervision of port facilities, government-owned shipyards, and the training of merchant seamen at governmental expense. It also provides operating and construction subsidies for merchant ships. Through the Army's Corps of Engineers and other agencies, the government controls flooding, makes the rivers navigable, and provides for irrigation. In 1973 the federal government spent $1.7 billion to operate airports and subsidize airline companies, and about $0.8 billion to assist the shipping industry.[17] The U.S. government has a virtual monopoly on postal communications and is the major shipper of small packages. In 1974 the U.S. postal service employed 710,000 workers, spent $11.3 billion, and delivered 90 billion pieces of mail, making it one of the largest corporations in the country.[18]

It should be noted, of course, that state ownership of the highways, post office, and electrical power plants also benefits the working people, and that the state would also own these institutions in a socialist society. But to understand why the state is involved in these activities (and not in running the computer or aircraft industries), how it historically came to be involved, and the ways these industries are run, one must understand that in capitalist society they serve primarily as infrastructure (or supportive services) for the private corporations, and only incidentally serve the interests of working people. For example, highways are more likely to get state support than mass transit (which would more effectively serve the interests of the people) because there are more private profit opportunities in highways. Moreover, highways are more likely to be built from the sources of raw materials and factories to industrial and consumer markets and from working-class neighborhoods to factories than from areas of population concentration to recreation areas.

Government support of credit

The government, in addition to expediting capital accumulation in the monopoly sector by spending vast sums, also expedites capital accumulation and maintains

---

[17] *The Budget of the United States*, 1974, p. 107.
[18] U.S. Department of Commerce, *Statistical Abstract of the United States*, 1973, pp. 511, 512.

buying power in the economy by facilitating the expansion of credit. One way to counteract underconsumption is for the government to facilitate buying on the installment plan. The federal government backs home mortgages and loans to cooperatives, businesses, and students. This allows credit to be extended to those who otherwise might not receive it (since the government promises to pick up the tab if a default occurs) and hence results in the expansion of purchasing power.

The federal debt itself is used as collateral on which banks can make loans (thus greatly expanding the basis on which private credit can be extended). Managed contraction and expansion of the outstanding federal debt, together with restrictions on the proportion of a bank's outstanding loans that must be kept as collateral, make credit easier or tighter as the state desires. The principal institution through which the U.S. state controls credit is the Federal Reserve Board (and the Federal Reserve Banking System through which it operates). In addition to directly guaranteeing loans, being an immense debtor itself, and manipulating the interest rate, the capitalist state encourages the expansion of debt through truth-in-lending laws and antiusury legislation (both of which encourage the expansion of debt through increasing consumer confidence), regulation of the credit industry, federal guarantees on bank deposits, and restrictions on the use of credit to speculate on the stock market.

The large governmental debt results in gigantic interest payments accruing to the capitalists. In 1973 interest on the state debt amounted to $25.1 billion, a sum equal to two-thirds of the total of all corporate income taxes for that year and about one-third of all after-tax corporate profits.[19] The manipulation of the federal debt (the buying and selling by the government of its own debt notes) also allows the government to influence greatly the interest rate in the economy and thus to influence the level of investments and savings.

The debt of the U.S. state (all levels of government) increases every year (it was $486 billion in 1950, and $2,777 billion in 1974). Since the end of World War II, it has risen slightly as a percentage of the GNP. It represented 171 percent of the GNP in 1950, and 199 percent in 1974.[20] Total private debt (that of corporations, individual mortgages, and consumer and other individual debt) increased in absolute terms from $246 billion in 1950 to $2,134 billion in 1974. In the period 1970 to 1974, the governmental debt increased by about $225 billion a year, while the private debt increased by about $190 billion.[21] Further, by guaranteeing private loans and implementing other measures to expand the credit structure, the U.S. state is largely responsible for the expansion in private credit.

A large part of governmental expenses are financed by taxing the working class. Thus, although purchasing power is added to the economy through state spending, it is subtracted by taxes decreasing the disposable income of the working

---

[19] U.S. Department of Commerce, *Statistical Abstract of the United States*, 1974, pp. 226, 253, 504.
[20] Ibid., p. 473.
[21] Idem.

class. However, a large share of what the government spends in fact represents a real addition to spending power — specifically the $225 billion a year financed by borrowing, and that spending financed by taxes actually incident on the profits and savings of the rich. It has been estimated that only about *one-half* of governmental expenditures can be considered a genuine addition to mass purchasing power.[22] Because the total level of governmental spending on all levels was about $320 billion in 1972, the impact of governmental spending in counteracting underconsumption is approximately equal to two-thirds of the effect of expanding credit. Both mechanisms by which the state encourages the continuation of the process of capital accumulation thus seem to be of about equal importance.

Countercyclical Policies

In addition to preventing long-term economic stagnation, the capitalist state since the 1930s has *attempted* (not always successfully) to stabilize the economic cycles endemic to capitalism — that is, to iron out or dampen the natural tendencies for periods of high investment, low unemployment, rapid rates of inflation, and high rates of growth to alternate with periods of low investment, high unemployment, low inflation, and low rates of growth. During periods of recession the state's monetary and fiscal policies are geared to increasing the supply of money by lowering interest rates (by decreasing legal bank reserve requirements, purchasing governmental securities to increase their price, and lowering the interest rate by which banks borrow from each other), increasing the volume of federal loans and loan guarantees, and increasing federal spending while reducing taxes. The net result of these policies is to increase purchasing power and hence reduce unemployment, increase investment, and increase the rate of growth. In periods of high inflation caused by too much demand for workers, raw materials, and credit for investment goods (which pressure wages and prices to rise rapidly), the state responds by reducing the demand for workers, raw materials, and credit by increasing taxes, decreasing governmental expenditures, decreasing the volume of federal loans and loan guarantees, and increasing interest rates (by increasing legal bank reserve requirements, selling governmental securities to depress their price, and increasing the rate by which banks must borrow money from each other). The purpose of following these "countercyclical" policies is to try to put the rate of inflation in balance with the rate of growth, thus avoiding both types of problems.

However, beginning in the early 1970s the Keynesian mechanisms that had been used rather successfully since the end of World War II to keep the United States (and the other capitalist economies) in balance began breaking down. Rapid inflation began occurring together with high unemployment and low rates of growth, thus negating Keynesian solutions. The capitalist state was unable to successfully deal with this "stagflation," since the traditional bromide for inflation

---

[22] Perlo, *The Unstable Economy*, Appendix II.

(that is, high rates of unemployment) contradicted the traditional bromide for high unemployment (that is, governmental stimulation of purchasing power). The capitalist state thus has to find more effective means by which to successfully "fine tune" the economy.

Direct and Indirect Subsidization of Private Corporations

There are several other means by which private enterprise is subsidized by the state, such as direct emergency loans to businesses that cannot otherwise obtain cheap credit. For example, in 1971 the Lockheed Aircraft Corporation applied to Congress for special legislation lending it $250 million dollars. The request was granted. Other corporations that are governmental contractors ask for and receive revisions in contracts to make more money than the original contracts called for, thereby gaining de facto subsidies. During both world wars and during the immediate post-World War II period, the U.S. government built factories and other facilities in such key sectors as steel, rubber, munitions, aerospace, and shipbuilding which it either sold at bargain-basement prices or continues to lease at a nominal sum to private enterprise, or in some cases operates itself to provide the corporations with cheap supplies and services. In 1954 the Department of Defense owned forty-eight shipyards employing 51 percent of all U.S. shipyard workers. In 1967, 1,900 different companies were using 209,598 pieces of federally owned industrial production equipment valued at over $2.5 billion.[23]

The U.S. state through the post-World War II period maintained vast stockpiles of a wide range of minerals and other materials labeled strategic commodities. The state bought up vast quantities of various materials to subsidize the raw material producers in times of slack international demand. Governmental purchases and inventory management of these strategic stockpiles have been designed normally to keep the market prices of these commodities as high as possible — for example, the government will not sell off a commodity in times of depressed markets. When great shortages and consequently skyrocketing prices for a raw material occurred, the government sold more than it bought of the scarce material. In the late 1960s and early 1970s, the value of the U.S. government raw material stockpile was approximately the same as the total value of all minerals (metals and nonmetals) mined in that year.[24] Clearly, then, the government's manipulation of its stockpiles has had a considerable influence on raw material markets.

The state also heavily subsidizes the agricultural industry. A considerable share of farm subsidies go to middle- and upper middle-class farmers (as a cost of

[23] U.S. Congress, *Hearings before the Joint Economic Committee; Economy in Government Procurement and Property Management*, 90th Cong., 1st sess., 1967.
[24] See Perlo, *The Empire of High Finance*, p. 264; and Percey W. Bidwell, *Raw Materials: A Study of American Policy* (New York: Harper and Brothers, 1958).

maintaining corporate upper-class control of the state in a formally democratic system). Large corporate farms, however, benefit significantly by such programs.[25] The state pays farmers not to grow food (that is, to keep their land idle), thereby decreasing the supply of agricultural goods, which forces their price up. It also purchases large amounts of basic commodities that it distributes overseas or domestically under various giveaway programs (always in such a fashion as not to undermine the markets of private agriculture). Other programs are available for various commodities that can be subsidized under various conditions. The total government payments to farmers in 1972 totaled $4.6 billion, but only $0.9 billion in 1975.[26] This subsidy has acted to constrain supply (by either taking land out of production or products off the market) and increase demand (through governmental purchases), thereby significantly increasing the price the public has to pay for agricultural goods. Because of the rapid growth in U.S. agricultural exports in the mid-1970s, the necessity for federal subsidies has declined drastically (at least for the time being). The governmental policy of keeping the price of agricultural goods high through enormous governmental subsidies secures an additional large indirect subsidy for the farm industry — which comes out of the pockets of working people, who must buy the artificially high-priced subsidized commodities. The commodities that the federal government supports are precisely those in which corporate agriculture has become most consolidated — the basic grains such as wheat, corn, oats, barley, and sorghum; and several other basic commodities such as cotton, tobacco, rice, peanuts, sugar beets, soybeans, and dairy products.

The government also acts to keep domestic prices artificially high by imposing tariffs on cheaper goods produced overseas that compete with goods produced in the United States, thereby enabling U.S. producers to sell their goods at a substantial profit. In general the United States admits duty free into the country raw materials that are in short supply (to encourage their importation and incorporation into U.S. manufactured goods), while imposing restrictive duties on those goods that compete with more expensive U.S. products. In the early 1970s about 60 percent of the goods imported into the United States (by value) were assessed an import tax.[27] Shoes, clothing, and other labor-intensive commodities traditionally have had the highest import duties (labor is much cheaper in Asia, Africa, and Latin America, where these imports increasingly originate). In recent years high duties have been placed on automobiles to guarantee the American market to the four U.S. auto corporations. Without a high tariff on Japanese and European cars, General Motors, Chrysler, and Ford would find it difficult to continue making adequate profits. The U.S. government also restricts the import of specific goods (such as sugar, uranium, and petroleum) into the United States, thereby

---

[25] James T. Bonnen, "The Absence of Knowledge of Distributional Impacts," in Richard Edwards et al., *The Capitalist System* (Englewood Cliffs, N.J.: Prentice-Hall, 1972), p. 240.
[26] *Statistical Abstract of the United States*, 1975, p. 227.
[27] *Statistical Abstract of the United States*, 1975, p. 810.

subsidizing domestic producers by keeping their prices very high. Furthermore, the government has made certain services, such as intra-United States cargo and passenger transportation, the monopoly of U.S. businesses.

The government sets artificially high prices for many commodities by placing legal limits on their production and actually setting their prices. For example, the price of petroleum products traditionally has been kept artificially high, not only by restrictions on their importation, but also through government-enforced restrictions on the amount of oil that can be pumped from the ground in a given month. Traditionally the Texas Railroad Commission, with the collaboration of other governmental units, estimates every month the amount of petroleum that can be sold at the artificially high price desired by the oil industry. Each production unit in the United States is then given a quota that cannot be exceeded legally. Oil is thus kept in short enough supply to force its price up.[28]

Other subsidies to business have included the giveaway of federal lands. Most of the railroads in the midwest and the west were built under an incentive system from the U.S. government that gave them not only the land on which they built the railroads, but also one-half of the land along their tracks. Federal land has also been given away in great quantities to mining interests, petroleum corporations, and land speculators. In the period 1860 to 1900, 90 percent of federally owned land was given away (including that given to small homesteaders).[29]

State-Sanctioned Self-Regulation of the Corporations

The federal regulatory commission was conceived under pressure from the corporations, which wanted to obtain the right to regulate their own industrial conditions. They needed to eliminate the internecine competition among themselves and erratic fluctuations in prices, demand, and profits. They had to develop the capacity to predict future developments in their markets so that they could rationally allocate their resources. They needed protection from the petty bourgeoisie, who were attacking the monopoly corporations for social irresponsibility.

State-sanctioned self-regulation gives the illusion of popular control over the corporations, thereby "cooling out" popular hostility. The logic underlying self-regulation is that it is better to make a high rate of profit over the long term than to attempt to make superprofits in the short term and risk shattering public faith in the capitalist system. Generally, the commissions allow for the rationalization of production and sales in each industry they regulate. Backed by the sanction of the law, the regulatory commissions coordinate corporate activities so that all companies can maximize their profits.[30] The regulatory commissions also act to even

[28] Robert Engler, *The Politics of Oil* (New York: Macmillan, 1961).

[29] Lundberg, *America's Sixty Families*, p. 53.

[30] For a discussion of the functioning of the regulatory commissions, see Gabriel Kolko, *Railroads and Regulation* (New York: Norton, 1970), and *The Triumph of Conser-*

out the rate of profit in the economy. Governmental regulation tends to drive up prices in more competitive markets and to ensure that profits in the markets where one firm has a natural monopoly (for example, telephones and railways) are not excessive to an extent that other corporations would have to pay exorbitant fees for their services.[31] The regulatory commissions thus allow self-regulation of important sectors of the economy, and regulate key sectors in the interests of all the monopoly corporations.

Although the regulatory commissions (such as the Interstate Commerce Commission, the Food and Drug Administration, the Federal Trade Commission, the Federal Aviation Administration, the Federal Communications Commission, the Federal Power Commission, the Federal Insurance Administration, the Federal Maritime Commission, and the Securities and Exchange Commission) are legally administrative agencies of the U.S. government, they function largely as part of the industries they regulate. The private corporations dominate them by controlling appointments to the commissions and providing staff, through official advisory committees and intensive lobbying, and by promises of jobs for retiring commissioners and leading staff people.[32] The governmental commissions reinforce and strengthen the private associations of corporations in each economic sector. They grant them legal powers to supervise, levy taxes, maintain internal courts, and impose sanctions, as well as the power to compel membership.[33]

The regulatory commissions control the airlines, trucking, railroad, shipping, electric power, pipeline, atomic power, petroleum, telephone, telegraph, interstate bus, and parts of the drug, food, retail, and other industries. These commissions also set prices, thus guaranteeing high profits because price competition — and in many cases all forms of competition — among enterprises in the same markets is prohibited. The ICC and the Civil Aeronautics Board establish which carriers can provide what services in given markets, as well as what rates they must charge. Competition is restrained to create artificial monopolies that will keep transportation rates high. In addition to setting high prices and limiting free competition under pain of state sanctions, these commissions mediate disputes among the corporations in each sector of the economy. Disputes about who should have the right to transport or distribute a commodity in an area are resolved by the commission, as are cases of mergers, consolidations, and reallocations of routes and services. Neither consumers nor small businesses have any significant say in how these commissions operate. They are run by, and in the interests of, the large corporations for whom they perform the essential functions of eliminating internecine competition and stabilizing profits at a high level.[34]

---

vatism; and Weinstein, *The Corporate Ideal in the Liberal State 1900-1918*.

[31] See Baran and Sweezy, *Monopoly Capital*, pp. 64-66.

[32] For documentation, see Tuckman, *The Economics of the Rich*, p. 105ff; David Serber, "Regulating Reform," *The Insurgent Sociologist* 5, no. 3 (Spring 1975); Domhoff, *Who Rules America?*, pp. 107-108; and *The New York Times*, September 7, 1975, p. 36.

[33] Kariel, *The Decline of American Pluralism*, chapter 7.

[34] Robert Fellmeth, *The Interstate Commerce Omission* (New York: Grossman, 1970).

Advancing the Overseas Interests of the Corporations

The foreign policy of the major capitalist countries is primarily designed to maximize those profits of its leading corporations that come from their international activities — that is, overseas direct and indirect investments, the obtaining of cheap and secure sources of raw materials, the securing of overseas export markets, and the subsidization of exports through various "foreign aid" programs.

An increasing percentage of the raw materials used by the major U.S. corporations must be imported from overseas. To obtain the competitive edge over Japanese and Western European corporations, the U.S. corporations must obtain the raw materials necessary for their production — not only cheaply, but also under conditions which ensure that they have primary and sustained access to these raw materials. Such preferred access to cheap raw materials can generally be obtained and secured only with the support of the U.S. government. The U.S. government uses economic sanctions, "foreign aid," and threats of military intervention to force the countries of Asia, Africa, and Latin America to allow U.S. raw material corporations to own, or at least dominate, the raw material supplies at their source. Even in areas such as the Middle East, where most of the raw materials (especially petroleum) are destined for Europe and Japan, the U.S. corporations secured a virtual monopoly of ownership and/or distribution, allowing them to make gigantic profits by supying the United States' competitors with oil.

The tendency for the U.S. economy to slip into stagnation and for capital accumulation to wither is combated not only by high levels of governmental spending and support of expanding private debt, but also by U.S. government encouragement and subsidization of corporate overseas exports (exports of their production that they are not able to sell profitably at home). The U.S. state directly subsidizes U.S. exports (as do all the major capitalist countries) through export credits (called "foreign aid") extended to various foreign countries. Virtually every cent of U.S. "foreign aid" is in the form of such export credits. A recipient receives credit with which to obtain the products of U.S. corporations that have been put on a special list of those materials that are currently having difficulties in overseas markets because of foreign competition. The recipients of "foreign aid" must pick from among such commodities. Government funds thus go directly to the major corporations, while the goods go overseas to the countries of Asia, Africa, and Latin America. To receive such aid, moreover, the local countries must agree to follow certain pro-U.S. economic and social policies that typically include the facilitation of U.S. corporations' profit-making opportunities in the local countries — for example, no restrictions on profit repatriation, no favoritism to local businesses over American businesses, discouragement of local industrialization (to prevent competition with U.S.-owned corporations), encouragement of raw material production (to increase supplies for U.S. corporations), low wage policies, and so on.

Although it is in the form of goods and not dollars, such foreign aid must generally be paid back with interest in dollars to the U.S. Treasury. Some "foreign aid" is even given to U.S.-owned corporations operating in the various Third World countries (rather than to the local governments or businesses owned by local citizens).[35] Foreign aid thus does double or triple service for the U.S. corporations. Beyond being a subsidy in the form of guaranteeing corporate exports, it also is used as a club by which to secure further profit-making opportunities in other countries. In 1974 "foreign aid" (which includes all economic and military grants and loans) to Asia, Africa, and Latin America amounted to approximately $8.8 billion. During that year U.S. exports to those countries came to about $14.5 billion.[36] Approximately 60 percent of U.S. exports to these countries thus were paid for by "foreign aid." Throughout the 1950s and 1960s the U.S. government paid for a similarly high percentage of such exports. Much of the remainder of U.S. exports has been a result of either the conditions for receiving "foreign aid" or has consisted of replacement parts for previously bought equipment. Note that in the mid-1970s the proportion of U.S. exports to these regions financed by the U.S. government has declined considerably because of the large funds now available to the oil-exporting countries to purchase U.S. exports. Without "foreign aid," the United States would apparently lose most of its competitive advantage in the export markets of Third World countries.

The major U.S. corporations increase their investments overseas considerably more rapidly than they do in the United States to take advantage both of cheaper labor costs overseas *and* to integrate themselves into foreign markets. The production of U.S. overseas enterprises around 1970 averaged about 30 percent of the U.S. gross domestic product, or about six times U.S. exports. The value of U.S. overseas production is sufficient to rank these investments in the aggregate as the second largest capitalist economy in the world (after the U.S. domestic economy). Although they account for only about 30 percent of the total value of all U.S. direct investments, U.S. investments in Asia, Africa, and Latin America bring in about 50 percent of all overseas earnings and 60 percent of all repatriated profits. The average rate of profit on all types of U.S. investments (including raw material and industrial operations) in the "developing countries" is approximately 15 percent on invested value.[37] In recent years the United States had repatriated about three times more from the Third World countries than it has invested in them.[38] Immense profits are made by using American technology to obtain superior positions in local markets, securing privileged access to rich deposits of raw materials, and exploiting the very cheap labor of Third World workers. But to ensure profitable operations for U.S. corporations, these countries must be subordinated by the U.S. state through its various international economic, military, and cultural

[35] See Harry Magdoff, *The Age of Imperialism* (New York: Monthly Review Press, 1969), chapter 4; and Teresa Hayter, *Aid as Imperialism* (Baltimore: Pelican, 1971).
[36] *The Statistical Abstract of the United States*, 1975, pp. 807, 814.
[37] Ibid., p. 801.
[38] Ibid., p. 802.

programs designed to advance the profit-making possibilities of private U.S. corporations around the world.

To facilitate its trade and promote and protect its investments, the United States maintains a system of embassies, consulates, and trade missions around the world. Such facilities function to advance U.S. business interests overseas. The U.S. government also runs a wide variety of supportive services designed to encourage foreign investment and trade. The U.S. government ensures overseas investments against expropriation, provides market research, facilitates financing, sponsors promotional trade fairs overseas and a wide range of technical services and advisory programs, as well as guarantees that its power will be used against those countries which do not allow themselves to be exploited by the U.S. corporations in ways which those corporations deem appropriate.[39]

The principal use of the U.S. military as well as the State Department is to support the overseas profit-making operations of U.S. corporations. A capitalist country without a strong military to protect and advance its overseas economic interests is helpless at the hands of its international opponents. Great Britain established itself as the leading economic power in the world in the seventeenth, eighteenth, and nineteenth centuries only because, being the leading economic power, it obtained naval hegemony in the world. Its chief competitors, first Spain, then Holland, then France, and then Germany were unable to best it because they failed to smash the British military. The immense profits accruing to British investment and trade interests around the world could not have been maintained without British military superiority. The French upper class in the eighteenth and early nineteenth centuries, and the German upper class in the first half of the twentieth century, attempted to displace Britain and greatly expand their economic interests through use of military force. The Japanese capitalists in the 1930s and 1940s attempted to secure economic hegemony throughout East Asia and the Pacific by military conquest. The United States succeeded in turning back the attempt of the Japanese and Germans in the 1940s, while at the same time dismembering the British empire and emerging as the unquestioned economic and military power in the world. Had German and Japanese or even British military power been superior, then one of these countries would have emerged from World War II as the hegemonic power in the world.

Military superiority is necessary to secure predominance for the capitalist class of a country. The upper class of the United States has been engaging in imperial adventures since the founding of the U.S. state.[40] A consistent imperialist policy was followed in the years before the Civil War under pressure from the slave-owning landlords of the South who desired more territory for the plantation system. A war with Mexico was fought that resulted in the annexation of one-half of Mexico's territory to the United States. The slave lords' designs on Cuba and

[39] See Magdoff, *The Age of Imperialism*.

[40] For a listing of most of the uses of the U.S. military overseas from 1783 to 1968, see *The Congressional Record*, June 23, 1969, pp. 16840–16843; and September 10, 1969, p. 25063.

Central America were frustrated only by their defeat in the Civil War. With the growth of industrial capitalism and the monopoly corporations in the generation after the Civil War, new forces operated on the U.S. state to bring it into a new era of imperialism in Latin America and the Pacific. Economic forces — now springing from the logic of monopoly capitalism rather than from that of the slave system — resulted in a war with Spain which deprived that country of all of its remaining colonies in Latin America (Cuba and Puerto Rico) and the Pacific (the Philippines and Guam). Hawaii and Samoa were annexed around the same time. During this same period the United States began an active policy of intervention in Central America, sending its Marines and Navy periodically to establish and preserve regimes that would do the bidding of the U.S. corporations.

The imperialist ventures of the U.S. government and corporations were largely restricted to northern Latin America and the Pacific until World War II. But in the post-World War II period, with economic and political interests everywhere outside of the Communist countries, the United States defined itself as the policeman of the world. It intervened throughout the world to preserve and advance its newly established hegemonic economic position.

To continue to secure sizable profits from its activities in Asia, Africa, and Latin America, the United States has had to continually intervene against attempts to establish Socialist, Communist, or nationalist regimes. U.S. foreign and military policy stresses the preservation of submissive regimes throughout the world. Nationalists who threaten to expropriate U.S. interests and turn them over to local capitalists are as dangerous as the Socialists and Communists who would turn them over to local workers or the state. All three alternatives threaten the profitability of American corporations, and therefore all are opposed by the U.S. government. The United States has helped overthrow such nationalist regimes as that of Mossadegh in Iran, Arbenz in Guatemala, Borsh in Santo Domingo, and Goulart in Brazil.

The U.S. capitalist state has been the hegemonic military power in the world since 1943. Throughout the 1960s and early 1970s the U.S. government spent roughly twice as much on its military as did *all* the other developed capitalist countries *combined*. In 1973 the United States spent $79 billion, while all other advanced capitalist countries (Canada, Japan, Australia, New Zealand, and the capitalist countries of Europe) spent only $48 billion.[41] U.S. military expenditures in 1973 were equal to 31 percent of the world's military expenditures. All the poor non-Socialist countries of Asia, Africa, and Latin America combined spent a total of $33 billion on their militaries in 1973. In this same year the United States and its allies in the advanced capitalist world spent 1.2 times as much on the military as did the Soviet Union and its military allies. In 1973 the military expenditures of the United States amounted to 6.1 percent of its GNP, compared with approximately the same percentage for the Warsaw Pact countries, and 3.3 percent for the NATO allies of the United States.[42] Except for Israel, the United

---

[41] *The Statistical Abstract of the United States*, 1975, p. 317.
[42] Ibid., pp. 317, 845.

States spends a higher proportion of its GNP on its military than does any other developed capitalist country in the world.

The United States is able to exert its military might in the world in many ways. The least subtle of these is through direct military intervention such as that against Santo Domingo in 1965, when the U.S. military was sent in to prevent the restoration of a democratically elected regime, and the intervention in Vietnam during the 1960s, when 500,000 American troops were used to attempt to suppress a Communist-led insurgency (as it turned out, without success). Under contemporary conditions, direct invasion is only used as a last resort when all else fails. The U.S. ruling class would much rather use the local military to put down opposition to capitalist interests or, failing that, to employ the armies of third countries to do the dirty work of the United States. The use of U.S. troops has the disadvantage of causing domestic opposition to arise in the United States and making U.S. dominance all the more obvious in the Third World. Use of nationals or natives of third countries has the advantage of obscuring U.S. involvement in the eyes of the peoples of the world and defusing domestic opposition to imperialist policies from the U.S. people.

The United States is able to use the militaries of various conservative regimes in Asia, Africa, and Latin America to intercede for U.S. interests because it provides them with most of their technologically advanced weapons, pays for a large share of their procurement and operating expenses, trains their officers, and provides advisers on all levels of the chain of command (especially at the highest levels). From 1950 to 1973 the U.S. government provided approximately $36 billion in arms to other countries and trained 428,476 foreign military personnel in the techniques of modern warfare (232,914 of these in the United States).[43] Since 1960 most of the arms and training have been for the armies of the more conservative regimes of Asia, Africa, and Latin America. In the period 1964 to 1973 the United States (private corporations and the state) supplied 53 percent of *all* arms purchased abroad by the less-developed countries of Asia, Africa, and Latin America.[44] Approximately 60 percent of these arms were paid for by the U.S. government.

The considerable assistance the United States gives to the militaries of Third World countries and the traditional guarantees of total U.S. support against Communist-led insurgencies ingratiates their ruling classes to the U.S. state and secures the conditions for the profitable operation of U.S. corporate interests in their countries. The local officer corps and those segments of the local upper classes who benefit the most from U.S. military programs usually are the most pro–United States. They become especially willing to collaborate with U.S. interests when they are subject to challenge by nationalistic and left-wing forces. The U.S.-organized training programs and their U.S. advisers pressure the

---

[43] U. S. Department of Defense, *Military Assistance and Foreign Military Sales Facts*, April 1974, pp. 11, 18.

[44] U. S. Arms Control and Disarmament Agency, *World Military Expenditures and Arms Trade*, 1963–1973, Washington, D.C., p. 67.

militaries of these countries to intervene against popularly elected governments that attempt to nationalize or otherwise interfere with the profit-making operations of U.S. corporations. The example of the Chilean military's overthrow of the popularly elected regime of Salvador Allende, which was expropriating U.S. business interests along with locally owned wealth, is only one of the most recent and blatant illustrations of the collaboration between the U.S. government and local reactionary forces in overthrowing a popular regime.

The United States or its local comprador regimes do not necessarily have to intervene militarily in countries where U.S. economic interests are threatened. It is often enough that an occasional *actual* intervention intimidates and terrorizes other oppositional movements. If such movements can be convinced that they would be defeated by the military strength of the United States and the mercenary armies of the local reactionary and conservative regimes it controls, demoralization may well set in and the attempt to make revolution never made. This is the logic behind the "domino theory" that was often invoked during the Vietnamese War. A defeat for U.S. imperialist policies in Vietnam, it was said, would result in the unleashing of domestic opposition movements throughout the world. Local nationalist and leftist forces would lose their fear of U.S. military might and attempt to imitate the Vietnamese. Conversely, a defeat for the Vietnamese insurgency, in spite of the NLF's sustained and heroic efforts, would have demoralized the opposition forces throughout Asia, Africa, and Latin America: many believed that if the Vietnamese had been unable to liberate themselves, they would have been unable to do so as well.

The necessity of containing threats to U.S. corporate profitability results in a foreign policy directed not toward a shortsighted defense of the corporate economic interests located in foreign countries, but rather toward the defense of the American imperial system's integrity. Thus the U.S. state will respond to antiimperialist movements anywhere in the world, regardless of whether the United States has any significant investments, markets, or raw material supplies in the area. The world system is defended at its weakest points, not where the U.S. stake is greatest. The U.S. ruling class views the world just as it views the United States. If an insurrection were to cause northern New Mexico to secede from the United States, the ruling class would stop at nothing to suppress it in spite of the fact that this area might (hypothetically) cost the corporations more to maintain in welfare costs than the economic benefit they derive from it. It is not the actual profits gained or lost in New Mexico that would motivate their suppression, but rather the potential repercussions of a successful secession on the rest of the country. Similarly, the United States before 1960 had no significant investments, markets, or raw material supplies in Vietnam. Nevertheless it committed itself totally for a very extensive period to try to prevent either Communists or genuine nationalists from forming a government there. U.S. Vietnam policies were designed not to maintain or secure profit opportunities in that country, but rather to prevent the reverberations of a successful revolution from resonating throughout the Third World and inspiring attempts to destroy the entire informal U.S. empire.

Summary

The most basic and elaborate function of the capitalist state is to guarantee the process of capital accumulation. The capitalist state accomplishes this function in many ways. The state regulates and in part provides a labor force willing and able to work under conditions that guarantee a healthy profit to private enterprise. It provides a wide variety of supportive services to private corporations, including the guarantee of the currency, weights and measures, roads, weather forecasting, navigational aids, communication and transportation aids, and so on. The state subsidizes private enterprise through agricultural programs, tariffs, price controls, and giveaway programs. Self-regulation of the corporations to ensure legal monopolies, high profits, and a dissipation of public hostility is sanctioned by the state. The state both attempts to regulate economic cycles and provide sufficient buying power to prevent the capitalist economy from sinking into economic stagnation. Finally, the state follows aggressive overseas military policies to promote the overseas interests of the giant corporations. The contemporary capitalist economy is absolutely dependent on these various forms of state involvement in the economy. Without support of the state, they would not be able to make a profit.

Many of the functions discussed in this and the previous chapter have their analogues in other types of society. The state in both precapitalist-class societies and in Socialist societies also is involved in training the labor force, promoting the legitimacy of the system, building roads and dams, facilitating the formation and tempering of the ruling-class will, collecting taxes, and so on. However, the type, extent, and mode of state involvement in the economy and society varies greatly among types of societies as a function of the requirements of a given social formation and its ruling class. It is to the specific type, extent, and mode of involvement in monopoly capitalist society that these chapters are addressed.

Contradictions among the functions

The need to satisfy all the five basic functions of the capitalist state puts *conflicting* demands on the state and can well result in the development or aggravation of social crises. It is impossible to realize fully the functions of legitimacy, capital accumulation and profit maximization, preserving capitalist-class rule, raising money to fund the state, and forming and preserving a unified capitalist-class will all at the same time. To maximize one necessarily undermines the maximization of others.

To advance the legitimacy of the state, the myth that the state is run by and in the interest of the people has to be made credible. But the more directly the state serves the interests of the capitalist class by acting to maximize profits and facilitate capital accumulation, the less credible this myth becomes. Similarly, the more the state acts to preserve the relationships of private property (such as facilitating the banks' foreclosures of mortgages during depressions, while harshly punishing those who steal food), the more the class nature of the state becomes obvious. The legitimacy of the state can also be undermined by the enormous and ever-rising share of their incomes people must pay in taxes to finance a state that spends most of its funds aiding the corporations. People are increasingly unwilling to vote for further taxes, thereby discrediting the state which raises taxes against their wishes. Last, the state's ability to formulate a unified capitalist-class will conflicts with the need to maintain legitimacy. Especially in crisis situations, when the people become mobilized, the state cannot easily "cool them out" as well as formulate a unified class will because of the diversity of interests and orientations in the upper class. In crises splits develop and attitudes about state policies polarize in the capitalist class.

The successful performance of the profit-maximizing and capital-accumulation functions can come into conflict with the need to maintain law and order. Maximizing profits can result in unemployment and poverty, which in turn bring drug addiction, burglary, robbery, and a whole range of crimes against property. Realizing the basic economic function can also come into conflict with the need to raise money to finance the state. Since people resist paying an ever increasing proportion of their income to finance the capital accumulation of the private corporations, the state must either finance itself by borrowing (at best only a temporary solution), cut back on its projects, or risk antagonizing the masses by continually raising taxes. Last, the economic function could come into conflict with the need to preserve capitalist-class unity. Given the relatively scarce financial resources at the disposal of the state, conflict among different segments of the capitalist class over the allocation of these resources is almost inevitable. Such conflict over scarce resources makes the development of a unified will difficult.

The need to preserve law and order and capitalist property relations can conflict with the function of raising taxes. If people become impoverished by taxes, or even if they become bitter toward the state because of such tax policies, they can be driven into crime to attempt to maintain their standard of living. At the same time they can become more willing to commit criminal acts against a system that is losing legitimacy in their eyes. Preserving capitalist property relations and law and order may also come into conflict with the function of unifying the capitalist class and developing a unified capitalist-class will. To maintain the system in the face of narrow-minded capitalist interests, the state sometimes must unite with a minority faction of the capitalist class to advance the entire system (see chapter 11). Under these conditions, the state will exacerbate the internal divisions within the capitalist class even while realizing its long-term class interests.

Raising tax money also can conflict with forming a unified capitalist-class will. As taxes rise, some groups will bear more of the tax burden than others, while some will benefit more from the allocation of tax money than others. Even when the state policies formulated serve the long-term interest of the entire capitalist class, the contest over who bears the burden and who benefits can undermine capitalist-class unity.

Although these conflicts among the functions of the capitalist state always exist to one degree or another, they are, of course, not always the primary aspect of the functioning of the capitalist state. Normally, in the absence of serious economic or social crisis the state is able to adequately perform all of its functions simultaneously even while generating minor frictions and problems. However, during crises the contradictions among the functions can become primary as the state becomes unable to perform simultaneously all its functions, and a general political crisis develops — the resolution of which calls for either fascist or military intervention on the one hand *or* a Socialist revolution on the other, if the crisis does not abate by its own logic (see chapters 12 and 13).

Whether a state will be able to work out a viable resolution of the contradictions among its functions during a crisis largely depends on the degree to which capitalist-state policy coincides with the general social interest. The greater this correspondence, the greater the probability of resolving the crisis and restoring social stability. When capitalist-state policy results in rapid economic growth, high levels of employment, rising real wages, the advance and preservation of basic liberties, and the advance of culture and education, the people as well as the capitalist class benefit more than not from these policies and hence give the state their support even when it is run by and for capital. Then again, when capitalist state policy results in unemployment, economic stagnation, no increases in real wages, the undermining of basic liberties, the contraction of education, welfare, and other public services, environmental destruction, and war the realization of capitalist functions comes into conflict with the popular interest. It becomes increasingly difficult to preserve the legitimacy of the system and avoid the development of revolutionary movements among the people. In other words, when there is a conflict between realizing the interests of the capitalist class and satisfying the basic needs of the people, stability is undermined. Only in such periods is a successful revolutionary movement possible.

10

The Mechanisms of Direct Domination of the State by Capital

To guarantee that the state in capitalist society performs its social functions, the state is dominated by capital. Most of the empirical literature available in the English language on capitalist-class domination of the state in the capitalist countries is on the U.S. state. The U.S. state is also the most powerful state in the world. Thus the focus of this discussion is mainly on the domination by capital of the U.S. state.

There are two fundamentally different ways by which capital is able to exercise domination over the state and thereby guarantee that it functions in support of the capitalist system:

1. The *direct mechanisms* of (a) putting members of the capitalist class or its loyal employees and servants into top governmental jobs; (b) lobbying and otherwise directly influencing the top governmental officials and decision makers; and (c) researching, formulating, and transmitting to the top state officials the social, economic, and foreign policies of the state through leading consensus seeking, policymaking bodies such as the Council on Foreign Relations;

2. The *indirect mechanisms* of control that act by structuring the environment within which state officials must make decisions — that is, by creating the attitudes of the masses, establishing the economic principles by which business operates, threatening direct intervention up to and including military takeovers, and being able to cause social disorder and unrest capable of "destabilizing" a government.

The relative importance of the direct and indirect mechanisms of state control has generated considerable debate among Marxists recently. The "instrumentalists" (perhaps the most prominent of whom are G. William Domhoff and Ralph Miliband) argue that the direct mechanisms (along with legitimation) play the central role.[1] The "structuralists" (represented by Nicos Poulantzas in France and the group around the journal *Kapitalistate* in the United States) argue that the state has considerable "relative autonomy" from direct control by the capitalist class, and that the mechanisms of domination by the capitalist class are mostly structural or indirect — that is, the logic of the process of capital accumulation creates the environment within which state officials must make and implement decisions.[2] In other words, the state in capitalist society is required to function in the interests of capital because of the nature of capitalist society.

This chapter is concerned only with those direct mechanisms emphasized by the "instrumentalists." The next chapter discusses the indirect mechanisms analyzed by the "structuralists." The position taken in this book is that different states at different times are dominated principally by direct mechanisms, and others at other times are dominated principally by indirect mechanisms. The types of direct or indirect mechanisms that are the most important vary. In chapter 11 the conditions under which different mechanisms become important are discussed.

The Selection of Top Governmental Personnel

Although few upper-class individuals ever hold top governmental positions, many top governmental positions are held by members of the upper class or individuals who have, through loyal service, risen to top jobs in the corporate institutions owned and controlled by the upper class. The presidency, the top cabinet positions, leading diplomatic posts, and membership on key special committees and the most important regulatory agencies are very often held by upper-class people or the top managers of the upper-class-owned corporate institutions (private corporations, banks, corporate law firms, foundations, and elite policy-formulating institutions). Many are the corporate executives who move back and forth between the top governmental and the top corporate positions. The top corporate executives of the leading corporations move into the government on the highest levels, while the leading executives of the second tier of corporations, or the second echelon of executives from the top corporations, take second-level governmental jobs. Fully 25

---

[1] Some of the best statements of this position are contained in Ralph Miliband, *The State in Capitalist Society* (New York: Basic Books, 1969); Domhoff, *Who Rules America?*, and *The Higher Circles*. The footnotes of this chapter contain numerous other works in this tradition. Note that Domhoff rejects the categorization of himself as an "instrumentalist." See his "I Am Not an 'Instrumentalist': A Reply to Kapitalistate Critics" in *Kapitalistate* no. 4-5 (Summer 1976).

[2] For perhaps the best summary statement of this position, see David Gold, Clarence Y. H. Lo, and Erik Olin Wright, "Recent Developments in Marxist Theories of the Capitalist State," in *Monthly Review* 27, no. 5-6 (October, November 1975).

percent of the heads of the leading corporations hold governmental positions at some point during their careers.[3] The corporate law firms, financial houses, and corporations that supply much of the top-level governmental personnel readily grant leaves for governmental service because of the advantages it brings the corporations. Business people in top governmental positions quite naturally bring in those they know and respect from the corporate world to serve under them. The various financial interest groups consequently tend to have influence in some part of the government at one time or another.[4]

Most of the earliest presidents were from the upper class. George Washington was alleged to be the richest man in the United States. Many of his immediate successors were, like him, rich Southern slave lords: Jefferson, Madison, and Monroe. From the 1830s, however, members of the upper class have been alternating in the presidency with individuals selected and financed by the upper class because of their ability to draw votes. The universal franchise has required a more sophisticated way to control the presidency than having always to run actual members of the upper class.

Nevertheless, members of the upper class are still very prominent among presidential candidates. Franklin Roosevelt was from an old-line upper-class family. John Kennedy and his brothers shared one of the larger fortunes in the United States. Of Nelson Rockefeller, nothing more need be said. Other prominent upper-class people who have run for president or "been available" for the presidency in recent years include Barry Goldwater, John Lindsay, Charles Percy, and William Scranton. When the actual members of the capitalist class do not themselves run for president, they locate, promote, and finance individuals with attractive political abilities as stand-in candidates. A common pattern is to engineer the nominations of widely known and respected heros (typically a military hero such as Andrew Jackson, John Tyler, Ulysses S. Grant, or Dwight Eisenhower), and occasionally a Hollywood actor such as Ronald Reagan or even an astronaut such as John Glenn. Usually (Reagan is an exception) such people have no particular understanding of political issues, interests, and political skills other than their public recognition, and can thus be easily manipulated by those who financed them. Another technique is to locate attractive candidates for the House of Representatives or governorships in the various states — ambitious lawyers are the most frequently selected — promote and finance their races for the nomination of one of the major parties, and then help them get elected. If they do well in upholding the interests of the local upper class *and* attract sufficient popular attention, they are then promoted and financed in campaigns for senatorial seats and eventually for the vice-presidency and presidency. The political careers of Harry Truman, Lyndon Johnson, Richard Nixon, and Gerald Ford are very similar in this regard. Each started as a small-time politician who, by linking his career to local upper-class interests, was able to rise from low-level office to the vice-presidency (usually by way of the Senate), and eventually to the presidency. Nixon throughout his career

---

[3] Linz and Lipset, "The Social Bases of Diversity," chapter 10, p. 25.
[4] Perlo, *The Empire of High Finance*, chapter 16.

was beholden to the Southern California military contractors, oil, and agribusiness interests that financed him. Johnson was similarly indebted to the Texas oil money that was responsible for his career.

Many key cabinet-level and under-secretarial positions are occupied by top managerial employees. Bankers, managers, and corporate lawyers normally directly control the three most important administrative agencies: the State Department, the Pentagon, and the Treasury. In the period 1933 to 1964, five of the eight secretaries of state were listed in the *Social Register* — that is, were from established wealthy families that were socially integrated into the capitalist class; eight of the thirteen secretaries of defense were listed, as were four of the seven secretaries of the treasury. Virtually all of the non-upper-class occupants of these three crucial cabinet positions were individuals with close ties throughout their careers to the richest interests in the United States. Since they are appointive jobs (and hence their incumbents need not have the popular recognition that it takes to win a national election), these three cabinet positions are traditionally even more closely held by the corporate rich than the presidency itself. The leading postwar secretaries of state have included John Foster Dulles (a senior partner of the Wall Street corporate law firm of Sullivan and Cromwell, the major law firm for EXXON); Dean Rusk (a chairman of the Rockefeller Foundation, and the director of a number of major Rockefeller-controlled corporations); Dean Acheson (a veteran corporate lawyer of a Morgan-associated corporate law firm); and Henry Kissinger (a long-time Nelson Rockefeller associate and employee, and member of the key upper-class foreign policy–formulating group, the Council on Foreign Relations).[5]

Since the early 1950s the State Department has largely been in the hands of people with close ties to the Rockefeller interests, whose concern for international relations stems largely from the immense wealth this family acquired from its interest in the Standard Oil companies and other investments in Asia, Africa, and Latin America. It is particularly important for this interest group to advance its overseas interests (which it sees as the interests of both the U.S. capitalist class and the United States itself) through control of U.S. foreign policy. Whether the president is a Democrat or a Republican, Rockefeller interests still usually control the State Department.

Since the end of World War II, the position of secretary of defense has been occupied by James Forrestal (the former head of the banking house of Dillon, Reed and Co., a firm which arranged important corporate loans for oil firms operating in the Middle East) and Robert McNamara (president of Ford Motor Company before he went into the government and president of the World Bank once he left). The position of secretary of the treasury has been occupied during this period by such individuals as George M. Humphrey (former head of M.A. Hanna and Co., to which he returned after his term with government), Robert B. Anderson (former president of Oil and Gas Association), and John Connally (closely tied to Texas oil interests).

Other cabinet-level governmental positions also have been frequently held by

[5] Domhoff, *Who Rules America?*, chapter 4.

members of the capitalist class and their top-level employees. Even the office of secretary of labor has been dominated by such types. For twenty-three of the years from 1933 to 1964, the secretary of labor was a member or top employee of the upper class. In addition to the top positions in the key governmental departments, the upper-class members and employees commonly hold the second-level jobs (such as under secretary and deputy secretary), at least in the key departments of Treasury, Defense, State, and Commerce. The control over the first and second levels of the most important departments of the federal government guarantees capitalist-class control over basic economic, military, and foreign policies.[6]

Beth Mintz studied the social backgrounds and business connections of all cabinet officials in all presidential administrations from McKinley to Nixon.[7] She defined a cabinet official as part of the social elite if he or she were listed in the *Social Register*, had attended one of an extremely small set of exclusive preparatory academies, or were a member of one of forty high-status social clubs or of one of the other social clubs listed in the front of the *Social Register*. If a cabinet member met one or more of these criteria, he or she was likely to have come from a proper well-connected background and have had upper-class social ties. Mintz defined a cabinet official as part of the business elite if at any time in his/her career (whether before or after his/her service in the cabinet) she or he were a member of a corporation's board of directors or had been a lawyer in a corporation-oriented law firm. Mintz found that from 1897 to 1973 approximately 90 percent of all cabinet officials were part of either (or both) the "social elite" or the "business elite," and that there was no consistent trend over time. She found that about 60 percent of all cabinet officials during the entire period were members of the "social elite" and 78 percent were part of the business elite (compared with 0.3 percent of the general population).

Cabinet officials are very frequently corporate lawyers, and to a lesser extent investment bankers. The corporate law firms perform a very important function for the major financial and industrial corporations. They are active in the merger and organization of corporations, do legal work involved in issuing new securities, act as go-betweens among the corporations, represent the corporations before various governmental agencies, and draft legislation offered by the corporations. As do the investment bankers, they usually have a much wider range of experience than does a top executive or director for a corporation (and can thus assume a truly *class* position), and have extensive experience in dealing with the government. Thus they are ideally suited to represent the entire corporate capitalist class (or at least very wide segments of it). The flexibility of these people is demonstrated by the frequency with which the incumbents of the various top-level cabinet jobs shift from being under secretary of this to secretary of that, and from being secretary of one department to being head of another.

The leading corporate law firms are more than just the lubricant of the cor-

---

[6] See Domhoff, *Who Rules America?*, chapter 4; Perlo, *The Empire of High Finance*, chapter 16; and Engler, *The Politics of Oil*.
[7] Beth Mintz, "The President's Cabinet," *The Insurgent Sociologist* 5, no. 3 (Spring 1975): 131-148.

porate system — they are themselves upper-class institutions. Of the 468 partners in the twenty largest Wall Street corporate law firms, 30 percent were listed in the *Social Register* and 72 percent got their law degrees from the *three* principal upper-class law schools (Harvard, Yale, and Columbia).[8] Note that while he had humble petty bourgeois origins, Richard Nixon eventually joined the prestigious corporate law firm of Mudge, Stern, Baldwin, and Todd (which became Nixon, Mudge, Rose, Guthrie, and Alexander).[9]

The president's inner circle is typically made up of many people with close ties to top business (for example, his top emissaries, advisers, speechwriters, and secretaries).[10] The very important National Security Council (NSC) is primarily composed of top-level business people. The NSC is a super-cabinet agency operating in secrecy and reporting only to the president. It is designed to assist the president in formulating and integrating policy planning for military and foreign affairs. It consists of the president, the vice-president, the secretary of state, the secretary of defense, the secretary of the treasury, the director of the CIA, the director of the office of civil defense mobilization, and several personal advisers to the president. The top-level staff of the NSC is typically headed by employees of the leading upper-class-run foundations, associations, and institutes. Its top advisers and consultants also are usually from the top strata of the corporate world.[11]

Occasionally the president appoints special committees to study and make policy recommendations on a pressing issue. The chairperson and leading members of such commissions and investigatory committees are typically upper-class-connected people. Two of the most famous have been the Gaither Committee, appointed by Dwight Eisenhower to reconsider U.S. military "preparedness," and the Clay Committee, appointed by John Kennedy to study U.S. foreign aid policies. Both were dominated by leading financiers, bankers, and corporate lawyers. In 1954 Eisenhower created a special Committee on Energy Supplies Resources to evaluate "all factors pertaining to the continued development of energy supplies and resource fuels in the United States with the aim of strengthening the national defense, providing orderly industrial growth, and assuring supplies for our expanding national economy in any future emergency." The research and findings of the committee were based on the work of a four-man task force that included the president of the Rochester and Pittsburgh Coal Company and the vice-president of the National City Bank of New York for petroleum affairs. Technical consultants for the task force consisted almost exclusively of experts from the private energy industry: the chief economist of Standard Oil of New Jersey, the chief foreign economist of The Texas Co., the chief economist of Continental Oil, the president of the Southern Natural Gas Co., the vice-presidents of the Texas Eastern Transmission Corporation, the vice-president of the United Gas Pipe

---

[8] See Domhoff, *Who Rules America?*, p. 59.
[9] North American Congress on Latin America, *Newsletter* 7, no. 9 (November 1973): 5–14.
[10] Domhoff, *Who Rules America?*, pp. 103–105.
[11] Domhoff, *The Higher Circles*, pp. 128–133.

Line Company, and so on. The composition of the staff of this committee is not untypical.[12]

The leading officials who are not from the corporate world (such as some members of the regulatory commissions and second- and third-level people in the various governmental agencies) serve the interests of the corporate rich in part because of their hopes of securing a plush job with the corporations once they leave the government. Behavior that antagonizes the business interests with which one deals every day can only hinder the advancement of one's personal career. Conversely, ingratiating oneself to business interests secures a good life in the future.

When the presidency is not occupied by upper-class people or by top corporate managers, it is occupied by those who are thoroughly indebted to upper-class people or top corporate managers for the financing and promotion that put them where they are. Once they get into the top governmental jobs, they are overwhelmed by the most intelligent, experienced, informed, well-connected, and generally impressive top business people who they have had to appoint to the top positions. They appoint such people because of the grip the wealthy have on the political parties that determine the presidential nominees and the process of financing the elections. And since they have no strong class interest or sophisticated position of their own, they have either authentically or cynically adopted that of their benefactors as the condition for their personal success. It is thus expected and natural to appoint the nominees of one's benefactors and their class. How can a politically naive general or a small-town schoolteacher or lawyer possibly dominate a group of people trained throughout their lives to command, who have the best staff money can buy providing them with information, and who have connections with the most powerful figures throughout the United States and the world? In spite of its formal powers, the presidency, when occupied by such people, functions primarily as a mediator among the various tendencies within the upper class. At best such a president can support this or that major faction within the higher circles. The presidency is thus essentially a facade for the actual power, represented by the top governmental officials and advisers who are from the corporate upper class — which, because of the formally democratic institutions through which it rules as well as the scarcity of talent, cannot always itself hold the top-level jobs.

Until the mid-1970s the capitalist class selected and promoted both celebrities and ambitious small-town politicians willing to serve its interests primarily by financing their campaigns. Although its impact has yet to be definitively evaluated, the Election Reform Act of 1974, which put stringent limits on both the size of political contributions and the total amount spent by candidates in federal elections, seems to have partially closed off this means of controlling the candidate selection process. The capitalist class thus seems to be, at least in part, falling back on the many alternative means of influencing the political process available to it.

To be elected to the presidency of the United States, as well as to the

[12] Engler, *The Politics of Oil*, p. 313. For a good case study of a standing governmental advisory agency, see Diana Roose, "Top Dogs and Top Brass," *The Insurgent Sociologist* 5, no. 3 (Spring 1975).

governorships and Senate in the larger states, has traditionally required a large amount of money. Even the governorships of the smaller states and seats in the House of Representatives have been beyond the reach of any but the richest of those who have had to finance their own campaigns. Nixon received over $70 million dollars in 1972 in his successful bid for reelection. McGovern received less than half that amount. This represented a considerable increase over the 1968 election, when the total reported spent in the presidential campaign was only about $67 million dollars (of which the Republicans spent $29 million and the Democrats $19 million).[13] The huge sums necessary to win political office have been caused by the extremely expensive use of television and radio. In 1964 a total of $35 million dollars was spent (just on political broadcasting) on all levels in the general election.[14]

To win a seat in the U.S. Senate in 1970 cost approximately $300,000. In the larger states, such as New York and California, the sum necessary was probably closer to $1 million.[15] To win a seat in the House of Representatives normally required only between $25,000 and $50,000, although in some urban districts it cost as much as $200,000.[16] The cost per vote in presidential elections rose from 19¢ in 1952 to 60¢ in 1968.[17]

Obviously, the campaign funds necessary to run for the presidency, Senate, and often the House were beyond the capacity of any but members of the upper class. There were two other ways to obtain the necessary funds: (1) to accumulate many small contributions from working-class and petty bourgeois people, either directly or indirectly (through unions and other mass organizations); or, (2) to solicit several substantial contributions from upper-class and, to a lesser extent, petty bourgeois people interested in financing candidates favorable to both their class and special interests. Approximately 85 percent of the money spent on presidential campaigns prior to 1974 came from business people and their families.[18]

As a rule most of the money for presidential campaigns came in sums of greater than $500. Approximately 30,000 people gave sums of this amount in 1968.[19] In 1968 the Republicans received $7,658,160 and the Democrats $4,290,561 in contributions in amounts of $10,000 or greater from only 400 individuals. Slightly over half of the money was from about ninety individual contributions in sums of over $30,000.[20] Several leading means of raising funds have been special fund-raising dinners, receptions, and picnics. While traditionally these

---

[13] Herbert Alexander, *Financing the 1968 Election* (Lexington, Mass.: D.C. Heath, 1971), p. 2.
[14] Thayer, *Who Shakes the Money Tree?*
[15] Ibid., p. 167.
[16] Ibid., pp. 166, 167.
[17] Mintz and Cohen, *America, Inc.*
[18] North American Congress on Latin America, *Newsletter* 6, no. 8 (October 1972): 26.
[19] See Mintz and Cohen, *America Inc.*, chapter 4; and Thayer, *Who Shakes the Money Tree?*, chapter 6.
[20] Alexander, *Financing the 1968 Election*, p. 168.

affairs cost $100 a plate, sums of $1,000 per plate have become increasingly popular. The rich have a special incentive to attend such events, since they get a chance to personally meet the presidential candidate. In 1964, Lyndon Johnson attended twenty-six fund raising events between March and November that raised a total of $7.9 million.[21] Of the 424 contributors of $10,000 or more in 1968, a core of twelve persons had also given at least that amount in every election since 1952.[22]

The capitalist class has provided most of the financing for the presidential campaigns. Although most of the leading upper-class families are Republican, they have also been major contributors to the Democratic party.[23] Many of the same individuals give to both parties. The logic of giving to both candidates in a single race is to ensure access to, and cooperation from, whichever probusiness candidate is elected.

Twenty-five individuals each contributed at least $150,000 to Richard Nixon's presidential campaign in 1972. The list was headed by W. Clement Stone (an insurance man), with a contribution of $2 million and Richard Scaife (an heir to the Mellon fortune), with $1 million.[24] Nixon also received a considerable number of illegal donations (at least fifteen of which were in the $100,000 range) from corporations.[25] George McGovern's campaign also had many large contributors. At least nine wealthy individuals contributed $100,000 or more. McGovern's list was topped by Stewart Mott (heir to one of the largest stockholders in General Motors), with $725,000.[26]

Also in 1972, John Lindsay (a member of the upper class) raised $500,000 from only 1,000 people to run in the Florida and Wisconsin primaries. Hubert Humphrey's campaign for the nomination raised $838,000 from 2,400 large contributions. Following his poor showing in the Wisconsin primary, Edmund Muskie invited 450 of his contributors to a meeting to reinvigorate his campaign. When only sixty-four showed up, he knew that the sources of his finance had dried up. He therefore withdrew from the campaign, stating correctly that he "did not have the money to continue."[27]

Contributions from business are in the form of gifts from rich individuals and relatives, illegal gifts from corporations, and contributions from industrial associations and their political action arms. Much of the money is "laundered" to hide its origins. A large contribution is broken down into small gifts to each state committee or made in the name of a multitude of different people.

The most potent of the political action associations associated with business have been the American Medical Political Action Committee (AMPAC); three large dairy lobbies (TAPE, SPACE, and ADEPT); the Business-Industry Political

[21] Thayer, *Who Shakes the Money Tree?*, p. 87.
[22] Ibid., p. 169.
[23] Alexander, *Financing the 1968 Election*, p. 170.
[24] Congressional Quarterly, *Weekly Report*, November 4, 1972, p. 2887, and October 6, 1973, pp. 2656, 2659-2660; and Thayer, *Who Shakes the Money Tree?*, pp. 114-115.
[25] Congressional Quarterly, *Weekly Report*, November 17, 1973, p. 3011.
[26] Congressional Quarterly, *Weekly Report*, October 6, 1973, p. 2654.
[27] Thayer, *Who Shakes the Money Tree?*, chapter 5.

Action Committee (BIPAC), which is associated with the right-wing National Association of Manufacturers; and the Bank PAC, the political action arm of the American Bankers Association.[28] These groups collect contributions in relatively small sums to advance the special interests of a given segment of the privileged. In 1972 AMPAC spent $731,035 and the Associated Milk Producers $674,000 for probusiness candidates on all levels in just eleven days in October 1972.[29]

Unlike the very richest families and largest corporations, the special interest groups have tended to concentrate their money on the specific members of Congress who can help them the most. The favorite targets of groups such as the AMA and the oil, real estate, securities, banking, public utilities, and trucking industries have been the members of the Ways and Means Committee of the House of Representatives. These industries are particularly interested in the tax bills or special legislation (such as the health insurance bills) that come before this committee.

Businesses also "encourage" their middle-level employees to donate to favorable candidates. Common practices include giving cash bonuses to employees with the understanding that a portion of the funds will be used as political contributions, using a portion of an employee's salary for campaign contributions, "lending" a corporation's employees to the staff of probusiness politicians (with the business continuing to pay their salaries), paying the professional fees of lawyers with the understanding that part of their fee will be contributed to a specified candidate, paying fake invoices supplied by a candidate and paying for phony consultations to candidates, and allowing the candidate to use company billboard space, airplanes, credit cards, and hotel rooms. Another common practice is to make a "loan" to a candidate which then is either forgotten or repaid at a small percentage of its face value after the election.[30] Note that the Campaign Reform Act of 1974, which set strict limits on contributions and spending, hardly affected these mechanisms of raising money for business candidates.

It is not at all surprising that those who have paid the bills have largely been able to call the tune. It is not that capitalist-class money cynically pulls the strings, but rather that it selects and co-opts the leading political contenders from the beginning of their political careers. If they did not accept the values of business, do the bidding of business as a matter of course, and sincerely believe that what's best for business is best for America, they never would advance. The continuing financing of candidates by business reinforces corporate values and the desire to serve business in them. The discretion available to politicians is delimited by the range of special interests within the corporate upper class. To the extent that there are real political differences among candidates, they typically reflect somewhat different attachments to different segments of the capitalist class. But most of the apparent differences among politicians merely reflect the various images projected by their Madison Avenue technicians, differences in personal styles or charisma, or slightly different political opinions about how best to advance the capitalist system.

[28] Ibid., pp. 210-221.
[29] Congressional Quarterly, *Weekly Report*, November 4, 1972, p. 2887.
[30] Mintz and Cohen, *Who Owns America?*, p. 206.

Because of the public outrage caused by the scandals of the Nixon administration, which included many revelations of both gigantic and illegal campaign contributions with apparent expectations of favors, Congress in 1974 passed a Campaign Reform Act to limit the ability of the wealthy to finance campaigns. A legal limit of $1,000 per individual for each candidate running in a primary, runoff, and general election was enacted with an aggregate limit of $25,000 in all federal election campaigns in a single year. Candidates together with their families were limited to spending $50,000 of their own funds in presidential campaigns, $35,000 in senatorial contests, and $25,000 in House races. The legal limit for a candidate's campaign spending was set at $10 million for a presidential primary, $20 million for the general presidential election, and $150,000 for a general Senate election. In addition, the national committee for each candidate can spend up to 2¢ per voter beyond these limits. The federal government also established a matching fund for presidential primaries and general presidential elections (with only the first $250 of each contribution matched). Strict reporting requirements were also enacted.[31]

During the two years after its passage, the federal courts have ruled part of the provisions of the act unconstitutional, while the election commission established by the Election Reform Act has liberally interpreted its restrictions.[32] These facts, together with the viability of the types of loopholes outlined above, leave open the question of just how effective this legislation will prove to be in restricting the ability of the rich to influence the outcome of elections through funding campaigns. It is possible, however, that because of public scandal (and the resultant loss of legitimacy of the system) produced by the blatant exercise of political power by the rich through this channel, campaign funding might well be reduced to a secondary means of determining political outcomes in the capitalist state. The implication of this possibility is that the other mechanisms of direct control of the state (outlined in this chapter) — and especially the mechanisms of indirect control (discussed in the next chapter) — will become all the more important.

Lobbying

There are approximately 4,000 registered lobbyists in Washington, D.C. (eight for every member of Congress). Most are employed by individual corporations, financial interests, or business associations to pressure legislators into adopting legislation favorable to business in general and to their special interest in particular. These lobbyists work in a number of ways:

1. They traditionally have financed a large part of the electoral campaigns of various members of Congress;
2. They promise good jobs or special business privileges to legislators and administrators for after they leave the government or Congress;

[31] Congressional Quarterly, *Weekly Report*, October 12, 1974, p. 2866.
[32] *New York Times*, September 12, 1976, p. 29.

3. They provide the legislators and administrators with well-researched studies that make convincing arguments for the business viewpoint, which is also supplemented by strong verbal cases from the lobbyists in person;

4. With their large expense accounts, they wine, dine, entertain, play golf and tennis with, and otherwise provide for, the Congress members and administrators they are interested in. While socializing with lobbyists — many of whom carry considerable prestige because of their backgrounds and connections — the middle-class Congress members and administrators usually are won over to the business viewpoint and personal friendships are established that translate into power for business;

5. Special services such as free consultation services and travel, as well as the channeling of business to a Congress member's law firm or other business — or simply phony fees — are provided to friendly Congress members and administrators.

The various personal favors done for Congress members and legislators tend to make these people beholden to business interests.[33] Many governmental departments have formally set up advisory committees composed principally of the business people most affected by the agency. Such semiofficial advisory parties have considerable impact on the policy of governmental agencies.

The techniques of lobbying have changed somewhat from those exercised in the 1930s. As corporations have grown larger, they have come to rely more on their own efforts and less on those of business associations. Business associations now are used by relatively smaller-business people, such as the dairymen, since no one of them individually could hope to exercise much clout. When acting together through the various dairymen's associations, they, however, are able to exert considerable influence. Another way in which the influence of the lobbies has changed is in their increasing reliance on influencing public opinion through institutional advertising — especially by means of television. The private electric power companies launched a very effective campaign against the expansion of publicly owned power by spending large sums for "public service" advertising for this purpose. Since the discovery of the environmental and energy "crises," the oil companies (most notably **EXXON**) have been spending large sums to convince us that they are operating in the best interest of the environment. Such sustained and well-financed efforts usually succeed in making public opinion more favorable to the various corporations that run these ads. People then pressure their representatives in Congress to oppose measures that big business does not like.[34]

Some of the most effective lobbyists are former members of Congress who now work for business interests. Because they have been legislators and know the ins and outs of the legislative process, have personal friends among members of

---

[33] Domhoff, *Who Rules America?*, pp. 111-114; and Lundberg, *The Rich and the Super Rich*, pp. 505ff.

[34] See Edwin Epstein, *The Corporation in American Politics* (Englewood Cliffs, N.J.: Prentice-Hall, 1969).

Congress, and have the status that commands respect, they make particularly good lobbyists. In 1970 the banking lobby employed five former members of the staff of the Senate Banking, Housing, and Urban Affairs Committee during its successful effort to weaken a bill to regulate one bank holding companies. The same is true of former members of the staff of other congressional committees and regulatory agencies. This process of personnel interchange also works the other way. Many Congress members and regulatory commission members and their staffs were formerly employed in important positions by private business. They thus have a special relationship with their former business associates, who in all probability they will rejoin one day. Consequently, the difference between lobbyists and staffers is blurred.[35]

In addition to the very influential milk lobbyists, the AMA, BIPAC, the National Association of Manufacturers (NAM), and the American Bankers Association, the following associations are among the most influential collective lobbies: the Association of American Railroads, the American Iron and Steel Institute, the American Petroleum Institute, the Air Transport Association, the Investment Bankers Association, the American Newspaper Publishers Association, the Edison Electric Institute, the American Farm Bureau Association, and the American Trucking Association. The AFL-CIO Committee on Political Education is a force on some questions, but is dwarfed by the ensemble of business associations, corporations, and rich individuals. Twelve individuals contributed as much to Nixon's campaign in 1972 as the labor unions contributed to *all* candidates in the 1968 elections.[36] The lobbying effort of the AFL-CIO has to be compared with the impact of any *one* of the larger special interest business groups; it cannot be compared with the influence of the business community as a whole.

Lobbyists expect special favors in return for their financial contributions to candidates for Congress and the presidency. For example, in early 1971 the dairy industry's Associated Milk Producers, Inc. (AMPI) agreed to contribute $2 million to the Nixon reelection campaign in exchange for an increase in the level of federal support for milk prices. Nixon increased the level of support after he received the pledge. AMPI also gave considerable financial support to Wilbur Mills's attempt to win the Democratic nomination for president in 1972. Since Mills chaired the House Ways and Means Committee and was thus perhaps the most powerful member of Congress in Washington, it was highly advantageous to flatter his presidential aspirations.[37] Hence, at least five persons on the AMPI payroll were assigned to work on the Mills campaign. AMPI also paid the rent on Mills's Washington apartment.

[35] See Mark Green et al., *Who Runs Congress?* New York: Bantam Books, 1972), pp. 43-46.
[36] See Alexander, *Financing the 1968 Election*, p. 2, for labor's total campaign contributions. For Nixon's top contributors, see Congressional Quarterly, *Weekly Report*, November 4, 1972, p. 2887, and October 6, 1973, pp. 2656, 2659-2660; and Thayer, *Who Shakes the Money Tree?*, pp. 114-115.
[37] Congressional Quarterly, *Weekly Report*, May 11, 1974, p. 1160.

The Process of Forming Public Policy

Most of the basic policy changes in U.S. foreign, economic, social, and governmental organization policy originate in a select group of private upper-class organizations set up to formulate state policies, obtain a consensus within the upper class, and have the state adopt its proposed policies. The most important organizations of this type are the key policy-planning and consensus-seeking groups: the Council on Foreign Relations (CFR), the Committee for Economic Development (CED), and the Business Council. There are other, less important groups of the same kind, such as the National Planning Council and the American Assembly. Other types of institutions are also very important in this process, such as certain key universities (for example, MIT, Harvard, Yale, Princeton, Johns Hopkins, University of Chicago, Berkeley, Stanford, and Caltech), the major foundations (for example, Carnegie, Ford, and Rockefeller), and the major "think tanks" (for example, the centers for international studies at various key universities, the Rand Corporation, the Brookings Institution, and the Stanford Research Institute).

The corporations and the corporate rich finance, run, and in part staff these various policy-forming institutions, which closely interact with one another in the process of developing policies and forming a consensus. Once policies are formulated, the consensus-seeking policy-planning groups (for example, the CFR, CED, and the Business Council) have the primary responsibility of getting the government to adopt these policies. They accomplish this primarily (1) by placing key members of their organizations in the top-level policymaking and implementing governmental jobs, and (2) by providing extremely well-argued and well-researched policy proposals to people in governmental jobs who identify with and/or are beholden to the interests in and behind the policy-planning groups (see figure 10-1 for an illustration of this process of influence).

The history of the role of the upper-class, consensus-seeking, policy-forming groups can be traced back to around 1900 and the founding of the American Economic Association (AEA), the National Civic Federation (NCF), and the American Association for Labor Legislation (AALL). The AEA was formed to encourage empirical research into practical economic problems that would be of use to governmental policymakers. The NCF, founded in the 1890s, was set up to develop a modus vivendi between labor and business that would not disturb the profitability of the capitalist system. It played a major role in resolving key labor disputes and encouraging welfare programs designed to make unions unnecessary. It was composed primarily of business executives, but also included many top labor leaders and sympathizers. Approximately one-third of the largest corporations had top executives represented in the NCF. The most famous member of this organization was Mark Hanna (a coal and steel magnate), who was also the principal figure behind the Republican party. During the next forty years, this organization played an important role in the push for welfare and labor legislation designed to integrate the working class into the system and to get the corporate rich to accept the measures necessary to accomplish this result. In 1906 another organization, the

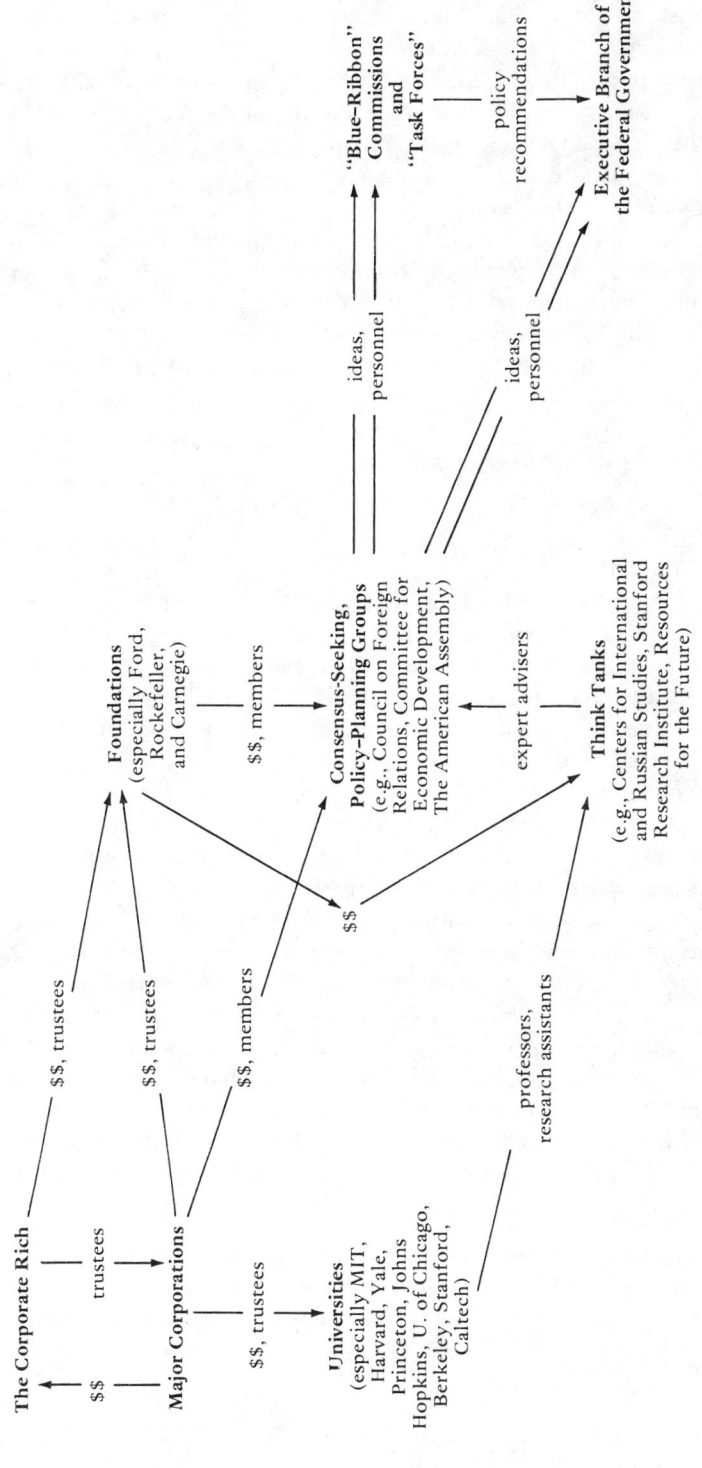

Figure 10–1 The Power Elite Policymaking Process

Source: From G. William Domhoff, "Answers to Radical Critics," *The Insurgent Sociologist* II, no. 2 (Spring 1972): 34.

AALL, was founded specifically to press for legislation designed to alleviate the worst abuses of the working class. It pressed for measures to compensate for industrial accidents; industrial diseases, unemployment, and old age, all of which were adopted during the 1930s. The AALL was founded by AEA types and had considerable overlap with the business leadership of the NCF.[38]

In the United States the political parties function almost exclusively to select individual candidates and not to formulate and implement governmental policies. In almost all of the other leading capitalist countries, the political parties do play a significant role in the policy process (see chapter 6). Consequently, the role of the consensus-seeking, policy-planning groups is especially important in the United States. These consensus-seeking, policy-planning groups are almost exclusively composed of the top bankers, corporate executives, corporate lawyers, and rich individuals who meet with several top experts in the appropriate fields to discuss specific problems, develop policy, and implement their recommendations.

The Council on Foreign Relations

The Council on Foreign Relations (CFR) was established after World War I, but became a central institution in establishing U.S. foreign policy during World War II.[39] The CFR had 1,450 members in 1970 — 725 of whom resided in New York City, and 725 in the rest of the country. A cardinal principle of the organization is that its members hold their deliberations in the strictest secrecy, which is necessary to help sustain the myth that foreign policy is formulated within the State Department. There are basically two types of members of the CFR. One type is composed of the corporate rich (the large majority), who provide direction, and the experts who provide them with expertise (a relatively small minority). Forty-eight percent of the members are listed in the *Social Register*, 41 percent are corporate executives and bankers, and 21 percent are corporate lawyers. The second type is composed of college presidents, political scientists, economists, and other scholars (22 percent of the total membership).[40] The president of the CFR in the early 1970s was David Rockefeller, the chairperson of the Chase Manhattan Bank and the principal figure in the most powerful financial interest group in the United States. Other leaders of the organization today (or in the recent past) include: John J. McCloy, Wall Street lawyer, former chairperson of Chase Manhattan, and head of the U.S. Arms Control and Disarmament Agency; Allen Dulles of the premier Wall Street law firm, Sullivan & Cromwell, and founder and director for many years of the CIA; Grayson Kirk, former president of Columbia University, director of Chase Manhattan, Consolidated Edison, IBM, Mobil Oil, and some others; Frank Altschul of the important Morgan Group holding company, General

---

[38] Domhoff, *The Higher Circles*, chapter 6. See also David Eakins, "The Development of Corporate Liberal Policy Research in the United States, 1885-1965" (Ph.D. diss., University of Wisconsin, 1966); and Weinstein, *The Corporate Ideal in the Liberal State*.
[39] For the best discussion of the CFR during the World War II years, see Lawrence H. Shoup, "Shaping the Postwar World," *The Insurgent Sociologist* 5, no. 3 (Spring 1975).
[40] Domhoff, *The Higher Circles*, pp. 116-117.

American Investors; Elliot V. Bell, director of Chase Manhattan, New York Life, and Chemical Bank; Gabriel Hague, director of Manufacturers Hanover Trust, Brooklyn-Union Gas Company, and others; George Ball, under secretary of state in the Kennedy administration, director of Standard Oil of California, leading public spokesperson for the CFR; Henry Wriston, president of Brown University; and Theodore Gates, head of Morgan Guaranty Trust, director of General Electric, Scott Paper Co., Campbell Soup, and secretary of defense in the Eisenhower administration.[41]

Both the Morgan and Rockefeller financial interest groups are especially strongly represented. Around 1970 the Morgan Group was represented by the directors of Morgan Guaranty Trust, nine directors of U.S. Trust Co., five directors of Banker's Trust, four directors of Lehman Brothers Investment Company, four directors of Brown Brothers, Harriman, and two directors of Marine Midland Bank. The Rockefeller interests are almost as strongly represented: thirteen directors of First National City Bank, eight directors of Chase Manhattan, three partners of Dillon, Read Investment, and two directors of the Chemical Bank were members of the CFR.[42]

The CFR is financed by membership dues, continuing grants from the Rockefeller, Ford, and Carnegie Foundations (which comprise about 25 percent of its income), subscriptions from its "corporate service" (at $1,000 to $10,000 a year), the profit from its publications, and individual gifts and bequests. Its corporate service provides for free consultation for the corporations, use of the CFR's library (second to none in its field), and the right to nominate executives to its study and discussion groups.

The CFR performs a number of important functions. It sponsors research on foreign policy issues with money from the major foundations; publishes *Foreign Affairs*, the most influential journal on foreign policy; sponsors the Committees on Foreign Relations in major cities around the country, which help mold the foreign policy views of the local rich; and serves as a training ground for new foreign policy leadership — many appointments to the State and Defense Departments are drawn from its ranks.

The most important activities of the CFR are its discussion groups and study groups. Each year the CFR organizes about ten discussion groups composed of twenty to twenty-five of its members, who hold a series of regular meetings, do background research and reading, and try to generate specific policy recommendations. Differences are ironed out and basic opinions formulated in these groups. From some of these general discussion groups come more focused study groups that are organized around the research of a specific council research fellow or staff member. A series of papers or reports are given by the "scholar," which are then discussed by CFR members and selected others. The goal of these study groups is the production of a book or article written by the "scholar" with the

---

[41] The Progressive Labor Party, *Who Rules the United States?* (Brooklyn, N.Y.: Progressive Labor Party, 1973), p. 34.
[42] Idem.

collaboration of his study group. Henry Kissinger was the center of one such study group in 1957 to 1958 that helped him research and write *Nuclear Weapons and Foreign Policy*. In his study group were two former chairpeople of the Atomic Energy Commission; two assistant secretaries of defense; and several second-level officials from the State Department, the CIA, and the three armed services.[43] From both types of groups evolved the strategies of U.S. imperialism.

In addition to its discrete discussion and study groups, the CFR normally has two long-range projects that involve a *set* of interrelated study groups. In the mid-1960s the two CFR projects were on U.S.–China relations (out of which emerged the U.S. policy of reconciliation with the Chinese that was implemented in the early 1970s) and on the "Atlantic Community," in which the problems of NATO, the Common Market, European competition with U.S. business, and political trends in Europe were discussed.[44]

The CFR has about 100 general meetings a year, some of which are addressed by top U.S. governmental officials, CFR staff members, or visiting foreign governmental leaders. The other meetings involve round-table discussions. It also sponsors special biannual seminars for leading corporate executives. These seminars include five meetings as well as round-table discussions. The chairpeople of most of the leading U.S. corporations with special interests in foreign affairs are brought together for a once-a-year, "off-the-record" dinner meeting. Of course, the proceedings of all these CFR functions are secret.[45]

The CFR can get the U.S. government to implement its policies in four ways: (1) by placing its own people in crucial governmental positions; (2) by holding "off-the-record" meetings with all levels of higher governmental officials — such members are especially important during periods of crisis; (3) through the joint participation of governmental officials, CFR staffers and scholars, and corporate executives in the various CFR functions; and (4) through the publication and targeted dissemination of books, articles, reports, and research findings, which become public or are simply channeled to the appropriate governmental agency. Because of the personal connections of CFR people with leading governmental officials, such publications and reports are almost always taken very seriously.

The most important of these four mechanisms of policy implementation is the placement of CFR people in top foreign policy posts. CFR people dominate the highest level of U.S. government foreign policymaking and policy implementation. There were at least twenty-five members of the CFR both in the Kennedy-Johnson administrations and in the Nixon administration.[46] Of John Kennedy's list of about eighty persons from which he filled the top State Department positions, three-fourths were members of the CFR. These included Dean Rusk and seven of the assistant and under secretaries of state actually selected.

The CFR has been a leading force in all basic U.S. foreign policy shifts in the postwar period. It was instrumental in establishing the United Nations, creating

[43] Domhoff, *The Higher Circles*, p. 119.
[44] The Progressive Labor Party, *Who Rules the United States?*, p. 36.
[45] Ibid., pp. 35-36.
[46] The Progressive Labor Party, *Who Rules the United States?*, p. 55.

the Marshall Plan, forming NATO, softening the U.S. position on German reparations, formulating the policy of nuclear confrontation and then detente, and most recently in changing U.S.-China policy.[47]

The domestically oriented policy-planning groups

The Committee for Economic Development (CED) serves much the same function for domestic (especially monetary and economic) policy that the CFR does for foreign policy. The control of the organization and the way in which it operates are much the same as the CFR.[48] Founded in 1942 by a group of businessmen, bankers, and advisors to Franklin Roosevelt, the organization was extremely influential in establishing the economic policy of the postwar U.S. state.[49] The early focus of the CED was on getting the government to adopt policies that would stabilize the level of employment, production, and prices to maximize the profit-making opportunities of the corporations and minimize the possibilities of social disorder.

The CED has been especially instrumental in developing the Marshall Plan (which was largely staffed by its trustees); the decision not to retire the huge federal debt after World War II, but rather to let it gradually expand (that is, the legitimization of deficit spending); the Bretton Woods agreement that established the International Monetary Fund (which allowed the United States to dominate world markets because the dollar was designated the international reserve currency); and the policy of using monetary and fiscal policies to add spending power to the economy by decreasing taxes and lowering interest rates when unemployment is high, and to reduce spending power by increasing taxes and raising interest rates in times of inflation. This latter policy successfully stabilized the economy from the end of World War II until it ran into difficulties in the mid-1970s.[50]

The CED is not as hegemonic in domestic economic policy as the CFR is in foreign policy. Several other very important consensus-seeking, policy-planning groups also operate in the area of domestic policy and have considerable influence over U.S. domestic economic and social policies. The most important of these are the National Planning Association (traditionally slightly more liberal than the CED), the American Assembly (which includes many more non-upper-class members than the CED), and the National Bureau of Economic Research.[51]

One other consensus-seeking, policy-planning group is especially important — the Business Council. It was established by business people sympathetic to Roosevelt's policies in 1933 to advise the government on its economic programs

[47] Domhoff, *The Higher Circles*, p. 121.
[48] The Progressive Labor Party, *Who Rules the United States?*, pp. 37-41; Domhoff, *The Higher Circles*, pp. 191-195, and *Fat Cats and Democrats*, pp. 158-166.
[49] Domhoff, *The Higher Circles*, p. 124.
[50] See Eakins, "The Development of Corporate Liberal Policy Research, 1885-1965"; and Schriftgiesser, *Business and Public Policy*.
[51] See Domhoff, *The Higher Circles*, p. 186ff; and Eakins, "The Development of Corporate Liberal Policy Research, 1885-1965."

and to act as a clearinghouse for individual business proposals concerning governmental policies affecting business. It was particularly active in formulating and pushing for the New Deal package of labor and social security legislation and regulation of the economy. Members of the Business Council worked closely with Roosevelt, to whom they turned over the council's proposals, which in many cases were then submitted by him to Congress.

Although its official connection with government was abolished in the early 1960s, it continues to play a key role in determining federal policies. The Business Council meets six times a year: members get together biannually for seminars that last several days at a fancy resort, and quarterly for one-day meetings. The Business Council staff also prepares elaborate studies and reports on topics of concern for big business that are transmitted to governmental agencies.[52] The Business Council has about seventy active members and a number of "graduates." Many of its members are from the Morgan and Rockefeller interest groups. Membership is limited to the top officers and directors of the very largest monopoly corporations.

The leaders of the Business Council, the CFR, and the CED are corporate liberals. Unlike the narrow-minded, shortsighted leadership of groups such as the National Association of Manufacturers (NAM), they understand the *class* interests of the capitalist class and act accordingly. Whether the presidency or the Congress was in the hands of Republicans or Democrats, the consensus-seeking, policy-planning groups have played the predominant role in governmental circles since the end of the Herbert Hoover administration. The leadership of these groups is unquestionably and totally in the hands of internationally minded, sophisticated, class-conscious people from the largest financial and industrial interests. However, groups such as the NAM, the Chamber of Commerce, the Farm Bureau, and many trade organizations such as the Iron and Steel Institute are often heavily influenced by relatively smaller big-business people without major international interests and/or a sophisticated capitalist-class consciousness. These latter groups normally pursue the special interests of various segments of the business community or the short-run interests of business as a whole without regard for the economic and social impact of shortsighted policies on the longer run interests of the entire upper class. Consequently, the leading consensus-seeking, policy-planning, upper-class groups that have been predominant since the 1930s in the United States have served as the guardians of the long-run interests of the entire capitalist class.

Summary

This chapter summarized the various direct ways by which the capitalist class in the United States is able to dominate the U.S. state. The role of the capitalist class in providing the candidates for top office, financing campaigns, lobbying the

---

[52] See the Progressive Labor Party, *Who Rules the United States?*, pp. 41–42; and Craig Kubey, "Notes on a Meeting of the Business Council," *Insurgent Sociologist* 3, no. 3 (Spring 1973).

legislative and executive branches, and organizing influential consensus-seeking and public policy-forming groups has been discussed. These are the mechanisms stressed by "instrumentalist" theorists of the capitalist state such as G. William Domhoff and Ralph Miliband, who argue that these are the principal ways in which the interests of capital are transmitted to the state. The strong and detailed evidence summarized in this chapter that they and other researchers in their tradition have provided would indicate that these channels are indeed important. People who have been brought up and have spent most of their lives serving the capitalist class are likely to have internalized the values and norms of this class, and thus are most likely to make political decisions within this framework. The massive funds that have been used to promote candidates and to lobby elected officials certainly play a major role in selecting, forming, and pressuring them to favor the interests behind them. The well-equipped and prestigious policy-forming groups are closely interlocked with top governmental agencies and exert considerable influence on the formulation of governmental policy. The question can still be raised, however, of whether these mechanisms are either the sufficient *or* necessary means by which the capitalist class dominates the capitalist state. The next chapter addresses the question of the role of "structural" factors in determining state policies.

11

The Mechanisms of Indirect Domination of the State by Capital

The capitalist system provides a structured environment within which the state administration and legislature must act. The decisions made by state officials have to take the essentials of this environment as the parameters within which they must work. These parameters — the basic logic of the capitalist system — impose firm and rather specific imperatives on the decision-making and administrative process of the state in capitalist society. State officials can ignore these imperatives only with the near certain risk of promoting economic, social, and political crisis and the probable end of their political careers.

The state in capitalist society cannot act any way other than to attempt to fulfill the basic functions required of it by the logic of capitalist society. Alternative forms of state policy — for example, genuine Socialist policies — can only be followed within a Socialist economy, where the state is required to respond to the logic of that form of economic organization. Attempts to straddle the fence with half-Socialist/half-capitalist policies within an essentially capitalist mode of production have universally failed, leading in rather short order to either military or fascist intervention, conservative electoral victories, the abandonment of Socialist politics on the part of left parties, *or* an increasingly serious social, economic, and political crisis culminating in an anticapitalist revolution and hence in a noncapitalist state (this latter course of historical events is rare).

There are basically four ways by which the state is induced into following capitalist policies independent of any direct mechanisms of state control by the capitalist class:

1. Capitalist ideological hegemony;
2. The logic of the economic laws of capitalist society within which the state must act;

3. The threat of military intervention in the event that the state does not adequately perform its functions;

4. The reality and threat of political and social crisis induced by the capitalist class in the event of its dissatisfaction with state policies.[1]

Ideological Hegemony as a Mechanism of Control

The politics of those people who are in the dominant positions of *stable* class societies are usually similar to the politics of the people in subordinate positions. In societies with parliamentary institutions this has often been interpreted as meaning that by voting, the masses determine what their leaders advocate. However, the transmission of political attitudes has generally been from the top down. By controlling the major "means of mental production" (that is, media, schools, and churches), the capitalist class normally is able to convince the masses to support the institutions that serve the capitalist class. The upper class thus is usually able to manipulate the masses into supporting its domination of the state. And at least in the United States, the capitalist class is able to get the masses to support the political parties it usually controls, the candidates it selects, the governmental policies it formulates, and the policies carried out by the state. Capitalist-class values and ideology permeate all aspects of life in capitalist society. The ideological hegemony of the capitalist class is probably the most important mechanism (direct or indirect) by which the capitalist class dominates the state and capitalist society.

A stable social order requires that its productive lower classes believe it to be legitimate. Power based on naked force or pure chicanery is notoriously unstable. In Max Weber's words, "organized domination . . . requires that human conduct be conditioned to obedience toward those masters who claim to be the bearers of legitimate power. . . . The very essence of the state is that most people accept its rule as being good and right. If the state is to exist the dominated must obey the authority claimed by the powers that be."[2] Every ruling class must justify its rule by

---

[1] The discussion that follows is indebted to Poulantzas, *Political Power and Social Classes*; Claus Offe, "The Abolition of Market Control and the Problem of Legitimacy, I and II," *Kapitalistate* no. 1 (1973): 109-116, and no. 2 (1973): 73-83; Claus Offe, "Advanced Capitalism and the Welfare State," *Politics and Society* 2, no. 4 (Summer 1972): 479-488; Sabine Sardei-Biermann et al., "Class Domination and the Political System: A Critical Interpretation of Recent Contributions by Claus Offe," *Kapitalistate* no. 2 (1973): 60-69; John Mollenkopf, "Theories of the State and Power Structure Research," *Insurgent Sociologist* 5, no. 3 (Spring 1975): 245-264; David Gold, Clarence Y. H. Lo, and Erik Olin Wright, "Recent Developments in Marxist Theories of the Capitalist State" in *Monthly Review* vol. 27, no. 5, 6 (October, November 1975); and to the panel presentations of, and informal discussions with the *Kapitalistate Collective* of the San Francisco Bay Area. I am especially indebted to discussions and correspondence with Erik Wright.

[2] Max Weber, "Politics as a Vocation" in Hans Gerth and C. Wright Mills, eds., *From Max Weber* (New York: Oxford University Press, 1946), pp. 78, 80.

basing it on some moral principle. Upper classes justify their hegemony as a logical and necessary consequence of the doctrines and beliefs that exist in a society and that are propagated by upper-class-controlled institutions (for example, the schools, media, and religion). Classical states and traditional ruling classes claimed legitimacy on the basis of God's will, the sanctification of the church (for example, the Pope would crown the emperor of the Holy Roman Empire), or simply age-old tradition. Modern states primarily rely on such factors as "the popular will" as expressed in elections, the high level of development of productive forces (for example, the American standard of living is "the highest in the world"), the personal (charismatic) characteristics of a leader, or nationalism and patriotism. Every ruling class attempts to consolidate its rule by attempting to monopolize all the means of mental production in the society to reinforce the underlying ideology on which the legitimacy of upper-class rule is based.

Voting is a powerful ideological mechanism. The ideology of "vote for your favorite candidate" permeates the media around election time. Having the majority of adults vote gives legitimacy to a system whose authority is supposedly derived from the will of the people. If only a small minority of eligible people vote, or if a declining percentage of those eligible vote (as has happened in the United States since the 1950s), this represents a danger signal, warning of a decline in legitimacy.

Another important factor helping the ruling class reinforce the legitimacy of its rule is the claim that it is responsible for the highest standard of living in the world and/or for very rapid economic advance; therefore it deserves to rule because of its contribution to the material well-being of the people. This factor is especially significant where the media reinforce the consumer ethic — the importance of possessing many material goods.[3]

Often an individual will capture the emotional spirit of a large part of a nation. He will be regarded as a "father" or as a "big brother" who has superhuman qualities and the ability to accomplish miracles for the people. The leadership of people with such electrifying qualities is in itself a basis for legitimate authority.[4] Hitler for the German petty bourgeoisie, Fidel Castro for the workers and peasants of Cuba, and perhaps the Kennedy brothers for large segments of the poor and the liberal middle classes in the United States have been such charismatic leaders.

The pursuit of the national interest in countries where the schools and media are permeated with the national idea is another important basis for the claim to legitimacy. The nationalist ideology claims that people should subordinate all other interests, including their class interest, to a more comprehensive national community. Where nationalism is strong, any group that persuades the people that it is best capable of realizing the nation's interests is assured of the people's support regardless of whether they are elected to power.

The more these four modern ways of establishing the authority of a ruling class are used the more secure is the legitimacy of the ruling class. If the ruling class

[3] Herbert Marcuse, *One Dimensional Man* (Boston: Beacon Press, 1964).
[4] Weber, "Politics as a Vocation," pp. 79-80.

can successfully claim that it is responsible for national prosperity and national aggrandizement, if it has been endorsed in a national referendum, and if it has a spokesperson with charismatic qualities, its rule is unchallengeable. A regime that is unable to consolidate itself by any of these claims to legitimacy must consequently rely on force to preserve its rule. Such regimes of necessity are unstable and short lived. Eventually such a situation will degenerate into rebellion and the regime will be overthrown, since every act of physical repression increases the resentment and alienation of the people. The rule of legitimate regimes, however, does not result in such alienation and accumulated resentment. Thus, the capitalist class's rule can only be secured by establishing the legitimacy of its rule among a willing and supportive underclass.

As was demonstrated earlier, upper-class ideological hegemony is never total. Both the day-to-day life experiences of and the active role of revolutionary organizations in the working class lead them to adopt political ideas counter to those being pushed onto them in the schools, churches, and mass media. In fact, in most capitalist countries an ideological battle continually goes on within the lower classes between radical and conservative political ideologies.[5] Even when members of the lower class accept capitalist-class values, they very often reinterpret them to suit their own situation.[6] Consequently the relative importance of ideological hegemony as an indirect structural mechanism of capitalist class control of the state varies from society to society and within a society over time with the degree of people's acceptance of what they are taught in the schools, hear on the radio and in sermons, see on TV, and read in the newspapers and magazines. How much of the capitalist ideology they accept is in turn a product of (1) the degree to which the media's message fits with their immediate and most strongly felt interests and experiences, and (2) the degree to which the counterideologies spread by radical organizations such as Marxist parties and revolutionary trade unions are pervasive and effective.

Note that it may not be necessary for working-class people to accept fully the capitalist values and ideologies propagated in the schools and media for these ideas to be effective instruments in securing capitalist-class domination of the state. While it is preferable that the masses be enthusiastic about the system, the barrage of procapitalist propaganda merely needs to neutralize alternative critical perspectives and demoralize those inclined to object to capitalist-class rule to guarantee social order and inoculate against the rise of mass revolutionary parties. Even if they sense that something is wrong, people constantly exposed to such procapitalist arguments can be deprived of the ability to successfully articulate their feelings and

---

[5] See Richard Hamilton, "Affluence and Workers: The West German Case," *The American Journal of Sociology* 71, no. 1 (September 1965): 144–152; Frank Parkin, *Class Inequality and Political Order* (New York: Praeger Publishers, 1971), chapter 3; and Walter P. Mills, "Lower Class Culture as a Generating Milieu of Gang Delinquency," *Journal of Social Issues* 14, no. 3 (1958): 5–19.

[6] See Parkin, *Class Inequality and Political Order*, chapter 3; and Hyman Rodman, "The Lower Class Value Stretch," *Social Forces* 42, no. 1 (October 1963): 205–215.

thus identify with revolutionary ideologies. Passivity, deference, and self-denigration can thus combine with bitterness and unarticulated class hatred as an alternative to conscious opposition to the system.[7]

The mass media

The three commercial TV networks, the four radio networks, the major popular magazines, and the mass circulation daily newspapers are all private corporations. As do all other private corporations, they exist to make a profit. In addition, the media corporations have the responsibility of disseminating the legitimizing capitalist-class ideology among the people.

The three commercial networks have a virtual monopoly on national and international news reporting and analysis on American television and (together with the Mutual network) radio. Each is fully integrated into the corporate world.[8] Of the 533 VHF TV stations in the early 1970s, 424 were affiliated with or owned outright by NBC, CBS, or ABC. The prime-time viewing and all of the national and international news and in-depth reporting of these stations is received from the three TV corporations. Of the remaining stations, eighty are NET affiliates and twenty-nine are independents. Although operated by a nonprofit corporation, NET is as closely tied to the upper class as any of the commercial networks. It was created by the Ford Foundation in 1953 and has been financed by it and several other closely allied upper-class foundations ever since. The Ford Foundation picks the board of directors and reserves the right to inspect NET programs produced with Ford money. The remaining twenty-nine independent VHF stations, all located in big cities where the other four networks have stations, produce virtually no programs of their own, relying on network reruns, old movies, and network-produced news footage.[9]

There are forty-two daily newspapers in the United States with a circulation greater than 300,000. Of these, thirty are owned by ten large newspaper chains. Ten of the others are controlled by independent millionaires. The other two are run by the Field Corporation, a company controlled by Chicago banks. The ten large chains are owned and controlled by leading upper-class financial interest groups or very wealthy upper-class families. The newspapers owned by these chains account for *62 percent* of the total newspaper circulation in the country.[10] The same corporations usually produce both newspapers and the leading magazines.[11]

[7] For a good discussion of these processes, see Richard Sennett and Jonathan Cobb, *The Hidden Injuries of Class*.
[8] For a detailed listing of the ties between the media corporations and various financial interests, see Howard Ehrlich, "The Politics of News Media Control," *The Insurgent Sociologist* 4, no. 4 (Summer 1974): 41-43.
[9] The Progressive Labor Party, *Who Rules the United States?*, p. 29.
[10] Mintz and Cohen, *America, Inc.*, p. 132.
[11] See The Progressive Labor Party, *Who Rules the United States?*, pp. 53-55 for a detailed list of the holdings of the dominant newspaper and magazine chains. See also Mintz and Cohen, *America, Inc.*, p. 132ff.

The major mass distribution newspapers targeted to the working-class market (the New York *Daily News*, the largest circulation daily in the country, being the primary example) restrict themselves to issues that deflect readers' concern away from class questions and mystify public events. Primary attention is given to petty scandals, sports, minor political corruption, and political demagogy. The papers are full of comic strips, inane features, contests, gossip columns, recipes, hobby columns, and right-wing political commentary and editorials. The news and editorial comment and the columns of all mass circulation dailies adopt the upper-class conservative or liberal orientations of the corporate owners and directors of the media corporations.

Leftist ideas are anathema to these papers, not only because they are against the interests of those who control the media, but also because the media need to attract advertising. The profits of the media corporations (TV, radio, and newspapers) come primarily from corporate advertising. Consequently, their programs and reporting must not offend advertisers. The corporations that are attacked by the media, either individually or as a class, are likely to withdraw their advertising from the media. Corporate advertisers thus hold life-or-death power over the media corporations, which they threaten to use if the media were ever to stop pursuing the interest of their owners. Advertisers have in many cases intervened in network programming directly or indirectly to prevent the showing of a program that was offensive to corporate interests.[12]

Although usually not owned by the large chains or members of the national upper class, small-town newspapers are nevertheless almost universally owned by wealthy local families. These families often have structured antagonisms with the largest financial interest groups; hence, these papers are even more conservative than the national papers that have close ties to the more liberal upper class. However, these smaller papers are forced to rely on the large newspaper chains and the two major wire services (which are, of course, also controlled by the capitalist class) for their national and international news, as well as for their columns and features. Even the editorials of most small-town papers are "canned" — that is, reproduced from editorials supplied by the national wire services or the special interests that send prepared editorials to the smaller papers throughout the country. Pressed for time and energy, smaller papers that are owned and controlled by the conservative local wealthy are usually happy to reproduce the right-wing positions supplied free to them by the various business groups. In the past the small-town newspapers were actually paid to use prepared editorials and commentary provided by such groups as the National Electric Light Association and National Coal Association.[13]

Competition among newspapers has decreased markedly during the course of the twentieth century. In 1910, 57 percent of all towns with newspapers had at

---

[12] See Miliband, *The State in Capitalist Society*, chapter 8; and Mintz and Cohen, *America, Inc.*, chapter 2, p. 113ff.

[13] Ferdinand Lundberg, *America's Sixty Families* (New York: Vanguard, 1937), chapter 7.

least two papers under different ownership. By 1970 this had been reduced to only 4 percent. In 1970 only sixty-four cities still had newspapers owned by different people.[14]

The upper class must maintain a virtual monopoly on the mass media. Only when the news, analysis, and attitudes disseminated to the masses are closely coordinated can the development of an independent position coinciding with one's class experiences and interests be arrested. Once media oriented to the interests of the working class (for example, mass circulation Socialist and Communist dailies, radio stations, and magazines) are allowed to compete effectively in the working class and among the other poorer classes, the ideological hegemony of the upper class is destroyed. When ideas compatible with working-class reality compete on essentially equal terms with upper-class ideas, the working class tends to adhere to the ideas organic to its own experience. Consequently, those who finance and advertise in the mass media are acutely sensitive to the necessity of maintaining a monopoly on attitude formation and act accordingly.

Note that the media do two things: (1) they reinforce and build up certain basic values and general attitudes in the masses of people, such as patriotism, respect for property, free enterprise, individualism, cynicism, desire for material affluence, anticommunism, competitiveness, fatalism, distrust, respect for authority, and racial, sexual, and working-class stereotypes;[15] (2) these values and general attitudes are then used by the media and state to mobilize support for specific policies and the individual leaders advanced by the upper class. Using such sentiments — established not only by the media but also by the worker's family, work, and social experiences — the upper-class media are able to manipulate the masses to support their specific programs such as the Spanish-American War, participation in World War I, the cold war, Korea, Vietnam, and its imperialist adventures in general, the Marshall Plan, NATO, the peacetime draft and massive military spending, the suppression of Communists and other radicals in the universities and unions in the 1950s, and detente with the Soviet Union and China. The various candidates of the two upper-class-controlled political parties are also able to utilize the basic sentiments established and reinforced by the media to befuddle the issue of class and make demagogic or irrational appeals to the masses to get their votes (and hence reconfirm the legitimacy of the existing class system).

The upper-class-controlled mass media set the limits on what legitimate issues arise. They establish the bounds within which discussion can take place. The range of columnists in newspapers, the range of panels on network shows, and the range of positions presented in documentaries are very narrow. Opinions falling outside of these bounds are discredited as too strange to be given serious consideration.[16] Issues such as workers' control of industry, military aid to the Viet Cong, the abolition of social classes, and the disbanding of the standing army and its replace-

[14] Mintz and Cohen, *America, Inc.*, pp. 131-132. See also Domhoff, *Who Rules America?*, pp. 79-83.
[15] See Wolfe, *The Seamy Side of Democracy: Repression in America*, pp. 144-145.
[16] See Domhoff, *Who Rules America?*, p. 80.

ment by a popular militia are simply never discussed. Since they seem beyond the pale of legitimate opinion, such issues are not taken seriously by the media corporations.

The most important upper-class-controlled media are closely linked with the capitalist class's consensus-seeking and policy-planning institutions — the CED and the CFR. The policy ideas formulated by such groups are thus disseminated by the leading mass media to be adopted by the American people as if they were their own. In the early 1970s seven of the directors of the *New York Times*, six directors of CBS, four directors of Time, Inc., and two each of the *Washington Post* and the *Los Angeles Times* were also members of the CFR. Four directors of both CBS and Time, Inc., were also trustees of the CED, as were three directors of the *Washington Post* and ABC and two directors of the *Los Angeles Times*.[17]

Political values and general attitudes are established and reinforced more in the general programs — and especially in the advertising — on television than in the overtly political commentary and news (which focuses on forming specific attitudes to concrete issues). TV programming (both the actual programs and the advertising) is permeated with upper-class values.[18]

The effect of the media on the formation of both general attitudes and values and specific opinions is immense. Studies have shown that people who are asked for their opinions about a domestic or international event after a president has addressed the nation over national television simply tend to paraphrase the president's position. Even people who neither read newspapers nor watch network news nevertheless acquire their political attitudes from these media indirectly. Opinion leaders or respected people exist in any community who are particularly attentive to world events. These people are often called upon to interpret news of world events, or, because of their interpersonal abilities, are able to sway people to their viewpoints. Such people acquire their personal political attitudes from the leading news magazines, the major papers, the network news, and special documentaries and panel discussions. Through informal networks of personal influence, they both reinforce each other's political attitudes (giving themselves confidence in the accuracy of the positions they have acquired from the mass media) and convince those who are not influenced directly by the media to accept their media-influenced viewpoints.[19] Thus, when they have a virtual monopoly on political information (as they do in the United States), the influence of the mass media corporations is thoroughly pervasive and one of the most important pillars of upper-class rule. If they are to be managed effectively, people need to believe that they are unmanaged. If their media control our heads, the powerful need not put guns to our backs.

Advertising in the mass media not only creates a popular demand for the

[17] The Progressive Labor Party, *Who Rules the United States?*, p. 57.
[18] See Miliband, *The State in Capitalist Society*, chapter 7; and Herbert Schiller, *The Mind Managers* (Boston: Beacon Press, 1973).
[19] See Katz and Lazarsfeld, *Personal Influence*; and Robert K. Merton, *Social Theory and Social Structure* (Glencoe, Ill.: Free Press, 1957), chapter 10.

products being advertised, it also is relentless propaganda for increased consumption of goods in general. The theme of this propaganda is that happiness is possessing many things. Further, by making material goods so important, advertising legitimatizes the economic and political system that is allegedly responsible for producing and delivering these goods. The cumulative effect of corporate advertising — at least as long as the standard of living improves — is to increase the prestige of capitalism and enhance the authority of the upper-class rule throughout the capitalist state.

The corporations also have mastered the techniques of public relations.[20] Most of the PR departments of the major corporations closely monitor public opinion (by conducting opinion surveys and reading letters-to-the-editor columns, the popular press and student newspapers) to detect any anticorporate or anti-upper-class sentiments (directed at either a specific or broad interest or corporation) that might be emerging. Once such sentiments are detected, the PR apparatus swings into full gear with rebuttal letters to the editor, demands for equal time, and local appearances of PR people to talk with the discontented or those likely to be influenced by them. However, if the situation is considered serious, this apparatus launches massive media campaigns to neutralize hostile attitudes and replace them with a renewed sense of the corporate interests' legitimacy and beneficence.[21]

The most significant example of this process in the early 1970s has been the petroleum corporations' (especially EXXON's) attempt to neutralize the rising hostility toward their role in creating and profiting from the pollution of the environment and the energy crisis. EXXON has sponsored a major and sustained PR effort focusing on the major TV networks' news programs to convince the opinion leaders among the masses that the oil company's major purpose is to clean up the environment and produce a guaranteed and cheap supply of energy for the American people. They have also been very sensitive to campus and community groups protests against the oil companies. They have assigned PR people to neutralize hostile sentiments by using letters and personal appearances. The techniques of manipulation of public opinion are by no means limited to the defensive. In the 1950s the privately owned electric power companies used a massive advertising campaign to marshall public opinion against governmental ventures into this economic sector in the form of publicly owned utilities.[22]

Empirical studies have shown that the more people are exposed to the media, the more conservative they become — at least in their attitudes about foreign policy. In 1968, 17 percent of those who regularly read newspapers and 22 percent of those who read "many" magazines favored pulling out of Vietnam, while 23 percent of those who read newspapers only occasionally or never, and 20 percent of

---

[20] See Glenn Hirsch, "Only You Can Prevent Ideological Hegemony," *The Insurgent Sociologist* 5, no. 3 (Spring 1975).

[21] Domhoff, *The Higher Circles*, pp. 255-256.

[22] See David Halberstam, *The Best and the Brightest* (New York: Random House, 1972) for several good examples of the use of public relations techniques by the U.S. government in the early and mid-1960s to sell the war in Vietnam to the American people.

those who read two, one, or no magazines did so.[23] These correlations remained the same across income categories and among Protestants and Catholics alike. The mass media in capitalist society does appear to have a conservatizing effect.

The capitalist class does not have to completely monopolize the media to secure its ideological hegemony. However, it does have to dominate the media to ensure that competition with alternative ideas is so lopsided as to virtually guarantee the outcome. In countries (such as France and Italy) where Communist newspapers and periodicals compete on essentially equal terms with those defending a capitalist ideology, the poorer classes tend to believe the material in the Communist press and the better-off classes tend to accept what they find in the capitalist press. In countries where the Marxist (or other radical) press is very small, few people of any class seriously consider its ideas even when such periodicals and literature can be easily obtained at any newsstand. The general indoctrination of the poorer classes can be massive enough to prevent them from taking such literature seriously. Further, the ready availability of such critical material, combined with the obvious fact that few bother to read it, is itself strong propaganda for the existing system, since people apparently have a free choice but choose to ignore Marxist material. The outlawing of critical material in countries where few would read it anyway would only stir curiosity and perhaps sympathy for those newspapers and writers that were repressed.

Schooling

The schools in capitalist society train people to acquire the proper respect for authority and the proper attitudes about class, nationalism, sex roles, and the rest of the core capitalist values and institutions. The primary schools emphasize the importance of discipline as much as they do the learning of concrete skills. The primary schools inculcate factory discipline in the working class. Standing in line, raising one's hand, getting permission to go to the bathroom, not talking, not eating in the classroom, unquestioned obedience to the teacher, unquestioned acceptance of what the teacher and textbooks say, punctuality, and regular attendance are just as important for the youngster to learn as reading, writing, and arithmetic if he or she is to be a good worker.

Both the primary and the secondary schools emphasize the internalization of the basic capitalist values and attitudes. Every morning a prayer is recited to the flag, patriotic songs are frequently sung, national holidays and rites are regularly celebrated, and all the textbooks — especially those in social sciences (American history and civics being the most overt) — are permeated with the values of capitalism and Americanism. It is in the primary and secondary schools that students learn many of the basic values and attitudes that will determine their behavior once they leave school. The mass media and the politicians have

[23] Richard Hamilton, *Restraining Myths*, p. 196. Part or even all of these relations could be due to the fact that those who pay more attention to the media are also the better educated (education is positively correlated with conservatism), and thus these results could possibly be spurious. Unfortunately, appropriate data could not be found that would determine whether this was in fact the case.

traditionally used the basic values and attitudes established in the schools to generate support for specific capitalist-class projects such as the war in Vietnam, wage controls, huge military expenditures, and cutbacks on welfare.

Compulsory public education in the United States was introduced explicitly for the purposes discussed here. During the period between the end of the Civil War and the beginning of World War I, it was introduced in the industrial areas to integrate the working-class immigrants into the capitalist system, build up patriotism and discipline in their children, and teach them the basic skills needed by an increasingly sophisticated industrial capitalist system. Control over the schools was carefully established so that the working class itself would be unable to determine what occurred in its schools. The primary and secondary schools were put under the control of city-wide boards dominated by local business people who selected the principals and textbooks and made the basic school policies that ensured that the schools would in fact realize the functions for which they were established. The new primary and secondary schools established for the working class differed in their purpose and orientation from the older schools designed to train the children of the upper and upper middle classes. Whereas the former stressed basic skills and discipline, the latter stressed the classical subjects such as Latin, Greek, history, philosophy and rhetoric — subjects thought to prepare these children for their future role as capitalists and leaders.[24]

The capitalist educational system continues to be greatly differentiated. On one extreme are the ghetto schools designed merely to keep children out of trouble. On the other extreme are the upper-class private schools designed to train the new generation of the capitalist class. In between are the large working-class schools, which emphasize discipline, elemental skills, and office and mechanical skills, and the middle-class schools, which emphasize creativity and preparation for college. Because the jobs for which their students are being trained require these attributes, upper-class and middle-class schools devote much less attention to discipline and respect for authority, and much more to student initiative and autonomy. In spite of the differences in their function and the type of student attending them, the ghetto, working-class, and middle-class schools are controlled by local business people who pick the textbooks, make basic policy, and select the top administrators.

Most universities in capitalist society train the managerial and highly skilled workers of the capitalist system. The elite universities, especially Harvard, Yale, and Princeton, specialize in training the new generation of the upper class — that is, those people who will occupy the top positions in the corporate world as well as

---

[24] See Samuel Bowles and Herbert Gintis, *Schooling in Capitalist America: Educational Reform and the Contradictions of Economic Life* (New York: Basic Books, 1976); David Tyack, *The One Best System* (Cambridge, Mass.: Harvard University Press, 1974); David Cohen and Marvin Lazenson, "Education and the Corporate Order," in *Socialist Revolution* no. 8 (March-April 1972); Michael Katz, *Class, Bureaucracy and Schools* (New York: Praeger Publishers, 1971); Michael Katz, *The Irony of Early School Reform* (Cambridge, Mass.: Harvard University Press, 1968); and Joel Spring, *Education and the Rise of the Corporate State* (Boston: Beacon Press, 1972).

the state. Those universities prepare people for work as lawyers, doctors, engineers, scientists, and teachers. Higher education continues the work of the primary and secondary schools in inculcating values and attitudes in students, although on a much more sophisticated level than is necessary in the latter schools. Political science, sociology, economics, history, philosophy, literature, and related fields train students to adopt the specific attitudes appropriate to the upper classes while reinforcing with highly sophisticated arguments the basic values and attitudes established in the primary and secondary schools. A college graduate is thus not only more skilled than a high school graduate, but also much more thoroughly indoctrinated in the system's values. Consequently, college graduates usually are more conservative (see table 11-1).

There are over 2,000 institutions of higher education in the United States. Most are small private (often denominational) colleges; approximately 800 are state owned. However, a handful of elite institutions set the academic standards and tone for the rest. Twenty-five universities grant 75 percent of all Ph.D.s in the

Table 11-1   The Effect of Formal Education on Leftism

	Italy[1] 1968 (C)[a]	West Germany[2] 1967 (S)[a]	Norway[3] 1965 (C+S+L)[a]	Britain[4] 1970 (L)[a]	Sweden[5] 1968 (C+S)[a]	Netherlands[6] 1968 (S)[a]	Australia[7] 1967 (L)[a]	Canada[8] 1965 (L)[a]	Japan[9] 1960 (S)[a]
All classes									
Only primary or equivalent education	30%	—	69%	—	64%	43%	—	10%	22%
Some college or equivalent education	5	—	30	—	21	36	—	11	35
Working class only									
Primary only	—	50	—	54	—	—	64	—	—
Some college	—	47	—	34	—	—	33	—	—

Sources:
1. Lipset and Rokkan, *Party Systems and Voter Alignments*, p. 168.
2. Rose, *Electoral Behavior*, p. 151.
3. Rose, *Electoral Behavior*, p. 335.
4. Rose, *Electoral Behavior*, p. 506.
5. Rose, *Electoral Behavior*, p. 404.
6. Rose, *Electoral Behavior*, pp. 244, 245.
7. Rose, *Electoral Behavior*, p. 460.
8. Rose, *Electoral Behavior*, p. 590.
9. Lipset and Rokkan, *Party Systems and Voter Alignments*, p. 449.

[a] Key to abbreviations:
(C): Support for the Communist party
(S): Support for the Social Democratic party
(L): Support for the Labor party

United States.[25] Ten receive 38 percent of all federal funds.[26] In many academic fields members of the top ten departments write over 50 percent of all the articles appearing in each field's major professional journals. Foundation grants are also concentrated in several leading institutions (in economics and business ten universities and research institutes received 78 percent of all Ford Foundation grants from 1951 to 1964).[27] Led by Harvard, Yale, Princeton, Columbia, the University of California at Berkeley, Stanford, Johns Hopkins, M.I.T., the University of Michigan, the University of Chicago, and a very few others, these elite schools thus establish the intellectual pattern for all the academic professions. The majority of graduate students emerging from these departments to become professors and researchers throughout the United States (and the world) are rather similar. They tend to share similar values, attitudes, and approaches to their subject matter. They then propagate the approaches and ideas hegemonic in the leading departments throughout the land. A minority, however, develop critical, even Marxist perspectives and often become the leaders of radical opposition movements in their academic disciplines.[28]

Virtually every institution of higher education is controlled directly by trustees representing the wealthiest and best connected interests in the areas they serve. Most schools and the less influential colleges are dominated by local small-business people. The elite universities, however, are directly controlled by the upper class and its leading employees. Of the 727 trustees of the thirty leading universities in the United States in the mid-1960s (fourteen of which are private and sixteen public), one-third were listed in *The Social Register* and 45 percent were corporate directors or executives. One-half of the top 200 industrial corporations and financial institutions were represented on the boards of these thirty schools.[29]

A study done of 306 trustees of the leading American universities in 1966 showed that only one was a labor official, one was black, ten were professors, and none were manual workers. Almost all others were big-business people.[30] Of the Lockheed corporation's eighteen directors in the early 1970s, ten were college trustees. The United California Bank's thirty directors included fifteen college trustees.[31] Directors of Chase Manhattan Bank sit on the boards of trustees of nine universities, including Harvard, Princeton, and Columbia; directors of General Motors sit on the boards of seven universities; directors of EXXON, on eight

---

[25] See David Horowitz, *The Universities and the Ruling Class* (San Francisco: Bay Area Radical Education Project, 1969) p. 5.

[26] James Ridgeway, *The Closed Corporation: American Universities in Crisis* (New York: Ballantine Books, 1968), p. 5.

[27] Horowitz, *The Universities and the Ruling Class*, p. 5.

[28] Everything said in the discussion of students' and scientists' politics in chapter 4 is relevant for understanding why this is so.

[29] Domhoff, *Who Rules America?*, p. 79.

[30] Troy Duster, "The Aims of Higher Learning and the Control of the Universities," Berkeley, Calif., booklet, (n.d.). p. 11, cited in David N. Smith, *Who Rules the Universities?* (New York: Monthly Review Press, 1974), pp. 49-50.

[31] Smith, *Who Rules the Universities?*, p. 55.

boards; and directors of General Electric, on eleven.[32] By staffing the boards of trustees of American colleges and universities, leading business people are able to directly control higher education. They select the higher officers of the colleges and universities and establish the basic educational policies which guarantee that faculty and administrators do the bidding of the upper class and that students are manipulated in the interests of the corporations.

The upper class is also able to control higher education through a number of other direct mechanisms, including the use of family endowments, personal gifts, foundation grants, and corporate gifts. They are also able to control them indirectly through the federal government, which heavily subsidizes the major universities.[33] A small percentage of the operating expenses of the leading universities comes from students' tuition. Government funds, foundation money (research grants, fellowships, and special grants), and gifts from the corporations and rich individuals account for most of their income. Schools vary considerably in the relative importance of these three sources of external funds. But all the leading schools are thoroughly dependent on the upper class because of their need for money.[34]

Universities are also integrated into the corporate world by virtue of being major corporations themselves. They have extensive stock holdings from which they derive much of their annual operating expenses. As does any other business, they buy and sell their stocks on the market to maximize their income. The universities and colleges are large-scale employers of office staff, ground and janitorial staff, and laboratory assistants in addition to their faculty. As is any large employer, they are interested in keeping wages down and productivity up. Moreover, universities are often directly and indirectly involved in several business ventures that are spin-offs of the research programs developed by their graduate faculties.[35]

The leading foundations play a very important role in controlling the leading universities. From around 1900 to 1932 the Rockefeller and Carnegie foundations played the leading role in creating large endowments for them. Through the mechanism of matching funds, these two foundations were responsible for creating $660 million in endowments during this period (about two-thirds of all endowments in 1932). Since World War II, the major foundations (especially the Ford Foundation) have been playing a major role in innovative programs designed to serve the upper class. Probably the most outstanding example of this has been the creation of the various institutes for international studies at the leading universities.[36]

The iron hand of the upper class has been felt whenever university faculties get out of line and conduct research, write, and teach in the interest of the working

---

[32] Ibid., p. 54.
[33] Domhoff, *Who Rules America?*, p. 77.
[34] See Ridgeway, *The Closed Corporation*, pp. 212-215, for an enumeration of the major universities' federal financial support.
[35] Ibid., chapter 3.
[36] Horowitz, *The Universities and the Ruling Class*.

class rather than the capitalists. There was a purge of the faculty of American universities who identified with the Populist movement in the 1890s. During World War I faculty who were antiwar were also purged (such prominent people as Thorstein Veblen and Charles Beard were dismissed).[37] During the McCarthy witch-hunt period in the 1950s, almost all Marxist professors were either fired or pressured (usually with success) to renounce their beliefs as the condition for continuing employment. The combination of the carrot (fat research grants, promotion opportunities, tenure, office space and resources, publication — and thereby the creation of a professional reputation — and other monetary and status inducements) with the stick (lack of promotion, impossibility of publication, deprivation of auxiliary services including research assistants, lack of grant money, and loss of jobs) has very effectively kept university faculty loyal to the capitalist class running the universities. This combination has also kept them performing their central functions, especially the development and propagation of a sophisticated ideological defense of the status quo — the specialty of the social science and humanities departments (which are well rewarded by their masters for their efforts).

Research money and promotions are used by the upper class to control the subject matter taught in the social sciences. Faculty and students who do the research desired by the capitalist class, come up with the "right" conclusions, and present positions compatible with upper-class interests in the classroom are rewarded, while professors who are critical of the status quo are punished and eventually eliminated. C. Wright Mills's experience is a classic example of the use of research grants and promotion to control the content of the social sciences. Mills, whose sociological projects had been well financed until his critical study of power in the United States, *The Power Elite*, appeared, was cut off from research grants after that book's publication. Leading Marxist scholars (such as Paul Sweezy) were unable to get tenure at American universities during the McCarthy period and were thus forced to find independent means of survival. The very few Marxists who survived the McCarthy period (such as Paul Baran at Stanford) were totally isolated in their departments by a hostile faculty interested in angling for favor with the sources of funding. During the early 1960s Stanford University forced the head of its institute of Hispanic-American and Luso-Brazilian Studies (Professor Ronald Hilton) to resign and the left-oriented journal he was publishing to fold so that Stanford could get Ford Foundation money.[38]

Empirical studies have demonstrated that virtually everywhere among the advanced capitalist countries education is negatively correlated with leftism — that is, the more education one has, the more conservative one becomes. This is true within the working class as well as within the whole population. Table 11-1 shows that this is true for Italy, West Germany, Norway, Britain, Sweden, the Netherlands, and Australia. The major exception to this relationship is Japan, the only country for which data could be located showing that the more educated are more leftist (in Japan this is true for the population as a whole). In France the

[37] Lundberg, *America's Sixty Families*, chapter 10
[38] Horowitz, *The Universities and the Ruling Class*, pp. 15-16.

workers with the *least* formal education are the most avid information gatherers, have the greatest interest in current events, and are the most leftist.[39] In the United States on basic issues such as the war in Vietnam, the more educated were the *most* likely to favor the war. For example, in 1969, 12 percent of those with a college education approved of immediately withdrawing all troops from Vietnam, compared with 18 percent of those with a high school education and 25 percent of those with only a grade school education.[40] Moreover, in 1968 people with only a grade school education were the most likely to call themselves "doves."[41] The schools thus seem to defuse potential discontent and conservatize the working class, thereby hindering it from developing class consciousness. Note, however, that both the quantity and quality of education appears to have a radicalizing effect on many of those who have trained for jobs they are unable to get. Both the knowledge gained and the bitterness resulting from frustrated expectations act to push some "overeducated" workers to the Left.

One could argue that education's almost universal negative correlation with leftism is a product of the high levels of education required for the highest paying professional and managerial jobs (which produce conservatism). However, the relationship between education and leftism seems to be as strong within the working class as within the entire population (see table 11-1). One could also argue that the negative correlation between education and leftism within the working class results from the more skilled and better-paid workers having more education. But little relationship between income level or skill and leftist politics within the working class seems to exist. It has been argued that the greater conservatism of the more educated workers could come from their resentment about being in working-class jobs (hence explaining their reluctance to identify with the working-class parties). This may partly explain the observed correlations. But it is unlikely to be as important as the effect of the content of the ideas and the personal goals that they have acquired through education — that is, its general conservatizing influence. One could argue that the resentment caused by having an education higher than that which is typical for one's occupation should produce greater, rather than lesser leftism.[42]

The churches and religion

Before the rise of the mass media and universal education, before general secularization, and before patriotism and nationalism came to have deep popular appeal, the major means of maintaining ideological hegemony was for the upper classes to control the churches. By doing so they controlled the process of building up and manipulating the basic values and attitudes of the working and peasant classes. Generally, religion preaches respect for authority, private property, and the law. It also persuades people to seek salvation in the afterlife by obeying God's

---

[39] Hamilton, *Affluence and the French Worker*, p. 113.
[40] George Gallup, *The Gallup Poll* (New York: Random House, 1972), p. 2223.
[41] Ibid., p. 2125.
[42] Lipset, *Political Man*, p. 254.

will, rather than in this life by acting on their own interests. Although not as important as it once was in preserving the class system, it still plays a major role as a conservatizing force in society. This is particularly true in the United States (the most religious of the advanced capitalist countries) and the more backward areas of the capitalist world where superstitions still have great strength because of the desperate condition of the poor.

The doctrine of the omnipotence of God and total submission to His will pervades the general world views of religious people, and hence is sublimated as submission to political rulers and the upper class. Religion provides a consolation for the suffering of people on earth and a deflection of one's hopes into the future. Combined with its advocacy of the earthly status quo, religion thus typically serves as a powerful legitimatizing force for upper-class rule.[43] Further, most religions, especially the religions of the working class and the poor — Baptism, Methodism, the Messianic sects, and Catholicism — in their sermons typically condemn radical political movements and preach instead either political abstention or submission to governmental authority.

The major denominations are usually controlled directly by upper-class families and institutions that supply much of their financing. The leading potentates of the churches are normally closely connected to the upper class and its corporations.[44] Although composed of, and generally led by, members of the oppressed classes, the sectarian Messianic sects and the fundamentalist Christian groups (for example, the Jehovah's Witnesses, the Jesus movement, and fundamentalist Baptists) are nevertheless also supported by the capitalist class and serve its ends.[45] Most of the "Jesus freak" groups of the 1970s are militantly apolitical and objectively conservative, while some sects, such as the "Moonies," are explicitly anti-socialist (the Children of God are a notable exception). Because of their orientation (especially in a crisis), such groups are financed and encouraged by the upper classes. Although they cannot control them directly, the upper classes use them to undermine the support of the Left in the lower classes.

The class-heterogeneous nature of most established churches acts as a further conservatizing influence on the working class. By bringing together people of all classes, participation in such religions confuses the lower classes and causes them to

---

[43] For studies of the connection between the capitalist class and the churches, see Jerome Davis, *Capitalism and Its Culture* (New York: Farrar and Rinehart, Inc., 1935); Roy H. Johnson, "American Baptists in the Age of Big Business," *Journal of Religion* 11, no. 1 (1931): 63-85; and Martin A. Larson, *Church Wealth and Business Income* (New York: Philosophical Library, 1965).

[44] Studies of the control of working-class churches by capital include Thompson, *The Making of the English Working Class*; and Pope, *Millhands and Preachers*.

[45] To a considerable extent salvation religion and revolutionary politics are functional substitutes for one another. Where such religions are strong, radicalism tends to be weak, and vice versa. See, for example, W. Phillips Davison, "Review of Sven Rydenfelt Kommunismen i Sverige," *Public Opinion Quarterly* 18 (Winter #4, 1954-1955): 375-88. Rydenfelt demonstrates a strong negative correlation between fundamentalist Christianity and support of the Communists by geographical areas within Sweden.

respect the middle- and upper-class leaders of their churches and, consequently, their political views (which are advanced as the church's views) as well.[46]

Religion almost universally acts as a conservatizing force on the common people's political consciousness and behavior (there is some evidence that religion also has a liberalizing influence on the better-off classes).[47] In France, West Germany, Italy, Belgium, the Netherlands, Sweden, Norway, Australia, and the United States the more religious people are, the less support they give the leftist parties (see table 11-2). This holds for the working class as well as for the entire population. Religious influence is considerable. Its greatest impact in undermining support of the Left occurs in those countries with strong Marxist parties — for example, France and Italy (as well as the Netherlands) — and its least impact occurs in countries with only moderately left labor parties or no true working-class parties at all — for example, Australia and the United States.[48]

[46] See Hamilton, *Class and Politics in the United States*, p. 320.

[47] As illustrations of the conservatizing effect of fundamentalist religion on the working class, see Benton Johnson, "Ascetic Protestantism and Political Preference," *Public Opinion Quarterly* 26 (Spring 1962): 34-46, and "Ascetic Protestantism and Political Preference in the Deep South," *American Journal of Sociology* 69 (January 1964): 359-366; and also Pope, *Millhands and Preachers*. Johnson's studies also show that church attendance has a liberalizing effect on the middle classes.

[48] Religious ideology itself need not necessarily have such a stabilizing social effect. There is a long history of uprisings inspired by religious ideologies which interpret Biblical preachments against injustice to imply not just retribution in the afterlife, but also the need for the righteous to act against the wicked in the here and now. Massive peasant insurrections occurred in Central Europe at the time of the Reformation which were inspired by revolutionary interpretations of the Gospels. The Puritan Revolution in England was similarly inspired.

Insurrections in Italy, China, and throughout the countries of the Third World have been inspired by similar inflammatory interpretations of Christianity. Such insurrectionary uses of Christianity (and other religions) always involve a reliance on God to play a crucial role in the success of the temporal revolutionary movement. Instead of relying on a scientific analysis of conditions, possibilities, strategies, and organizational forms, religiously inspired insurrections place their faith in divine intervention. As a consequence, such movements have always failed. Religious insurrections, although often triumphant for short periods, are always crushed in relatively short order and consequently are either completely exterminated by the authorities or become apoliticized, retreating by necessity back to the conception of salvation in the afterlife — or in some cases to the establishment of religious communes that do not challenge the existing authorities but instead attempt to establish the life of brotherhood *only* among the community of believers.

See, for example, Thomas O'Dea, *The Sociology of Religion* (Englewood Cliffs, N.J.: Prentice-Hall, 1966); Friedrich Engels, "Peasant War in Germany," in Friedrich Engels, *The German Revolutions* (Chicago: University of Chicago Press, 1967); and Norman Cohn, *The Pursuit of the Millennium* (New York: Harper & Row, 1961); Hill, *Puritanism and Revolution*, and *The Century of Revolution*; Viltorio Lanternari, *The Religions of the Oppressed* (New York: The New American Library, 1965); Peter Worsley, *The Trumpets Shall Sound* (New York: Schocken, 1968); Eric Hobsbawm, *Primitive Rebels* (New York: W. W. Norton, 1965); and Eric Wolf, *Peasant Wars of the Twentieth Century*.

Table 11–2 The Effect of Religion on Leftism

	France[1] 1952 (C)[a]	West Germany[2] 1967 (S)[a]	Italy[3] 1968 (C+LS+S)[a]	Belgium[4] 1968 (S)[a]	Netherlands[5] 1968 (S)[a]	Sweden[6] 1968 (C+S)[a]	Norway[7] 1965 (C+S+L)[a]	Australia[8] 1967 (L)[a]	United States[9] 1964 (D)[a]
All classes									
Regular churchgoers	—	—	—	12%	—	26%	22%	—	—
Nonchurchgoers	—	—	—	50	—	72	57	—	—
Working class only									
Regular churchgoers	0%	31%	14%	22	15%	—	—	50%	57%
Nonchurchgoers	44	60	47	69	72	—	—	70	82

Sources:
1. Linz, "The Social Bases of West German Politics," p. 256. These data are for nominally Catholic men only.
2. Rose, *Electoral Behavior*, p. 148.
3. Rose, *Electoral Behavior*, p. 190.
4. Rose, *Electoral Behavior*, pp. 81, 85.
5. Rose, *Electoral Behavior*, p. 249.
6. Rose, *Electoral Behavior*, p. 417.
7. Rose, *Electoral Behavior*, p. 331.
8. Rose, *Electoral Behavior*, p. 462.
9. Hamilton, *Class and Politics in the United States*, p. 320.

[a] Key to abbreviations:
(C) : Communist party support
(S) : Social Democratic party support
(L) : Labor party support
(D) : Democratic party support
(LS) : Left Socialist party support

Religious workers are less politically active than nonreligious workers. In 1953 a study of West German workers showed that roughly 44 percent of the nominal Christian male workers who never attended church seldom discussed politics, but roughly 53 percent of the regular attenders never discussed politics.[49] In general, religious workers have less of an understanding of politics and demonstrate less concern for political issues than do nonreligious workers.

Although religious workers are far more likely than nonreligious workers to support the working-class parties of the Left, they are only somewhat more conservative in their general political attitudes than nonreligious workers (see table 11-3). For example, although nonreligious workers were ten times more likely to vote for the Marxist parties in Italy in 1959, they were only twice as likely to believe that the interests of the majority were ignored by the government. In Germany in the same year the religious and nonreligious workers did not differ in their belief that the interests of the majority were ignored by the government; however, the nonreligious workers were almost three times as likely as the religious workers to vote for the Social Democratic party. That religion has a considerably greater effect on voting than on general political attitudes suggests that the Christian Democratic parties are able to mobilize the religious sentiments of discontented

[49] Linz, "The Social Bases of West German Politics," p. 279.

Table 11-3 The Effect of Religion on Leftist Attitudes (Men Only), 1959

	Germany		Italy	
	Religious Workers	Nonreligious Workers	Religious Workers	Nonreligious Workers
Percent voting for the Left parties	27%	72%	7%	75%
Percent expressing lack of confidence in the ruling Christian Democratic party	16	37	13	32
Percent believing that the interests of the majority are ignored by the government	51	49	20	39
Percent believing that voting decides how the country is run	88	85	49	56
Percent feeling that the economic situation of their family is satisfactory	68	55		
Percent feeling they could influence their local government	35	26	29	15

Source: Calculated from Gabriel Almond and Sidney Verba's data used for their *Civic Culture* study, *Civic Culture* (Princeton, N.J.: Princeton University Press, 1963).

people — who otherwise might support the Left — to get them to vote for "God and the Church."

Normally the most economically backward and traditional areas of a country are the most susceptible to the hold of religion and other "opiates" that prevent the rise of class-conscious ideology and behavior. Poverty and the stability of traditional relationships can discourage hope for basic improvement in "this life" as well as the belief that collective action can produce basic social changes — hope is channeled into prayers for salvation in an afterlife instead. Ignorance and illiteracy mitigate against intraclass communication and cause the people to rely more on religious authorities for information and social analyses. The relatively most oppressed workers of the backward regions usually are the most loyal to the traditional ways. The generally more conservative attitudes of Southern workers in the United States is only one example of the grip traditional religion, racism, and nationalism have on the more backward regions of the industrial capitalist countries.[50]

[50] Lipset, *Political Man*, pp. 273-278.

However, once radicalism catches on in such regions, they typically become the most leftist in a country. Once workers break out of the stranglehold that the upper-class-manipulated traditional ideologies have over them, their oppression (perhaps combined with the bitterness of having long been used by the upper class) manifests itself in extremely militant opposition to the system. Such a phenomenon occurred in the Andalusian region of Spain, where during the nineteenth century the traditional Catholic peasant's conservatism was transformed into an extreme anarchism and hatred of class society.[51] A breakthrough from enslavement to tradition and conservative politics has also been occurring in southern Italy. Support for the Communist Party has grown very rapidly in the postwar period, transforming this area from the bastion of Italian conservatism to a hotbed of discontent.[52]

Nationalism and racism

Racism, nationalism, and religion have similar effects on people. The more workers think of themselves as first members of a national community, racial group, or religious sect containing all classes of people, the less likely they are to develop class-conscious attitudes and behavior. Adherents of such perspectives see national events as well as their felt oppression as the manifestation of the struggle between nations or races. "Only the supremacy of the Aryan, white, or the black race, only the world hegemony of Germany, England, or the United States can set things right." As do established religions, such attitudes defuse class consciousness and struggle, obfuscate the causes of oppression, and mystify the possibility of solutions. Such ideologies benefit the upper class, which generally propagates and manipulates them to mobilize the working masses to support capitalist-class policies.

The upper class's use of racism and national chauvinism to maintain its rule was enhanced by the entry of the working class into politics during the nineteenth and early twentieth centuries. To win elections and thus preserve the institutions of formal democracy, thereby giving the people the illusion of popular rule, the ruling class has had to develop methods of making conservatism popular. A formally democratic system, in which the working class and other lower class groups greatly outnumber the middle and upper classes, requires the upper class to secure a large proportion of the votes of the lower classes. Given the forces operating on the working class and all oppressed groups that facilitate the development of class consciousness and support of radical efforts to abolish inequality, this has not been easy. If they are to win elections, conservative parties must reduce the salience of the class question. They therefore stress non-class issues that mystify and obscure social relations. By appealing to the masses' emotions rather than to their reason and class interest, the upper class usually can prevent the working-class parties from winning a majority of the vote.

---

[51] Gerald Brenan, *The Spanish Labyrinth* (Cambridge: The University Press, 1964), chapters 7 and 8.
[52] Sidney Tarrow, *Peasant Communism in Southern Italy* (New Haven: Yale University Press, 1967).

The landed upper class in the South destroyed the Populist party in the U.S. South in the 1890s by resorting to massive race baiting.[53] The Populist party temporarily united large segments of the poorest Southern black and white sharecroppers and independent farmers around a radical program that included nationalization of the railways, banks, and agricultural storage and distribution facilities. This interracial leftist movement was crushed by the Southern upper class only by means of a most vicious and prolonged campaign of race baiting, which culminated in the institution of Jim Crow laws and the disenfranchisement of blacks in the South.

The Southern upper class has largely been able to maintain its unchallenged rule for many years thereafter by using the tactic developed so skillfully at that time. Many of the poorest and most oppressed white workers are persuaded to stay out of unions and away from anything that is vaguely radical or hints of class action. The upper class accomplishes this by associating these things with "niggers" and "un-Americanism." The doctrine of "white skin privilege" (which the upper class encourages) claims that no matter how poor a white worker might be, at least he or she has white skin (which he or she shares with the capitalists) and is hence better than any black. This racist ideology can be stubbornly held in face of the most overwhelming evidence that the principal cause of the poor whites' poverty is their reluctance to join unions, engage in class action, and support radical causes designed to further their interests. The South continues to send the most reactionary Congress members to Washington. And the most reactionary presidential aspirants (for example, Barry Goldwater and George Wallace) get disproportionate support from the South — even though it is a highly industrialized and poverty stricken region. Although the percentage of the economically active population engaged in manufacturing was higher in both North and South Carolina in 1970 than in any other state, these states were among the most conservative and least unionized in the United States.

Racism and nationalism are, of course, not restricted to the U.S. South. These conservatizing ideologies are entrenched throughout the United States and are used by conservative politicians (such as George Wallace, Richard Nixon, and Gerald Ford) as well as by liberal Democrats (albeit in more sophisticated ways) to obscure class questions. Busing, "black welfare cheaters," trade with Communist countries, "softness on communism," Communists in the State Department, opposition to immigration, anti-big-city influences, Catholicism, and "the loss of China" have a long history of being the most salient issues in American politics.[54] These issues are fabricated by the upper class and the politicians in its employ to overwhelm the real issue — the question of class.

The most effective use of nationalist and racist appeals occurs when they are used together with a pseudoleftist rhetoric. The use of pseudoleftist language is, however, potentially dangerous for the upper class, in that it gives some credence to

---

[53] See C. Vann Woodward, *The Strange Career of Jim Crow* (New York: Oxford University Press, 1957).

[54] For a good discussion of the irrational, nonclass appeals of conservatism, see Linz and Lipset, "The Social Bases of Diversity," chapter 5.

the issues raised by the Left. Consequently, it is not used until the situation becomes desperate. As its best practitioners, the Nazis, so clearly demonstrated, its successful use can grab hold of the masses and defeat their challenge to class society. The Nazis talked of Germany as a "proletarian nation." Adolf Hitler called his movement National *Socialism*. He adopted much of the Marxist symbolism, such as red for his flag and May Day as a national day.

Anti-Semitism has traditionally been used as a pseudoleftist tactic to appeal to the oppressed and thereby deflect class hostility from the upper class.[55] The Czarist regime used anti-Semitism to stabilize its rule during its declining years of the last part of the nineteenth and early twentieth centuries. When class opposition to the regime increased, as it did around the time of the 1905 Revolution, local officials were instructed to promote pogroms against the Jews to channel the resentment of the masses against them. The Nazis used anti-Semitism in an identical way. The evils of capitalism were identified with Jewish bankers and middlemen largely because in many areas of Central and Eastern Europe the Jews were the traditional middlemen between the workers and peasants and the upper class (that is, the small merchants and the money lenders). The peasants and workers became embittered in their dealings with those who were used by the actual ruling class to perform the odious functions of petty buying, selling, lending, and foreclosing on mortgages. It was thus rather easy for the upper class to stir up anti-Semitism and blame the Jews for all the problems of the oppressed during a crisis. In the absence of a working-class political party with sophisticated analyses and roots in the masses, unsophisticated workers are likely to succumb to such diversions as anti-Semitism.

Patriotism

The cult of patriotism is taught in the schools through the pledge of allegiance to the flag, the singing of patriotic songs ("America," "The Star Spangled Banner"), American history and geography, civics, Americanism, and so on. It is reinforced in all the mass media and at mass activities attended primarily by working people such as football, baseball, and basketball games, where it is standard ritual to play the national anthem and have a flag present. It is reinforced on every national holiday (President's Day, Memorial Day, the Fourth of July, Labor Day, Veterans Day, and Thanksgiving) in the ceremonies, parades, symbolism, and recitations of American greatness and glory. It is normally intensified and concretized in military training and in the military experience in general. The sentiments of patriotism are strengthened in the course of every successful war. The basic values of patriotism have been consciously inculcated in the working classes over generations so that they would willingly respond to the call to die in the wars fought in the interests of the ruling class. It has also been used to motivate underclasses to work in their mines, fields, and factories without major complaint, and generally acquiesce to capitalist-class rule since this rule is promoted as Americanism. The patriotism so carefully inculcated in the working class is one of the most important weapons used by the capitalist class to get the working class to support its rule.

[55] See Paul Massing, *Rehearsal for Destruction* (New York: Harper and Brothers, 1949).

Un-Americanism is used by the upper class vis-à-vis the schools and media to refer to militant trade unionism, a significant increase in the standard of living, antiwar sentiments, antiimperialism, the belief in the essential equality of people, the idea that working people ought to run the places where they work and rule the state instead of the capitalist class — that is, anything in the interests of the working class. Conversely, Americanism is equated with racism, sexism, militarism, overseas adventures, oppression of other nations, opposition to unions, willingness to work long hours for low pay, support of inequality and lack of authentic democracy — that is, support of capitalist-class rule. Patriotism is a very powerful weapon in the hands of the upper class. It is a major source of obscurantism and is certainly one of the major barriers to the development of class consciousness in the American working class.

The family's role in socializing children

The basic values and general attitudes (especially those relating to authority), as well as many specific social and political attitudes of a person are very heavily influenced by his/her childhood experience. The effect of the family is of a different order than that of the mass media, the schools, religion, and the cult of patriotism, because it mostly tends to reproduce in children the values and attitudes acquired or reinforced in these latter ways, as well as the values and attitudes that come from the life experiences of the working classes on the job. Children typically adopt the political attitudes of their parents.[56] Their parents (or their parents' parents) in turn acquire their political attitudes largely from the means of mental production controlled by the upper class (or in the case of class-conscious working people, from radical organizations and media as well as from their own experience).

The authoritarian structure of the family — in which the parents are the totalitarian rulers over the children and the arbiters of whether and in what manner the children can satisfy their basic needs and desires — fosters a characteristic way of relating to authority that typically stays with them all their lives. The helpless child must develop a mode of dealing with the conflicting demands of parents and body. This typically involves adopting traits of shyness, obedience, fear of authority, and respect for people in positions of power. The ways worked out to both please one's parents and to reasonably satisfy one's desires become permanently imprinted as the core of one's personality or character structure. When people are faced with authorities outside of the home who make demands on them later on in life, they tend to respond to those external authorities in the *same manner* as they did to their parents as children. Strong political leaders (for example, Adolf Hitler, Benito Mussolini, John Kennedy, and most effective presidents, kings, and dictators) thus are able to manipulate this residual childhood response to authority to incite emotions in people characteristic of their childhood relationship to their parents, such as a submissive attitude and willingness to follow them in an unthinking emotional manner. The authoritarian response to charismatic leadership can strongly inspire the working classes and other oppressed groups to follow the

[56] Herbert Hyman, *Political Socialization* (Glencoe, Ill.: Free Press, 1959).

leadership of the upper class. By using such means people often internalize the political ideas of their leaders just as they internalized their parents' attitudes as children. Charismatic leadership has its other side. The childlike love of the people for their leader can change to hatred if the behavior of the leader demolishes the myth of his superhuman or fatherlike qualities — for example, the public outrage against Richard Nixon after two years of Watergate, or the rejection of Benito Mussolini by Italians after 1943.

The establishment of authoritarian personalities in the capitalist family is a result of the functional requirements of the family for capitalism. The demand for unquestioned obedience on the part of the parents and the suppression of the children's basic desires and needs according to the parents' conception of what is right and proper is a product of class society. Primitive nonclass society usually has very permissive parent-child relationships that do not restrain the child's instincts as much. These nonauthoritatian family forms produce a very different type of individual than does the family in class society — one who is more autonomous, less respectful of arbitrary authority, and far less likely to give irrational emotional support to a strong father figure. The oppressive experience of capitalist society calls out for compensation in the form of mastery over one's children. A psychological compensation is found both in establishing oneself as unquestioned master in one's own house (the only place where one can hope for real respect and control) and in preventing uninhibited gratification on the part of children (which would invoke unconscious feelings of envy and resentment from those deprived of opportunities for gratification).

The family, to paraphrase Wilhelm Reich, acts as the germ cell of conservative consciousness in the working class. The authoritarian personality established in the family is an important prop of the capitalist order. The key role the traditional hierarchical family plays in the preservation of class society is revealed during a crisis when rightist regimes and movements call for strengthening the bonds of the family and marriage, respect for parents, disciplining of children, and repression of sexual "immorality."[57]

Summary of the role of ideological hegemony

Ideological hegemony is probably the most important mechanism by which the capitalist mode of production structures an environment that causes the state to follow policies in the interest of the capitalist class. To a considerable degree the political ideas of common people in a capitalist society — especially one similar to the United States — are those of the dominant economic class. Since the working

---

[57] See Wilhelm Reich, *The Mass Psychology of Fascism* (New York: Farrar, Straus and Giroux, 1970); "The Imposition of Sexual Morality," in *Sexual Politics: Essays 1929-1934* (New York: Vintage Books, 1972); and *The Sexual Revolution* (New York: Farrar, Straus and Giroux, 1974); also, Erich Fromm, *Escape from Freedom* (New York: Holt, Rinehart and Winston, 1940); *The Crisis in Psychoanalysis* (Greenwich, Conn.: Fawcett Publications, 1971); *The Dogma of Christ and Other Essays* (Garden City, N.Y.: Doubleday, 1966); and Sigmund Freud, *Civilization and Its Discontents* (New York: W. W. Norton, 1962).

people willingly accept capitalist values, they freely elect politicians who publicly promise to implement and support capitalist-class policies. This "ideological hegemony" of the capitalist class is secured by a virtual (but not usually total) monopoly of the "means of mental production" by the capitalist class. Control of the newspapers, magazines, book publishing houses, radio and television stations, schools, universities, and churches allows the capitalist class to use these institutions to propagate the ideas indigenous and beneficial to it. In the absence of any appreciable amount of anticapitalist ideology being propagated by radical organizations, and especially when the economy is relatively stable, the common people by default largely accept the ideas with which they are bombarded from all sides. The actual role that ideological hegemony plays in securing political domination by the capitalist class varies with the degree of acceptance of capitalist values by the masses. The rest of the chapter examines the other three structural mechanisms by which the interests of capital are transformed into state policies.

The Logic of Capitalist Relations as a Mechanism of Control

The second most important indirect mechanism of control of the state is the logic of capitalist economic relations. This mechanism largely dictates the policies the state must follow (or provides the very *limited range* of options that are workable) given the persistence of the capitalist mode of production. These laws of capitalism dictate the causes and effects of inflation, unemployment, economic growth, increases in productivity, the rate of investment, the most effective size of firms, investment patterns, and so on. If it wants to maximize productivity, investment, and growth, and minimize unemployment, inflation, the probability of recessions, and crises, the state must pursue the very limited range of options dictated to it by these laws and their manifestations in the rational profit-seeking behavior of individual capitalists. The capitalists respond to state policies in a manner designed to maximize their profits, taking into consideration the rate of unemployment, the rate of inflation, and the rate of investment and growth. If the state were to follow policies designed to increase labor's share of the value of the product, the level of profit could be reduced to such a level that business might cut back on production and refuse to make new investments, thereby inducing a recession and creating massive unemployment. Business's decision to take these actions might occur after a conscious collective decision to sabotage state policy — or it might simply be the unintended consequence of profit-maximizing decisions of many individual businesses acting independently. In either event both the root cause and the effect are the same — immense pressure on the state to change its policy and reduce the level of wages. This will be the case, unless the state has the massive popular support necessary to expropriate the major businesses that cut back on production and run them itself (or allow the workers to run them directly) according to non-profit-maximizing principles. Hence the state in capitalist society is forced to perform the requisite functions for capitalism. It must preserve law and order and facilitate profit maximization and capital accumulation.

Among the weapons used by business against a recalcitrant state that attempts to implement policies unfavorable to it are refusal to invest, curtailment of production, refusal to provide the state with needed supplies, relocation of some or all of its productive plants to areas outside of the state's jurisdiction, and massive noncompliance with state regulations (perhaps legitimatized by long court battles). The Allende regime in Chile from 1970 to 1973 and the leftist regimes in Portugal from 1974 to 1975 were faced with such problems and, of course, suffered severely.

Domestic and international banks have the additional clout of insisting that the state follow certain types of economic and social policies in exchange for loans. In the habit of regularly operating on a deficit, modern capitalist states get increasingly in debt to the domestic and international banks as well as to the international financial institutions such as the World Bank and the International Monetary Fund. The deeper in debt a state (or its subunits) becomes, the more desperate it becomes for more loans to finance not only current expenses, but the payments on past loans as they come due. A form of debt bondage then tends to develop, in which the financial institution's power over the state grows in proportion to the size of the state's debt. The governmental units thus have the choice of either agreeing to the increasingly demanding conditions the banks impose to obtain more loans *or* repudiating their debt or going bankrupt. Unless the state is willing to violate such a basic principle of capitalism as debt obligations, it has no choice but to comply. It cannot violate the basic rules of private property without either becoming socialist *or* destabilizing all capitalist economic agreements and threatening the viability of the stock and bonds market and all contracts. This latter course would mean massive economic disruption. Thus unless the state can find other ways to finance its activity that do not result in increasing debt, it must comply with the banks' demands.[58]

New York City's situation in the 1970s is an excellent illustration of this process. When New York City's ability to borrow to pay off its previous debts became impaired, New York's leading bankers stepped in and set up a Municipal Assistance Corporation to supervise the city's policies. The banks agreed to attempt to raise money for the city on the condition that the city follow very stringent economic policies agreeable to them. New York had little choice but to comply. Among the conditions imposed by the banks for further loans to alleviate the city's financial crisis were the firing of city workers, a freeze on the salaries of certain categories of city workers over a certain amount, an increase in transit fares, drastic cutbacks in the city's university program, cutbacks in sanitation and fire protection, considerable cutbacks in the city's capital construction programs, and a freeze on the expansion of public services.[59] These policies had to be followed by the city to avoid bankruptcy independently of what the voters of the city and the local business interests (outside of the major banks) wanted. Whether New York City

---

[58] For a discussion of international debt bondage, see Magdoff, *The Age of Imperialism*, chapters 3 and 4; and Cheryl Payer, *The Debt Trap: The IMF and the Third World* (New York: Monthly Review Press, 1975).

[59] *The Guardian*, August 27, 1975, p. 4.

had a Republican, Democratic, Conservative, Liberal, Socialist, or even Communist administration, its response would have had to be the same.

Most of the countries of the capitalist world are subjected to the domination of international banks (many based in the United States) and the international financial institutions such as the International Monetary Fund (IMF) and the World Bank. When countries run persistent and large balance-of-payments deficits, run up excessive debts to international financial institutions, or run domestic governmental deficits greater than the local banks are willing or able to finance, they are often forced to turn to these international institutions. The international private banks, the IMF, and World Bank, as well as the foreign assistance lending agencies of the various leading capitalist states (such as the U.S. Agency for International Development and the Export-Import Bank) impose certain economic conditions on the borrowing government. Organizations such as the USAID also typically impose political conditions, such as requiring support of U.S. economic and international policies. Typical requirements of such international loans include insistence on devaluation of the local currency (to encourage exports and discourage imports), liberalization of trade (reduction of tariffs and other restrictions), restrictions of domestic credit, cutbacks on governmental expenditure, decreases in wages, increases in taxes, the elimination of governmental subsidies to business, the elimination of price controls, and — at least in the Third World countries — encouragement of raw material production, abandonment of restrictions on the convertibility of currency, and the ending of any restrictions on foreign investment or the repatriation of profits.[60] In short, policies that are most favorable to the transnational corporations are insisted on as the condition for international funding. Whether the government of a country is Conservative, Liberal, Progressive, Social Democratic, Labor, or even Communist (for example, Yugoslavia), it must meet similar conditions or face the most dire domestic consequences.

It should be emphasized that it makes no difference whether the major banks and international financial institutions are merely acting rationally to maximize their rate of return on loans, or whether they have the added motive to consciously force changes in economic and social policies independently of maximizing their own profits (that is, are acting as instruments of the entire capitalist-class interest), the effect and ultimate cause is the same: to maximize the interest of capital.

Military Intervention as a Mechanism of Control

A third mechanism of indirect control of the capitalist state is the threat of military intervention in the form of a domestic military coup d'état, military invasion from abroad, or foreign support for subversive movements within the country. The high-level officer corps of the military establishment in most capitalist societies is

---

[60] See Magdoff, *The Age of Imperialism*, chapter 4; Steve Weissman et al., *The Trojan Horse* (San Francisco: Ramparts Press, 1971); and Hayter, *Aid as Imperialism*.

integrally linked with capitalist interests. Military ideology is authoritarian, conservative, imperialistic, and resonates well with capitalist ideology. Top military officers typically have close personal and business (and sometimes blood) connections with the leading corporations and capitalist families. Consequently, the leading generals typically look unfavorably on any attempts at radical change in the society — especially on such changes accompanied by massive disorders and threats to the military supremacy of the armed forces' bureaucracy they control (that is, the development of popular militias and the arming of workers).

In Spain in 1936, a few months after a Popular Front government of Socialists and progressives was elected to office, the military revolted and fought a victorious three-year civil war to overthrow the elected leftist government. In Chile in 1973 the military revolted against the elected Socialist government of Salvador Allende to roll back his Socialist reforms. The Greek military effected a coup d'état in the late 1960s against a leftist-inclined government. The German military gave its support to Adolf Hitler during the crucial early years of the Nazi regime in Germany. Leading generals of the Russian army attempted to establish a military regime in Russia in 1917 after the initial successes of the Revolution and again in 1919, provoking a bitter civil war. Throughout the countries of Eastern Europe in the post-World War I period and throughout the countries of Asia, Africa, and Latin America in the post-World War II period, conservative general staffs made coups d'états against many democratic and popular regimes that were either attempting to institute progressive reforms or were unwilling to implement unpopular measures required by capital.[61] The democratic regimes in Poland, the Baltic countries, Hungary, Romania, and Greece were overthrown by their militaries to frustrate popular forces. In the post-World War II period, the popular governments of Indonesia, Cambodia, Iran, Guatemala, the Dominican Republic, Brazil, Argentina, and Venezuela have been overthrown for the same reason.

It is, of course, not necessary for the military to actually overthrow a progressive government for it to have a considerable effect on governmental policies. That the military establishment has something approaching a monopoly of military force and that the rank-and-file soldiers will obey orders is sufficient to stop most governments from attempting to implement anticapitalist policies if the general staff of the military makes its strong opposition known. Even if an overwhelming majority of the people want a democratically elected government to implement radical policies, the government would be unable to implement such policies as long as the general staff is opposed *and* willing to intervene militarily if its will is denied. The power of the general staff can only be neutralized if a government is part of a general revolutionary movement *and* is in a position to raise

---

[61] For analyses of the post-World War I coups in Central and Eastern Europe, see Polanyi, *The Great Transformation*, chapter 20; and Daniel Mitrany, *Marx Against the Peasant* (Chapel Hill, N.C.: University of North Carolina Press, 1951). For an interesting cross-national statistical study of the incidence of coups d'états, see Douglas A. Hibbs, *Mass Political Violence: A Cross-National Causal Analysis* (New York: John Wiley and Sons, 1973), chapter 6.

a popular militia *or* subvert the authority of the generals among the rank-and-file soldiers to exert superior counterforce in the event of an attempted military coup. A state government that is not in a revolutionary situation has no choice but to capitulate to the demands of the military (or go down in a heroic suicide, such as Allende did in Chile in 1973).

Note that military officers are not always conservatives and do not always defend the status quo against progressive governments. Sometimes military officers pressure conservative, undemocratic governments to implement reforms. Such officers even occasionally make coups d'états in support of popular reform. Such was the case, for example, in Portugal in 1974, Ethiopia in 1974, Peru in 1968, and Egypt in 1952. Such leftist interventions are rather rare and usually occur in societies where: (1) serious domestic crises are occurring; (2) ossified, unpopular, and backward ruling classes exist; *and* (3) the officer corps is connected by blood, friendship, and interest more with the people (normally the intermediate strata) than with the clearly bankrupt and stagnant upper classes. Such progressive military coups are normally led and inspired by junior officers, not the top generals, even when a leading general (such as Spinola in Portugal) is the figurehead. Junior officers usually are closer to the people and have more of a personal stake in revolutionary change.

In the post–World War II period the U.S. military (and occasionally the militaries of the other leading capitalist countries) together with the U.S. Central Intelligence Agency have been active in supporting conservative elements in the military establishments of other countries. Support is given in the form of arms, advisers, and training to such militaries. In exchange they are encouraged to intervene against popular governments in their countries. The interventions in the Dominican Republic, Brazil, Guatemala, Indonesia, and Iran, for example, were clearly of this kind. When unpopular military regimes are faced with the rise of popular insurgent movements, the United States typically steps in to arm, supply, advise, and train the local military establishments to prevent their overthrow. Such was the case in China in the late 1940s, and Indochina from the 1950s through 1975, as well as throughout Latin America in the post–World War II period.

When the local troops are unable to contain rebellion, the U.S. military has been willing to send its troops to a country to put down local popular insurgency. Thus the United States sent its troops into Vietnam in the 1960s and the Dominican Republic in 1965. The credibility established by these direct interventions serves to intimidate insurgent movements and progressive governments around the world because of their fear of U.S. military intervention, either direct or indirect.

Political and Social Disruption as a Mechanism of Control

A fourth mechanism of indirect control is the capitalist class's ability to create a political and social crisis. Even though the capitalist class may be outvoted in an election, its great financial and moral resources allow it to cause considerable disruption if it should choose to do so. It can stir up and finance petty bourgeois groups (such as the independent truckers and shopkeepers in Chile, who demonstrated very effectively against the Allende regime in 1973; or the independent small farmers in northern Portugal, who in the summer of 1975 went on a rampage against the Communist Party) that riot, strike, burn, and generally disrupt the operation of leftist governments. Such disruptions made in the name of religion, the nation, and anticommunism, by appealing to the traditional ideologies and being backed by wealth and respected figures (often with the implicit collusion of the military and police), can have a devastating effect on a popular government's ability to rule.

To avoid such disruption and the undermining of its authority, an elected anticapitalist regime might avoid taking measures that would provoke such devastating opposition. Again, capitalist-class disruption can be avoided only by people mobilizing themselves to engage in a revolutionary process against capital. A state whose mandate to govern comes *only* from winning an election (that is, is not part of a firmly rooted revolutionary process) is unable to successfully cope with such crises and is thus pressured to comply with the demands of capital. Of course, the capitalists also have the option of heavily financing, promoting, and otherwise supporting antigovernment candidates in future elections. This also represents a substantial threat to progressive politicians in nonrevolutionary situations.

The United States government can also induce political and social disruption by utilizing its Central Intelligence Agency or similar agencies of other leading capitalist countries. These agencies act in concert with transnational corporations and local capitalist elements to "destabilize" local progressive regimes. Money is channeled to right-wing opposition parties and associations (such as the Socialist party in Portugal in the summer of 1975, or the truckers association in Chile in the year before the military overthrow of Allende) to encourage their disruptive actions. "Destabilization" of a government also occurs by refusing to refinance loans as they come due, eliminating trade preferences, slowing the supply of spare parts or fulfilling contracts, boycotting trade (such as the Cuban trade embargo of 1960, which was instituted to bring pressure on the Cuban Revolutionary Government), transnational corporations refusing to invest in or obey the regulations and commands of the progressive government (such as the refusal of the U.S.-owned oil companies to refine Soviet oil, even when the government of Cuba ordered them to do so in 1960), and laying off workers and cutting back essential production. All such actions are designed to create sufficient social disruption to create political movements inside and outside of the military of a given country that can pressure the government to change its anticapitalist policies or be overthrown.

Structural Determination of State Policies

Whether the state is led by members of the capitalist class or those indebted to them, whether the lobbying and campaign financing efforts of business interests are the dominant force in determining the output of legislatures and administrative agencies, and whether groups such as the Council on Foreign Relations (CFR) are in fact formulating governmental policies, the state nevertheless will act in the interests of the capitalist class in capitalist society because the structure of its environment requires it to perform its functions for capital. This is true whether the occupants of state office and the majority in the legislatures are conservatives, fascists, liberals, Social Democrats, Socialists, or even Communists, just as long as the basic mode of production in the economy remains capitalist.

The examples of the Ramsey McDonald governments in Britain during the 1920s and 1930s as well as of the Labour party majority government from 1945 to 1951 show that avowed Socialists are forced to behave as good capitalists when in office.[62] The earlier governments followed the same sort of conservative economic policies vis-à-vis balancing the budget, reducing the trade deficits, and resisting workers' demands for wage increases as the Conservative and Liberal governments that came before and after. The main difference between the two types of government was that a Labour prime minister was better able to get the working class to accept the sacrifices required of them to make capitalism work, whereas an explicitly procapitalist government would have provoked considerably more opposition in implementing the same policies. In other words, the presence of avowed Socialists in leading governmental positions within a capitalist economy can stabilize a volatile political situation, thereby making the economic policies dictated by the logic of capitalism work.

The policies followed by the British Labour government from 1945 to 1951 — especially the institution of National Health Insurance, the expansion of other welfare programs, the increased state management of the economy, and the policy of liquidating the empire (while remaining firmly anti-Communist in foreign policy) — was dictated by the logic of British capitalism in a period of decline and challenge from the Left, not by the preferences of the members of the Labour party. The Conservative or Liberal parties would have been required to follow essentially the same policies because the same pressures would have acted on them. That similar policies were adopted during the same period in Italy, West Germany, the Netherlands, and elsewhere in Western Europe where Social Democratic or Labor parties were not in power indicates that it is not the political program of parties but rather the imperatives of the situation that determine state policies within capitalist society.

Social Democratic governments in France in the 1930s and the post-World War II period, the government of the Social Democrats in Germany in the post-World War I period and in the 1960s and 1970s, and the Social Democrats in Scandinavia followed basic policies only slightly different from those of the Gaullists in France, the Christian Democrats in Italy or Germany, or for that matter the policies of any of the non–Social Democratic regimes in the advanced capitalist countries. In fact, in spite of their rather radical Socialist origins, early aspirations, and the continuing sentiments of many of their supporters, the very

[62] See Ralph Miliband, *Parliamentary Socialism* (New York: Monthly Review Press, 1964), for a good discussion of the Labour governments in Britain.

ideology and program of the Social Democratic parties has evolved to the point of being imperceptibly different from that of the Gaullists, Christian Democrats, and other centrist capitalist parties. Again, this reflects not only the need to follow certain policies, but also the need to win elections on such programs within capitalist society.[63]

Socialist governments that have attempted to do more than just implement the policies dictated by the logic of capitalism have found themselves in very serious crises from which they have not been able to extricate themselves. The moderate Socialist policies of the Blum Popular Front government in France in the mid-1930s, the government led by Kerensky in Russia in 1917, and the Social Democratic governments in Germany after World War I, as well as Nkrumah's in Ghana, Sukarno's in Indonesia, Goulart's in Brazil, Peron's in the 1950s in Argentina, Borsh's in the Dominican Republic, Arbenz' in Guatemala, and Mossadegh's in Iran attempted to implement something less than all-out procapitalist policies, all without the massive support for a social revolution that could have replaced capitalist production practices. All resulted in internal economic and political crises followed by the overthrow of these regimes (all except the Russian) by explicitly right-wing forces willing and able to do what the logic of capitalism required of the situation.

Even the presence of Communists (avowed enemies of the capitalist mode of production) in governments in capitalist society makes very little difference. The Communists were part of the Popular Front government in France and Chile in the late 1930s as well as part of the immediate postwar governments in France and Italy from 1944 to 1947, yet their role was limited to increasing welfare measures, protecting or restoring parliamentary forms and liberties, and expanding state control over the economy (in the interest of the private corporations). They even (until the end of their participation in these governments) pressured the working class not to strike, not to ask for "unreasonable" wage increases, and to increase productivity for the sake of "the nation." All these policies were essentially identical to those followed by the Christian Democrats and similar parties in the other capitalist countries at the same time. This does not reflect on whether the Communist Party and its cadre actually wanted revolution and were prepared to act on their beliefs if they had decided to do so; rather, it suggests that once the Communists agreed to participate in the government in any role other than a disruptive one, they were required to participate "constructively" — that is, pursue the policies dictated by the situation to decrease unemployment and inflation, earn foreign exchange, reconstruct industry, and so on. The choice in the immediate postwar period in Western Europe was either to attempt an all-out revolution against capitalism or make capitalism work. There was no middle ground, neither then nor at any other time, that could in fact do anything other than precipitate serious crises and very possibly reaction. Once the Communists decided not to make

---

[63] For a good critical analysis of the Social Democratic state in Sweden, see Paul Stevenson, "Monopoly Capital and Inequalities in Swedish Society," *The Insurgent Sociologist* 5, no. 1 (Fall 1974): 41–58. Stevenson shows that there is no essential difference between U.S. and Swedish monopoly capitalism.

revolution, the only alternative would have been to sit on the sidelines (their policy after 1947) and wait. Instead, they helped stabilize the capitalist system by legitimatizing the immediate postwar parliamentary restorations.[64]

Short of a revolutionary situation with massive popular mobilization, then, governmental officials — regardless of their personal political inclinations and philosophies — must behave in the same way. If they desire to stay in office and to enhance their careers, they must act in ways designed to maximally realize the essential functions of the capitalist state. To promote economic prosperity, avoid military intervention, and prevent massive social and political disruption, they must act to maximize the interests of capital. All this is true whether members of the capitalist class or their close protégés occupy top governmental positions and whether or not the mechanisms of lobbying, policy formation, and campaign contributions are operating to directly secure control of the state for the capitalist class.

The personal chances of success of politicians thus is closely linked with the successful performance of the functions of the capitalist state. Consequently, it is not a matter of good or bad intentions, or the desire to realize the popular will or serve the narrow interests of the rich, but rather a matter of the imperatives of the system being exerted through the state officials. The policies of these officials are determined by the environment, structured by the capitalist mode of production, in which they must act to advance the interests of capital on the pain of being thrown out of office or demoted.

It is not only the leading national politicians who are required to realize capitalist state functions because of the logic of the capitalist mode of production and the ideological, military, and social hegemony of the capitalist class. Even local governmental units that are run by working people can be subjected to the same pressures. For example, a school board run entirely by working-class parents (again assuming a nonrevolutionary situation) would be strongly inclined to run the school in the same manner as a school board run by business people. Given the logic of the capitalist system, parents have as much motivation as business executives to want the schools to be coordinated with the needs of capital. Executives as well as working-class parents want children to get "good" jobs after their graduation. Both tend to view the school primarily as a means of training for postschool jobs. Neither the parents nor the executives normally want to train children for jobs that will not exist. Both want to train children for the jobs the corporations will have open upon their graduation. Thus, training in practical math, typing skills, mechanical drawing, and shop will be stressed by both parents and executives for the many children destined for skilled working-class and white-collar jobs, while engineering, teaching, and business management are stressed at the college level. As long as the corporate system structures the life chances of children and the current division of labor prevails (where people have one type of job all their lives), the short-term interests of parents will appear to be essentially the same as those of capital, and hence the decisions they make about education

---

[64] For an insightful analysis of the pressures acting on the large Communist parties of Western Europe, see Paul Sweezy and Harry Magdoff, "The New Reformism," *Monthly Review* (June 1976).

will be identical.[65] Direct business domination of school boards, then, is another example of "overdetermination" or double control over education by the capitalist class.

The formulation and implementation of state policies do not generally correspond in a one-to-one fashion to specific demands or pressures from specific capitalist-class interests or even to the policies of groups such as the CFR in the United States (although these latter groups come considerably closer than the former). No concrete demand to preserve law and order to facilitate commerce, provide basic education, and welfare is usually made; rather, there is a vaguely defined pressure to perform the basic functions necessary so that the system can prosper. The interest groups that engage in the lobbying process may not even know exactly what must be done to realize the basic capitalist functions. More likely, specific demands on the state to perform its functions, in contrast to merely satisfying the demands of interest groups, may not be felt until the failure to perform its functions is manifested in serious crises within the system. Many state-related activities exist that are not manipulated by specific capitalist interests, but are rather a result of the state bureaucracy analyzing the system to find out what makes it work, or alternatively are merely a result of trial and error.

Many reforms, such as many of those of the New Deal in the 1930s, cannot be fully explained as initiatives of the capitalist class, even when each can be traced to a business person or business-related association. In fact, business people have ties to a wide range of political programs, and there are many business-related associations from rather left-liberal to extremely conservative. But why does the state occasionally select a policy, especially in a crisis situation, formulated by a minority bloc over that of the biggest business bloc? Thus, studies that attempt to account for the New Deal as a manifestation of business-formulated policies are incomplete. These studies beg the question of why policies initially developed by the National Civic Association, the American Association for Labor Legislation, or the Business Council were adopted over those developed and pursued by the National Association of Manufacturers or the Chamber of Commerce (groups that during the 1930s were considerably larger than the former groups). Only by recognizing that the state bureaucracy has (at least at times) some autonomy from direct control by the majority bloc among the capitalist class, and hence is able to implement policies in the interest of the entire capitalist class, can this be made understandable. Because of the narrow-mindedness and internal antagonisms of business in some crisis situations, state bureaucracy must sometimes develop policies that advance the interests of the system even when the primary beneficiaries of these policies drag their feet. State officials and their allies in a minority of the business community can often foresee the growing economic and social crisis that could develop from following the shortsighted policies of the

---

[65] One would expect that education in a truly Communist society would be quite different. Here where the life-long division of labor has broken down, students would receive a general education in a very wide range of both mental and manual skills suiting them to many jobs rather than preparing them for one narrow niche as in the capitalist division of labor.

majority bloc of business. Concerned about their own political futures and the pressures that will be brought against them in the event of an increasingly growing crisis, state officials can develop class-conscious, capitalist-class policies.

The Role of Direct and Indirect Mechanisms of Domination of the State

The role of the direct and indirect mechanisms of capitalist-class rule varies considerably among capitalist countries as well as over time. In France, for example, it is often argued that the state bureaucracy is not directly controlled by capitalist interests because the capitalist class in France is rather fractionated; whereas in Great Britain, where the capitalist class has a tradition of unity, the state machinery is directly controlled by the upper class.[66] The more fractionated the capitalist class, the less it is able to formulate a common class will in its own institutions outside of the state apparatus (that is, in groups such as the CFR and the Business Council) as well as in the legislatures. Therefore, the state bureaucrats must formulate the general interest of the entire capitalist class by combining foresight with trial and error. This process can occur even against the opposition of a majority of the members of the capitalist class, whose narrow self-interest or lack of sufficient foresight to understand the long-term interests of the entire system can impede their development of a class-conscious will.

Something similar to this happened in the United States during the New Deal. A majority of the capitalist class at first opposed (some rather militantly) much of FDR's program (although a significant minority around the Business Advisory Council actively supported it). Nevertheless, the state implemented policies in the face of this resistance that served the long-term capitalist-class interest. The state occasionally finds itself selecting among the various competing capitalist interests a policy that serves the interests of the entire capitalist class.

In the United States since World War II there has been no significant autonomy of the U.S. state. Throughout this period the capitalist class has maintained direct control of the state apparatus. Through class-wide institutions such as the Business Council, the CFR, the Brookings Institution, the major foundations and universities, and all the other institutions of the corporate liberal upper class, the capitalist class has been able to develop sufficient foresight and class consciousness to formulate the appropriate rational class policies in advance of the state apparatus and then transmit them successfully to the state. The interests of the state officials have coincided with the class-conscious policies developed in these private bodies, and hence there is no attempt by these officials to side with a minority faction of the upper class (either of the Right or Left) against the corporate liberal center. The careers and political futures of state officials have thus been closely tied to the explicit will of the capitalist class to produce an "overdetermination" of state

[66] See, for example, Poulantzas, *Political Power and Social Classes*, part IV, chapter 5 and part V, chapter 13.

policy and a rather smoothly functioning state apparatus.

The degree of relative autonomy of the state bureaucracy from direct capitalist-class domination can either decrease *or* increase drastically during an economic and social crisis. A state that is too directly dominated by the majority bloc of the capitalist class may be unable to handle such a crisis, because the narrow-minded self-interest of this bloc prevents the state it dominates from adopting the policies necessary to save and advance the system. Domination of the state by these groups also tends to discredit the state, which because of such control is obviously not alleviating an economic crisis. The legitimating function of the state thus comes into increasing conflict with direct capitalist-class control. One solution to such a contradiction is for the majority bloc to lose direct control of the state (as it did with the election of FDR in 1933), thereby greatly enhancing the legitimacy of the state and allowing for the state to develop long-term class-conscious policies.

Then again, a state that is relatively autonomous from capitalist-class control may not be able to give the appropriate response to an economic and social crisis quickly enough to avoid a serious aggravation of the crisis, and thus risks provoking a possible revolution. Since a state not directly controlled by capital often has to develop its policies on a trial-and-error basis, and since it often relies on analyzing situations rather than immediately capitulating to the demands of capital, it could make some very serious mistakes in the short run that might disequilibrate the political and economic system. This in turn could increase support for popular revolutionary action, rather than for capitalist-class policies. In such crisis situations the state might not be able to respond to the needs of the capitalist system, and hence direct intervention would be needed to put the state back on its course. Such a situation was a primary motive of the fascist takeovers in Italy in 1922 and Germany in 1933, and the military takeovers of most of the countries of Eastern Europe after World War I and of many Third World countries in the post–World War II period. It was not that the governments in these countries got into the hands of revolutionaries. Rather, it was that the state officials who had considerable autonomy from direct rule by the majority bloc of the capitalist class were unable to effectively develop viable policies to adequately perform the basic capitalist functions.

The state may even function in the interest of capital when the capitalist class itself is very weak economically and politically. Such was the case in Germany and Japan in the last half of the nineteenth century.[67] To enhance the international position of these countries, their bureaucratic ruling groups were forced to encourage industrialization and the rapid growth of an industrial capitalist class by using the state bureaucracy to accumulate capital, which was then transferred to private enterprise, as well as to perform all the usual functions of the capitalist state. The structure of the international capitalist system thus can induce capitalist-state policies even in the absence of a strong domestic capitalist class.

[67] On capitalist development of Germany and Japan, see Moore, *The Social Origins of Dictatorship and Democracy*, chapters 5 and 8; and Baran, *The Political Economy of Economic Growth*, chapter 5.

12

Fascism

There are two social movements within monopoly capitalist society that *aim* to alter fundamentally the balance and the institutional forms of class forces: revolutionary left movements (Communist, left-Socialist, anarchist, syndicalist) and fascist movements (because of the nationalism of the latter movement, fascist groups — unlike the internationalist left movements — are typically known by different names in each country). Movements of the revolutionary Left are based primarily in the working class and poorer peasantry, whereas fascist and similar movements are typically based in the petty bourgeoisie and other middle strata. While the various forms of revolutionary leftism fight for control of society by the common working people, the fascist and fascistic movements fight for the "little man" (the paradigm of which is the family farmer, independent business person or artisan) against both big business *and* the organized power of the working class. Fascist movements, then, represent extremism of the center.

Fascist and semifascist movements originate and grow up in the petty bourgeoisie and other intermediate strata of the population, attracting marginal and socially unintegrated malcontents from all classes as they grow. Fascistic movements are characterized by their hostile rhetoric *both* against the monopolies, big business, big banks, and the oligarchy on the one side, *and* against the powerful unions, Socialists, Communists, anarchists, cooperatives, radical intellectuals, and working-class militants on the other. These movements thus reflect the class interest of the petty bourgeoisie and other middle groups, which in fact are under extreme pressure from the monopoly capitalist class as well as the organized working class. The pressures operating on them are especially intensely felt during economic crises (when fascist movements grow). Fascist movements are also characterized by (1) an extreme jingoism, nationalism, and/or racism (which is offered as a counterideology to the international class solidarity appeal of the revolutionary Left), and (2) a readiness to use systematic violence and terror against the working class, leftist organizations, and individuals. (This readiness is reflected in the propaganda and rhetoric of fascist organizations and leaders.)

As long as the capitalist class can dominate the state, it contains fascist and fascistic movements, which, of course, raise demands that seriously threaten its interests as well as question the political institutions serving the capitalist class. However, during a prolonged social crisis in which anticapitalist sentiment grows and permeates the masses of people, the capitalist class is no longer able to rule successfully through parliamentary forms, and especially is unable to resolve the economic and social crisis (for example, restore profitability and industrial discipline) through such mechanisms. When both the revolutionary left and the fascist movements are strong and when both appear to have an actual chance of coming to power, the upper class usually allies itself with the fascists. The condition of such alliances is that the fascists will be allowed to carry out the anti-Marxist and anti-working-class aspects of their program (which, of course, benefits the capitalist class) but cannot execute their anti-monopoly-capitalist program. In return, the capitalist class, after guaranteeing itself the appropriate safeguards (for example, maintaining control over the army), brings the fascist leaders into the government, abolishes parliamentary rule, and suppresses the unions and working-class parties.

Fascist Movements

Fascism normally appeals primarily to the intermediate classes ("the little people"). Under capitalism these classes come under increasing pressure from big capital, which, because it can produce and sell goods at lower prices than can the small producers, drives them into the proletariat. Conversely, the manual working class is able to form unions, cooperatives, and other organizations that not only shield it from the harshest manifestations of capitalism, but also put pressure on the petty bourgeoisie (the cooperatives deprive them of business, the unions sometimes organize their workers, and so on). The petty bourgeoisie grows increasingly bitter about what is happening to it, and consequently develops a strong desire to be rid of both big capital *and* the organized working class. This crisis is greatly accelerated during an economic depression as buying power diminishes and bankruptcies mushroom. The petty bourgeoisie, now restless and discontent, yearns for the mythical days when it was the leading class in society. Consequently, the fascists' romantic and mystical rhetoric appeals to the petty bourgeoisie. Its anticapitalist and anti-Socialist appeal and its glorification of the "little man" are music to the ears of the petty bourgeoisie, who can easily be recruited into its ranks. Fascism publicly proposes a third course, different from that advocated by both big business and Socialist revolution. The petty bourgeois fascist movements thus can blossom, gain the support of the capitalist class, smash working-class organization, and abolish parliamentary forms. But in reality the fascist leaders (being opportunists) stand willing to do the bidding of big business when called upon to share in political power.[1]

[1] See Leon Trotsky, *The Struggle Against Fascism in Germany* (New York: Pathfinder, 1971), chapters 11 and 19; Corey, *The Crisis of the Middle Class*, chapter 12; R. Palme

Although fascism appeals primarily to the middle classes, during a crisis it can win considerable support throughout the population. White-collar workers, underemployed professional workers, and domestic servants have historically also been sympathetic. Fascist support in the manual working class is greatest among those workers who are *least* integrated into working-class organizations, culture, and networks of interpersonal relations — for example, workers in small towns and small firms, the downwardly mobile, and nonunion members. Being essentially petty bourgeois phenomena, fascist movements generally derive their greatest support from those segments of the working class most amenable to petty bourgeois influence. When strong, however, fascism finds some support throughout the working class.

During social and economic crises (caused, for example, by economic depression or defeat in war), the class struggle typically heightens, and the revolutionary Left builds considerable working-class support and flexes its muscles. The growing strength of the revolutionary Left produces a climate of excitement and fear among its opponents and results in the increasing instability of the capitalist state. As the ascendant working class advances its revolutionary program, it wins over large segments of the population (including much of the rural population, petty bourgeoisie, and intellectuals) as they become convinced of the bankruptcy of capitalist-class rule because of its inability to solve the social crisis. But if the proletariat does not act while enjoying its maximum popular support, its self-confidence and the support of other segments of the population wane.

The Left's failure to lead the people to a revolutionary resolution of the crisis, when it has the opportunity, prepares the historical stage for the ascendancy of the fascists. The first fascist groups are organized to push back the offensive of the revolutionary Left and to prevent social revolution (and here they do play a major role). But once the revolutionary tide turns, the fascists, greatly strengthened by their participation in the successful struggle against the revolutionaries, now go on the offensive, advancing their own solution to the crisis which the capitalist class remains unable to resolve. The fascists thus are able to win over the petty bourgeoisie and segments of the demoralized working class (for they are very badly in need of a solution to their problems). It also wins the support of the capitalist class, which fears a revival of insurrectionary agitation and desires to smash the Left completely and forever. Moreover, because of the unpopularity of the measures necessary to accomplish this purpose within a capitalist framework, the capitalist class needs to solve the crisis in a manner enabling it to abolish democratic forms.

The victory of fascism in a country must thus be in part attributed to the leaders of the socialist movements, who by making a bid for power terrified the

---

Dutt, *Fascism and Social Revolution* (San Francisco, Proletarian Publishers, 1934, 1974), chapter 4; Guerin, *Fascism and Big Business*, 1973, chapter 2; Lipset, *Political Man*, chapter 5; and Rudolf Heberle, *From Democracy to Nazism* (New York: Grosset and Dunlap, 1945, 1970), p. 121.

upper class and much of the petty bourgeoisie. So, if Socialist parties do not successfully act when they have their chance, the working class becomes demoralized and their struggle is paralyzed, thereby allowing the fascists to take the initiative and eventually assume power.[2]

Fascism's answer to the problem of acute economic depression is to shift the burden of economic recovery onto the working people. Its program includes the reduction of wages, the elimination of independent unions, and increased productivity, as well as heavy state spending on military projects, overseas adventures to secure markets and raw materials, and the institution of rigid coordination and regulation of the economy (by, and in the interests of, the upper class). Fascism becomes possible in a monopoly capitalist society when its economy is faced with chronic stagnation, unemployment, underconsumption, and the consequent social upheaval.[3]

Fascistic movements developed in virtually all the major capitalist countries in response to the universal social upheaval, economic crisis, and offensive of the Left at the end of World War I. The *Freikorps* in Germany, Mussolini's fascists in Italy, and the Ku Klux Klan in the United States were all different manifestations of the same phenomena. With the defeat of the Left's offensive and the subsiding of the world economic and political crisis, the various fascist movements in the world largely withered away. Even the one movement that had actually come to power (that of Mussolini) acted like a respectable capitalist military dictatorship. The worldwide economic collapse of 1929 to 1931 again created the socioeconomic conditions for a reinvigoration of fascist movements — this time becoming major forces in several capitalist countries.[4] As a rule, the more intense the economic and political crisis and the greater the revived strength of the revolutionary Left in the working class, the greater the growth of fascism.

Fascist Regimes

Once opposition to capitalist-class rule increases to a point where its rule through the preferred parliamentary forms is untenable, it is forced to find new nonelectoral forms with which to secure its interests. Traditionally, an upper class resorted to military intervention in such situations. Such is still the norm in the less industrialized capitalist countries of Asia, Africa, and Latin America. Military

---

[2] Georgi Dimitrov, *The United Front Against Fascism* (New York: Gamma Publishing, 1974), chapter 1; Dutt, *Fascism and Social Revolution*, chapters 2-4 and 8; Polanyi, *The Great Transformation*, chapter 20; Guerin, *Fascism and Big Business*, chapter 1; and Trotsky, *The Struggle Against Fascism in Germany*, part I.

[3] See Dimitrov, *The United Front Against Fascism*, chapter 1; Polanyi, *The Great Transformation*, chapter 20; and Guerin, *Fascism and Big Business*, p. 284.

[4] For descriptions of the various European fascist movements of the 1920s and 1930s, see Eugene Weber, *Varieties of Fascism* (New York: Van Nostrand, 1964); Hans Rogger and Eugene Weber, *The European Right* (Berkeley, Calif.: University of California Press,

intervention has also been used in the twentieth century in the more industrialized (but relatively less developed) capitalist countries of Greece, Portugal, Spain, and most of the countries of Eastern Europe between the two world wars. In all these areas, the upper class's personal ties to the leading military officers (blood and economic ties, similar interests and ideologies) have been used to get the military to intervene to reassert unquestioned capitalist rule. The military general staff (often unlike junior officers) is typically a conservative body with considerable respect for tradition and is fully committed to defending the capitalist system.

The more developed a capitalist country and the more involved the masses are in political life, the less effective a military regime can be in securing capitalist-class control. Once they have been brought into politics, the masses do not easily relinquish their participation. Consequently, military regimes in the most developed capitalist countries — especially those with an active democratic life in the past (for example, Argentina and Greece) — are particularly unstable and ineffective. Securing the legitimacy of the capitalist state in such countries is difficult. The instability of such military regimes leads to the restoration of democratic forms — not because the capitalist class will be able to control the situation any better than it could before the military coup, but because the alternative might well be violent revolution. In desperate situations the upper class in the most developed capitalist countries thus often uses fascism as a tool to maintain its control over the state.

If recourse must be had to nonparliamentary forms, the upper class would prefer to rule through military dictators who did not have an independent political base in the population. But generals are notorious for lacking the charismatic qualities and political skills necessary to dominate a population. Moreover, the army lacks the ability to coordinate the people successfully (they are specialists in violence, not politics). Herein lies the vulnerability of military dictatorships and the resultant preference of the capitalist class in the most industrialized countries for fascism.

Fascism can save capitalist rule only by mobilizing the masses (especially the petty bourgeoisie, but also marginal working-class people) behind the leadership and program of a fascist strongman (for example, Hitler and Mussolini) who is not from the upper class, but who is able to establish a partnership with the capitalists allowing this class to maintain its control of the economy. Bringing fascists to power can be very dangerous for the capitalists — as they found out during World War II when Mussolini took Italy into the war against the desires of large segments of Italian industry, and Hitler followed his Götterdämmerung policies until the end even though the capitalist class favored a settlement with the Allies. The capitalist class in both Germany and Italy sponsored coups against the fascists. In Italy they succeeded in 1943, but in Germany the general's plot on

---

1965); and S. J. Woolf, ed., *The Nature of Fascism* (New York: Random House, 1969). For what is probably the best treatment of the Italian fascist movement in English, see Angelo Tasca, *The Rise of Italian Fascism 1918-1922* (New York: Fertig, 1966).

Hitler's life failed.⁵ Because of its inherent dangers the upper class resorts to fascism only during very serious crises when the use of police and military repression is no longer adequate and the open use of systematic terror is required to master the situation.

In fascist regimes all nonfascist parties and mass organizations are suppressed. The cutting edge of fascism is terror against the working class and the Left. The autonomous working-class and leftist organizations that are destroyed are replaced with fascist-run organizations that closely supervise and monitor the working class. Unrelenting and uncontested propaganda is used together with terror (for example, assassinations, beatings, jailings, and persecutions) to demoralize all opposition to capitalism and to the new regime and to build up further mass support for its procapitalist policies. The fascists and the fascist regimes in the capitalist state use appeals to nationalism, base prejudice, and irrationalism of all kinds to disguise that it is actually a dictatorship of the capitalist class.⁶

Fascism uses popular demagogy (including Socialist terminology and symbolism) to appear as if it represents the interests of the people. It appeals to both the rebellious *and* the authoritarian sentiments of the people. It presents itself as revolutionary, but in fact it reduces to a sham rebellion conducted with the approval of the upper class. Fascism links reaction to popular traditions, prejudices, hopes, and fears to give conservatism a popular appeal. It reinvigorates the capitalist order by manipulating the masses, who are brought into motion ostensibly to further their interests and to establish a new order. In reality, however, the fascists use the masses only to strenghten the old order against the attack of the Left. Fascism performs the miracle of transforming discontent and disillusionment with capitalism into enthusiasm for the status quo.

By mastering the techniques of mass propaganda and charismatic leadership, the fascists portray themselves as having mythical and magical qualities. Fascist mass ceremonies often take on the qualities of religious revivals and energizing sacraments and rites. Personal allegiance to the fascist leaders is encouraged and grows. The fascists demagogically promise prosperity, an equalitarian community, national pride, and order to all. The mysticism, the leadership cult, and the popular appeals provide the needed stabilization and result in the preservation of capitalism.⁸

⁵ Guerin, *Fascism and Big Business*, preface to the 1945 French edition.
⁶ See Corey, *The Crisis of the Middle Class*, chapter 12; Dimitrov, *The United Front Against Fascism*, chapter 1; Dutt, *Fascism and Social Revolution*, chapter 4; Guerin, *Fascism and Big Business*, chapter 4.
⁷ Tasca, *The Rise of Italian Fascism*; Dutt, *Fascism and Social Revolution*, chapter 4; Polanyi, *The Great Transformation*, chapter 20; Moore, *The Social Origins of Dictatorship and Democracy*, chapter 8; and Franz L. Neumann, *Behemoth: The Structure and Practice of National Socialism, 1933-1944* (New York: Harper & Row, 1944, 1966), part I.
⁸ See Neumann, *Behemoth*, part I, chapter 6; Guerin, *Fascism and Big Business*, chapter 3; Dimitrov, *The United Front Against Fascism*, chapter 1; and Theodore Abel, *The Nazi Movement: Why Hitler Came to Power* (New York: Athelon Press, 1965), chapter 8.

The Nazis

The paradigm of a fascist movement was the German National Socialist party, which came to power in Germany in 1933. The German Nazi movement was preceded by a fascist-type organization, the *Freikorps*, composed largely of anti-Communist nationalist veterans in the immediate post-World War I period. These early predecessors of the Nazis assassinated some of the most prominent leftist leaders of the revolutionary upheavals of 1919 (Rosa Luxemburg and Karl Liebknecht) and were responsible for smashing Communist-led insurrections in various parts of Germany as well as intimidating much of the revolutionary movement.[9]

The Nazi party grew out of a part of the *Freikorps* movement. It attempted a coup of sorts in the early 1920s, which was easily suppressed by the government, and played a vocal but minor part in German politics until the onslaught of the Great Depression, when its vote in the general elections blossomed from less than 3 percent of the total to approximately 44 percent in just five years. The depression hit Germany particularly hard. It opened up the old wounds caused by the loss of World War I, strengthened the Communist movement, and placed intolerable strains on the petty bourgeoisie. At the same time it undermined the profit-making opportunities of the big corporations. Unable to cope with the growing economic, social, and political crisis within parliamentary forms, big business turned to Adolf Hitler and the Nazi party (which a minority of them had been supporting for some years) as the best hope for solving the crisis, restoring the profitability of German capitalism, and going on the offensive against the Left and the working class.[10] Business support of Hitler increased considerably in 1931, when arrangements were made to provide enough financial support (especially from the heavy industrialists of the Ruhr) for the Nazis to blitz German politics and emerge as the leading party of the Reich.[11]

The basis of Hitler's popular support, however, was found in the German middle classes. It was the small shopkeepers, the artisans, professionals, low-level managerial personnel, the small farmers, and the civil servants that gave him their overwhelming support. While most of the industrial working class remained loyal to the working-class parties (the Socialists and the Communists), many of the more marginal workers joined the Nazis, along with many domestic servants, white-collar workers, and lumpen proletarians (who were isolated from the working-class movement and under the influence of the middle and upper classes).

The Nazis recruited primarily from the middle-class parties (whose sup-

---

[9] See Robert Waite, *Vanguard of Nazism: The Free Corps Movement in Postwar Germany, 1918-1923* (New York: W. W. Norton, 1969), chapter 4; and Guerin, *Fascism and Big Business*, pp. 106-107.

[10] Calvin Hoover, *Germany Enters the Third Reich* (New York: Macmillan, 1933), chapter 4.

[11] Arthur Schweitzer, *Big Business and the Third Reich* (Bloomington, Ind.: Indiana University Press, 1964), p. 101.

porters were heavily petty bourgeois), which declined drastically in the period 1928 to 1933. The working-class parties largely held their own, with the Communists gaining the support the Social Democrats were losing during this same period. While the non-Catholic middle-class parties held only 21 percent of their vote from 1928 to 1932, the working-class parties held 92 percent of theirs.[12] The eclectic class appeal of German Nazism is also illustrated by the proportional presence of the different classes in the Nazi party. The male, independent petty bourgeoisie was overrepresented in the Nazi party by a factor of 1.87, male domestic servants by 1.78, male white-collar and employed professionals by 1.69, and male civil servants by 1.46. But male manual workers were underrepresented by a factor of .68.[13]

The Nazis achieved especially strong support among the small farmers in the heavily Protestant areas of Germany. In rural districts where the Protestant small farmers predominated, the Nazi support in the elections of 1932 and 1933 approximated 100 percent. Their overwhelming support in areas essentially devoid of farm workers, unions, and significant Socialist or Communist organizations indicates that the small farmers were seeking solutions to the crushing economic crisis that was ruining them and not to any threat of Communist revolution. Thus, Nazism appears to have had the same meaning for the small German farmers as did the populist movement for similarly pressed U.S. farmers in the late nineteenth century. With the proper leadership from working-class organizations, these farmers could have just as easily been mobilized by the Left as by the Right. It was a matter of which class was able to most effectively offer a solution to the victims of the economic collapse. The failure of the Left allowed the Right to win their support.[14]

Although the Nazis were given state power by big business through legal channels, they called a state of emergency at the first opportunity and abolished parliamentary forms. Hitler was made dictator, responsible to no one but the army and big business. Hitler's first act was the banning of unions, working-class cooperatives, and the Socialist and Communist parties. This was soon followed by the violent repression of his own militant left wing (the storm troopers), which was pushing for the implementation of the anti–big business part of the Nazi program. The agreement between the Nazis and the big capitalists that brought Hitler to power was thus consolidated.[15]

Nazi economic policies were designed and implemented by representatives of the big-business people that brought them to power. These policies shortly resulted in the virtual abolition of unemployment, the restoration of high levels of production, the construction of a wide range of synthetic industries (to reduce

---

[12] Lipset, *Political Man*, p. 139.

[13] Ibid., p. 147.

[14] Heberle, *From Democracy to Nazism*, chapters 3 and 4; and Charles Loomis and J. Allan Beegle, "The Spead of German Nazism in Rural Areas," *American Sociological Review* 11 (December 1946): 724-734.

[15] See Schweitzer, *Big Business and the Third Reich*, chapters 3, 4, and 5; and Hoover, *Germany Enters the Third Reich*, chapters 5 and 6.

dependence on the world market), the restoration of a high level of profit, the restoration of unquestioned managerial prerogatives in industry, and the general strengthening of capitalist hegemony.

The Nazis strengthened the cartel structure of German industry. Business people's membership in the various industrial associations was made mandatory. These business associations were delegated state authority and allowed to determine most of what happened in the industrial sectors over which they had jurisdiction (for example, which firms received how much raw material, which received how many laborers and what prices they could charge). These associations were run by the largest capitalists and consequently were used to subordinate the smaller enterprises to the monopolies and speed up the process of monopolization within the German economy by driving many of the smaller firms to merge with the larger. The business associations centralized decision making about production, wages, prices, allocation of materials, and marketing, thereby ensuring full utilization of resources while guaranteeing high profits for all major enterprises. The associations enforced the synchronization and coordination of business, integrated the various enterprises, and allowed capital accumulation to proceed according to an economic plan.[16]

While markets continued to exist as a mechanism through which the various sectors of the economy related to one another, the Nazis greatly constricted their operation. The allocation of raw materials was moved from the free market to the governmental allocation agencies and the business associations. The various associations and enterprises within the associations had to fight it out within these bodies rather than on the market. Wage rates were set by the governmental and business associations, and the right of workers to change jobs without the permission of their employer or the state labor exchange was restricted. The capital market was virtually absorbed by the state, which also reduced dividend payments. This was done to increase the retained earnings of the corporations used for capital accumulation. The Nazi state restricted the issue of stock and restricted the stock market to force new investment funds into governmental bonds. Rather than relying on the private capital markets for new funds for capital investment, the industrial enterprises were financed by the state through its generous military and public works contracts and subsidies. The exclusion of private firms from capital markets resulted in the relative decline of finance capital and the strengthening of industrial capital as the productive sector became reliant on state assistance and internal funds rather than borrowing for financing capital accumulation.[17]

The state and the business associations, synchronized with one another, largely replaced free markets with a centralized command economy. However,

---

[16] See Schweitzer, *Big Business and the Third Reich*, especially chapters 9 and 10 and pp. 524-547; Robert Brady, *Business as a System of Power* (New York: Columbia University Press, 1943), chapter 1; Neumann, *Behemoth*, part II; and Guerin, *Fascism and Big Business*, chapter 9.

[17] See Guerin, *Fascism and Big Business*, chapter 9; Neumann, *Behemoth*, part II; Schweitzer, *Big Business and the Third Reich*, chapter 10; and Brady, *Business as a System of Power*, chapter 1.

neither the role of profit nor the law of value was discarded as the guiding principles of economic enterprise. Profit remained the primary goal of the business associations. Never were any state controls placed on profits.[18] Wages and prices, however, were rigorously controlled, as was just about every other aspect of the economy, including foreign trade and international money dealings. Prices were not set at arbitrary levels, however, but rather at levels designed to rationalize the economy and facilitate monopolization. Prices continued to play a decisive role in determining production and in allocating resources.[19]

When the Nazis first came into power, they turned several state-owned industries over to private capital. The state-owned sector of the economy was never significantly expanded by the Nazis. Beginning in 1937, however, various party organizations and individuals transformed themselves into private capitalists. Hermann Göring assembled a steel corporation, and the Nazi Labor Front established several businesses. The expansion of party activities into the private sector secured a stable basis for party financing and integrated party leaders into the capitalist class. The party's move into business was equivalent to that of the American Mafia, which first accumulated funds through illegal activities, and then invested this money in legitimate capitalist enterprises. As with the Mafia, the Nazi leadership coalesced with the previously established capitalists.[20]

The Nazis' labor policy utterly smashed the trade unions and all other autonomous working-class organizations and restored the unquestioned hegemony of the capitalists in their own enterprises. Workers were punished by the state for "disturbing labor peace" (for example, striking, sabotaging, or otherwise resisting the orders of their capitalists), interfering with management, or even "repeatedly making frivolous appeals." Employer-worker relations were militarized as army discipline was instituted in the factories. Wages were set by the state and business associations, and the right to change jobs became dependent on the employer or the state labor exchange. Workers were transferred from one enterprise to another as labor demands changed. Although full employment was achieved, real wages declined by 6 percent during the first four years of the Nazi regime.[21] The German working class was reduced to a form of semiserfdom (where the burden of reproducing labor power still lay on the individual worker, and the workers' nonwork time was still their own).

The Nazis compensated for the complete defeat of the working class with an intense propaganda campaign designed to win over the workers by playing on the themes of the German "race" and nation. Hitler claimed Germany was a "proletarian nation" exploited by the world, made May Day into a Nazi holiday, called himself a (national) socialist, utilized red in his flags and banners, used an equalitarian rhetoric, and blamed the Jews for all the problems caused by capitalism. Nazi propaganda stressed social harmony among all Germans, the

[18] Neumann, *Behemoth*, part II, chapter 4.
[19] See Schweitzer, *Big Business and the Third Reich*, chapter 7; Neumann, *Behemoth*, part II, chapter 11; and Guerin, *Fascism and Big Business*, chapter 9.
[20] Neumann, *Behemoth*, part III, chapter 4, appendix, part III.
[21] Schweitzer, *Big Business and the Third Reich*, chapter 7.

strength of the German people, and pride in the German "race" and traditions. Many were taken in by the rhetoric and few could resist feeling some pride in Germany's economic and military achievements. The Nazis' appeal won over a rather large segment of the working class and neutralized much of the rest.

The intensive Nazi propaganda was supplemented by a very effective campaign of isolating and destroying radical and revolutionary militants within the working class. Marxist cadres were rounded up, sent to concentration camps, and eventually executed. Without Marxist leadership and autonomous organizations to provide alternatives, the Nazi monopoly on the interpretation of events after 1933 proved to be quite effective. Just how successful their efforts were is shown by the virtual absence of massive resistance in the working class to Hitler even in the later years of World War II, and by the relatively weak showing of the Communist Party in West Germany in the immediate postwar period. This was particularly significant because the German Communist Party had been the strongest in the world outside of the Soviet Union before 1933, and because defeat in war typically fosters revolutionary movements (as it had in Germany in 1918 to 1919).[22]

The restrictions on the labor market — especially on the free movement of workers (implemented in the first years of the Nazi regime) — and the institution of virtual state slavery for "non-Aryans" from both the conquered territories and Germany itself during World War II meant that Nazi Germany was well on the way to transforming itself from an authentically monopoly capitalist economy (with very heavy state coordination) to a state-dominated and centralized but essentially private system of industrial serfdom/slavery, with the old monopoly capitalist class (infused with new blood from the Nazi elite) as the exploiting class. Similarly, although it brought Hitler to power in 1933, the old monopoly capitalist class by the late 1930s lost control over the state, and until the latter years of the war, it was no longer the ruling class. The last years of the Nazi state and economy may have simply represented a temporary condition made necessary by the extreme emergency of the war. But Nazi success in World War II may also have possibly resulted in a truly unique mode of economic organization qualitatively different from either private or state monopoly capitalism, with a continuation of industrial serfdom and slavery as the primary relations of production. Whether this would have been true after a World War II with a different outcome, or whether the Nazi empire would have reverted to monopoly capitalism of either the private or state types (such as clearly existed in Franco's Spain), with essentially free movement of labor and either or both the old private and new state capitalists as the ruling class, will never be known.[23]

The Nazi party increased in strength as it consolidated its independent social and economic base, and became increasingly able to act independently of the old

---

[22] Guerin, *Fascism and Big Business*, chapter 8; Brady, *Business as a System of Power*, chapter 9; Neumann, *Behemoth*, part III; and Fromm, *Escape From Freedom*, chapter 6.
[23] For a discussion of the categorization of modes of production and social formations, see Albert Szymanski, "The Class Nature of the Soviet Union," University of Oregon, mimeographed, 1976, chapter 1.

monopoly capitalist class that brought it into power. Although the imperial policies of the Nazis were at first motivated primarily by the needs and interests of German big business, which needed secure markets, cheap labor, and access to raw materials, the irrational and suicidal pursuit of that end after the early German blitzkrieg victories in World War II were motivated primarily by the power hunger and world hegemonic romantic aspirations of Hitler and the Nazi party. These policies resulted not only in the complete defeat of the German state, but in the triumph of socialism in eastern Germany. The risk assumed by the German capitalists when they decided to rely on the Nazis to preserve their rule did not pay off.

Fascistic Movements in the United States

Fascism and fascistic movements have by no means been limited to the period between the two world wars. There were similar movements before 1918, and there have been many since 1945.[24] Fascism as a massive phenomenon is endemic to the monopoly stage of capitalism. Fascist movements, which do not necessarily come to power, can be expected to become significant social phenomena whenever the revolutionary left or militant working-class organizations are perceived as a threat by the middle classes *and* the upper class during a period of social crisis in which the Left is unable to mobilize the middle classes.

The United States has a long history of right-wing movements with fascistic characteristics, although never anything of the order of the German or Italian fascist parties. These rightist movements have always been a response to the Left and the organized working class. In the later part of the nineteenth century, an organization called the American Protective Association (APA) grew up. This group stressed native Americanism and expressed opposition to the migrants who were coming into the industrial working class from East Asia and Southern and Eastern Europe. Data are available on the class backgrounds of the membership of the APA for the cities of Oakland, Minneapolis, and San Francisco. In these three cities nonmanual occupations were overrepresented by a factor of about 20 percent while the manual working class was similarly underrepresented by a factor of about 20 percent.[25] This group's opposition to the new manual working class, its superpatriotism, and its appeal to the middle classes suggest that the APA was a semifascist organization.

In the aftermath of World War I, the Ku Klux Klan (the KKK, whose historical namesake had originally been a southern organization set up to combat Reconstruction in the late 1860s) was revived in the North. The KKK attacked

---

[24] See, for example, Weber, *Varieties of Fascism*; and Lipset, *Political Man*, chapter 5. Also see Weber, *Varieties of Fascism*; Rogger and Weber, *The European Right*; Woolf, *The Nature of Fascism*; and Tasca, *The Rise of Italian Fascism*.

[25] Seymour Martin Lipset and Earl Raab, *The Politics of Unreason* (New York: Harper & Row, 1970), pp. 79-92.

everything "un-American": foreign workers (the heart of the U.S. industrial proletariat in the 1920s), Catholicism (the religion of the Poles, Italians, and many other nationalities in the new industrial working class), Judaism (the religion of many of the non-Catholic immigrant workers, traditionally associated with moneylenders and bankers — the direct exploiters of small-business people), trade unions, and Socialists, Communists, and radicals of all kinds. The Klan also expressed hostility against the powerful Eastern interests that were betraying the "little man" and his nation by supporting foreign migration, Catholicism, internationalism, and other profitable but "un-American" things. The Klan and its various parallel organizations of the time played an important role in smashing (by using violence and terror) various left-wing working-class organizations in the early 1920s. The Klan demonstrated its greatest strength in the urban areas of the most industrial part of the country — the Midwest. It also showed strength in the urban areas of the Southwest and West. The Klan recruited mainly from struggling independent business people, male white-collar workers, and nonunion Protestant workers who, in the absence of a powerful Socialist working-class movement, were mobilized by the fascist program of the Klan. This organization used patriotism and fundamentalist religion to win such workers to the cause of smashing unions, revolutionary organizations, and their fellow workers of European or Asian birth.[26] The activities and program of the Klan closely paralleled the fascist movements of Europe during the same period.

During the 1930s fascist organizations such as the Black Legion and the Silver Shirts appeared, principally in the Midwest, to harass the growing unions and radical organizations in the industrial heartland. These groups picked up many of the former supporters of the KKK and demonstrated the same superpatriotism and antiimmigrant sentiments as did that organization. In 1936 the Black Legion was estimated to have about 40,000 members.[27] Other fascistic movements also developed in the 1930s. These movements advanced various proposals to grapple with the extreme economic crisis of capitalism, stop the growth of the Left, and "bring the country back together again." One of the most influential of these was that of the radio priest Father Coughlin and his National Union for Social Justice. Coughlin emphasized patriotism, anticommunism, and a strong state role in bringing the country out of the depression. After 1937, he became increasingly anti-working class, anti-Semitic, and overtly pro-Hitler and Mussolini.[28]

The post–World War II period in the United States witnessed an anti-Communist hysteria that peaked in the Joseph McCarthy phenomenon. While McCarthy's support never manifested itself in an actual organization, it nevertheless did bear many similarities to a fascist-type movement. It, like all fascist movements, was violently anti-Communist, superpatriotic, *and* hostile to the

---

[26] Lipset and Raab, *The Politics of Unreason*, chapter 4; John Moffat Mecklin, *The Ku Klux Klan* (New York: Harcourt Brace Jovanovich, 1924); and Kenneth Jackson, *The Ku Klux Klan in the City, 1915–1930* (New York: Oxford University Press, 1967).
[27] Lipset and Raab, *The Politics of Unreason*, pp. 150–167.
[28] Ibid., pp. 167–189.

establishment (which it accused of being pro-Communist). By attacking both the Left and the powers that be, it was able to mobilize much of the petty bourgeoisie and large segments of the working class (who were without revolutionary leadership or organizations) to support it. As do most fascist movements that have any degree of success, McCarthy had the backing of the capitalist class (who benefited considerably from his attacks on the Left) until he attacked the establishment itself. When he turned on his powerful supporters, he was promptly crushed and discarded. McCarthyism found its support disproportionately among small-business people and the better-paid manual and white-collar workers.[29]

The most important American right-wing movement in the late 1950s and early 1960s was the John Birch Society. Unlike the others discussed here, this organization did *not* have fascist characteristics. It did not attack big business; instead, it focused its attack exclusively on the Left and those it accused of being its dupes. Its appeal was disproportionately to the better-off predominantly upper-level petty bourgeois groups in society. It was an extremist, nationalist, right-wing group.[30]

Wallace

The most important fascist-type phenomenon of the 1960s and 1970s was the movement of Governor George Wallace of Alabama. As do fascists, Wallace appealed to "the little man" caught between the lower-class groups (national minorities, lumpen proletarians) and radicals on the one side, and the big financial interests on the other. And similar to the fascists, his appeal was to superpatriotism and tradition against the threats of social upheaval, economic crisis, and the Left. Unlike traditional fascist movements, however, Wallace's greatest support came from the manual working class. Outside of the South, 5 percent of white nonmanual, but 9 percent of white manual workers voted for Wallace, and in the South 22 percent of white nonmanual, but 53 percent of white manual workers voted for him. His appeal among whites was greatest in the more rural areas, among the least skilled, least educated, and the lowest income strata.[31]

The considerable strength of Wallace in the white manual working class (especially in its lowest strata) must be attributed largely to a lack of an alternative in the United States. In other capitalist countries the Communists or Socialists would pick up much of the support that went to him in the United States. In the absence of a significant leftist movement within the United States, working-class resentment against the oppressive life led by working people is channeled into right-wing "radical" movements. In the absence of a significant working-class Left, Wallace and those like him are able to verbalize the discontent of much of the working class and lead this class's attempt to find a solution to the growing crisis of capitalism.

[29] See Martin Trow, "Small Businessmen and Support of McCarthy," *The American Journal of Sociology* 64, no. 3 (November 1958): 270–281; Lipset, *Political Man*, pp. 170–173; and Lipset and Raab, *The Politics of Unreason*, chapter 6.
[30] Lipset and Raab, *The Politics of Unreason*, chapter 8.
[31] Ibid., pp. 384–390.

That the support of Wallace does not indicate traditionalist conservative politics can be demonstrated by the attitude of his supporters on various social questions. Of Wallace supporters in 1968, 46 percent believed that the United States needed more welfare programs (compared with 67 percent of Humphrey supporters, and 40 percent of Nixon supporters.) Of non-South manual workers who voted for Wallace, fully 50 percent wanted an expansion of governmental welfare programs. Forty-four percent of Wallace supporters, as against 24 percent of the Humphrey supporters and 22 percent of the Nixon supporters, felt that blacks were making too much progress.[32] These data suggest that Wallace's *main* appeal was neither to racism nor to opposition to the state, but rather to "the little man" unable to cope with the crisis of capitalism.

Wallace consciously appealed to the interests of the "average," white, native-born, working man with his presidential campaign planks advocating expanded social security, more job retraining, a 100 percent tax deduction for medical expenses for those over sixty-five, improved Medicare benefits, guarantees for collective bargaining, and public works to create jobs when necessary, as well as by his continuing jibes at the Eastern establishment and his equalitarian rhetoric. As a result, the social basis of the Wallace appeal shifted from its more traditional, conservative, petty bourgeois supporters (such as those who had earlier supported the John Birch Society) increasingly to the white working class — which, lacking any better alternative to articulate their problems, turned to the only significant force addressing their problems in their own language.

The Wallace appeal in 1964 was primarily to the petty bourgeoisie. Wallace's strength in the primaries of that year was greatest in the suburban areas of the northern industrial cities and in traditionally conservative and middle-class areas.[33] Even in 1968 when Wallace showed great strength in the manual working class, his support demonstrated much of the classic fascist appeal to middle groupings. The fear of, and hostility toward blacks, Latins, and other recent immigrant workers, the social upheavals (such as rioting and demonstrations) this hostility fostered, and the revival of the Left as manifested in the student antiwar movements created considerable hostility among the relatively well-off white workers and the petty bourgeoisie. Then again, the pressure exerted on these middle groups by monopoly capitalism, which was forcing ever larger numbers of them into the unskilled proletariat, and the pressures on the better-off workers to increase productivity resulted in increasing frustration with the "Eastern establishment" and the "Washington bureaucrats" who were doing their bidding.

As did the Nazis in Germany and the Fascists in Italy, Wallace appealed primarily to youth (especially nonstudents). In October 1968, 25 percent of young people aged 18 to 24 not in college supported Wallace. Overall, about 35 percent of youth who had never been to college supported Wallace. (Among college students, however, only 7 percent supported Wallace.) In the November

[32] Lipset and Raab, *The Politics of Unreason*, pp. 400–405.
[33] Michael Rogin, "Politics, Emotion and the Wallace Vote," *British Journal of Sociology* 20, no. 1 (March 1969): 27–49, and "Wallace and the Middle Class: The White Backlash in Wisconsin," *Public Opinion Quarterly* 30, no. 1 (Spring 1966): 98–108.

1968 election 17 percent of whites between the ages of 21 and 25, compared with 11 percent of those over 50, voted for Wallace.[34]

The Wallace phenomenon in the United States was not full-fledged fascism. But it had enough in common with both traditional fascist movements in Europe and with the most fascist of American mass movements (the KKK of the 1920s) to warrant its consideration as a quasi-fascist movement that could have easily developed into a full-fledged fascist movement if the social crisis of the late 1960s had been intensified and prolonged. Wallace made the same general types of appeals to those who were in part the same type of people in what was becoming a similar type of situation as that which gave birth to Hitler's and Mussolini's movements in Europe.

Remember that just before the economic collapse of German capitalism, Hitler in the election of 1928 received less than 3 percent of the vote; five years later he was in office. George Wallace received 13 percent of the vote in 1968 during a period of only minor crisis (caused by a stalemated war in Vietnam and the social upheaval of blacks and students at home). In the face of a major economic or other crisis in U.S. society, Wallace (or someone like him) can be expected to do considerably better. None of the right-wing fascistic movements in the history of the United States has ever received any significant support from a wide segment of the U.S. capitalist class, because since 1861 it has been able to rule through parliamentary forms, and thus has had no reason to run the risk of building up and putting a fascist dictatorship in power. The revolutionary Left in the United States has never presented a major challenge to the rule of the capitalist class. Even during the very serious economic crisis of the 1930s, the hegemony of the capitalist class was never seriously threatened. If in a future crisis hostility to capitalist-class rule should grow and the strength of the revolutionary Left becomes manifest, the U.S. capitalist class can be expected to behave in the same manner as did the German and Italian (and many other) capitalist ruling classes, and provide the financing and support to build up a strong fascist movement that it would attempt to bring into power. Whether it will succeed hinges on the degree to which the revolutionary Left can build a massive revolutionary working-class movement capable of winning the leadership of the intermediate strata, thus depriving a future fascist movement of its base of support and the upper class of an opportunity to make reaction popular, thereby saving its neck. If the Left should try, but fail, as it did in Germany, Italy, France, Spain, and Chile, fascism of one form or another will be on the historical agenda of the United States.

Summary

This chapter examined one of the two radical social movements that aim to transform monopoly capitalist society. We have seen that the social base of fascism lies primarily in the petty bourgeoisie, although fascist movements also attract some

[34] Lipset and Raab, *The Politics of Unreason*, pp. 367-368, 382.

support from all classes of the population. Fascism out of power is extremism of the center. Fascists are hostile to *both* big business and organized working-class movements. The growth of fascist movements among the petty bourgeoisie reflects the pressure from both sides that middle-class people suffer, especially in times of economic crisis.

Fascist movements tend to come to power in times of social crisis in countries where the revolutionary working-class Left is strong and has recently made an unsuccessful attempt to come to power. Fascist movements typically originate as a defense against a working-class challenge to class society. Then, when the social crisis persists past the point of the left threat, they tend to go on the offensive, advancing their own solution to the crisis. Fascist groups only come to power in coalition with monopoly capitalists, who see the fascists as the best hope for the consolidation of the interests of monopoly capital. In times of extreme social crisis, when the bourgeoisie is no longer able to rule effectively by parliamentary forms, it is forced to cooperate with those who have the ability to mobilize the population to "make reaction popular." Fascist regimes tend to come to power in the more advanced capitalist countries where the masses have a substantial history of political involvement, while classic military dictatorships (which rely much less on popular mobilization and manipulation) tend to come to power in the least advanced capitalist countries.

Fascist and fascistic movements were not unique to Europe in the period between the two world wars. Such movements occur wherever monopoly capitalism exists, especially in times of prolonged social crisis. Among the important fascistic movements in modern U.S. history have been the Ku Klux Klan (a very powerful force in the 1920s) and the Wallace movement of the late 1960s and early 1970s. Both exhibited most of the classic features of fascist movements, such as the appeal to intermediate groups, hostility to both the "Eastern establishment" and the Left, and extreme nationalism.

13

Revolution and Socialist Movements in the Capitalist State

The capitalist class's domination of the state and the capitalist state's domination of society is by no means immutable. Capitalist society is vulnerable to working-class-based movements whose goal is a Socialist transformation. Just as forces within the capitalist economy give rise to the capitalist state as a necessary organ of capitalist hegemony, they also give rise to Socialist movements. To be successful, however, Socialist movements must know how best to utilize advantageous situations.

Revolutionary and other radical movements of the oppressed classes in capitalist society have arisen throughout the history of capitalism — for example, the movements of 1848, the Paris Commune of 1871, the rapid growth of the Socialist parties of Europe in the last decades of the nineteenth century, the revolutionary insurrections of 1917 to 1923 in Central Europe,[1] the revolutionary upsurge of 1944 to 1948 in Europe, the French upheaval of 1968, and the Portuguese Revolution of 1974 to 1975. The success of such attempts depends on the full development of the contradictions in capitalist society, on the full development of all progressive possibilities in the old society (that is, in its reaching the dead end

---

[1] For discussions of the European revolutions of the period from 1919 to 1923, see Werner Angress, *Stillborn Revolution: The Communist Bid for Power in Germany* (Princeton, N.J.: Princeton University Press, 1963); A. Joseph Berlau, *The German Social Democratic Party 1914-1921* (New York: Columbia University Press, 1949); David Caute, *The Left in Europe Since 1789* (New York: McGraw-Hill, 1966); Rudolf Coper, *Failure of a Revolution: Germany 1918-1919* (Cambridge, England: Cambridge University Press, 1955); and Ralph Lutz, *The German Revolution 1918-1919* (Stanford, Calif.: Stanford University Press, 1922).

of its historical development), and the technological and social possibilities of building a new society.²

The ripeness of the material conditions for social revolution against capitalism manifests itself on a number of levels. The oppression of the working class and the other nonprivileged classes is increasingly felt to be unnecessary and intolerable (as the technological and social possibilities of living differently become more apparent). The ideological hegemony of the capitalist class spontaneously breaks down. And the masses become increasingly bitter and disillusioned with their present existence. The capitalist class itself becomes cynical about its ability and right to rule. It increasingly resorts to manipulation rather than to patriotism, religion, and popularly supported violence to preserve its rule. Internally, it becomes increasingly divided and demoralized, and hence incapable of adequately dealing with the movements of the oppressed. Also, the various alternative solutions being offered as solutions to the oppression of the working classes and other oppressed groups (such as nationalism, fascism, liberal reformism, Social Democracy, and Christian Democracy) lose credibility among the oppressed as these solutions reveal themselves to be bankrupt (that is, incapable of actually relieving oppression). Last, revolutionary organizations develop that can mobilize both the working class *and* the other oppressed classes into a common united front, provide them with a realistic analysis of the causes of their oppression, a proposal about the historical alternatives, and a program to realize an alternative — that is, an organizational form, a strategy, and a set of tactics to make revolution. It is the contradictions of capitalism itself that generate the conditions for the development of movements designed to replace capitalism.³

² In Marx's words:

> *No social order ever perishes before all the productive forces for which there is room in it have developed; and new, higher relations of production never appear before the material conditions of their existence have matured in the womb of the old society itself. Therefore mankind always sets itself only such tasks as it can solve; since, looking at the matter more closely, it will always be found that the task itself arises only when the material conditions for its solution already exist or are at least in the process of formation.*

From the preface to a contribution to the *Critique of Political Economy*, in Marx and Engels, *Selected Works*, vol. I, p. 363.

³ As Marx and Engels argued:

> *These conditions of life, which different generations find in existence, decide also whether or not the periodically recurring revolutionary convulsion will be strong enough to overthrow the basis of all existing forms. And if these material elements of a complete revolution are not present (namely, on the one hand the existence of productive forces, on the other the formation of a revolutionary mass, which revolts not only against separate conditions of society up till then, but against the very "production of life" till then, the "total activity" on which it was based), then, as far*

The Conditions for Revolution

Felt oppression

The root of revolutionary opposition to the capitalist system lies not in the reality of hunger or other forms of material deprivation. In fact, the truly hungry are too desperate and demoralized to be truly revolutionary. Similarly, many people in primitive nonclass society regularly suffer serious material deprivation without being oppressed. Oppression is a consequence of the artificial creation of hunger among the masses by the society's economic organization even though the productive forces are sufficiently developed to eliminate it. In other words, oppression exists when the gluttony of some (the upper class) causes the hunger of the masses. Hunger in class society is oppressive because it implies that the hungry are not fully human nor as good as those who are responsible for their hunger. As long as capitalism exists, the potential for its dissolution through revolutionary action will also exist. The humiliation and degradation produced by society is the motive force of revolution. Revolutionaries feel in their bones the truth of the maxim that "it is better to die on your feet than to live on your knees."

Revolution in capitalist society is a revolt against authoritarian relations, the onslaught against human dignity, and coercion and lack of self-determination. This is equally true of the revolutionary movements that triumphed in the less developed capitalist countries such as China, Russia, Vietnam, and Cuba as it is for those movements currently operating in the most developed, such as Italy and France. Revolutions in both the less and the most developed capitalist countries typically assault the full range of authoritarian class institutions in these societies — the religions, the state, all forms of private business, the schools, the family, and the culture. All revolutions of the oppressed have been strongly leveling, democratizing, and liberating in their immediate impact.

Oppression is relative to the possible, not to an abstract ahistorical standard. The potential for radicalization of a class is a function of the difference between what *is* and what realistically *could be* when the state of the society's technology is considered. It is *not* a function of the absolute deprivation of a group, but rather of a group's deprivation *relative* to what could be achieved. Thus the potential for radicalization is independent of the absolute level of economic development of a country; rather, it is a function of the amount of inequality in a society. The potential for radicalization is a function of the difference between how the masses in a society live and how they *could* live given the state of technological development.

Massive felt oppression has been the precondition of the major revolutionary movements of the twentieth century. The revolutions in Russia, China, and Cuba,

---

> as practical development is concerned, it is absolutely immaterial whether the "idea" of this revolution has been expressed a hundred times already....

Karl Marx and Friedrich Engels, *The German Ideology* (New York: International Publishers, 1947), pp. 29, 30.

for example, all occurred in societies where the masses were both outrageously oppressed *and* where they came to feel that they were in fact oppressed.

In prerevolutionary Russia, the vast majority of the population were poor peasants who had only recently been released from serfdom, but who still bore the burden of considerable payments for taxes, rents, and manumission to the state and aristocracy. The expansion of commerce into the countryside together with the hostility of the state to the communal institutions of the village destroyed many of the traditional protective institutions of the peasantry and resulted in the concentration of land in fewer hands (that is, in the growth of the rich peasants or kulaks).

An industrial working class had been created in Russia in the later half of the nineteenth century. Although it represented only a few percent of the population in 1917, it was concentrated in several heavily industrialized areas and often worked in technologically advanced factories as large and modern as those in Western Europe. Their low wages, long hours, miserable working conditions, and barbarous housing arrangements, combined with the knowledge that foreigners had a considerable stake in these enterprises, caused the workers to be hostile to the capitalist system that had uprooted them from the countryside and transformed them into a propertyless proletariat. The economic oppression suffered by both the peasantry and the urban working class was greatly enhanced by the political oppression experienced not only by these classes, but by the intermediate classes and sectors of the wealthy as well. The czarist autocracy was the last major absolutism in Europe, and as such denied basic democratic liberties as well as ruled in a most capricious manner.[4]

Since the 1830s, China had been increasingly humiliated by the Western imperial powers. Britain, France, Russia, and the others demanded that China open itself to trade with them, grant them extraterritorial rights in its coastal cities, and otherwise subject itself to foreign domination. Foreign business dominated the Chinese economy and humiliated the Chinese in virtually every way. With the collapse of the imperial regime around the turn of the century, a series of warlord/gangster regimes culminating in the rule of Chiang Kai-shek emerged. These warlords were totally indifferent to the needs and aspirations of their people. During the invasion of China in the 1930s and 1940s, Chiang preferred to either fight the Communists or hold his troops in reserve to reduce casualties, rather than fight the Japanese. As a result, the Japanese were able to overrun most of China and humiliate the Chinese once again.

Meanwhile, the commercialization of Chinese society induced by the forced trade with the West accelerated the decay of the old imperialist institutions and gave impetus to the development of a rich merchant class as well as its corollaries:

---

[4] Good discussions of the oppressive conditions of the peasants and workers as well as of the czarist autocracy can be found in Leon Trotsky, *History of the Russian Revolution* (Ann Arbor: University of Michigan Press, 1967); Wolf, *Peasant Wars of the Twentieth Century*, chapter 2; Marcel Liebman, *The Russian Revolution* (New York: Vintage Books, 1970); Jerome Blum, *Lord and Peasant in Russia: From the Ninth to the Nineteenth Century* (Princeton, N.J.: Princeton University Press, 1961); and V. I. Lenin, *The Development of Capitalism in Russia* (Moscow: Foreign Languages Publishing House, 1956).

massive rural and urban poverty, and the concentration of land and wealth in few hands. Rents rose as the land was commercialized and the drive for profits accelerated. Some of the peasants, forced off the land by massive famines that killed millions, migrated to the cities to stay alive. The lucky ones found work as coolies or as factory or dock hands under the most menial of conditions, earning barely enough to stay alive. Many of the urban workers worked in foreign-owned enterprises, which added insult to injury. Even the merchants, smaller capitalists, and smaller landlords suffered under the domination of the foreigners, who tried to secure most of the profits to be made for themselves. As a result there existed a substantial material basis for an alliance of the working class, peasantry, small landlords, and smaller bourgeoisie against both foreign domination and the oppressive structure of Chinese society.[5]

During the 1950s, Cuba was dominated by American transnational corporations more than any other country of the world (aside from the United States itself). In the mid-1950s, 40 percent of Cuba's sugar was produced in U.S.-owned mills; 90 percent of electric power production, the phone company, and 50 percent of the railways were owned by Americans. During this decade about 60 percent of all of Cuba's exports and about 75 percent of all her imports were with the United States. The average annual rate of unemployment was 25 percent. Eight percent of the farms contained 71 percent of all the land (six sugar companies occupied 60 percent of the sugar land). In 1956 the average annual per capita income of the peasants was $91 (one-third of the national average).

Most Cubans were proletarians. The rural land was primarily owned by the sugar companies, which employed cane cutters and sugar refinery workers. While the conditions of work and the standard of living of the workers in Havana was considerably better than that of the rural and small-town workers, very few workers were able to lead the comfortable life of the better-off petty bourgeoisie and upper class of Havana. The humiliations suffered under the domination of the ever-present American corporations, the abject poverty (especially in the rural areas), and the tyrannical rule of the Batista dictatorship in the 1950s (his secret police were responsible for the murder of approximately 20,000 people) combined to drive the population of the country into opposition to the existing government and to U.S. domination and the extreme inequities of Cuban society as well.[6] (Note

---

[5] Good discussions of the oppressive conditions of peasants and workers in China as well as of the humiliation suffered at the hands of the imperialist countries can be found in Franz Schurmann and Orville Schell, *Imperial China* (New York: Vintage Books, 1967); Franz Schurmann and Orville Schell, *Republican China* (New York: Vintage Books, 1961); John Fairbank, *The United States and China* (Cambridge, Mass: Harvard University Press, 1971); Wolf, *Peasant Wars of the Twentieth Century*, chapter 3; Barrington Moore, *Social Origins of Dictatorship and Democracy* (Boston: Beacon Press, 1966), chapter 4; and R. H. Tawney, *Land and Labour in China* (Boston: Beacon Press, 1966).

[6] On the oppressive conditions of the Cuban masses and the role of U.S. imperialism in Cuba, see Maurice Zeitlin and Robert Scheer, *Cuba: Tragedy in Our Hemisphere* (New York: Grove Press, 1963); Wolf, *Peasant Wars of the Twentieth Century*, chapter 6; C. Wright Mills, *Listen Yankee* (New York: McGraw-Hill, 1960); Leo Huberman and

that even the Cuban middle class was alienated from the oppressive Batista regime and supported the 26th of July Movement of Fidel Castro until it adopted a clearly Socialist course. In fact, it was from this group as well as from the peasantry that most of the recruits for the guerillas that fought the Batista regime were drawn. The manual working class did not play an active and direct role in the actual overthrow of the old regime, although it did play a major role in the evolution of the policies of the Castro regime after it had come to power.)

Neither oppression (that is, the existence of a low living standard caused by the organization of production) nor the lack of dignified treatment as full human beings is a sufficient condition for revolution. If it were, the productive classes would have been in constant revolt for the past 5,000 years. That the oppressed historically have not often challenged the system politically indicates that certain other material conditions must be present before oppression (which *is* a *necessary* condition for revolution against capitalism) can realize itself in popular revolutionary movements.

It is not enough that oppression and its consequent bitterness exist. Such oppression often causes the masses to look for personal salvation in various religious cults, hope for escape for oneself or one's children into the upper petty bourgeoisie, various consciousness-contracting drugs, sex cults, or numerous other diversions offering salvation.[7] Throughout the history of class society, such solutions usually have been more popular than revolution. Only under certain material conditions does felt oppression manifest itself in seeking political solutions.

Oppression must be felt as socially caused for it to be manifested in revolutionary movements. As long as people conceptualize their condition as the product of personal flaws or failings (not enough brains, education, or ambition) and as being inevitable (for example, that they are sinners, that there have always been poor, or that it is God's will for them to be poor), they will not feel their oppression as oppression by society's organization. To feel oppressed, they must understand that their miserable lot is a social product *and* that alternative ways of living are realistically possible and obtainable through collective action. Once oppression is recognized as socially determined rather than historically necessary, popular bitterness is transformed into collective action against capitalism.

Decline of the upper class's ideological hegemony

Before oppressed people will turn away from the existing institutions of class society and withdraw their support from the capitalist state, they must believe that

---

Paul Sweezy, *Cuba: Anatomy of a Revolution* (New York: Monthly Review, 1961); Robert Smith, *Background to Revolution* (New York: Alfred Knopf, 1966); Robert Smith, *The United States and Cuba* (New Haven, Conn.: College and University Press, 1960); and James O'Connor, *Origins of Socialism in Cuba* (Ithaca, N.Y.: Cornell University Press, 1970).

[7] For good discussions of the role of religion in expressing the oppression of the lower classes, see Lanternari, *The Religions of the Oppressed*; Worsley, *The Trumpet Shall Sound*; and Hobsbawm, *Primitive Rebels*.

the state is responsible for maintaining their oppression and that the present political order is neither good nor necessary. The ideological hegemony of the upper class normally prevents this awareness from occurring. The working class is exhorted to respect authority and is conditioned to follow orders, accept its subordinate social position, and feel incapable of self-determination.[8]

Just as class society produces the oppression of the working class and other groups, it also undermines its own ideological hegemony. The normal operation of capitalist society undermines respect for authority, the sacredness of tradition, and the belief that happiness can be found within capitalist social relations. This happens in a number of ways, among which are the undermining of religious faith, the shock of defeat in war, sustained and widespread corruption and scandal in the upper class, and economic depression.

For capitalism, nothing is sacred except the pursuit of profit. Sunday work, lying, and stealing are commonplace capitalist activities in pursuit of increased profits. The transparent use of the churches by capitalists to manipulate the masses, and the fact that the industrial proletariats' lives provide an experience less compatible with religious mysticism than do the lives of rural peasants or workers, contribute to the workers' alienation from religion.

Every state makes claims to its people about its greatness. Such claims tend to evaporate when a state engages in war and loses. People become disillusioned not only with the leadership that took them into an unsuccessful war, but also with the system that was responsible for it and the patriotism and nationalism that had been used to manipulate them into supporting it. The rapid delegitimation of the upper class's rule that follows an unsuccessful war has historically been one of the leading sparks for revolution. The loss of the 1904 to 1905 Russian war with Japan sparked the 1905 Russian Revolution. The losing Russian war with Germany was the catalyst for the 1917 revolutions (both in February and October). The impetus for the Chinese Revolution came from the continuing conquest of China by the Japanese, and the unwillingness and inability of the Kuomintang to cope with it. Crises produced by military defeat are perhaps the most important catalysts transforming the masses' oppression into revolutionary action.

Sustained scandals and political corruption involving both the leading officials of the state and prominent members of the upper class can also result in the discrediting of the ruling class and the capitalist state — particularly since the people have been so carefully conditioned to respect authority because of its moral superiority. Once the upper class and a series of state officials become exposed as venal, immoral, and guided by the pettiest, most egotistic, and self-seeking of motives, the masses' previous trust in their rule can be transformed into disillusionment and hatred. For this to happen, such scandals must appear to be not just the product of immoral individuals, but rather the norm for these groups. The more people of the ruling class who are exposed as corrupt, and the wider the range of their political affiliations, the more likely are the masses to conclude that the

---

[8] For discussions of the role of legitimacy, see Lipset, *Political Man*, chapter 3; Linz and Lipset, "The Social Bases of Diversity," chapter 6; and Leggett, *Class, Race and Labor*, chapter 4.

system is morally bankrupt and hence to withdraw from it their belief in its legitimacy.

Sustained economic depression is another form of crisis that can cause the rule of the capitalist class and its state to be discredited and the consequent rapid rise of a revolutionary movement. A state that bases its claim for popular support on its ability to ensure general affluence and jobs for all, but which is unable to deliver for a sustained period of time, is in trouble (as is the capitalist class which continues to live at high levels during a general depression). The more a ruling class has rooted the legitimacy of its rule on the claim that capitalism is responsible for prosperity, jobs, and "the highest standard of living in the world," the more endangered is its position during depressions (especially when depressions do not affect the noncapitalist countries).

Another factor that undermines the legitimacy of the capitalist state is exposure of the ruling classes' behavior as self-interested and callous rather than guided by the best interests of all the people. A factor that contributed to the Russian Revolution of 1905 was a march of peasants on the czar's palace to protest the treatment of the peasantry by the czar's officials that was fired upon by the palace guards. This event resulted in the rapid disillusionment of wide segments of the peasantry with the czarist system — the peasants' own experience was worth a million speeches and leaflets denouncing the czar.

Rapid changes in the economic institutions of society produced by industrialization, or the development or transformation of local production into production for capitalist markets, is another potentially delegitimating factor. Rapid economic change induced by capitalism, and the resultant social dislocations undermining the traditional basis of authority, persuade people that nothing is sacred and that change is in the nature of things. The capitalist state and the upper class, which are (and are eventually *perceived* to be) responsible for the social dislocations and the increasing exploitation and brutalization that normally come with them, are consequently discredited. The European countries that most rapidly became industrialized experienced some of the most bitter class war on that continent.[9] One of the essential factors leading to the growth of revolutionary movements in Third World countries (such as China) was the rapid growth of commercial relationships and the resultant dislocation and brutalization in these countries.[10]

The increasing inability of the state — for whatever reason — to cope with the demands of the working class and other groups in society can produce delegitimation. If the economic demands on the state grow more rapidly than the state is able to increase its revenues to satisfy such demands, people will become increasingly disenchanted with the state and will increasingly oppose it. The demands of the world market and the need to preserve the legitimacy of the capitalist system force the state to appropriate and spend an ever-growing proportion of the national

---

[9] Lipset, *Political Man*, pp. 53-58.
[10] See Erich Jacoby, *Agrarian Unrest in South East Asia* (New York: Columbia University Press, 1949); J. D. Boeke, *The Interests of the Voiceless Far East* (Leiden: Universitaire Presse, 1948); and Clifford Gertz, *Agricultural Involution: The Process of Ecological Change in Indonesia* (Berkeley, Calif.: University of California Press, 1970).

income. At the same time, resistance to increasing taxation grows as taxes take an increasing bite out of wages, thereby reducing living standards. This growing "fiscal crisis of the state" could develop into a serious crisis of legitimacy for the capitalist state, against which people feel increasingly resentful for increasing taxes and for not delivering the goods demanded of it.[11]

The prerevolutionary periods in Russia, China, and Cuba serve as an example of the delegitimation of tyrannical regimes. Students and intellectuals became increasingly alienated from czarism from the mid-nineteenth century on, when they formed movements to overthrow it. Many people of the educated classes adopted various revolutionary ideologies and rejected the dominant values. Their influence on the rest of the population became considerable once they were able to build organizations that could take their ideas to the people. The great power of the mystical and demented monk Rasputin over the czarina, and the arbitrary and tyrannical rule of the czar along with the general backwardness of Russia alienated large segments of even the wealthy classes from the czarist system. The defeats of the 1904 and 1914 wars, the harsh discipline of the army, and the disintegration of the Russian economy combined to produce massive insubordination in the military, as well as spontaneous strikes, riots, and land seizures throughout Russian society.[12]

In China the traditional legitimacy of the state had been largely destroyed in the late nineteenth and early twentieth centuries with the collapse of the imperial system and its replacement by warlords who usurped state power. Even before the collapse of the imperial system in 1912, the authority of the state had disintegrated. This was manifested in the universal predominance of graft among state officials and in the replacement of the old merit examination system for entry into the imperial bureaucracy by the new system of buying one's way in. Respect for the old ruling classes had evaporated as racketeers, warlords, and shady characters rose to fill the vacuum. In the period from 1872 to 1949, over 100,000 Chinese students went abroad, where they were exposed to various Western ideas. These students were the seeds of oppositional currents upon their return. The ineffective resistance of the Chinese state to the Japanese encroachments on Chinese territory added considerably to the delegitimation of the state.[13]

---

[11] See O'Connor, *The Fiscal Crisis of the State*. In this context, note that the capitalist class is increasingly trying to "lower people's expectations" to stabilize the system. Jerry Brown, the governor of California, emphasizes this approach, as did Gerald Ford's WIN program. See Daniel Bell, *The Cultural Contradictions of Capitalism* (New York: Basic Books, 1976).

[12] On the process of the delegitimating of authority in prerevolutionary Russia, see Trotsky, *History of the Russian Revolution*; Wolf, *Peasant Wars of the Twentieth Century*, chapter 2; Liebman, *The Russian Revolution*; Lenin, "Left-Wing Communism: An Infantile Disorder," in *Selected Works*; and Crane Brinton, *The Anatomy of Revolution* (New York: Vintage Books, 1965), chapter 2.

[13] On the process of the delegitimating of authority in prerevolutionary China, see Wolf, *Peasant Wars of the Twentieth Century*, chapter 3; Moore, *The Social Origins of Dictatorship and Democracy*, chapter 4; Schurmann and Schell, *Imperial China*; and Schurmann and Schell, *Republican China*.

The delegitimation of the Cuban regime during the 1950s occurred largely because of the tyrannical rule of the Batista dictatorship, which alienated many segments of Cuban society. That the revolution progressed far beyond the mere ending of the Batista tyranny was largely a product of the heavy-handed response of the U.S. government and the transnational corporations to Cuba's attempt to gain control over its own economy, and the weakness of the upper class's ideological hegemony in rural areas (there were very few rural schools or churches). Moreover, most rural residents in Cuba were rural proletarians who had long since lost the traditional conservatism of most peasantries.[14]

The failure of nonrevolutionary solutions to a social crisis

It is not enough that the ideological hegemony of the capitalist class is undermined; other alternatives must be similarly discredited. Before oppressed people will turn to revolutionary solutions to their problems, all other nonrevolutionary solutions must be discredited in their eyes. Revolution is a grave action, never engaged in lightly, and never without serious consequences. Religious, personal, cultist, and reformist solutions that do not appear to incur the wrath of the upper class are much easier to pursue, and consequently are typically tried before people turn to revolution as a last resort. Of course, not everyone has to personally experience the failure of other solutions. It is only necessary that the working class and other oppressed groups in capitalist society authentically understand the lessons of those who tried these other solutions and failed. The more direct the actual experiences, or the closer the identification with those who tried them, the more the point is driven home that salvation from oppression does *not* lie in these directions.

Once the attraction of the nonpolitical alternatives to revolution is discredited, people tend to pursue the various reformist solutions typically offered by representatives of various intermediate groups who are seeking a middle road between the course offered by the upper class and social revolution. All sorts of reforms, such as breaking up the large corporations, nationalizing the banks and railways, public financing of elections, guaranteeing an annual minimum income, expanding welfare services, giving away land for homesteading or communes, closer regulation of the corporations, decreasing military spending, increasing the power of unions, and subsidizing and protecting small independent businesses, are advanced as goals. Running candidates and winning elections is advanced as the principal way in which such reforms can be won. Such proposed solutions have considerable popular appeal because of the perceived ease with which they can be implemented.

The direct experience of the attempts — both successful and unsuccessful — to find reformist solutions to the working class's oppression typically results in disillusionment and turns people to more revolutionary solutions. The attempt to implement such reforms often runs up against the bitter resistance of the upper

---

[14] On the process of the delegitimating of authority in prerevolutionary Cuba, see Wolf, *Peasant Wars of the Twentieth Century*, chapter 6; and Zeitlin and Scheer, *Cuba: Tragedy in Our Hemisphere*.

class. And yet once such reforms (often in a diluted form) are implemented, they seem to make little difference. The essential oppressive features of the capitalist system remain. Consequently, the working class tends to move to the Left under capitalism. This tendency is, however, combated by the capitalist state's conscious attempt to neutralize it by reinvigorating the cult of the flag, expanding welfare programs, repressing those individuals and movements that refuse to desist from their attacks on the state and the capitalist class, and so on.

Decline of the ruling class's ability to solve a social crisis and counter the growth of revolutionary movements

A revolutionary movement may grow on the basis of the felt oppression of the working class, together with the delegitimation of nonrevolutionary alternatives. But it cannot succeed unless the ruling class is unable to solve the social crisis that is delegitimating the capitalist state and deal with the rising revolutionary movement. Lenin, a proved expert in these matters, argued:

> *The fundamental law of revolution, which has been confirmed by all revolutions, and particularly by all three Russian revolutions in the twentieth century, is as follows. It is not enough for revolution that the exploited and oppressed masses should understand the impossibility of living in the old way and demand changes; it is essential for revolution that the exploiters should not be able to live and rule in the old way. Only when the "lower classes" do not want the old way, and when the "upper classes" cannot carry on in the old way — only then can revolution triumph. This truth may be expressed in other words: revolution is impossible without a nation-wide crisis (affecting both the exploited and the exploiters). It follows that for revolution it is essential, first, that a majority of the workers (or at least a majority of the class-conscious, thinking, politically active workers) should fully understand that revolution is necessary and be ready to sacrifice their lives for it; secondly, that the ruling classes should be passing through a governmental crisis, which draws even the most backward masses into politics (a symptom of every real revolution is a rapid, tenfold and even hundredfold increase in the number of members of the working and oppressed masses — hitherto apathetic — who are capable of waging the political struggle), weakens the government and makes it possible for the revolutionaries to overthrow it rapidly.*[15]

The ruling class's inability to cope with a social crisis is a necessary aspect of the revolutionary process.

The ability of the ruling class to handle both a social crisis and a rising revolutionary movement is a product of its internal cohesion, the intensity of its belief in the legitimacy of its rule, and its willingness to use force when necessary.

---

[15] Lenin, "Left-Wing Communism: An Infantile Disorder," in *Selected Works*, vol. III, pp. 430-431.

When a ruling class cannot unify around and implement a rational program to handle the crisis or revolutionary movement (because of a loss at war, the disaffection of many upper-class youth and their rejection of upper-class traditions, widespread corruption, encroaching decadence and loss of will, or demoralizing internal antagonisms that cannot be contained by a strong sense of class solidarity), it is likely to be overthrown. Even if a ruling class has a reasonably high level of internal cohesion and sense of purpose, it may still fail to resolve a crisis and cope with the revolutionary movement unless it adopts the appropriate strategies. The capitalist class's ability to handle crises is limited by the historical possibilities of any given situation — for example, its ability to successfully manipulate the economy. It may also make serious errors of judgment in handling opposition movements.

The ruling classes in Russia, China, and Cuba were hopelessly split and largely demoralized on the eve of these countries' respective revolutions. As a result, they were unable to effectively exert themselves to save their regimes. In Russia, the wealthy and powerful were sharply divided on the question of preserving czarism; in China, on the question of fighting the Japanese, eliminating foreign influence, and the ineffective policies of the Kuomintang; and in Cuba, on the tyrannical policies of Batista. The ruling class was not able to develop a policy that could mobilize the people and bring the country out of its extreme crisis in any of these countries. In Russia only the Bolsheviks were able to actively pursue the people's needs — peace, land, and bread. In China only the Communists actively fought both the Japanese and all foreign dominance, and pursued genuine land reform. In Cuba only the Fidelistas effectively opposed the Batista dictatorship and sought economic development.

In all three the strategies followed by the state in handling the insurgent movements backfired. The repressive measures of the Kuomintang in China and the Batista regime in Cuba only further alienated large segments of the population and drove them to support the rebels. The vacillating policies of the czarist government until February 1917 and the provisional government from February to October — at some points making concessions, and at others being overtly oppressive — produced in the masses feelings of both confidence *and* outrage. It was certainly ineffective.[16]

The basic strategies and tactics available to the capitalist state include repression, manipulation, co-option, and combinations of these. Different circumstances and different periods in the development of a crisis or movement require different responses. At times the most effective response is to adopt as hard a line as possible, put down demonstrations with force to demoralize the revolutionaries, refuse to meet any of the demands of the working class to discredit their strategy and leaders, and kill, jail, or drive into exile the revolutionary leaders, thereby

[16] For good discussions of the roles of splits in the ruling class and the ruling class's inability to make the appropriate defensive moves in a revolutionary crisis, see Pareto, *The Mind and Society*; Lenin, "Left-Wing Communism; An Infantile Disorder"; Trotsky, *The History of the Russian Revolution*; and Brinton, *The Anatomy of Revolution*, chapters 2 and 5.

demoralizing the movement and depriving it of guidance. At other times, it is most appropriate to offer a number of nonessential concessions to a movement (which may be withdrawn or undercut once the movement subsides), reward its leaders with governmental jobs and status, change the governmental leaders on whom the blame for the people's grievances is laid, and so on. Most often it is wisest for the state to follow a mixed policy of nonsubstantial concessions and the buying off of the less revolutionary leaders, while at the same time repressing the most revolutionary organizations and their leaders. Such a strategy is designed to split the mass of the movement from its leaders and organizations.

This was the strategy followed by the U.S. state in the late 1960s to deal with the black movement. The state employed a wide range of relatively nonsubstantial concessions — for example, various antidiscrimination laws (which barely touched the vast majority of working-class blacks), governmental jobs, and expanded welfare programs — to buy off the more moderate black leaders and the black masses. The state also violently suppressed the most militant of the black organizations, such as the Black Panther Party — much of whose leadership was assassinated, jailed, or driven into exile. Similar policies were followed by the U.S. state in previous historical periods to handle the discontent of the small farmers in the early years of the Republic, the working-class movements and discontent of the post–Civil War period, the Socialist party and the Industrial Workers of the World during World War I, and the Communist Party during the 1950s. There is no rule of thumb on how best to deal with revolutionary movements. The wise ruling class must learn from its successes and failures as well as the experiences of other ruling classes.

Following a hard-line policy of repression may work well when the revolutionary forces have little sympathy in the general population and can thus be terrorized into submission without risking widespread alienation from the state, and hence facilitating recruitment into the revolutionary movement. Hard-line policies, however, can totally backfire, creating sympathizers and supporters for those who are repressed and making martyrs out of their leaders. If a movement has widespread sympathy, it might be wise to appease rather than repress it. Under some circumstances, though, policies of appeasement also backfire. Concessions can reinforce a strong movement and hence encourage it to keep asking for more until it gets everything it wants. The ruling class must carefully judge the resolve of the masses and their leaders, the degree of support they have in the general population, and the ease with which they are demoralized by defeats or encouraged by victories.

When utilizing a hard-line repressive policy, there are several methods of handling revolutionary leaders. Jailing the leaders of a movement has the disadvantage of creating living martyrs to their cause. The incarcerated people, who are continuing to suffer for their dedication to the people, become a cause célèbre around which to mobilize popular support. The black leaders jailed in the late 1960s (Angela Davis, Bobby Seale, and Huey P. Newton) were used in this manner. Buying leaders off, both to quiet them down and to discredit them in the eyes of the people, is normally an effective response — at least for leaders that have widespread popular support. Failing this, another efficient method generally is to drive them into exile. Leaders driven into exile normally do not become martyrs, because while they are enjoying a relatively comfortable life in some other country, their followers back home are still facing the day-to-day punishments of being associated with the movement. Moreover, they typically lose touch with developments in their countries and often just fade away. Such is not necessarily the case for particularly important leaders such as Lenin, nor with non-revolutionary leaders such as Peron, whose exiles in fact served as popular rallying points.

In spite of the risks, assassination is sometimes the most efficient technique for eliminating opponents of the state. If the assassination is not blamed on the state, but rather on a deranged individual or on a small group of extremists, the state can get rid of its opponents without creating a great public outcry. Assassination has the additional advantage of avoiding public trials and the long period of appeals before a legal execution, during which support can be mobilized for those to be executed (as happened in the cases of Sacco and Vanzetti, the Chicago Haymarket Anarchists, and the Rosenbergs in the United States).[17] The major drawback of assassination is that should it ever be exposed as the work of the state or the capitalist class, a very serious legitimacy crisis could ensue. Moreover, it could also create martyrs whose heroic dedication to the cause of the oppressed will inspire others to struggle even more than they would have had the martyred leaders been alive.

Efficient organization and scientific strategy and theory

It is not enough that the working class and other oppressed groups should cease to regard the capitalist state as legitimate. If they are to succeed, they must also adopt a class-conscious revolutionary ideology *and* organize themselves to actually overthrow the capitalist state. Otherwise their bitterness against the system will eventually turn to nonpolitical forms, such as drugs, religion, and personalistic solutions. To be successful, revolutionary ideology (today, generally Marxism) must be developed that explains felt oppression as an outcome of capitalist society, suggests an alternative way of living where social relationships would be based on equality, and gives guidance about how to overthrow the capitalist state.

Such ideologies, and especially Marxism, have in our time been originally developed by intellectuals who initially formed organizations to propagate their ideas and became the early leaders of the popular struggles of the oppressed. Marx, Engels, Lenin, Mao, and many others were converted to Marxism as students and elected to reject the professional lives for which they were being trained to dedicate their lives to making revolution. Although Marxism was originally formulated by intellectuals, it quickly became the ideology of the working class as working people developed class consciousness under the prodding of revolutionary organizations. The revolutionary organizations (such as the Russian and Chinese Communist par-

---

[17] For discussions of these three latter cases, see Richard O. Boyer and Herbert M. Morais, *Labor's Untold Story.*

ties), which began as small circles of students and intellectuals, eventually became predominantly composed of working-class people and peasants.[18] A revolutionary party comes to perform the intellectual function. It counters the intellectual hegemony of the capitalist class and propagates in its place a working-class culture of resistance. The Leninist parties (described in chapter 6) have proved to be the most effective at both propagating a revolutionary ideology and leading the struggles of the oppressed.

Class-conscious revolutionary ideology must be brought to the oppressed classes by revolutionary organizations to combat the hegemony of capitalist ideology.[19] Battered all their lives with ideas reinforcing the status quo, oppressed people cannot easily or spontaneously become conscious about those things removed from their direct experiences without outside help. Working people, whose critical abilities are blunted by the daily oppressions of life under capitalism, and whose alienated labor is so mentally and physically exhausting, do not often have the time or energy to seek out alternative explanations for their lot.

To counterbalance the monopoly of the capitalists' media, a revolutionary party must maintain its own press, education classes, cultural events, and rallies to propagate a class-conscious ideology. A class-conscious revolutionary ideology will only be accepted by the oppressed when they are approached with patience, respect, caution, and a scientific understanding of the peculiar psychology of each stratum. If they are to be successful in winning people over, revolutionaries cannot browbeat or be overbearing, nor insist on subordination to their leadership. They instead have to establish the moral and political authority of their organization and its ideology, winning the respect of the masses through hard work, seriousness,

---

[18] On the development of the revolutionary movement in Russia, see Liebman, *The Russian Revolution*; Lenin, *Selected Works in Three Volumes*; Trotsky, *The History of the Russian Revolution*; Joseph Stalin, *History of the Communist Party of the Soviet Union* (Bolsheviks), (New York: International Publishers, 1939); E. H. Carr, *A History of Soviet Russia* (London: Macmillan, 1950); and Richard Pipes, ed., *Revolutionary Russia: A Symposium* (Garden City, N.Y.: Doubleday, 1969). On the development of the Chinese revolutionary movement, see Schurmann and Schell, *Republican China*; Harold R. Isaacs, *The Tragedy of the Chinese Revolution* (Stanford, Calif.: Stanford University Press, 1951); Suyin Han, *Morning Deluge: Mao Tse-tung: The Chinese Revolution* (Boston: Little, Brown, 1972); Mao Tse-tung, *Selected Works in Four Volumes*; and Wolf, *Peasant Wars of the Twentieth Century*, chapter 3. On the development of the Cuban revolutionary movement, see Huberman and Sweezy, *Cuba: Anatomy of a Revolution*; and Zeitlin and Scheer, *Cuba: Tragedy in Our Hemisphere*.

[19] According to Lenin:

> *Class political consciousness can be brought to the workers* only from without, *that is, only from outside the economic struggle, from outside the sphere of relations between workers and employers. The sphere from which alone it is possible to obtain this knowledge is the sphere of relationships of all classes and strata to the state and the government, the sphere of the interrelations between all classes.*

Lenin, "What Is to Be Done?" in *Selected Works*, vol. I, p. 190.

knowledge, compassion, and the authentic respect *they* show for the oppressed, their problems and ideas. The validity of the "counterculture" advocated by a revolutionary party is shown by the extent to which the oppressed classes, exposed to both it and the bourgeois media, accept it. In fact, such revolutionary ideas acquired something like hegemony in the mainstream of the working classes of most European countries during the first half of the twentieth century.

Revolutionary organizations have differed greatly on the tactics and strategy to be followed by popular movements. Among the major alternative strategies for seizing power are general strikes (all workers refuse to work until the capitalists turn power over to the working class), insurrection (the committed seize the key centers of the society — communication and transportation centers, radio stations, and governmental buildings — encouraging the masses and the army to support them in the streets), guerrilla warfare (the committed conduct low-keyed hit-and-run warfare against the system to inspire an insurrection or defeat of the capitalist armies in battle), terrorism (governmental leaders are killed and crucial buildings damaged with the hope of mobilizing popular support or breaking the will of the capitalists to fight), military coups (the revolutionaries work within the army to get it to seize power), and elections (the movement runs candidates that it hopes will win a majority of votes and — if such were to happen — be allowed to take power and implement the party's program). Frequently, a revolutionary group will combine several of these strategies or move from one to another as their estimate of conditions changes. No simple rule dictates when one or the other is the best course to follow. Rather, if it is to win, a movement must make intelligent choices on the basis of its past experience and historical understanding, always being ready to modify its strategy within the context of its successes or failures.[20]

The attempt to develop a rule defining the strategy and tactics that apply in all situations is what is referred to by revolutionaries as *dogmatism*. Dogmatism can be leftist (for example, inflexible advocacy of bombing and guerrilla warfare) or rightist (for example, inflexible advocacy of nonviolence or the electoral process). No revolutionary organization can succeed unless it can successfully adapt its strategies and tactics to the consciousness of the oppressed people whom it is organizing, as well as to the repressive and co-optive potentials of the state. A successful movement must be both flexible and have adequate intelligence on the mood of the masses and the likely moves of the state if it is to adopt the best strategies and tactics.

[20] Good discussions of the various strategies advocated by Marxist revolutionaries are found in the works of Lenin. See his *Selected Works*, especially his "What Is to Be Done?", "The State and Revolution," and "Left-Wing Communism: An Infantile Disorder"; and Joseph Stalin, *The Foundations of Leninism* (Peking: Foreign Languages Publishing House, 1965); Katharine Chorley, *Armies and the Art of Revolution* (Boston: Beacon Press, 1974), chapter 1; Trotsky, *History of the Russian Revolution*, vol. III, chapter 6; and Mao Tse-tung, "Problems of Strategy in China's Revolutionary War," in *Selected Works*, vol. I, and "Problems of Strategy in Guerrilla War Against Japan," in *Selected Works*, vol. II. The Marxist-Leninist position on effective revolutionary organization can be found in Lenin, "What Is to Be Done?"; Stalin, *The Foundations of Leninism*; and Selznick, *The Organizational Weapon*.

Related to the mistake of dogmatism are the mistakes of what revolutionaries call *left-adventurism* and *right-opportunism*. Left-adventurism is the uncompromising tendency within revolutionary organizations to advocate the seizure of power and the use of violence even when the masses are not ready to follow such a course and/or when the state would be sure to successfully repress such efforts. Right-opportunism is the tendency to maintain always that the masses are not ready for revolution and therefore advocate compromise and accommodation. The same strategy can at one time be adventurist, at another time appropriate, and at still another time opportunist. Again, there can be no rule of thumb for those interested in making a revolution.

Future Revolutionary Possibilities in the United States

Applying the schema of the causes of the rise and success of revolutionary movements to American society, the rise of a revolutionary working-class movement in the next generation appears to be a distinct possibility. The United States is virtually the only advanced capitalist country in the world that never developed a large-scale Socialist or Labor party based primarily in its working class. It is one of the few advanced capitalist countries where the working class never developed a Socialist consciousness. Although Socialist sentiments and parties had significant strength in the United States until the World War I period, socialism was never able to extend hegemony over the working class as it generally did in Europe.

The failure of a large-scale Socialist movement to develop in the United States was *not* because American workers were especially well off; the conditions of their labor are essentially the same as elsewhere, as is their lack of control over the state.[21] Nor was it due to a greater chance of succeeding through hard work (that is, greater individual upward mobility).[22] The rates of upward mobility are much the same in all the advanced capitalist countries. (Since 1950, in fact, they have in all probability been more rapid in Europe than in the United States, since the United States has had such a slow rate of economic growth in the last generation.)[23]

Some have argued that the failure of socialism in America has had to do with the endemic sectarianism of American radicals.[24] While this certainly has played a

---

[21] Among those who have argued that socialism never had a raison d'être in America is Daniel Bell, *Marxian Socialism in the United States* (Princeton, N.J.: Princeton University Press, 1952).

[22] Among those who have argued that an exceptionally rapid rate of upward mobility has been a major factor in the lack of a Socialist tradition in the U.S. working class are Stephan Thernstrom, "Socialism and Social Mobility," in *Failure of a Dream*, John Laslett and Seymour Martin Lipset, eds. (Garden City, N.Y.: Doubleday, 1974); and Werner Sombart, "American Capitalism's Economic Rewards," in Laslett and Lipset, *Failure of a Dream*.

[23] Seymour Martin Lipset and Reinhard Bendix, *Social Mobility in Industrial Society* (Berkeley, Calif.: University of California Press, 1959), chapter 2.

[24] See, for example, Weinstein, *The Decline of Socialism in America: 1912-1925.*

role, this factor cannot be accepted as the ultimate explanation. It must be explained in turn by the material conditions that produce sectarianism. Sectarianism existed during the early stages of the development of the Socialist movement in other countries as well, but it tended to be dissipated as the movement succeeded. In fact, sectarianism is not so much a cause of failure as it is a result. The frustrations of failure are manifested in divisive internal squabbling among the hard core. Similarly, explanations of the failure in terms of faulty leadership or being too leftist or too rightist miss the point.[25] Other movements in other countries had bad leaders and made rightist and leftist errors without destroying the possibilities of a mass Socialist movement. A movement that has an immediate potential for growth becomes rooted enough in the masses to be able to correct its errors and develop appropriate leadership. Again, inadequate leadership and rightist and leftist errors are more a result than a cause of the failure of early Socialist/revolutionary movements to develop in the United States.

The reasons for the past failures of American socialism to develop stem from the unique position of the United States in the world: the divisiveness of the race and national questions (a product of the numerous immigrant groups within the American working class), its economic affluence, and its world hegemonic position since World War II. The bitterness of the various national groups within the working class (whites and blacks, as well as Irish, Poles, Italians, and Protestant native born) was channeled into mutual antagonisms and eventually into patriotism (proving they were "real Americans") rather than into Socialist class consciousness, as happened virtually everywhere else in the capitalist countries. In part this was an unintended consequence of the massive migrations; but it was also a result of a conscious policy implemented by employers to encourage and manipulate national and racial sentiments to their own advantage.

By endlessly proclaiming that the United States is the "richest country in the world" and has provided its working class with "the highest standard of living anywhere," the capitalist class has been effectively able to win the support of working people for the system. People who came from "the old country" (or whose parents or grandparents did) are able to compare their poor and desperate backgrounds with their new lives in America, contrast the two, and (with years of hindsight) pronounce the new country good. That the system has been able to regularly increase the real wages of workers (at least until around 1965), meeting at least some of their demands for a better life, has defused much of the hostility that otherwise might have been transformed into class consciousness.

The world hegemonic position of the United States since World War II has permeated the consciousness of the American people. The feelings that "we are number one" peaked during World War II, when the United States achieved a position of virtually unquestioned dominance in the world by means of a

---

[25] Among those who have argued that the Socialist party failed in the United States because its line was not left enough is Ira Kipnis, *The American Socialist Movement, 1897-1912* (New York: Columbia University Press, 1952). Among those who have argued that the failure of the Socialist party lay in its line being too left is Bell, *Marxian Socialism in the United States.*

domestically popular war. The world system largely organized by the United States after the war gave Americans great pride in the achievements of "their country." The universal American economic and military presence defended and glorified by the mass media instilled an imperial consciousness in the American people.

Felt oppression in the United States

Even though the standard of living of the U.S. working class rose steadily from the later part of the nineteenth century until the mid-1960s, and the numbers of hours worked declined from the 1870s until the 1930s, the masses in the United States continue to be oppressed. Although income rose, the wealth distribution has changed little. A few wealthy corporations control an increasingly larger share of the economy. Working people have as little control over the work process, what they produce, and how it is disposed of as they ever did. Autonomy, creativity, and job control are perhaps even less present today than ever before. As always, the working class sells its labor power, which then is at the almost total disposal of the corporations that buy it. Alienation of labor is complete.[26] Discontent with the nature of industrial labor remains high even when workers feel relatively satisfied with the level of wages (since they compare themselves with others making less, and with their parents' past). Although the oppression of the working class has not been alleviated, the size of the working class relative to the other classes in society has grown. In 1940 approximately 22 percent of the economically active people were self-employed (75 percent sold their labor power). But by 1970 only 9 percent were still self-employed, and 90 percent were wage and salary earners.[27] Although some of the wage and salary earners are managers who have positions of authority as well as high salaries, a considerable proportion of the 9 percent of the self-employed are either franchise holders (for example, doughnut shops or gas stations) and have little real independence, or are marginal farmers and small-business people heavily in debt to the banks and just barely keeping their heads above water. The independent middle class thus has largely dropped out as society becomes increasingly polarized between a very small class of capitalist owners of the means of production, and a proletariat of those who neither own *nor* control the means of production.[28]

The major trends within the class structure in the last generation have been the radical reduction in the relative number of farmers, farm laborers, and domestic workers, and the relative increase in salaried professionals (the "new" middle class). Another very important change that has occurred has been the socialization and industrialization of housework and childcare. This change has released working-class women from the home just in time to fill the state's and corporations' expanding needs for more sales and clerical personnel (thereby pulling

---

[26] For an excellent discussion of alienated labor under conditions of contemporary capitalism, see Andre Gorz, *Strategy for Labor* (Boston: Beacon Press, 1967), part I.
[27] See Szymanski, "Trends in the American Class Structure."
[28] For a good analysis of the effect of the shrinkage of the independent bourgeoisie on the support for the capitalist system, see Schumpeter, *Capitalism, Socialism and Democracy.*

them into the labor force as white-collar workers). In 1974 over two-thirds of all clerical and sales jobs were held by women. The resultant "proletarianization" of working-class women has been a major force undermining the traditional isolating effect of housework, producing both feminist and class consciousness among working-class women.[29] The potential for a division of the working class along sex lines (as occurs in the Catholic countries during political crises, when the church tends to mobilize the more religious women to vote against the revolutionary parties) is thus continually diminishing.

The great reduction in farmers, farm laborers, and domestics and their transfer into the manual working class isolates these groups from the conservatizing experiences of living in small towns and working in the immediate physical proximity of the better-off classes. Instead, they now work in highly socialized work environments (for example, a food processing center, rather than a rich woman's kitchen; a large cannery, rather than as a hired hand on a small farm) that are far more conducive to the development of class consciousness.

In addition to remaining fundamentally oppressed in their economic life, the American common people are subjected to a wide range of other forms of oppression that stem from the nature of the capitalist mode of production. Blacks, Latins, and other people of Third World extraction suffer the humiliations of racism and racial discrimination, while women of all colors suffer the degradation of sexism. Militarism and aggressive wars for which working-class people pay both in lives and in taxes are endemic to the system, as is environmental destruction, competitive individualism, neglect of collective needs (such as creative leisure and the popular arts), and the general meaninglessness of life. Politically, the state continues to be run by, for, and in the interests of capital. The potential for revolution remains. The question is whether it will be realized.

Remember that oppression is relative to the possible. It is not the absolute level of living or working standards that drives people to rebellion, but rather the gap between what is possible (especially in the eyes of the common people) and what the present reality provides — it is the gap between people's expectations and what they in fact receive that measures the potential for revolution. If James C. Davies' theory of the "J-curve" is correct — that is, if revolutions occur when a lengthy period of rising expectations confirmed by actual improvements is followed by a sharp downturn in people's real situations and the consequent rapidly developing gap between expectations and reality — then the potential for the rise of a revolutionary movement is ever present even in the richest society (provided that expectations do rise, and that the economy or political system can in fact suffer a sudden dramatic and sustained downturn).[30]

Note that actual wages have been essentially stagnant in the United States since 1965, while the workweek has been constant since the end of World War II. Safety conditions on the job have not improved significantly during this period, and the percentage of the labor force in unions (and thus workers having a modicum

---

[29] See Szymanski, "The Socialization of Women's Oppression."
[30] James C. Davis, "Toward a Theory of Revolution," in William Lutz and Harry Brent, eds., *On Revolution* (Cambridge, Mass.: Winthrop Publishers, 1971).

— however small — of job control and job security) has declined significantly since the early 1950s.

Decline of legitimacy in the United States

The legitimacy of the American way of life (for example, capitalism, imperialism, racism, and patriotism) has declined considerably since the mid-1950s — the peak of the "Great American Celebration." Virtually all signs point to the deterioration in people's faith in the system and the major institutional pillars of the society — religion, the family, respect for private property, the state, and so on.[31] In 1972 the lowest proportion of the voting age population (51 percent) voted than in any other presidential election since 1932 (except for that of 1948).[32] A Gallup poll taken in 1972 found that 32 percent of persons 18 to 20 years old would prefer to settle in another country besides the United States.[33] In 1971 one in fourteen members of the army deserted (that is, were AWOL for more than thirty days)[34] — this was the highest figure in modern times. From 1960 to 1972 the number of army inductees refusing induction increased by a factor of twenty.[35] During the course of the Vietnam War, drug use, "fragging" of officers, and refusals to obey orders became endemic. The military was considerably weakened by the deterioration in morale and discipline, which reflected a general loss of faith in American values by soldiers. Church attendance has also declined significantly since the 1950s. In 1955 according to the Gallup poll, 49 percent of adult Americans said they went to church regularly; but in 1975, only 40 percent said they did so.[36]

The declining legitimacy of the American way of life is also reflected in changing attitudes toward work. Young working people are becoming less willing to be pushed around without resistance and to suffer patiently a miserable job. Quit rates, the changing of jobs, spontaneous resistance to foremen, drug use, and the decline in the work ethic (the serious lifelong commitment to getting ahead by hard work, together with contempt for welfare and other means of surviving without hard work) are becoming common among young workers.[37]

The undermining of authority in American society is also reflected in the weakening of the family — an institution that ties workers to their work (to support wives and children) as well as hinders the development of broad social ties by delimiting the sphere of solidarity to small units. The ratio of divorces to marriages

---

[31] See Albert Szymanski, "The Decline and Fall of the American Eagle," *Social Policy* 4, no. 5 (March-April 1974).

[32] U.S. Department of Commerce, *The Statistical Abstract of the United States*, 1975, p. 450.

[33] *Gallup Opinion Index*, May 1972, p. 25.

[34] U.S. Department of Commerce, *The Statistical Abstract of the United States*, 1975, p. 327.

[35] Ibid., p. 331.

[36] *The Gallup Opinion Institute Report*, no. 130, 1975, p. 26.

[37] Data on the trends in quit rates can be found in the U.S. Department of Labor, *Handbook of Labor Statistics*, 1975.

increased five times from 1910 to 1974, while the percentage of all births that are "illegitimate" increased over three times from 1950 to 1974.[38]

Rapidly rising crime rates are another sign of the undermining of the system's legitimacy. In the period 1960 to 1974, virtually all forms of major crime at least doubled in their incidence — for example, the number of murders rose from 5 to 10 per 100,000 people, and the number of robberies rose from 60 to 209 per 100,000 in this period.[39] Statistics on the incidence of mental illness and narcotics addiction reflect the same trend. The loosening of the social bonds tying people to capitalist social relations results in increasingly antisocial (although, of course, nonpolitical) behavior.

The three major pillars that have tied the consciousness of American working people to the capitalist system and its state for the last two generations are disintegrating. Antiblack racism, the unique economic position of American workers, and the world hegemonic political and military position of the United States are all decaying. Capitalism is itself undermining the bases of racial antagonism in the working class — an antagonism that has divided the class and prevented the development of class consciousness. The greatest profit comes from creating the largest pool of mutually substitutable employees. This places maximum pressure on the employed to ensure industrial discipline and keep wages down as well as maximize labor force flexibility. Insistence on discrimination against blacks means that white wages are kept artificially high. The hiring of blacks for all jobs for which whites are eligible means that the maximum pressure is placed on the whites. Consequently, both their wages and job security decline. This has been demonstrated in the construction industry, where the construction companies (in contrast to the predominantly white unions) have been encouraging the integration of the unions to decrease wages. The logic of this process results in the genuine integration of the work force and the leveling out of the economic differences between blacks and whites. As a result, in the period 1950 to 1970 virtually all of the income gap between white and black women working full time was eliminated, along with about one-quarter of the gap between black and white men working full time. At the same time, occupational discrimination decreased significantly for both men and women in almost all the major occupational categories.[40]

As the internal caste-like boundaries are undermined by the very logic of capitalism, the material basis is being established for genuine black-white solidarity within the working class. People who work side-by-side (and thus have identical economic interests as well as more of an opportunity to get to know each other) are more likely to form relationships of solidarity and develop a class consciousness. There is, however, a possibility that as a new immigrant group, such as

---

[38] U.S. Department of Commerce, *The Statistical Abstract of the United States*, 1975, p. 51, 57.

[39] U.S. Department of Commerce, *The Statistical Abstract of the United States*, 1975, p. 150.

[40] See Albert Szymanski, "Race, Sex and the U.S. Working Class," *Social Problems* 25, no. 5 (June 1974): 706-725, and "Trends in Racial Discrimination in the United States," *The Review of Radical Political Economics* 7, no. 3 (Winter 1976).

Latins from South and Central America (who have been displacing southern blacks as the major source of new "dirty workers"), migrates to the urban industrial areas of the United States, it may replace the blacks as the pariah group against which racial hatred is directed. Whether this will happen is still open. The outcome could well be a product of whether a new form of class consciousness develops in the U.S. working class that will channel frustration against the system before a consolidated anti-Latin racism arises to channel it elsewhere.

In the 1950s the wages of American workers averaged about four times higher than those of the other leading capitalist countries. By 1975 the wages of workers (including social security benefits) in many of the countries of Northern and Northwestern Europe approximated those of U.S. workers.[41] Actual wages in the United States were stagnant from 1965 to 1977, and the much more rapid rates of growth of most of the other capitalist countries were manifested in vast improvements in the living standards of their workers. Swedish, Danish, and other European workers can now brag that they have "the highest standard of living in the world." No more can the American workers' affluent conditions be cited as evidence of the superiority of the American system. Rather, the stagnation in U.S. workers' living standards can increasingly be contrasted with the rising living standards of workers elsewhere to the detriment (and discredit) of the American system.

The era of "Pax Americana" (1945 through 1968), during which the United States dominated the capitalist world, was probably the shortest period of world domination by any country in history. The domination of Rome lasted over five hundred years; that of Britain over one hundred; that of the United States a mere generation. During the 1950s the United States dominated world production as well as the world export and import trade. But by the early 1970s the exports and imports of Germany and Japan were of the same order as those of the United States. Since 1950 the rates of economic growth of all the other leading capitalist countries except Great Britain have been consistently higher than that of the United States. This has been reflected in the constant deterioration in the U.S. international economic position during this period.[42] Although the United States in the 1970s has far and away the largest and best equipped military establishment in the capitalist world, its ability to maintain its military superiority is being undermined by the deterioration of its economic position. To maintain world military hegemony, large amounts of money, resources, and technical expertise must be expended to innovate, replace military hardware, and simply to maintain the massive military establishment. This immense cost is mostly unproductive and results in a very serious drag on the rate of increase in productivity in American industry.[43] Here we have a true contradiction. The course necessary to reproduce the military hegemony of the United States is precisely that course which undermines the possibility of the United States holding onto its military hegemony.

---

[41] See the United Nations, *Statistical Yearbook*, 1974.
[42] See Szymanski, "The Decline and Fall of the American Eagle."
[43] See Melman, *Our Depleted Society*; and Szymanski, "Military Spending and Economic Stagnation."

One additional factor working to undermine the inoculation of the American working class against Marxism stems from the increasingly difficult international economic position of the United States. As the United States's international competitors (such as Japan, France, and West Germany) have secured an increasing share of the world export market, the United States has been pushed out of many foreign markets. As a result, it has found it impossible to continue its cold war policies of refusing to trade with the "centrally planned economies," especially since its major competitors have few such restraints. As the Soviet and Chinese economies grow, they have come to offer an attractive market for U.S. exports, which U.S. capital can decline only at considerable cost to itself. Consequently, in the early 1970s the United States's relationship with China was normalized, and greater attempts were made to secure detente with the Soviet Union. Trade expanded considerably with both countries.

A corollary of the rapidly expanding trade with the Soviet Union and China, as well as of detente and normalization of relations with the Soviet Union which this expanding trade requires, is a lessening of anticommunism in the United States. The rabid anticommunism promoted by both the corporations and the state during the cold war to mobilize support for high levels of military spending and the overseas adventures of the U.S. government is becoming dysfunctional now that the primary thrust of international economic policy is increasingly toward expanding trade with the Soviet Union and China. Rabid anticommunism results in phenomena such as consumer boycotts of goods made in Socialist countries with "slave labor," popular opposition to grain deals with the Soviet Union, refusal of right-wing unions to handle commodities in transit between the United States and the Socialist countries, and congressional opposition to extending trade credits to China. Consequently, rabid anticommunism has to be undermined and China and the Soviet Union portrayed in somewhat sympathetic terms by the mass media and the government. The radical change in the attitudes of the American mass media in the early 1970s toward China must be explained in these terms. The unintended consequence of the changed official attitude toward the Socialist countries is to make Marxism a less outrageous alternative in the United States. Indeed, the following that the People's Republic of China attained in the United States in the mid-1970s is a sign of the increasing potential for Marxist ideas to take hold in America.

Summary and Conclusion

Socialist movements and revolutions develop because of the contradictions of capitalism (that is, social structural problems generate movements to change society), but such movements do not arise and triumph automatically. The success of such movements is very much a result of *both* the best use of organizational forms, strategy, and ideology on the part of the oppressed, *and* the failure of the privileged classes to organize themselves to suppress insurgency effectively.

Three sets of conditions exist that are necessary and sufficient for the growth and success of revolutionary movements:

1. The lower classes in society must feel their oppression. The denial of human dignity to the oppressed gives them the energy to resist. The denial of dignity bears no necessary relation to the level of the economic development of a country, but rather only to the degree of social inequality in the society. Revolutionary movements are thus equally likely to occur in rich or poor societies that have a comparable degree of social inequality.
2. The denial of dignity is not transformed into political opposition to the system until the ideological hegemony of the ruling class is broken and the appeal of alternative nonrevolutionary solutions to oppression is lost. Before people become revolutionary, they must reject the authority of class institutions and lose faith in the various sacred institutions of capitalism.
3. Massive popular revolutionary sentiment will not be realized in a successful revolutionary transformation until it can be successfully organized around a winning strategy guided by a sound theory or ideology to inspire and lead the masses. Neither will it be successfully realized until the ruling class either makes fatal mistakes in its counterstrategy, becomes internally divided against itself, or becomes demoralized and loses the will to preserve its privileges.

The political situation in the United States seems to be becoming increasingly ripe for the long overdue development of a widespread Socialist class consciousness in the working class. The exceptional conditions that halted and then reversed the development of Socialist consciousness — which came to fruition in most other advanced capitalist countries in the generation before World War I — are rapidly going out of existence. The special economic and world hegemonic position of the United States, along with the peculiar racial/national composition of the U.S. working force, are disappearing. Their disappearance creates the precondition for the rise of a revolutionary movement. How soon this movement will arise and how effective it will be in the short run is a product of the effectiveness of the ideology (or counterconsciousness) advanced by radicals, and the ineffectiveness of the response of the ruling class to the growth of such a movement.

Marxist ideology and Leninist organizational forms are likely to become major factors in the United States. Not only are the conditions that have acted as a prophylactic against "foreign ideologies" ending, but the continuing worldwide success of Marxist-Leninist organizational forms as the twentieth century progresses is becoming increasingly impressive.

The major social fact of the twentieth century seems to be revolution: first the growth of large Socialist working-class movements in Europe in the pre–World War I period; then the Russian Revolution and the movements it inspired all around the world; then the great advances of communism in the aftermath of World War II, both in the Chinese and Eastern European revolutions (for example, Yugoslavia, Albania, and Czechoslovakia) and in the growth and strengthening of the Communist parties in Western Europe and in the Third World areas.

The 1960s and 1970s witnessed the growth of Communist-led and inspired movements in Latin America (Cuba, Chile, and the guerrilla movements throughout the continent), Asia (especially Indochina, where Communist-led insurgent movements came to power in three countries in 1975), and Africa (where Marxist-inspired movements triumphed in Guinea-Bissau, Mozambique, and Angola). The late 1960s and the 1970s have also seen the revitalization of the militant working-class movement in Europe, with a near insurrectionary general strike in France in 1968, the growth of a near revolutionary situation in Italy, a revolution based in the working class in Portugal, the ending of the Spanish dictatorship, and the increased militancy among British workers. Given the international trend, which is more difficult than ever to hide from the American working class because of television news and the spread of higher education, it is most likely that the ideas of these movements will filter through the ever-loosening ideological screen of the ideological hegemony of the capitalist class.

The rapid development of the student New Left in the 1960s (from the liberal pacifism of the early 1960s, to the revolutionary Marxism of the late 1960s), together with the evolution of the black movement (from the civil disobedience/integrationist orientation of the early 1960s, through the nationalist black-power orientation of the mid-1960s, to Marxism-Leninism in the late 1960s — for example, the Black Panthers, the League of Revolutionary Black Workers, and the Black Workers Congress) indicated the potential for the development of a revolutionary Marxism in the United States.

The mid- and late 1960s might well be a precursor of the future. Forces that were gradually building up in the United States were greatly accelerated in their development by the war in Vietnam. As a result, events moved much faster than the underlying development of material forces justified, and the "movement" burned itself out without being able to establish and maintain firm roots among the working people. The maturing crisis of American capitalism, together with the undermining of the legitimacy of the system, however, suggest that the underlying material forces are becoming ripe. They also suggest that the next time there is a development of a student and cadre-based revolutionary Left comparable to that of the late 1960s, firm roots in the masses will be established and a massive revolutionary movement built.

How soon this can be expected to happen and how quickly events will come to fruition depends primarily on how prepared the Left is, how effectively it can overcome sectarianism, and how effective its leadership will be, *as well as* on the development of unforeseen crises (wars or depressions) and bungling on the part of the ruling classes. Given American society's momentum, a genuine mass-based fascist movement does not seem to be a short-run possibility. But the rapid growth of a massive leftist movement that tries but fails to come to power, or even merely threatens to come to power without decisively making the attempt, could easily produce a revival of patriotic sentiments and promote the rise of a fascist movement. And such a movement could attain power in the United States as it did under similar conditions in Italy and Germany. The future is open.

Index

A

ADEPT, 223
AFL—CIO, 5, 46, 176
    Committee on Political Education, 227
Acheson, Dean, 218
Advertising, 242, 244
Aerospace industry, 40, 45—46, 194
    and politics, 48, 49
Africa, 18
    and corporations, 36, 45, 206
    foreign aid, 207
    imports, 44
    military, 265, 278
    revolution, 318
    and U.S., 210
African Blood Brotherhood, 112
Agricultural societies, 138, 139
Agriculture
    crops, 95—96
    factories, 77—78
    subsidies, 202—203
    tenure systems, 92—95
    workers, 64—65, 76—78, 82, 92—93
Alcoa Aluminum, 169
Allende, Salvador, 263, 265, 266, 267
Altschul, Frank, 230
American Airlines, 169
American Assembly, 228, 233
American Association for Labor Legislation (AALL), 186, 228, 230, 271

American Bankers Association, 224, 227
American Communist Party, 181
American Economic Association (AEA), 228—229
American Legion, 177
American Medical Association (AMA), 173, 194, 227
American Medical Political Action Committee (AMPAC), 223
American Motors, 169
American Nazi party, 52
American Negro Labor Congress, 112
American Protective Association (APA), 286
American Telephone and Telegraph (AT&T), 36
American Woman Suffrage Association (AWSA), 105
Americans for Democratic Action (ADA), 52
Anderson, Robert B., 218
Angola, 318
Anthony, Susan B., 105
Anti-Duhring (Engels), 22n
Arbenz, 209, 269
Argentina, 265, 269, 279
Articles of Confederation, 153
Artists, 88
Asia, 18
    corporations, 36, 45, 206
    foreign aid to, 207
    imports, 44
    military, 265, 278

Asia *(cont.)*
    revolution, 318
    and U.S., 210
Assassination, 306
Associated Milk Producers, 224
Athens, 148
Atlantic Community, 232
Atomic Energy Commission (AEC), 232
August 29th Movement, 110
Australia, 116, 209, 254
Automobile industry, 43, 46–47, 195
    strikes, 114
    workers, 61

B

Bacon, Nathan, 152
Ball, George, 231
Baltzell, E. Digby, 11, 39
Bank of America, 169
Bank PAC, 224, 227
Banks, 24–25
    and corporations, 36n
    and credit, 200
    and foreign policy, 230–231
    and housing, 194
    lobbying, 224, 227
    and politics, 47–48, 212
    regulation, 189
    and state policy, 263–264
Baptists, 253
Baraka, Amiri, 113, 114
Baran, Paul, 251
Batista, Fulgencio, 297, 304
Beard, Charles, 251
Beecher, Henry Ward, 105
Belgium, 103, 116
Bell, Elliot V., 231
Bentley, Arthur, 2–3
Berelson, Bernard, 18
Berkeley, 91, 228
Bill of Rights, 115
Black Legion, 287
Black Muslims, 113
Black Panthers, 110, 113–114, 181, 305, 318
Black Star Lines, 111

Black Workers Congress, 114, 318
Blacks, 17, 51
    class consciousness, 108–109, 114–115
    and criminal justice, 179, 180
    and Marxism, 108–109, 112, 114
    and politics, 51, 52
    in U.S., 110–115, 154, 155, 258, 305, 312, 314, 318
    and women, 106–107
Bloor, Ella Reeve, 107
Blum, Leon, 269
Bolsheviks, 70n, 132–135, 304
Bonapartism, 22
Borsh regime, 209, 269
Branch party, 130–131
Brazil, 209, 265, 266, 269
Bretton Woods agreement, 233
Brookings Institution, 175, 228, 272
Brotherhood of Sleeping Car Porters, 112
Business, 22. *See also* Corporations
    and blacks, 109
    and fascism 282–284, 286, 290
    and pluralism, 2, 3, 4, 5
    and politics, 23–24, 30, 40–53
    small, 83–85
    and state, 24–25, 233–234
Business Council, 50, 51, 122, 128, 233–234
    and capitalist class, 175, 190, 228, 271, 272
Business-Industry Political Action Committee (BIPAC), 224

C

CASA, 110
CED. *See* Committee for Economic Development
CFR. *See* Council on Foreign Relations
CIA. *See* Central Intelligence Agency
CORE, 176
California Institute of Social Welfare, 118
Cambodia, 265
Campbell, Angus, 18
Canada, 209
    elections, 125–126
    U.S. investment, 45

Capital gains, 169—170
Capitalist class
 and Congress, 174—175
 conservatism, 40
 and courts, 180—181
 and education, 248—252
 and election expenses, 220—225
 and fascism, 275—277, 282—284, 286, 290
 and government, 216
 ideology, 238—241, 243—244, 258—260
 and petty bourgeois, 81—82
 and politics, 40—53, 172—173, 217—218
 and religion, 452—457
 and revolution, 294
 social culture, 28—30
 and state policy, 173—175, 228—234, 238—239, 265—273
 taxation, 169—170
 and U.S., 33—38, 151—161, 168—178, 310
 wealth, 33—38
 and white-collar workers, 74
 will, 171—176
Carmichael, Stokely, 113
Carnegie Foundation, 228, 231, 250
Castro, Fidel, 114, 239
Catholics, 40, 50, 51, 287
Central Intelligence Agency (CIA), 73, 230, 266, 267
Chamber of Commerce, 51, 175, 234
Charles I, 149
Chase Manhattan, 169, 230, 249
Chiang Kai-shek, 296
Children of God, 253
Chile, 265, 266, 267, 318
 Communists, 99, 263
China, 22, 296—297
 Communists, 94, 95, 132, 135, 304
 revolution, 178, 295—296, 299, 301, 314
 trade, 144, 316
 and U.S., 232, 316
Christian Democratic parties, 122, 123, 131, 132, 255—256
Cigar makers, 62
Cities and class, 69, 75—76
Civil Aeronautics Board (CAB), 205
Civil rights groups, 176
Civil servants, 88—89

Class. *See also* Capitalist class; Middle class; Working class
 and capitalism, 144—145
 and communication, 62—66, 74, 79
 consciousness, 26, 39, 61, 64—68, 78, 79, 131, 306, 307—308, 312
 and fascism, 276—277
 in history, 138—139
 and Marxism, 16, 21—22
 social, 26—28
 and state, 9—10, 21, 25—26, 138—143
 struggles, 26—27
Cleaver, Eldridge, 305
Clothing industry, 45
Columbia University, 91
Committee for Economic Development (CED), 50, 51, 122, 128
 and capitalist class, 172, 173, 175
 and economic policy, 190, 228, 233—234
 and media, 242
Committee on Energy Supply Resources, 220
Committees of Correspondence, 152
Common Cause, 52
Common Sense (Paine), 151
Communism, 269—279
 and age, 116
 and artists, 88
 and blacks, 108—109, 112, 114—115
 and farm workers, 78
 fear of, 12
 parties, 28, 31, 40, 59, 65, 88, 112, 124, 127, 129, 132—135, 267, 285
 repression, 181—182
 and Third World, 27, 114
 and unions, 186
 and U.S., 61—62, 72—73, 114—115, 127, 181—182, 305, 316
 and working class, 72—76
Communist League, 114
Communist Manifesto, 21
Congress of Afrikan Peoples, 113, 114
Congressional Union of Woman's Suffrage (CUWS), 106
Connally, John, 218
Conservatism, 6
 and class, 26, 40, 67
 and education, 248, 249—250
 and elitism, 13—14
 and extremists, 52

Index / 321

Conservatism (cont.)
  and income, 56–57, 83, 85
  and industry, 48–49
  and masses, 13
  and media, 242, 245–246
  parties, 28–30, 31–32n, 50–53, 122, 123, 127, 130
  and petty bourgeois, 84–88
  and professionals, 86–89
  and women, 99–102, 105
Consumer industries, 41–43, 46, 53
Continental Congress, 153–154, 155
Contradictions, 10
  and capitalism, 212–214, 293, 316–317
  and production, 27–28
Corporations
  and education, 247–250
  and elections, 221–225
  and foreign aid, 174, 206–208
  and government personnel, 216–225
  managers, 36n, 81
  and military, 10–11, 45, 208–211
  and politics, 5, 40–53
  public relations, 245
  regulation, 204–205, 212
  and state, 42, 82, 188–192, 198, 202–204, 228–234
  stockholders, 34–36, 170
  and taxation, 168–171
Coughlin, Father, 287
Council of Economic Advisors, 161, 171, 174
Council on Foreign Relations (CFR), 24, 50, 51, 122, 128
  and capitalist class, 172, 173, 175, 218, 230–231, 268
  members, 242
  power, 5, 228, 231–233
"Cowboys," 40, 49
Credit, 190, 199–201
Crime, 28, 314. *See also* Law and order
Cromwell, Oliver, 82, 149
Cuba
  blacks, 108
  revolution, 78, 295–296, 298, 302, 304, 318
  and U.S., 208, 209, 267, 297
  and working class, 61, 77, 78, 79, 117
Currency, 188, 189

D

Davies, James C., 312
Davis, Angela, 305
Davis, Benjamin, 112
Death penalty, 101, 109
Defense industry, 41–42, 45–46, 53, 192–193
Deficit financing, 164, 166–167
Democracy, 7, 13–14, 16, 18
  primitive, 139–141
Democratic party, 30, 123, 128
  and capitalist class, 40–41, 45, 50, 51, 52, 222, 223
  expense, 222
  and foreign policy, 122
  and petty bourgeois, 83
  and white-collar workers, 73
Democratic-Republicans, 129–130
Denmark, 315
Detroit, 108–109, 114, 117
Divorce, 102–103, 313–314
Doctors, 86–87
Dodge Revolutionary Union Movement (DRUM), 114
Dogmatism, 308
Domhoff, G. William, 38n, 39, 216, 235
Dominican Republic, 265, 266, 269
Du Bois, W. E. B., 111, 112
Dulles, Allen, 230
Dulles, John Foster, 218
DuPont family, 34, 46, 51
Duverger, Maurice, 102

E

Eastern Airlines, 169
Education, 150
  and capitalist values, 247–252
  and communism, 271n
  and conservatism, 248–250
  and patriotism, 176–177, 246–247
Egypt, 266
Eighteenth Brumaire, The (Marx), 23
Eisenhower, Dwight, 23, 217, 220
Elderly, politics of, 115–119
Election Reform Act, 221, 224, 225

Elections. *See* Politics; Voting
Electronics industry, 40, 45, 46, 49, 195
Elitism, 11–12, 20
  critiques, 14–15
  and democracy, 13–14, 18
  and functionalism, 7–8
Embourgeoisment, 17–18, 56–57
Engels, Friedrich, 22–23, 139, 140–141n, 163, 294n, 306
Environmental policy, 52
Equal Rights Amendment (ERA), 102, 107
Equality, 7, 105
Equity League of Self-Supporting Women, 106
Ethiopia, 266
Ethnic groups, 49–50, 51
Ethnographic Atlas (Murdock), 138, 139
Export-Import Bank, 264
Export industry, 44, 316
EXXON, 245, 249–250

F

FBI, 181–182
Family
  decline, 313–314
  fortunes, 34–36, 51
  and socialization, 260–261
Fanon, Frantz, 113–114
Farm Bureau, 175, 227, 234
Farmer-Labor movement, 94
Farmers, 17, 26, 81
  crops, 95–96
  family, 93–94
  and fascism, 282
  migration, 68–70
  politics, 92–96, 151, 155
  and state, 196, 202–203, 305, 311
Fascism, 6, 275–291
  and militarism, 178
  parties, 129, 132, 281
  and petty bourgeois, 82–83, 85, 275, 276
  in U.S., 46, 286–290, 318
Federal Reserve Board, 200
Federalist Papers, The, 154
Federalist party, 129–130
Feudal society, 21, 143–144, 148

Field Corporation, 241
Finland, 78, 116
Ford family, 34
Ford Foundation, 231, 241, 250
Ford, Gerald, 24, 102, 217, 258
Ford Motor Co., 41, 43, 169
Foreign Affairs, 231
Foreign aid, 168, 174, 206
Foreign policy, 45, 48, 52, 53, 206–210, 230–233
Forman, James, 114
Forrestal, James, 218
Foundations, 51, 52, 170, 174
  and education, 250
  and public policy, 228, 231, 272
France, 144, 268
  capitalist class, 272
  communism, 40, 56, 78, 126, 246, 318
  farm workers, 78, 92
  imperialism, 208, 296
  Popular Front, 269
  religion, 103, 254
  revolution, 82, 95, 150, 318
  state, 144, 148–149
  and War for Independence, 152
  women, 103
  working class, 61, 78, 251–252
Freikorps, 278, 281
Friedan, Betty, 107
Functionalism, 6–9, 20, 32
  critiques, 9–11
  and Marxism, 26

G

Gaither Committee, 220
Gardner, John, 52
Garvey, Marcus, 111, 113
Gastonia, N.C., strike, 65
Gates, Theodore, 231
General Electric, 41, 43, 46, 250
General Motors, 41, 43, 223, 249
Germany, 23, 145, 197, 268, 315
  communism, 62, 116
  farmers, 92, 273
  fascism, 178, 193, 278, 279–280, 281–286

Germany (cont.)
  imperialism, 208
  petty bourgeois, 85
  religion, 255
  women, 99–100, 102, 103
  working class, 59, 62, 67, 73, 76
Ghana, 269
Gilman, Charlotte Perkins, 106
Glenn, John, 23, 217
Goldman, Emma, 107
Goldwater, Barry, 30, 50, 52, 217, 258
Göring, Hermann, 284
Goulart regime, 209, 269
Grant, Ulysses, 217
Gray Panthers, 118
Great Britain, 144, 315
  capitalism, 145, 272
  crime, 145–146
  economic policies, 6
  elections, 125–126
  imperialism, 193, 200, 296
  Labour party, 40, 83, 102, 268
  parliament, 149–150
  petty bourgeois, 83
  and War for Independence, 151–152
  women, 102
  World War I, 48
Greece, 265, 279
Greensboro, N.C., sit-in, 113
Grumman Aircraft, 45–46
Guam, 209
Guatemala, 209, 265, 266, 269
Guerrilla warfare, 308, 318
Guinea-Bissau, 318
Gulf and Western, 43, 169

H

Hague, Gabriel, 231
Ham and Eggs movement, 117–118
Hamilton, Richard, 18, 61, 69, 73
Hanna, Mark, 228
Hanseatic League, 148
Harvard, 91, 228, 247
Hawaii, 209
Haymarket Massacre, 105, 306
Highways, 195, 199
Hilton, Ronald, 251

Hitler, Adolf, 72–73, 82, 239, 281–286
  charisma, 260
  and military, 265, 279–280
Holy Roman Empire, 148, 239
Honeywell, 169
Horticultural societies, 137, 138
Housing, 193–194
Hughes, Howard, 49
Humphrey, George M., 218
Humphrey, Hubert, 30, 50, 223, 289
Hungary, 265
Hunt, H.L., 49
Hunting and gathering societies, 137, 138

I

IBM, 43, 46
ICC, 205
ITT, 169
Immigrants, 187–188, 286, 287, 314–315
Imperialism, 48, 53, 208–211, 296
Imperialism: The Highest Stage of Capitalism
  (Lenin), 56
Income
  equality, 7
  and politics, 56–57, 83, 85, 91
  and taxation, 168–171, 213
India, 22
Individual
  and capitalism, 28
  and democracy, 13–14
  and elitism, 11–12
  and pluralism, 4
  and religion, 13
  values, 6
Indochina, 266
Indonesia, 265, 266, 269
Industrial Workers of the World (IWW),
  181, 305
Inflation, 46–47, 153, 167
Infrastructure, 168, 191–192, 198–199
Inner City Voice, 114
Instrumentalists, 215–216, 235
Interest groups, 2–3, 10, 173, 234
International Monetary Fund (IMF), 50, 233,
  264
Internationalism, 52

Investments, 24–25
 foreign, 45, 264
Iran, 209, 265, 266, 269
Ireland, 90, 95, 187
Iron and Steel Institute, 227, 234
Israel, 209–210
Italy, 90, 268
 communism, 40, 56, 78, 116, 126, 246, 255, 318
 farm workers, 78, 92
 fascism, 6, 178, 272, 278, 279
 income, 99
 religion, 254

J

J-curve theory, 312
Jackson, Andrew, 217
Jackson, George, 179
Jackson, Henry, 46
Jacobins, 82
Japan, 145, 196, 273, 315
 imperialism, 208
 military spending, 209
 socialism, 116
Jefferson, Thomas, 217
Jeffersonian democracy, 7, 83
Jesus freaks, 253
Jews
 and capitalist class, 40
 and Marxism, 108
 persecution, 259, 284, 287
 and politics, 50, 51, 108
Jim Crow laws, 110, 111, 112–113, 258
John Birch Society, 52, 288, 289
Johnson, Andrew, 158
Johnson, Lyndon, 6, 24, 217, 218, 223
Jones, LeRoi. *See* Baraka, Amiri
Jones, Mother, 107
Jungle, The (Sinclair), 74

K

Kapitalistate, 216
Karenga, Ron, 113
Kennedy, Edward, 102, 239
Kennedy, John, 23, 217, 232, 239

Kerensky government, 269
Keynesian economics, 201–202
Keyserling, Leon, 171
King, Martin Luther, Jr., 113
Kissinger, Henry, 218, 232
Korean War, 178, 243
Kornhauser, William, 13
Ku Klux Klan (KKK), 108, 111, 278, 286–287
Kuhn, Maggie, 118

L

Labor, 43. *See also* Unions
 division, 140
 legislation, 186
 migration, 187–188
 and minorities, 44
 and pluralism, 2, 3, 4
 regulation, 25, 283–287
 skill, 58–60, 184–185
 and state, 145–146, 183–187
Labor parties, 28, 31, 127, 268
 and petty bourgeois, 83
 and women, 102
Land regulation, 189, 204
Landlords, 21, 93, 95, 151
Laos, 101, 109
Latin America, 18
 and corporations, 36, 45, 206
 foreign aid to, 207
 imports, 44
 military, 265, 278
 revolution, 318
 and U.S., 192, 209, 210
Latins, 17, 51, 312, 315
Law and order, 25, 124, 179–181, 213
Lawrence, Mass., strike, 65
Lawyers, 86–87
 corporation, 217, 218, 219–220
Lazarsfeld, Paul, 18
Leaders, 15, 22, 23
 and capitalism, 22
 charisma, 239, 260–261
 revolutionary, 305–306
League of Revolutionary Black Workers, 110, 114, 318
League of Struggle for Negro People, 112

Left-adventurism, 309
Leftism
    and age, 116–117
    and communication, 62–66, 74, 79
    and education, 251–252
    and fascism, 277–278, 290–291
    and income, 56–57, 79
    and media, 242
    and minorities, 108–109
    and mobility, 66–70
    parties, 123, 124
    and religion, 254
    and scientists, 87–88
    and sex, 99–101, 106–107
    and skill level, 58–60, 79
    and students, 90
    and unemployment, 60–62
    and unions, 70–73, 79
    and U.S., 72–73
    and white-collar workers, 73–76
Leggett, John, 61, 69, 108–109, 117
Leisler, Jacob, 152
Lenin, 21, 56–57, 306
    and party organization, 133–135
    on revolution, 303
Liberal party, 127, 130
Liberalism, 6
    and industry, 50, 234
    politics, 28–30, 50–53, 127
Liebknecht, Karl, 281
Lincoln, Abraham, 158
Lindsay, John, 217, 223
Linz, Juan, 75, 85
Lipset, Seymour Martin, 13, 14, 16–17, 87n
Lobbyists, 4, 24, 194
    and capitalist class, 172, 173, 225–227, 234–235
Lockheed, 45–46, 169, 202, 249
Lumpen proletariat, 26, 180
Luxemburg, Rosa, 281

M

McCarthy, Joseph, 85, 251, 287–288
McCloy, John J., 230
MacDonald, Ramsey, 6, 268
McDonnell-Douglas, 45–46, 169
McGovern, George, 6, 50, 52, 102, 222
McLain, George, 118
McNamara, Robert, 218
Madison, James, 217
Mafia, 284
Malcolm X, 113
Manual workers, 16, 276, 286. *See also* Working class
    and petty bourgeois, 84
    politics, 30–31, 55–56, 284, 289
    and revolution, 298
    training, 184
Mao Tse-tung, 114, 306
Marshall Plan, 233, 243
Marx, Karl, 23, 163, 294, 306
Marxism, 20–32, 306–307
    and blacks, 108–109, 112, 114
    and education, 249
    and group pressures, 19–20
    and minorities, 108–109, 112
    political parties, 56, 126
    repression, 72–73
    and state, 20–21, 25–28, 215–216
    and U.S., 19, 317, 318
    and universities, 251
    and women, 107
    and working class, 16–18, 21, 27, 28, 72, 215–216
Mass society, 11–13, 14–15, 150–151
    and fascism, 280, 290
Materialism, 25–26
Media, 4, 31
    and elections, 222, 239
    and ideology, 240, 241–246
    and working class, 150
Mellon family, 34
Mexican war, 208
Michels, Roberto, 11. 13, 14, 18
Middle class, 81–82. *See also* Petty bourgeoisie
    and democracy, 16, 18
    and fascism, 281–282
    and religion, 250n
    and U.S., 311
    and working class, 17–18
Migrant workers, 77
Milbank family, 51
Miliband, Ralph, 216, 335
Military, 10
    conscription, 166
    and corporations, 10–11, 45, 208–211

Military *(cont.)*
  decline, 313
  expenditures, 44, 45, 52, 161, 192–195, 209–210
  foreign intervention, 25
  indoctrination, 31
  and patriotism, 177–178, 259
  and state, 23, 131, 142, 264–266, 278–279
  U.S., 10–11, 45, 47, 177–178, 182, 192–195, 209–210, 311
Milliken family, 51
Mills, C. Wright, 8, 11, 12–13, 251
Mills, Wilbur, 227
Minorities, 17
  and labor force, 44
  and politics, 49–50, 108–115
Mintz, Beth, 219
Mississippi Summer, 52
Mobil Oil, 43, 169
Mobility, 66–70, 309–310
Monopolies, 42–43, 46, 151
  and buying power, 190
  and fascism, 284, 285, 286
  foreign, 206
  and price, 20
  and state, 165–166, 199
Monroe, James, 217
Montgomery, Ala., boycott, 113
Moonies, 253
Morgan financial interests, 48, 50, 51, 218, 230, 234
Mosca, Gaetano, 11, 13, 14
Mossadegh, Muhamad, 209, 269
Mott, Lucretia, 105
Mott, Stewart, 223
Mozambique, 318
Mudge, Stern, Baldwin, and Todd, 220
Murdock, George, 138, 139
Muskie, Edmund, 50, 223
Mussolini, Benito, 82, 260, 261, 278, 279

N

NATO, 209, 232, 233, 243
NET, 241
National American Woman Suffrage Association (NAWSA), 105, 106
National Association for the Advancement of Colored People (NAACP), 11, 176
National Association of Manufacturers (NAM), 51, 175, 224, 227, 230
National Bureau of Economic Research, 233
National Civic Association, 271
National Civic Federation, 186, 228
National Coal Association, 242
National Committee for an Effective Congress, 52
National Consumer League, 106
National Electric Light Association, 242
National Guard, 182
National Ham and Eggs, 117–118
National Labor Relations Act, 186
National Liberation Front (NLF), 211
National Negro Congress (NNC), 112
National Organization of Women (NOW), 107
National Planning Association, 233
National Planning Council, 228
National Security Council (NSC), 220
National Socialist party. *See* Nazis
National Union for Social Justice, 287
National Urban Coalition, 52
National Urban League, 111, 176
National Woman Suffrage Association (NWSA), 105
National Women's Trade Union, 105–106
Nationalism, 23, 239, 257–259
  and blacks, 111
  and corporations, 208, 211
  and fascism, 280
  and minorities, 108
  parties, 123
  students, 90
Nationalization, 45
  and Populist party, 82, 160, 161, 258
Nazi Labor Front, 284
Nazis, 193, 259, 281–286
Nebraska People's party, 96
Negro World, 111
Netherlands, 116, 144, 148, 268
  imperialism, 208
  religion, 254
  and War for Independence, 152
New Deal, 50, 160, 234, 271, 272
New Left, 318
New York, 152, 155, 222

New York City, 263–264
  Communists, 127
New York *Daily News*, 242
New Zealand, 209
Newspapers, 241–243
Newton, Huey, 113, 305
Nisbet, Robert, 13
Nixon, Mudge, Rose, Guthrie, and Alexander, 220
Nixon, Richard, 6, 24, 122, 217–218, 220, 222, 223, 225, 227, 258, 260, 289
Nkrumah, Kwame, 269
Noble, Robert, 117
North Carolina, 155
Norway, 59, 116
  Labour party, 40
Nuclear Weapons and Foreign Policy (Kissinger), 232

O

Obscurantism, 67
Organization of African American Unity, 113

P

Paine, Tom, 151
Pareto, Vilfredo, 11, 13, 14
Paris Commune, 160, 293
Parks, Mrs. Rosa, 112–113
Parliamentary government, 147–151, 172–173
  and fascism, 276
Parsons, Talcott, 6–11
Patriotism, 12, 25, 195, 259–260
  and education, 176–177, 246, 259
Paul, Alice, 106
Peasantry, 92, 150, 184
People's party, 160
Percy, Charles, 217
Peron, Juan, 269, 306
Peru, 266
Petroleum industry, 43
  and government policies, 220–221
  and politics, 42, 45, 48, 49
  subsidies, 204
  taxation, 170
Petty bourgeoisie, 16, 21–22, 26. *See also* Middle class
  and blacks, 111
  and fascism, 82–83, 85, 275, 276
  and minorities, 110
  political attitudes, 26, 67, 81–97, 128
  rural, 81
  and upper class, 81–82
Pew family, 34, 51
Philippines, 95, 209
Plantation workers, 76–77
Pluralism, 1–3, 32
  critiques, 4–6
  and functionalism, 10
  and group pressures, 2, 3, 4, 10, 18–20
Poland, 90, 187, 265
Political Man (Lipset), 16–18, 87n
Politics
  and capitalism, 22, 23–24, 33–53, 121–124, 128–132, 135–136, 217–218, 221–224, 270
  electoral systems, 121–128
  parties, 122–124, 128–135, 221
  and petty bourgeois, 81–97
  repression, 181–182
  and working class, 55–79, 128, 131–132, 175–176
Populist party, 82, 127, 230
  and farmers, 94, 96
  and South, 258
  and universities, 251
Portugal, 266, 267, 279, 293, 318
Poulantzas, Nicos, 216
Power Elite, The (Mills), 8, 251
Private property, 139
  protection, 25, 155, 159–160, 179–181, 212
Process of Government, The (Bentley), 2–3
Production industries, 41–43, 53, 283
Professionals, 22, 26, 81
  and fascism, 277
  politics, 30, 31, 83, 86–89
  training, 184
  women, 107
Progressive era, 160–161
Progressive party, 52
Proletariat. *See* Working class

Protestants, 50, 51, 118, 282, 287
Puerto Rico, 209
Puritan Revolution, 82, 254n

R

RCA, 46
Racism, 28, 123, 150, 312, 314
   and capitalist class, 257–258
   and fascism, 275
Radicalism
   and age, 115–116
   and farmers, 94, 95
   and income, 91
   and poverty, 251
   and women, 106–107
   and working class, 72–73
Ranch workers, 77
Rand Corporation, 228
Randolph, A. Philip, 112
Rasputin, 301
Raw materials, 264
   imports, 42, 44–45, 53, 206
   and state, 189, 202, 283
   taxation, 170
Reactionaries, 83
Reagan, Ronald, 23, 102, 217
Reconstruction era, 110, 127, 286
Regulation, 204–205
   agencies, 25, 161, 189, 205
   policies, 45, 183–188, 283, 284
Reich, Wilhelm, 261
Religion, 31
   and capitalist class, 252–257, 299
   and masses, 12, 13, 150
   and pluralism, 2, 3
   and politics, 50, 70n, 123
   and state, 23, 313
   and women, 101, 103
   and working class, 253–255, 299
Republic of New Africa, 113
Republican party, 123, 128
   and capitalist class, 40–41, 45, 50–51, 222–223
   expenses, 222
   foreign policy, 122
   and Reconstruction, 127, 158–159
   and white-collar workers, 73

Research and development, 10–11, 197–198, 251
Revolution, 27
   and capitalist state, 283, 298–305
   and corruption, 299–300
   and farmers, 99
   ideology, 306–307
   and oppression, 295–298, 311–313
   and petty bourgeois, 82
   and repression, 305–306
   and U.S., 309–318
   and war, 299, 301
Revolution, 105
Revolutionary Communist League, 114
Rhode Island, 155
Right-opportunism, 309
Robeson, Paul, 112
Rockefeller, David, 230
Rockefeller family, 34–36
   and politics, 48, 50, 51, 218, 231, 234
Rockefeller Foundation, 218, 228, 231, 250
Rockefeller, Nelson, 50, 217
Romania, 265
Romano, Paul, 58
Rome, 148, 315
Roosevelt, Franklin, 160, 161, 217, 233, 234, 272, 273
Rosenbergs, 306
Rural Electrification Commission, 199
Rural workers, 65, 68–70
Rusk, Dean, 218, 232
Russian revolution, 70, 132, 178, 264, 269, 295–296, 303, 304. *See also* Soviet Union.
   of 1905, 299, 300

S

SPACE, 223
Sacco and Vanzetti, 306
Samoa, 209
San Francisco State, 91
Santo Domingo, 209, 210
Scaife, Richard, 223
Schooling. *See* Education
Schumpeter, Joseph, 13–14
Scientists, 87–88, 91
Scottsboro boys, 112

Scranton, William, 217
Seale, Bobby, 113, 305
Securities and Exchange Commission (SEC), 189, 205
Self-employed, 311
Serfs, 21, 22, 92, 184
Shays' Rebellion, 94, 153
Silver Shirts, 287
Sinclair, Upton, 74
Slavery, 92
    classes, 21
    and imperialism, 208–209
    owners, 151–152, 153, 185, 216
    regulation, 184
    and women's movement, 105
Small business, 196
    politics, 83–85
    workers, 75
Social Democratic parties, 56, 59, 122, 268–269
    and age, 116, 130
    and petty bourgeois, 85, 90, 282
    and religion, 255
    and white-collar workers, 75, 76
    and women, 103
Social expenditures, 195–198
Social Register, 33, 218, 219, 230, 249
Social security, 118, 161
Socialism, 237
    and age, 116
    and capitalism, 268–269, 293
    and farmers, 96, 277–278
    history, 10
    minorities, 109–110
    parties, 28, 31, 65, 125, 131–132
    sectarianism, 310
    and U.S., 72, 309
    and women, 102
Sons of Liberty, 152
South, the, 185
    politics, 41, 51, 127–128, 158–159, 258
    religion, 256
    slavery, 151–152
Southern Christian Leadership Conference (SCLC), 113
Southern Regional Council, 52
Soviet Union, 44, 53, 209, 316. *See also* Russian revolution

Space program, 194
Spain, 148–149, 208, 279, 285
    revolution, 265, 318
    and U.S., 209
    and War for Independence, 152
Special interest. *See* Interest groups
Spinola, General, 266
Standard Oil, 43, 169, 218
Stanford Research Institute, 228
Stanford University, 251
Stanton, Elizabeth Cady, 105
State
    absolutism, 149, 173
    bureaucracy, 22, 25, 82, 88–89, 145, 146, 164–168
    and class, 9–10, 21, 25–26, 138–143
    and commerce, 188–189
    and corporations, 42, 82, 188–192, 198, 202–204, 228-234
    definitions, 7
    direct control mechanisms, 215–235, 272–273
    and education, 246
    foreign policy, 206–211
    ideology, 238–262, 298–302
    indirect control mechanisms, 237–273
    legitimacy, 23, 176–179, 182, 239–240, 300, 313–316
    and Marxism, 20–21, 25–28, 215–216
    and masses, 13
    monopolies, 165–166, 199
    and parliamentary government, 147–150
    rise of, 137–143
    and taxation, 164, 166, 167, 194, 213
    values, 6, 10, 23
State policy
    and capitalist class, 173–175, 228–234, 238–239, 265–273
    and class, 27
    and elections, 121–124
    and pluralism, 2, 3, 5–6
Statistical services, 188
Stock market, 189
Stone, Lucy, 105
Stone, W. Clement, 49, 223
Strikes, 65, 106, 114, 308
    public sector, 89
    and state, 146, 186

Structuralism, 216
Student Nonviolent Coordinating Committee (SNCC), 52, 106–107, 113
Students, 89–91, 289, 301, 307, 318
   women, 107
Students for a Democratic Society (SDS), 106–107
Subsidies, 168, 197, 202–204
Sugar workers, 77, 78
Sukarno, 269
Sullivan and Cromwell, 218
Sweden, 59, 116, 315
Sweezey, Paul, 251
Switzerland, 144

T

TAPE, 223
Taft-Hartley Act, 186
Tariffs, 4, 45, 46, 160, 202, 264
Taxation, 145
   and corporations, 168–171
   property, 85, 169
   and revolution, 301
   and state, 164, 166, 167, 194, 213
   working class, 168–171, 200
Television, 241
Tennessee Valley Authority, 199
Terrorism, 308
Texaco, 43, 169
Texas Railroad Commission, 204
Textile industry, 41, 45, 49, 64–65
Think tanks, 228
Third World
   communism, 27, 114
   fascism, 273
   foreign aid, 206–207
   investments in, 48, 53
   raw materials, 42, 48, 53, 206
   religion, 254n
   revolution, 300, 317–318
   students, 90
Tobacco workers, 78
Townsend, Dr. Francis, 117
Townsend movement, 117, 118
Trade, 141–142
   U.S., 44, 45, 46, 203–204
Truman, Harry, 171, 217
26th of July movement, 90, 298
Tyler, John, 217

U

Unemployment, 60–62, 167, 186–187
Union
   agricultural, 82
   and blacks, 110, 111, 112
   and communism, 70–71
   and fascism, 282, 284
   and industry, 46, 50
   and politics, 56, 57, 227
   power, 5
   and rural migrants, 69–70
   and state policy, 42, 50, 161, 176, 185–186
   and women, 105–106
   and working class, 70–73, 79
United Nations, 50, 232–233
United States. *See also* South, the
   blacks, 110–115, 154, 155, 258, 305, 312, 314
   bureaucracy, 164
   capitalist class, 33–38, 151–161, 168–178
   communism, 61–62, 72–73, 114–115, 127, 181–182, 305, 316
   and credit, 190, 199–201
   debt, 200
   education, 176–177, 247–252
   elections, 30, 121–124, 125–126, 127
   farmers, 92, 94, 96, 151, 155, 196, 202–203
   fascism, 46, 286–290, 318
   government expenditures, 188–202
   government personnel, 216–225
   government services, 189
   imperialism, 48, 53, 208–211
   infrastructure, 168, 191–192, 198–199
   labor, 185–188
   manpower training, 184–185
   military, 10–11, 45, 47, 177–178, 182, 192–195, 209–210, 315
   mobility, 67–68
   petty bourgeois, 82

United States *(cont.)*
  political parties, 129—130
  president, 156, 217, 221—222
  research and development, 10—11
  revolution, 309—318
  socialism, 72, 309
  trade, 44, 45, 46, 203—204
  women, 101, 102, 104—107, 311—312
U.S. Agency for International Development (USAID), 264
U.S. Army Corps of Engineers, 199
U.S. Bureau of Land Management, 189
U.S. Congress, 25, 40, 52, 156—157
  and capitalist class, 173—174, 180, 220—223
  and elections, 222, 224—225
  and lobbyists, 225—227
U.S. Constitution, 106, 154—157, 158
U.S. Department of Defense, 193, 202, 218
U.S. Department of Interior, 189
U.S. Department of State, 208, 218, 230—232
U.S Postal Service, 199
Universal Negro Improvement Association, 111
Universities, 228, 243, 247—252, 272
  students, 89—91
Upper class. *See* Capitalist class
US, 113
Utilities, 64, 199

V

Values, 6, 10, 23, 244
Veblen, Thorstein, 251
Venezuela, 265
Venice, 148
Veterans of Foreign Wars (VFW), 177
Veto groups, 3—4
Viet Cong, 114, 243
Vietnam
  attitudes toward war, 115, 178, 318
  communism, 135
  U.S. policy, 6, 101, 109, 210, 211, 243, 266
Virginia, 155
Voluntary associations, 4—5, 19

Voting
  and capitalism, 121—124, 125—132
  and class, 30—31
  franchise, 150, 151, 154, 159, 162
  and legitimacy, 239
  and state policy, 14, 121
  U.S., 121—124, 125—126, 127
  women, 102

W

Wages
  and conservatism, 41, 56—57
  minorities, 44
  regulation, 183, 186, 283, 284
  subsidies, 198
  and U.S. Congress, 174, 310, 312—313
Wallace, George, 85, 102, 258, 288—290
Wallace, Henry, 52
War of Independence, 82, 151—152
Warsaw Pact, 209
Washington, Booker T., 110—111
Washington, George, 156, 217
Watson, John, 114
Wealth
  capitalist class, 33—38, 311
  and democracy, 17
  family, 34—36
  and primitive society, 139
Weber, Max, 238
Welfare
  and capitalist class, 175
  expenditure, 194, 195—198
  and industry, 44, 46, 50, 53
  and politics, 52, 85
  and state, 146—147, 150, 170, 178—179, 184
  and U.S. Congress, 174
Whiskey Rebellion, 94
White-collar workers, 16, 65, 73—76, 184
  and fascism, 277
  women as, 75, 104, 312
Weights and measures, 188
Westinghouse, 41, 43
Williams, Robert, 113
Woman's Journal, 105
Women, 118—119
  conservatism, 99—102, 105

Women *(cont.)*
  and politics, 99–107
  rights, 101–103, 104–107, 311–312
  and white-collar work, 75, 104, 312
Women's Political Union, 106
Working class, 26
  conservatism, 64–68, 78, 253–254, 265, 266
  crime, 179–180
  culture, 66
  and elections, 222
  embourgeoisment, 17–18, 56–57
  and fascism, 280, 284, 286
  ideology, 240
  income, 42, 56–57
  intolerance, 18
  and Marxism, 16–18, 72
  mobility, 66–70
  petty bourgeois, 84
  and politics, 55–79, 128, 131–132, 175–176
  and religion, 253–255, 299
  and revolution, 307
  taxation, 168–171, 200
  training, 184
  unions, 70–73
  and white-collar workers, 73, 76
  and women, 105–106
World Bank, 50, 264
World War I, 46, 48, 243, 251
World War II, 193, 285, 310
Wriston, Henry, 231

Z

Zeitlin, Maurice, 18, 61, 109, 117
Zionism, 108